The G.K. Chesterton Collection

Volume 1

The Defendant
Varied Types
Heretics
All Things Considered

By G.K. Chesterton

Henderson Publishing

Copyright ©2024 by Henderson Publishing.
Published July 2024.
Version: 1.0.
ISBN: 978-1-964170-79-4.

If you have a question or have found an error concerning this manuscript, please email: contact@hendersonpublishing.com

Book cover designed by Christian Caudill.
Book designed by Jeremy Hausotter.
This book is typeset in IM FELL English.
The Fell Types are digitally reproduced by Igino Marini. www.iginomarini.com

Henderson Publishing | San Antonio, Texas

Table of Contents

The Defendant   I

Varied Types   59

Heretics

All Things Considered   261

Book Catalog

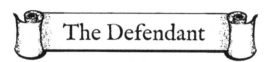

The Defendant

In Defence of a New Edition

he reissue of a series of essays so ephemeral and even superfluous may seem at the first glance to require some excuse; probably the best excuse is that they will have been completely forgotten, and therefore may be read again with entirely new sensations. I am not sure, however, that this claim is so modest as it sounds, for I fancy that Shakespeare and Balzac, if moved to prayers, might not ask to be remembered, but to be forgotten, and forgotten thus; for if they were forgotten they would be everlastingly re-discovered and re-read. It is a monotonous memory which keeps us in the main from seeing things as splendid as they are. The ancients were not wrong when they made Lethe the boundary of a better land; perhaps the only flaw in their system is that a man who had bathed in the river of forgetfulness would be as likely as not to climb back upon the bank of the earth and fancy himself in Elysium.

If, therefore, I am certain that most sensible people have forgotten the existence of this book—I do not speak in modesty or in pride—I wish only to state a simple and somewhat beautiful fact. In one respect the passing of the period during which a book can be considered current has afflicted me with some melancholy, for I had intended to write anonymously in some daily paper a thorough and crushing exposure of the work inspired mostly by a certain artistic impatience of the too indulgent tone of the critiques and the manner in which a vast number of my most monstrous fallacies have passed unchallenged. I will not repeat that powerful article here, for it cannot be necessary to do anything more than warn the reader against the perfectly indefensible line of argument adopted at the end of p. 28. I am also conscious that the title of the book is, strictly speaking, inaccurate. It is a legal metaphor, and, speaking legally, a defendant is not an enthusiast for the character of King John or the domestic virtues of the prairie-dog. He is one who defends himself, a thing which the present writer, however poisoned his mind may be with paradox, certainly never dreamed of attempting.

Criticism upon the book considered as literature, if it can be so considered, I should, of course, never dream of discussing—firstly, because it is ridiculous to do so; and, secondly, because there was, in my opinion, much justice in such criticism.

But there is one matter on which an author is generally considered as having a right to explain himself, since it has nothing to do with capacity or intelligence, and that is the question of his morals.

I am proud to say that a furious, uncompromising, and very effective attack was made upon what was alleged to be the utter immorality of this book by my excellent friend Mr. C.F.G. Masterman, in the 'Speaker.' The tendency of that criticism was to the effect that I was discouraging improvement and disguising scandals by my offensive optimism. Quoting the passage in which I said that 'diamonds were to be found in the dust-bin,' he said: 'There is no difficulty in finding good in what humanity rejects. The difficulty is to find it in what humanity accepts. The diamond is easy enough to find in the dust-bin. The difficulty is to find it in the drawing-room.' I must admit, for my part, without the slightest shame, that I have found a great many very excellent things in drawing-rooms. For example, I found Mr. Masterman in a drawing-room. But I merely mention this purely ethical attack in order to state, in as few sentences as possible, my difference from the theory of optimism and progress therein enunciated. At first sight it would seem that the pessimist encourages improvement. But in reality it is a singular truth that the era in which pessimism has been cried from the house-tops is also that in which almost all reform has stagnated and fallen into decay. The reason of this is not difficult to discover. No man ever did, and no man ever can, create or desire to make a bad thing good or an ugly thing beautiful. There must be some germ of good to be loved, some fragment of beauty to be admired. The mother washes and decks out the dirty or careless child, but no one can ask her to wash and deck out a goblin with a heart like hell. No one can kill the fatted calf for Mephistopheles. The cause which is blocking all progress today is the subtle scepticism which whispers in a million ears that things are not good enough to be worth improving. If the world is good we are revolutionaries, if the world is evil we must be conservatives. These essays, futile as they are considered as serious literature, are yet ethically sincere, since they seek to remind men that things must be loved first and improved afterwards.

G. K. C.

Chapter 1
Introduction

I n certain endless uplands, uplands like great flats gone dizzy, slopes that seem to contradict the idea that there is even such a thing as a level, and make us all realize that we live on a planet with a sloping roof, you will come from time to time upon whole valleys filled with loose rocks and boulders, so big as to be like mountains broken loose. The whole might be an experimental creation shattered and cast away. It is often difficult to believe that such cosmic refuse can have come together except by human means. The mildest and most cockney imagination conceives the place to be the scene of some war of giants. To me it is always associated with one idea, recurrent and at last instinctive. The scene was the scene of the stoning of some prehistoric prophet, a prophet as much more gigantic than after-prophets as the boulders are more gigantic than the pebbles. He spoke some words—words that seemed shameful and tremendous—and the world, in terror, buried him under a wilderness of stones. The place is the monument of an ancient fear.

If we followed the same mood of fancy, it would be more difficult to imagine what awful hint or wild picture of the universe called forth that primal persecution, what secret of sensational thought lies buried under the brutal stones. For in our time the blasphemies are threadbare. Pessimism is now patently, as it always was essentially, more commonplace than piety. Profanity is now more than an affectation—it is a convention. The curse against God is Exercise I. in the primer of minor poetry. It was not, assuredly, for such babyish solemnities that our imaginary prophet was stoned in the morning of the world. If we weigh the matter in the faultless scales of imagination, if we see what is the real trend of humanity, we shall feel it most probable that he was stoned for saying that the grass was green and that the birds sang in spring; for the mission of all the prophets from the beginning has not been so much the pointing out of heavens or hells as primarily the pointing out of the earth.

Religion has had to provide that longest and strangest telescope—the telescope through which we could see the star upon which we dwelt. For the mind and eyes of the average man this world is as lost as Eden and as sunken as Atlantis. There runs a strange law through the length of human history—that men are continually tending to undervalue their environment, to undervalue their happiness, to undervalue themselves. The great sin of mankind, the sin typified by the fall of Adam, is the tendency, not towards pride, but towards this weird and horrible humility.

This is the great fall, the fall by which the fish forgets the sea, the ox forgets the meadow, the clerk forgets the city, every man forgets his environment and, in the fullest and most literal sense, forgets himself. This is the real fall of Adam, and it is a spiritual fall. It is a strange thing that many truly spiritual men, such as

General Gordon, have actually spent some hours in speculating upon the precise location of the Garden of Eden. Most probably we are in Eden still. It is only our eyes that have changed.

The pessimist is commonly spoken of as the man in revolt. He is not. Firstly, because it requires some cheerfulness to continue in revolt, and secondly, because pessimism appeals to the weaker side of everybody, and the pessimist, therefore, drives as roaring a trade as the publican. The person who is really in revolt is the optimist, who generally lives and dies in a desperate and suicidal effort to persuade all the other people how good they are. It has been proved a hundred times over that if you really wish to enrage people and make them angry, even unto death, the right way to do it is to tell them that they are all the sons of God. Jesus Christ was crucified, it may be remembered, not because of anything he said about God, but on a charge of saying that a man could in three days pull down and rebuild the Temple. Every one of the great revolutionists, from Isaiah to Shelley, have been optimists. They have been indignant, not about the badness of existence, but about the slowness of men in realizing its goodness. The prophet who is stoned is not a brawler or a marplot. He is simply a rejected lover. He suffers from an unrequited attachment to things in general.

It becomes increasingly apparent, therefore, that the world is in a permanent danger of being misjudged. That this is no fanciful or mystical idea may be tested by simple examples. The two absolutely basic words 'good' and 'bad,' descriptive of two primal and inexplicable sensations, are not, and never have been, used properly. Things that are bad are not called good by any people who experience them; but things that are good are called bad by the universal verdict of humanity.

Let me explain a little: Certain things are bad so far as they go, such as pain, and no one, not even a lunatic, calls a tooth-ache good in itself; but a knife which cuts clumsily and with difficulty is called a bad knife, which it certainly is not. It is only not so good as other knives to which men have grown accustomed. A knife is never bad except on such rare occasions as that in which it is neatly and scientifically planted in the middle of one's back. The coarsest and bluntest knife which ever broke a pencil into pieces instead of sharpening it is a good thing in so far as it is a knife. It would have appeared a miracle in the Stone Age. What we call a bad knife is a good knife not good enough for us; what we call a bad hat is a good hat not good enough for us; what we call bad cookery is good cookery not good enough for us; what we call a bad civilization is a good civilization not good enough for us. We choose to call the great mass of the history of mankind bad, not because it is bad, but because we are better. This is palpably an unfair principle. Ivory may not be so white as snow, but the whole Arctic continent does not make ivory black.

Now it has appeared to me unfair that humanity should be engaged perpetually in calling all those things bad which have been good enough to make other things better, in everlastingly kicking down the ladder by which it has climbed. It has appeared to me that progress should be something else besides a continual parricide; therefore I have investigated the dust-heaps of humanity, and found a treasure in all of them. I have found that humanity is not incidentally engaged, but eternally and systematically engaged, in throwing gold into the gutter and diamonds into the sea. I have found that every man is disposed to call the green leaf of the tree a little less green than it is, and the snow of Christmas a little less white than it is; therefore I have imagined that the main business of a man, however humble, is defence. I have conceived that a defendant is chiefly required when worldlings despise the world—that a counsel for the defence would not have been out of place in that terrible day when the sun was darkened over Calvary and Man was rejected of men.

Chapter 2
A Defence of Penny Dreadfuls

ne of the strangest examples of the degree to which ordinary life is undervalued is the example of popular literature, the vast mass of which we contentedly describe as vulgar. The boy's novelette may be ignorant in a literary sense, which is only like saying that a modern novel is ignorant in the chemical sense, or the economic sense, or the astronomical sense; but it is not vulgar intrinsically—it is the actual centre of a million flaming imaginations.

In former centuries the educated class ignored the ruck of vulgar literature. They ignored, and therefore did not, properly speaking, despise it. Simple ignorance and indifference does not inflate the character with pride. A man does not walk down the street giving a haughty twirl to his moustaches at the thought of his superiority to some variety of deep-sea fishes. The old scholars left the whole under-world of popular compositions in a similar darkness.

To-day, however, we have reversed this principle. We do despise vulgar compositions, and we do not ignore them. We are in some danger of becoming petty in our study of pettiness; there is a terrible Circean law in the background that if the soul stoops too ostentatiously to examine anything it never gets up again. There is no class of vulgar publications about which there is, to my mind, more utterly ridiculous exaggeration and misconception than the current boys' literature of the lowest stratum. This class of composition has presumably always existed, and must exist. It has no more claim to be good literature than the daily conversation of its readers to be fine oratory, or the lodging-houses and tenements they inhabit to be sublime architecture. But people must have conversation, they must have houses, and they must have stories. The simple need for some kind of ideal world in which fictitious persons play an unhampered part is infinitely deeper and older than the rules of good art, and much more important. Every one of us in childhood has constructed such an invisible *dramatis personæ*, but it never occurred to our nurses to correct the composition by careful comparison with Balzac. In the East the professional story-teller goes from village to village with a small carpet; and I wish sincerely that anyone had the moral courage to spread that carpet and sit on it in Ludgate Circus. But it is not probable that all the tales of the carpet-bearer are little gems of original artistic workmanship. Literature and fiction are two entirely different things. Literature is a luxury; fiction is a necessity. A work of art can hardly be too short, for its climax is its merit. A story can never be too long, for its conclusion is merely to be deplored, like the last halfpenny or the last pipelight. And so, while the increase of the artistic conscience tends in more ambitious works to brevity and impressionism, voluminous industry still marks the producer of the true romantic trash. There was no end to the ballads of Robin

Hood; there is no end to the volumes about Dick Deadshot and the Avenging Nine. These two heroes are deliberately conceived as immortal.

But instead of basing all discussion of the problem upon the common-sense recognition of this fact—that the youth of the lower orders always has had and always must have formless and endless romantic reading of some kind, and then going on to make provision for its wholesomeness—we begin, generally speaking, by fantastic abuse of this reading as a whole and indignant surprise that the errand-boys under discussion do not read 'The Egoist' and 'The Master Builder.' It is the custom, particularly among magistrates, to attribute half the crimes of the Metropolis to cheap novelettes. If some grimy urchin runs away with an apple, the magistrate shrewdly points out that the child's knowledge that apples appease hunger is traceable to some curious literary researches. The boys themselves, when penitent, frequently accuse the novelettes with great bitterness, which is only to be expected from young people possessed of no little native humour. If I had forged a will, and could obtain sympathy by tracing the incident to the influence of Mr. George Moore's novels, I should find the greatest entertainment in the diversion. At any rate, it is firmly fixed in the minds of most people that gutter-boys, unlike everybody else in the community, find their principal motives for conduct in printed books.

Now it is quite clear that this objection, the objection brought by magistrates, has nothing to do with literary merit. Bad story writing is not a crime. Mr. Hall Caine walks the streets openly, and cannot be put in prison for an anticlimax. The objection rests upon the theory that the tone of the mass of boys' novelettes is criminal and degraded, appealing to low cupidity and low cruelty. This is the magisterial theory, and this is rubbish.

So far as I have seen them, in connection with the dirtiest book-stalls in the poorest districts, the facts are simply these: The whole bewildering mass of vulgar juvenile literature is concerned with adventures, rambling, disconnected and endless. It does not express any passion of any sort, for there is no human character of any sort. It runs eternally in certain grooves of local and historical type: the medieval knight, the eighteenth-century duellist, and the modern cowboy, recur with the same stiff simplicity as the conventional human figures in an Oriental pattern. I can quite as easily imagine a human being kindling wild appetites by the contemplation of his Turkey carpet as by such dehumanized and naked narrative as this.

Among these stories there are a certain number which deal sympathetically with the adventures of robbers, outlaws and pirates, which present in a dignified and romantic light thieves and murderers like Dick Turpin and Claude Duval. That is to say, they do precisely the same thing as Scott's 'Ivanhoe,' Scott's 'Rob Roy,' Scott's 'Lady of the Lake,' Byron's 'Corsair,' Wordsworth's 'Rob Roy's Grave,' Stevenson's 'Macaire,' Mr. Max Pemberton's 'Iron Pirate,' and a thousand more works distributed systematically as prizes and Christmas presents. Nobody imagines that an admiration of Locksley in 'Ivanhoe' will lead a boy to shoot Japanese arrows at the deer in Richmond Park; no one thinks that the incautious opening of Wordsworth at the poem on Rob Roy will set him up for life as a blackmailer. In the case of our own class, we recognise that this wild life is contemplated with pleasure by the young, not because it is like their own life, but because it is different from it. It might at least cross our minds that, for whatever other reason the errand-boy reads 'The Red Revenge,' it really is not because he is dripping with the gore of his own friends and relatives.

In this matter, as in all such matters, we lose our bearings entirely by speaking of the 'lower classes' when we mean humanity minus ourselves. This trivial romantic literature is not especially plebeian: it is simply human. The philanthropist can never forget classes and callings. He says, with a modest swagger, 'I have invited twenty-five factory hands to tea.' If he said 'I have invited twenty-five chartered accountants to tea,' everyone would see the humour of so simple a classification. But this is what we have done with this lumberland of foolish writing: we have probed, as if it were some monstrous new disease, what is, in fact, nothing but the foolish and valiant heart of man. Ordinary men will always be sentimentalists: for a sentimentalist is simply a man who has feelings and does not trouble to invent a new way of expressing them. These common and current publications have nothing essentially evil about them. They express the sanguine and heroic truisms on which civilization is built; for it is clear that unless civilization is built on truisms, it is not built at all. Clearly, there could be no safety for a society in which the remark by the Chief Justice that murder was wrong was regarded as an original and dazzling epigram.

If the authors and publishers of 'Dick Deadshot,' and such remarkable works, were suddenly to make a raid upon the educated class, were to take down the names of every man, however distinguished, who was caught at a University Extension Lecture, were to confiscate all our novels and warn us all to correct our lives, we should be seriously annoyed. Yet they have far more right to do so than we; for they, with all their idiotcy, are normal and we are abnormal. It is the modern literature of the educated, not of the uneducated, which is avowedly and aggressively criminal. Books recommending profligacy and pessimism, at which the high-souled errand-boy would shudder, lie upon all our drawing-room tables. If the dirtiest old owner of the dirtiest old bookstall in Whitechapel dared to display works really recommending polygamy or suicide, his stock would be seized by the police. These things are our luxuries. And with a hypocrisy so ludicrous as to be almost unparalleled in history, we rate the gutter-boys for their immorality at the very time that we are discussing (with equivocal German Professors) whether morality is valid at all. At the very instant that we curse the Penny Dreadful for encouraging thefts upon property, we canvass the proposition that all property is theft. At the very instant we accuse it (quite unjustly) of lubricity and indecency, we are cheerfully reading philosophies which glory in lubricity and indecency. At the very instant that we charge it with encouraging the young to destroy life, we are placidly discussing whether life is worth preserving.

But it is we who are the morbid exceptions; it is we who are the criminal class. This should be our great comfort. The vast mass of humanity, with their vast mass of idle books and idle words, have never doubted and never will doubt that courage is splendid, that fidelity is noble, that distressed ladies should be rescued, and vanquished enemies spared. There are a large number of cultivated persons who doubt these maxims of daily life, just as there are a large number of persons who believe they are the Prince of Wales; and I am told that both classes of people are entertaining conversationalists. But the average man or boy writes daily in these great gaudy diaries of his soul, which we call Penny Dreadfuls, a plainer and better gospel than any of those iridescent ethical paradoxes that the fashionable change as often as their bonnets. It may be a very limited aim in morality to shoot a 'many-faced and fickle traitor,' but at least it is a better aim than to be a many-faced and fickle traitor, which is a simple summary of a good many modern systems from Mr. d'Annunzio's downwards. So long as the coarse and thin texture of mere current popular romance is not touched by a paltry culture it will never be vitally immoral. It is always on the side of life. The poor—the slaves who really stoop under the burden of life—have often been mad, scatter-brained and cruel, but never hopeless. That is a class privilege, like cigars. Their drivelling literature will always be a 'blood and thunder' literature, as simple as the thunder of heaven and the blood of men.

Chapter 3
A Defence of Rash Vows

F a prosperous modern man, with a high hat and a frock-coat, were to solemnly pledge himself before all his clerks and friends to count the leaves on every third tree in Holland Walk, to hop up to the City on one leg every Thursday, to repeat the whole of Mill's 'Liberty' seventy-six times, to collect 300 dandelions in fields belonging to anyone of the name of Brown, to remain for thirty-one hours holding his left ear in his right hand, to sing the names of all his aunts in order of age on the top of an omnibus, or make any such unusual undertaking, we should immediately conclude that the man was mad, or, as it is sometimes expressed, was 'an artist in life.' Yet these vows are not more extraordinary than the vows which in the Middle Ages and in similar periods were made, not by fanatics merely, but by the greatest figures in civic and national civilization—by kings, judges, poets, and priests. One man swore to chain two mountains together, and the great chain hung there, it was said, for ages as a monument of that mystical folly. Another swore that he would find his way to Jerusalem with a patch over his eyes, and died looking for it. It is not easy to see that these two exploits, judged from a strictly rational standpoint, are any saner than the acts above suggested. A mountain is commonly a stationary and reliable object which it is not necessary to chain up at night like a dog. And it is not easy at first sight to see that a man pays a very high compliment to the Holy City by setting out for it under conditions which render it to the last degree improbable that he will ever get there.

But about this there is one striking thing to be noticed. If men behaved in that way in our time, we should, as we have said, regard them as symbols of the 'decadence.' But the men who did these things were not decadent; they belonged generally to the most robust classes of what is generally regarded as a robust age. Again, it will be urged that if men essentially sane performed such insanities, it was under the capricious direction of a superstitious religious system. This, again, will not hold water; for in the purely terrestrial and even sensual departments of life, such as love and lust, the medieval princes show the same mad promises and performances, the same misshapen imagination and the same monstrous self-sacrifice. Here we have a contradiction, to explain which it is necessary to think of the whole nature of vows from the beginning. And if we consider seriously and correctly the nature of vows, we shall, unless I am much mistaken, come to the conclusion that it is perfectly sane, and even sensible, to swear to chain mountains together, and that, if insanity is involved at all, it is a little insane not to do so.

The man who makes a vow makes an appointment with himself at some distant time or place. The danger of it is that himself should not keep the appointment. And in modern times this terror of one's self, of the weakness and mutability of one's self, has perilously increased, and is the real basis of the objection to vows of any kind. A modern man refrains from swearing to count the leaves on every third tree in Holland Walk, not because it is silly to do so (he does many sillier things), but because he has a profound conviction that before he had got to the three hundred and seventy-ninth leaf on the first tree he would be excessively tired of the subject and want to go home to tea. In other words, we fear that by that time he will be, in the common but hideously significant phrase, *another man*. Now, it is this horrible fairy tale of a man constantly changing into other men that is the soul of the Decadence. That John Paterson should, with apparent calm, look forward to being a certain General Barker on Monday, Dr. Macgregor on Tuesday, Sir Walter Carstairs on Wednesday, and Sam Slugg on Thursday, may seem a nightmare; but to that nightmare we give the name of modern culture. One great decadent, who is now dead, published a poem some time ago, in which he powerfully summed up the whole spirit of the movement by declaring that he could stand in the prison yard and entirely comprehend the feelings of a man about to be hanged:

'For he that lives more lives than one
More deaths than one must die.'

And the end of all this is that maddening horror of unreality which descends upon the decadents, and compared with which physical pain itself would have the freshness of a youthful thing. The one hell which imagination must conceive as most hellish is to be eternally acting a play without even the narrowest and dirtiest greenroom in which to be human. And this is the condition of the decadent, of the aesthete, of the free-lover. To be everlastingly passing through dangers which we know cannot scathe us, to be taking oaths which we know cannot bind us, to be defying enemies who we know cannot conquer us—this is the grinning tyranny of decadence which is called freedom.

Let us turn, on the other hand, to the maker of vows. The man who made a vow, however wild, gave a healthy and natural expression to the greatness of a great moment. He vowed, for example, to chain two mountains together, perhaps a symbol of some great relief, or love, or aspiration. Short as the moment of his resolve might be, it was, like all great moments, a moment of immortality, and the desire to say of it *exegi monumentum oere perennius* was the only sentiment that would satisfy his mind. The modern aesthetic man would, of course, easily see the emotional opportunity; he would vow to chain two mountains together. But, then, he would quite as cheerfully vow to chain the earth to the moon. And the withering consciousness that he did not mean what he said, that he was, in truth, saying nothing of any great import, would take from him exactly that sense of daring actuality which is the excitement of a vow. For what could be more maddening than an existence in which our mother or aunt received the information that we were going to assassinate the King or build a temple on Ben Nevis with the genial composure of custom?

The revolt against vows has been carried in our day even to the extent of a revolt against the typical vow of marriage. It is most amusing to listen to the opponents of marriage on this subject. They appear to imagine that the ideal of constancy was a yoke mysteriously imposed on mankind by the devil, instead of being, as it is, a yoke consistently imposed by all lovers on themselves. They have invented a phrase, a phrase that is a black and white contradiction in two words— 'free-love'—as if a lover ever had been, or ever could be, free. It is the nature of love to bind itself, and the institution of marriage merely paid the average man the compliment of taking him at his word. Modern sages offer to the lover, with an ill-flavoured grin, the largest liberties and the fullest irresponsibility; but they do not respect him as the old Church respected him; they do not write his oath upon the heavens, as the record of his highest moment. They give him every liberty except the liberty to sell his liberty, which is the only one that he wants.

In Mr. Bernard Shaw's brilliant play 'The Philanderer,' we have a vivid picture of this state of things. Charteris is a man perpetually endeavouring to be a free-lover, which is like endeavouring to be a married bachelor or a white negro. He is wandering in a hungry search for a certain exhilaration which he can only have when he has the courage to cease from wandering. Men knew better than this in old times—in the time, for example, of Shakespeare's heroes. When Shakespeare's men are really celibate they praise the undoubted advantages of celibacy, liberty, irresponsibility, a chance of continual change. But they were not such fools as to continue to talk of liberty when they were in such a condition that they could be made happy or miserable by the moving of someone else's eyebrow. Suckling classes love with debt in his praise of freedom.

> 'And he that's fairly out of both
> Of all the world is blest.
> He lives as in the golden age,
> When all things made were common;
> He takes his pipe, he takes his glass,
> He fears no man or woman.'

This is a perfectly possible, rational and manly position. But what have lovers to do with ridiculous affectations of fearing no man or woman? They know that in the turning of a hand the whole cosmic engine to the remotest star may become an instrument of music or an instrument of torture. They hear a song older than Suckling's, that has survived a hundred philosophies. 'Who is this that looketh out of the window, fair as the sun, clear as the moon, terrible as an army with banners?'

As we have said, it is exactly this backdoor, this sense of having a retreat behind us, that is, to our minds, the sterilizing spirit in modern pleasure. Everywhere there is the persistent and insane attempt to obtain pleasure without paying for it. Thus, in politics the modern Jingoes practically say, 'Let us have the pleasures of conquerors without the pains of soldiers: let us sit on sofas and be a hardy race.' Thus, in religion and morals, the decadent mystics say: 'Let us have the fragrance of sacred purity without the sorrows of self-restraint; let us sing hymns alternately to the Virgin and Priapus.' Thus in love the free-lovers say: 'Let us have the splendour of offering ourselves without the peril of committing ourselves; let us see whether one cannot commit suicide an unlimited number of times.'

Emphatically it will not work. There are thrilling moments, doubtless, for the spectator, the amateur, and the aesthete; but there is one thrill that is known only to the soldier who fights for his own flag, to the ascetic who starves himself for his own illumination, to the lover who makes finally his own choice. And it is this transfiguring self-discipline that makes the vow a truly sane thing. It must have satisfied even the giant hunger of the soul of a lover or a poet to know that in consequence of some one instant of decision that strange chain would hang for centuries in the Alps among the silences of stars and snows. All around us is the city of small sins, abounding in backways and retreats, but surely, sooner or later, the towering flame will rise from the harbour announcing that the reign of the cowards is over and a man is burning his ships.

Chapter 4
A Defence of Skeletons

ome little time ago I stood among immemorial English trees that seemed to take hold upon the stars like a brood of Ygdrasils. As I walked among these living pillars I became gradually aware that the rustics who lived and died in their shadow adopted a very curious conversational tone. They seemed to be constantly apologizing for the trees, as if they were a very poor show. After elaborate investigation, I discovered that their gloomy and penitent tone was traceable to the fact that it was winter and all the trees were bare. I assured them that I did not resent the fact that it was winter, that I knew the thing had happened before, and that no forethought on their part could have averted this blow of destiny. But I could not in any way reconcile them to the fact that it *was* winter. There was evidently a general feeling that I had caught the trees in a kind of disgraceful deshabille, and that they ought not to be seen until, like the first human sinners, they had covered themselves with leaves. So it is quite clear that, while very few people appear to know anything of how trees look in winter, the actual foresters know less than anyone. So far from the line of the tree when it is bare appearing harsh and severe, it is luxuriantly indefinable to an unusual degree; the fringe of the forest melts away like a vignette. The tops of two or three high trees when they are leafless are so soft that they seem like the gigantic brooms of that fabulous lady who was sweeping the cobwebs off the sky. The outline of a leafy forest is in comparison hard, gross and blotchy; the clouds of night do not more certainly obscure the moon than those green and monstrous clouds obscure the tree; the actual sight of the little wood, with its gray and silver sea of life, is entirely a winter vision. So dim and delicate is the heart of the winter woods, a kind of glittering gloaming, that a figure stepping towards us in the chequered twilight seems as if he were breaking through unfathomable depths of spiders' webs.

But surely the idea that its leaves are the chief grace of a tree is a vulgar one, on a par with the idea that his hair is the chief grace of a pianist. When winter, that healthy ascetic, carries his gigantic razor over hill and valley, and shaves all the trees like monks, we feel surely that they are all the more like trees if they are shorn, just as so many painters and musicians would be all the more like men if they were less like mops. But it does appear to be a deep and essential difficulty that men have an abiding terror of their own structure, or of the structure of things they love. This is felt dimly in the skeleton of the tree: it is felt profoundly in the skeleton of the man.

The importance of the human skeleton is very great, and the horror with which it is commonly regarded is somewhat mysterious. Without claiming for the human skeleton a wholly conventional beauty, we may assert that he is certainly not uglier than a bull-dog, whose popularity never wanes, and that he has a vastly more cheerful and ingratiating expression. But just as man is mysteriously ashamed of the skeletons of the trees in winter, so he is mysteriously ashamed of the skeleton of himself in death. It is a singular thing altogether, this horror of the architecture of things. One would think it would be most unwise in a man to be afraid of a skeleton, since Nature has set curious and quite insuperable obstacles to his running away from it.

One ground exists for this terror: a strange idea has infected humanity that the skeleton is typical of death. A man might as well say that a factory chimney was typical of bankruptcy. The factory may be left naked after ruin, the skeleton may be left naked after bodily dissolution; but both of them have had a lively and workmanlike life of their own, all the pulleys creaking, all the wheels turning, in the House of Livelihood as in the House of Life. There is no reason why this creature (new, as I fancy, to art), the living skeleton, should not become the essential symbol of life.

The truth is that man's horror of the skeleton is not horror of death at all. It is man's eccentric glory that he has not, generally speaking, any objection to being dead, but has a very serious objection to being undignified. And the fundamental matter which troubles him in the skeleton is the reminder that the ground-plan of his appearance is shamelessly grotesque. I do not know why he should object to this. He contentedly takes his place in a world that does not pretend to be genteel—a laughing, working, jeering world. He sees millions of animals carrying, with quite a dandified levity, the most monstrous shapes and appendages, the most preposterous horns, wings, and legs, when they are necessary to utility. He sees the good temper of the frog, the unaccountable happiness of the hippopotamus. He sees a whole universe which is ridiculous, from the animalcule, with a head too big for its body, up to the comet, with a tail too big for its head. But when it comes to the delightful oddity of his own inside, his sense of humour rather abruptly deserts him.

In the Middle Ages and in the Renaissance (which was, in certain times and respects, a much gloomier period) this idea of the skeleton had a vast influence in freezing the pride out of all earthly pomps and the fragrance out of all fleeting pleasures. But it was not, surely, the mere dread of death that did this, for these were ages in which men went to meet death singing; it was the idea of the degradation of man in the grinning ugliness of his structure that withered the juvenile insolence of beauty and pride. And in this it almost assuredly did more good than harm. There is nothing so cold or so pitiless as youth, and youth in aristocratic stations and ages tended to an impeccable dignity, an endless summer of success which needed to be very sharply reminded of the scorn of the stars. It was well that such flamboyant prigs should be convinced that one practical joke, at least, would bowl them over, that they would fall into one grinning man-trap, and not rise again. That the whole structure of their existence was as wholesomely ridiculous as that of a pig or a parrot they could not be expected to realize; that birth was humorous, coming of age humorous, drinking and fighting humorous, they were far too young and solemn to know. But at least they were taught that death was humorous.

There is a peculiar idea abroad that the value and fascination of what we call Nature lie in her beauty. But the fact that Nature is beautiful in the sense that a dado or a Liberty curtain is beautiful, is only one of her charms, and almost an accidental one. The highest and most valuable quality in Nature is not her beauty, but her generous and defiant ugliness. A hundred instances might be taken. The croaking noise of the rooks is, in itself, as hideous as the whole hell of sounds in a London railway tunnel. Yet it uplifts us like a trumpet with its coarse kindliness and honesty, and the lover in 'Maud' could actually persuade himself that this abominable noise resembled his lady-love's name. Has the poet, for whom Nature means only roses and lilies, ever heard a pig grunting? It is a noise that does a man good—a strong, snorting, imprisoned noise, breaking its way out of unfathomable dungeons through every possible outlet and organ. It might be the voice of the earth itself, snoring in its mighty sleep. This is the deepest, the oldest, the most wholesome and religious sense of the value of Nature—the value which comes from her immense babyishness. She is as top-heavy, as grotesque, as solemn and as happy as a child. The mood does come when we see all her shapes like shapes that a baby scrawls upon a slate—simple, rudimentary, a million years older and stronger than the whole disease that is called Art. The objects of earth and heaven seem to combine into a nursery tale, and our relation to things seems for a moment so simple that a dancing lunatic would be needed to do justice to its lucidity and levity. The tree above my head is flapping like some gigantic bird standing on one leg; the moon is like the eye of a Cyclops. And, however much my face clouds with sombre vanity, or vulgar vengeance, or contemptible contempt, the bones of my skull beneath it are laughing for ever.

Chapter 5
A Defence of Publicity

t is a very significant fact that the form of art in which the modern world has certainly not improved upon the ancient is what may roughly be called the art of the open air. Public monuments have certainly not improved, nor has the criticism of them improved, as is evident from the fashion of condemning such a large number of them as pompous. An interesting essay might be written on the enormous number of words that are used as insults when they are really compliments. It is in itself a singular study in that tendency which, as I have said, is always making things out worse than they are, and necessitating a systematic attitude of defence. Thus, for example, some dramatic critics cast contempt upon a dramatic performance by calling it theatrical, which simply means that it is suitable to a theatre, and is as much a compliment as calling a poem poetical. Similarly we speak disdainfully of a certain kind of work as sentimental, which simply means possessing the admirable and essential quality of sentiment. Such phrases are all parts of one peddling and cowardly philosophy, and remind us of the days when 'enthusiast' was a term of reproach. But of all this vocabulary of unconscious eulogies nothing is more striking than the word 'pompous.'

Properly speaking, of course, a public monument ought to be pompous. Pomp is its very object; it would be absurd to have columns and pyramids blushing in some coy nook like violets in the woods of spring. And public monuments have in this matter a great and much-needed lesson to teach. Valour and mercy and the great enthusiasms ought to be a great deal more public than they are at present. We are too fond nowadays of committing the sin of fear and calling it the virtue of reverence. We have forgotten the old and wholesome morality of the Book of Proverbs, 'Wisdom crieth without; her voice is heard in the streets.' In Athens and Florence her voice was heard in the streets. They had an outdoor life of war and argument, and they had what modern commercial civilization has never had—an outdoor art. Religious services, the most sacred of all things, have always been held publicly; it is entirely a new and debased notion that sanctity is the same as secrecy. A great many modern poets, with the most abstruse and delicate sensibilities, love darkness, when all is said and done, much for the same reason that thieves love it. The mission of a great spire or statue should be to strike the spirit with a sudden sense of pride as with a thunderbolt. It should lift us with it into the empty and ennobling air. Along the base of every noble monument, whatever else may be written there, runs in invisible letters the lines of Swinburne:

'This thing is God:
To be man with thy might,

To go straight in the strength of thy spirit, and live
out thy life in the light.'

If a public monument does not meet this first supreme and obvious need, that
it should be public and monumental, it fails from the outset.

There has arisen lately a school of realistic sculpture, which may perhaps be
better described as a school of sketchy sculpture. Such a movement was right and
inevitable as a reaction from the mean and dingy pomposity of English Victorian
statuary. Perhaps the most hideous and depressing object in the universe—far
more hideous and depressing than one of Mr. H.G. Wells's shapeless monsters of
the slime (and not at all unlike them)—is the statue of an English philanthropist.
Almost as bad, though, of course, not quite as bad, are the statues of English
politicians in Parliament Fields. Each of them is cased in a cylindrical frock-coat,
and each carries either a scroll or a dubious-looking garment over the arm that
might be either a bathing-towel or a light great-coat. Each of them is in an
oratorical attitude, which has all the disadvantage of being affected without even
any of the advantages of being theatrical. Let no one suppose that such abortions
arise merely from technical demerit. In every line of those leaden dolls is expressed
the fact that they were not set up with any heat of natural enthusiasm for beauty
or dignity. They were set up mechanically, because it would seem indecorous or
stingy if they were not set up. They were even set up sulkily, in a utilitarian age
which was haunted by the thought that there were a great many more sensible
ways of spending money. So long as this is the dominant national sentiment, the
land is barren, statues and churches will not grow—for they have to grow, as much
as trees and flowers. But this moral disadvantage which lay so heavily upon the
early Victorian sculpture lies in a modified degree upon that rough, picturesque,
commonplace sculpture which has begun to arise, and of which the statue of
Darwin in the South Kensington Museum and the statue of Gordon in Trafalgar
Square are admirable examples. It is not enough for a popular monument to be
artistic, like a black charcoal sketch; it must be striking; it must be in the highest
sense of the word sensational; it must stand for humanity; it must speak for us
to the stars; it must declare in the face of all the heavens that when the longest
and blackest catalogue has been made of all our crimes and follies there are some
things of which we men are not ashamed.

The two modes of commemorating a public man are a statue and a biography.
They are alike in certain respects, as, for example, in the fact that neither of them
resembles the original, and that both of them commonly tone down not only all a
man's vices, but all the more amusing of his virtues. But they are treated in one
respect differently. We never hear anything about biography without hearing
something about the sanctity of private life and the necessity for suppressing the
whole of the most important part of a man's existence. The sculptor does not
work at this disadvantage. The sculptor does not leave out the nose of an eminent
philanthropist because it is too beautiful to be given to the public; he does not

depict a statesman with a sack over his head because his smile was too sweet to be endurable in the light of day. But in biography the thesis is popularly and solidly maintained, so that it requires some courage even to hint a doubt of it, that the better a man was, the more truly human life he led, the less should be said about it.

For this idea, this modern idea that sanctity is identical with secrecy, there is one thing at least to be said. It is for all practical purposes an entirely new idea; it was unknown to all the ages in which the idea of sanctity really flourished. The record of the great spiritual movements of mankind is dead against the idea that spirituality is a private matter. The most awful secret of every man's soul, its most lonely and individual need, its most primal and psychological relation-ship, the thing called worship, the communication between the soul and the last reality—this most private matter is the most public spectacle in the world. Anyone who chooses to walk into a large church on Sunday morning may see a hundred men each alone with his Maker. He stands, in truth, in the presence of one of the strangest spectacles in the world—a mob of hermits. And in thus definitely espousing publicity by making public the most internal mystery, Christianity acts in accordance with its earliest origins and its terrible beginning. It was surely by no accident that the spectacle which darkened the sun at noonday was set upon a hill. The martyrdoms of the early Christians were public not only by the caprice of the oppressor, but by the whole desire and conception of the victims.

The mere grammatical meaning of the word 'martyr' breaks into pieces at a blow the whole notion of the privacy of goodness. The Christian martyrdoms were more than demonstrations: they were advertisements. In our day the new theory of spiritual delicacy would desire to alter all this. It would permit Christ to be crucified if it was necessary to His Divine nature, but it would ask in the name of good taste why He could not be crucified in a private room. It would declare that the act of a martyr in being torn in pieces by lions was vulgar and sensational, though, of course, it would have no objection to being torn in pieces by a lion in one's own parlour before a circle of really intimate friends.

It is, I am inclined to think, a decadent and diseased purity which has inau-gurated this notion that the sacred object must be hidden. The stars have never lost their sanctity, and they are more shameless and naked and numerous than advertisements of Pears' soap. It would be a strange world indeed if Nature was suddenly stricken with this ethereal shame, if the trees grew with their roots in the air and their load of leaves and blossoms underground, if the flowers closed at dawn and opened at sunset, if the sunflower turned towards the darkness, and the birds flew, like bats, by night.

Chapter 6
A Defence of Nonsense

here are two equal and eternal ways of looking at this twilight world of ours: we may see it as the twilight of evening or the twilight of morning; we may think of anything, down to a fallen acorn, as a descendant or as an ancestor. There are times when we are almost crushed, not so much with the load of the evil as with the load of the goodness of humanity, when we feel that we are nothing but the inheritors of a humiliating splendour. But there are other times when everything seems primitive, when the ancient stars are only sparks blown from a boy's bonfire, when the whole earth seems so young and experimental that even the white hair of the aged, in the fine biblical phrase, is like almond-trees that blossom, like the white hawthorn grown in May. That it is good for a man to realize that he is 'the heir of all the ages' is pretty commonly admitted; it is a less popular but equally important point that it is good for him sometimes to realize that he is not only an ancestor, but an ancestor of primal antiquity; it is good for him to wonder whether he is not a hero, and to experience ennobling doubts as to whether he is not a solar myth.

The matters which most thoroughly evoke this sense of the abiding childhood of the world are those which are really fresh, abrupt and inventive in any age; and if we were asked what was the best proof of this adventurous youth in the nineteenth century we should say, with all respect to its portentous sciences and philosophies, that it was to be found in the rhymes of Mr. Edward Lear and in the literature of nonsense. 'The Dong with the Luminous Nose,' at least, is original, as the first ship and the first plough were original.

It is true in a certain sense that some of the greatest writers the world has seen—Aristophanes, Rabelais and Sterne—have written nonsense; but unless we are mistaken, it is in a widely different sense. The nonsense of these men was satiric—that is to say, symbolic; it was a kind of exuberant capering round a discovered truth. There is all the difference in the world between the instinct of satire, which, seeing in the Kaiser's moustaches something typical of him, draws them continually larger and larger; and the instinct of nonsense which, for no reason whatever, imagines what those moustaches would look like on the present Archbishop of Canterbury if he grew them in a fit of absence of mind. We incline to think that no age except our own could have understood that the Quangle-Wangle meant absolutely nothing, and the Lands of the Jumblies were absolutely nowhere. We fancy that if the account of the knave's trial in 'Alice in Wonderland' had been published in the seventeenth century it would have been bracketed with Bunyan's 'Trial of Faithful' as a parody on the State prosecutions of the time. We fancy that if 'The Dong with the Luminous Nose' had appeared in the same period everyone would have called it a dull satire on Oliver Cromwell.

It is altogether advisedly that we quote chiefly from Mr. Lear's 'Nonsense Rhymes.' To our mind he is both chronologically and essentially the father of nonsense; we think him superior to Lewis Carroll. In one sense, indeed, Lewis Carroll has a great advantage. We know what Lewis Carroll was in daily life: he was a singularly serious and conventional don, universally respected, but very much of a pedant and something of a Philistine. Thus his strange double life in earth and in dreamland emphasizes the idea that lies at the back of nonsense—the idea of *escape*, of escape into a world where things are not fixed horribly in an eternal appropriateness, where apples grow on pear-trees, and any odd man you meet may have three legs. Lewis Carroll, living one life in which he would have thundered morally against any one who walked on the wrong plot of grass, and another life in which he would cheerfully call the sun green and the moon blue, was, by his very divided nature, his one foot on both worlds, a perfect type of the position of modern nonsense. His Wonderland is a country populated by insane mathematicians. We feel the whole is an escape into a world of masquerade; we feel that if we could pierce their disguises, we might discover that Humpty Dumpty and the March Hare were Professors and Doctors of Divinity enjoying a mental holiday. This sense of escape is certainly less emphatic in Edward Lear, because of the completeness of his citizenship in the world of unreason. We do not know his prosaic biography as we know Lewis Carroll's. We accept him as a purely fabulous figure, on his own description of himself:

> 'His body is perfectly spherical,
> He weareth a runcible hat.'

While Lewis Carroll's Wonderland is purely intellectual, Lear introduces quite another element—the element of the poetical and even emotional. Carroll works by the pure reason, but this is not so strong a contrast; for, after all, mankind in the main has always regarded reason as a bit of a joke. Lear introduces his unmeaning words and his amorphous creatures not with the pomp of reason, but with the romantic prelude of rich hues and haunting rhythms.

> 'Far and few, far and few,
> Are the lands where the Jumblies live,'

is an entirely different type of poetry to that exhibited in 'Jabberwocky.' Carroll, with a sense of mathematical neatness, makes his whole poem a mosaic of new and mysterious words. But Edward Lear, with more subtle and placid effrontery, is always introducing scraps of his own elvish dialect into the middle of simple and rational statements, until we are almost stunned into admitting that we know what they mean. There is a genial ring of commonsense about such lines as,

> 'For his aunt Jobiska said "Every one knows
> That a Pobble is better without his toes," '

which is beyond the reach of Carroll. The poet seems so easy on the matter that we are almost driven to pretend that we see his meaning, that we know the peculiar difficulties of a Pobble, that we are as old travellers in the 'Gromboolian Plain' as he is.

Our claim that nonsense is a new literature (we might almost say a new sense) would be quite indefensible if nonsense were nothing more than a mere aesthetic fancy. Nothing sublimely artistic has ever arisen out of mere art, any more than anything essentially reasonable has ever arisen out of the pure reason. There must always be a rich moral soil for any great aesthetic growth. The principle of *art for art's sake* is a very good principle if it means that there is a vital distinction between the earth and the tree that has its roots in the earth; but it is a very bad principle if it means that the tree could grow just as well with its roots in the air. Every great literature has always been allegorical—allegorical of some view of the whole universe. The 'Iliad' is only great because all life is a battle, the 'Odyssey' because all life is a journey, the Book of Job because all life is a riddle. There is one attitude in which we think that all existence is summed up in the word 'ghosts'; another, and somewhat better one, in which we think it is summed up in the words 'A Midsummer Night's Dream.' Even the vulgarest melodrama or detective story can be good if it expresses something of the delight in sinister possibilities—the healthy lust for darkness and terror which may come on us any night in walking down a dark lane. If, therefore, nonsense is really to be the literature of the future, it must have its own version of the Cosmos to offer; the world must not only be the tragic, romantic, and religious, it must be nonsensical also. And here we fancy that nonsense will, in a very unexpected way, come to the aid of the spiritual view of things. Religion has for centuries been trying to make men exult in the 'wonders' of creation, but it has forgotten that a thing cannot be completely wonderful so long as it remains sensible. So long as we regard a tree as an obvious thing, naturally and reasonably created for a giraffe to eat, we cannot properly wonder at it. It is when we consider it as a prodigious wave of the living soil sprawling up to the skies for no reason in particular that we take off our hats, to the astonishment of the park-keeper. Everything has in fact another side to it, like the moon, the patroness of nonsense. Viewed from that other side, a bird is a blossom broken loose from its chain of stalk, a man a quadruped begging on its hind legs, a house a gigantesque hat to cover a man from the sun, a chair an apparatus of four wooden legs for a cripple with only two.

This is the side of things which tends most truly to spiritual wonder. It is significant that in the greatest religious poem existent, the Book of Job, the argument which convinces the infidel is not (as has been represented by the merely rational religionism of the eighteenth century) a picture of the ordered beneficence of the Creation; but, on the contrary, a picture of the huge and undecipherable unreason of it. 'Hast Thou sent the rain upon the desert where no man is?' This simple sense of wonder at the shapes of things, and at their exuberant independence of our intellectual standards and our trivial definitions, is the basis of spirituality as it is the basis of nonsense. Nonsense and faith (strange as the conjunction may seem) are the two supreme symbolic assertions of the truth that to draw out the soul of things with a syllogism is as impossible as to draw out Leviathan with a hook. The well-meaning person who, by merely studying the logical side of things, has decided that 'faith is nonsense,' does not know how truly he speaks; later it may come back to him in the form that nonsense is faith.

Chapter 7
A Defence of Planets

book has at one time come under my notice called 'Terra Firma: the Earth not a Planet.' The author was a Mr. D. Wardlaw Scott, and he quoted very seriously the opinions of a large number of other persons, of whom we have never heard, but who are evidently very important. Mr. Beach of Southsea, for example, thinks that the world is flat; and in Southsea perhaps it is. It is no part of my present intention, however, to follow Mr. Scott's arguments in detail. On the lines of such arguments it may be shown that the earth is flat, and, for the matter of that, that it is triangular. A few examples will suffice:

One of Mr. Scott's objections was that if a projectile is fired from a moving body there is a difference in the distance to which it carries according to the direction in which it is sent. But as in practice there is not the slightest difference whichever way the thing is done, in the case of the earth 'we have a forcible overthrow of all fancies relative to the motion of the earth, and a striking proof that the earth is not a globe.'

This is altogether one of the quaintest arguments we have ever seen. It never seems to occur to the author, among other things, that when the firing and falling of the shot all take place upon the moving body, there is nothing whatever to compare them with. As a matter of fact, of course, a shot fired at an elephant does actually often travel towards the marksman, but much slower than the marksman travels. Mr. Scott probably would not like to contemplate the fact that the elephant, properly speaking, swings round and hits the bullet. To us it appears full of a rich cosmic humour.

I will only give one other example of the astronomical proofs:

'If the earth were a globe, the distance round the surface, say, at 45 degrees south latitude, could not possibly be any greater than the same latitude north; but since it is found by navigators to be twice the distance—to say the least of it—or double the distance it ought to be according to the globular theory, it is a proof that the earth is not a globe.'

This sort of thing reduces my mind to a pulp. I can faintly resist when a man says that if the earth were a globe cats would not have four legs; but when he says that if the earth were a globe cats would not have five legs I am crushed.

But, as I have indicated, it is not in the scientific aspect of this remarkable theory that I am for the moment interested. It is rather with the difference between the flat and the round worlds as conceptions in art and imagination that I am concerned. It is a very remarkable thing that none of us are really Copernicans in our actual outlook upon things. We are convinced intellectually that we inhabit a small provincial planet, but we do not feel in the least suburban. Men of science have quarrelled with the Bible because it is not based upon the true astronomical system, but it is certainly open to the orthodox to say that if it had been it would never have convinced anybody.

If a single poem or a single story were really transfused with the Copernican idea, the thing would be a nightmare. Can we think of a solemn scene of mountain stillness in which some prophet is standing in a trance, and then realize that the whole scene is whizzing round like a zoetrope at the rate of nineteen miles a second? Could we tolerate the notion of a mighty King delivering a sublime fiat and then remember that for all practical purposes he is hanging head downwards in space? A strange fable might be written of a man who was blessed or cursed with the Copernican eye, and saw all men on the earth like tintacks clustering round a magnet. It would be singular to imagine how very different the speech of an aggressive egoist, announcing the independence and divinity of man, would sound if he were seen hanging on to the planet by his boot soles.

For, despite Mr. Wardlaw Scott's horror at the Newtonian astronomy and its contradiction of the Bible, the whole distinction is a good instance of the difference between letter and spirit; the letter of the Old Testament is opposed to the conception of the solar system, but the spirit has much kinship with it. The writers of the Book of Genesis had no theory of gravitation, which to the normal person will appear a fact of as much importance as that they had no umbrellas. But the theory of gravitation has a curiously Hebrew sentiment in it—a sentiment of combined dependence and certainty, a sense of grappling unity, by which all things hang upon one thread. 'Thou hast hanged the world upon nothing,' said the author of the Book of Job, and in that sentence wrote the whole appalling poetry of modern astronomy. The sense of the preciousness and fragility of the universe, the sense of being in the hollow of a hand, is one which the round and rolling earth gives in its most thrilling form. Mr. Wardlaw Scott's flat earth would be the true territory for a comfortable atheist. Nor would the old Jews have any objection to being as much upside down as right way up. They had no foolish ideas about the dignity of man.

It would be an interesting speculation to imagine whether the world will ever develop a Copernican poetry and a Copernican habit of fancy; whether we shall ever speak of 'early earth-turn' instead of 'early sunrise,' and speak indifferently of looking up at the daisies, or looking down on the stars. But if we ever do, there are really a large number of big and fantastic facts awaiting us, worthy to make a new mythology. Mr. Wardlaw Scott, for example, with genuine, if unconscious, imagination, says that according to astronomers, 'the sea is a vast mountain of water miles high.' To have discovered that mountain of moving crystal, in which the fishes build like birds, is like discovering Atlantis: it is enough to make the old world young again. In the new poetry which we contemplate, athletic young men will set out sturdily to climb up the face of the sea. If we once realize all this earth as it is, we should find ourselves in a land of miracles: we shall discover a new planet at the moment that we discover our own. Among all the strange things that men have forgotten, the most universal and catastrophic lapse of memory is that by which they have forgotten that they are living on a star.

In the early days of the world, the discovery of a fact of natural history was immediately followed by the realization of it as a fact of poetry. When man awoke from the long fit of absent-mindedness which is called the automatic animal state, and began to notice the queer facts that the sky was blue and the grass green, he immediately began to use those facts symbolically. Blue, the colour of the sky, became a symbol of celestial holiness; green passed into the language as indicating a freshness verging upon unintelligence. If we had the good fortune to live in a world in which the sky was green and the grass blue, the symbolism would have been different. But for some mysterious reason this habit of realizing poetically the facts of science has ceased abruptly with scientific progress, and all the confounding portents preached by Galileo and Newton have fallen on deaf ears. They painted a picture of the universe compared with which the Apocalypse with its falling stars was a mere idyll. They declared that we are all careering through space, clinging to a cannon-ball, and the poets ignore the matter as if it were a remark about the weather. They say that an invisible force holds us in our own armchairs while the earth hurtles like a boomerang; and men still go back to dusty records to prove the mercy of God. They tell us that Mr. Scott's monstrous vision of a mountain of sea-water rising in a solid dome, like the glass mountain in the fairy-tale, is actually a fact, and men still go back to the fairy-tale. To what towering heights of poetic imagery might we not have risen if only the poetizing of natural history had continued and man's fancy had played with the planets as naturally as it once played with the flowers! We might have had a planetary patriotism, in which the green leaf should be like a cockade, and the sea an everlasting dance of drums. We might have been proud of what our star has wrought, and worn its heraldry haughtily in the blind tournament of the spheres. All this, indeed, we may surely do yet; for with all the multiplicity of knowledge there is one thing happily that no man knows: whether the world is old or young.

Chapter 8
A Defence of China

here are some things of which the world does not like to be reminded, for they are the dead loves of the world. One of these is that great enthusiasm for the Arcadian life which, however much it may now lie open to the sneers of realism, did, beyond all question, hold sway for an enormous period of the world's history, from the times that we describe as ancient down to times that may fairly be called recent. The conception of the innocent and hilarious life of shepherds and shepherdesses certainly covered and absorbed the time of Theocritus, of Virgil, of Catullus, of Dante, of Cervantes, of Ariosto, of Shakespeare, and of Pope. We are told that the gods of the heathen were stone and brass, but stone and brass have never endured with the long endurance of the China Shepherdess. The Catholic Church and the Ideal Shepherd are indeed almost the only things that have bridged the abyss between the ancient world and the modern. Yet, as we say, the world does not like to be reminded of this boyish enthusiasm.

But imagination, the function of the historian, cannot let so great an element alone. By the cheap revolutionary it is commonly supposed that imagination is a merely rebellious thing, that it has its chief function in devising new and fantastic republics. But imagination has its highest use in a retrospective realization. The trumpet of imagination, like the trumpet of the Resurrection, calls the dead out of their graves. Imagination sees Delphi with the eyes of a Greek, Jerusalem with the eyes of a Crusader, Paris with the eyes of a Jacobin, and Arcadia with the eyes of a Euphuist. The prime function of imagination is to see our whole orderly system of life as a pile of stratified revolutions. In spite of all revolutionaries it must be said that the function of imagination is not to make strange things settled, so much as to make settled things strange; not so much to make wonders facts as to make facts wonders. To the imaginative the truisms are all paradoxes, since they were paradoxes in the Stone Age; to them the ordinary copy-book blazes with blasphemy.

Let us, then, consider in this light the old pastoral or Arcadian ideal. But first certainly one thing must be definitely recognised. This Arcadian art and literature is a lost enthusiasm. To study it is like fumbling in the love-letters of a dead man. To us its flowers seem as tawdry as cockades; the lambs that dance to the shepherd's pipe seem to dance with all the artificiality of a ballet. Even our own prosaic toil seems to us more joyous than that holiday. Where its ancient exuberance passed the bounds of wisdom and even of virtue, its caperings seem frozen into the stillness of an antique frieze. In those gray old pictures a bacchanal seems as dull as an archdeacon. Their very sins seem colder than our restraints.

All this may be frankly recognised: all the barren sentimentality of the Arcadian ideal and all its insolent optimism. But when all is said and done, something else remains.

Through ages in which the most arrogant and elaborate ideals of power and civilization held otherwise undisputed sway, the ideal of the perfect and healthy peasant did undoubtedly represent in some shape or form the conception that there was a dignity in simplicity and a dignity in labour. It was good for the ancient aristocrat, even if he could not attain to innocence and the wisdom of the earth, to believe that these things were the secrets of the priesthood of the poor. It was good for him to believe that even if heaven was not above him, heaven was below him. It was well that he should have amid all his flamboyant triumphs the never-extinguished sentiment that there was something better than his triumphs, the conception that 'there remaineth a rest.'

The conception of the Ideal Shepherd seems absurd to our modern ideas. But, after all, it was perhaps the only trade of the democracy which was equalized with the trades of the aristocracy even by the aristocracy itself. The shepherd of pastoral poetry was, without doubt, very different from the shepherd of actual fact. Where one innocently piped to his lambs, the other innocently swore at them; and their divergence in intellect and personal cleanliness was immense. But the difference between the ideal shepherd who danced with Amaryllis and the real shepherd who thrashed her is not a scrap greater than the difference between the ideal soldier who dies to capture the colours and the real soldier who lives to clean his accoutrements, between the ideal priest who is everlastingly by someone's bed and the real priest who is as glad as anyone else to get to his own. There are ideal conceptions and real men in every calling; yet there are few who object to the ideal conceptions, and not many, after all, who object to the real men.

The fact, then, is this: So far from resenting the existence in art and literature of an ideal shepherd, I genuinely regret that the shepherd is the only democratic calling that has ever been raised to the level of the heroic callings conceived by an aristocratic age. So far from objecting to the Ideal Shepherd, I wish there were an Ideal Postman, an Ideal Grocer, and an Ideal Plumber. It is undoubtedly true that we should laugh at the idea of an Ideal Postman; it is true, and it proves that we are not genuine democrats.

Undoubtedly the modern grocer, if called upon to act in an Arcadian manner, if desired to oblige with a symbolic dance expressive of the delights of grocery, or to perform on some simple instrument while his assistants skipped around him, would be embarrassed, and perhaps even reluctant. But it may be questioned whether this temporary reluctance of the grocer is a good thing, or evidence of a good condition of poetic feeling in the grocery business as a whole. There certainly should be an ideal image of health and happiness in any trade, and its remoteness from the reality is not the only important question. No one supposes that the mass of traditional conceptions of duty and glory are always operative, for example, in the mind of a soldier or a doctor; that the Battle of Waterloo actually makes a private enjoy pipeclaying his trousers, or that the 'health of humanity' softens the momentary phraseology of a physician called out of bed at two o'clock in the morning. But although no ideal obliterates the ugly drudgery and detail of any calling, that ideal does, in the case of the soldier or the doctor, exist definitely in the background and makes that drudgery worth while as a whole. It is a serious calamity that no such ideal exists in the case of the vast number of honourable trades and crafts on which the existence of a modern city depends. It is a pity that current thought and sentiment offer nothing corresponding to the old conception of patron saints. If they did there would be a Patron Saint of Plumbers, and this would alone be a revolution, for it would force the individual craftsman to believe that there was once a perfect being who did actually plumb.

When all is said and done, then, we think it much open to question whether the world has not lost something in the complete disappearance of the ideal of the happy peasant. It is foolish enough to suppose that the rustic went about all over ribbons, but it is better than knowing that he goes about all over rags and being indifferent to the fact. The modern realistic study of the poor does in reality lead the student further astray than the old idyllic notion. For we cannot get the chiaroscuro of humble life so long as its virtues seem to us as gross as its vices and its joys as sullen as its sorrows. Probably at the very moment that we can see nothing but a dull-faced man smoking and drinking heavily with his friend in a pot-house, the man himself is on his soul's holiday, crowned with the flowers of a passionate idleness, and far more like the Happy Peasant than the world will ever know.

Chapter 9
A Defence of Useful Information

t is natural and proper enough that the masses of explosive am-
munition stored up in detective stories and the replete and solid
sweet-stuff shops which are called sentimental novelettes should
be popular with the ordinary customer. It is not difficult to realize
that all of us, ignorant or cultivated, are primarily interested in
murder and love-making. The really extraordinary thing is that the most appalling fictions are not actually so popular as that literature which deals with the
most undisputed and depressing facts. Men are not apparently so interested in
murder and love-making as they are in the number of different forms of latchkey
which exist in London or the time that it would take a grasshopper to jump from
Cairo to the Cape. The enormous mass of fatuous and useless truth which fills
the most widely-circulated papers, such as *Tit-Bits, Science Siftings*, and many
of the illustrated magazines, is certainly one of the most extraordinary kinds of
emotional and mental pabulum on which man ever fed. It is almost incredible
that these preposterous statistics should actually be more popular than the most
blood-curdling mysteries and the most luxurious debauches of sentiment. To
imagine it is like imagining the humorous passages in Bradshaw's Railway Guide
read aloud on winter evenings. It is like conceiving a man unable to put down an
advertisement of Mother Seigel's Syrup because he wished to know what eventually happened to the young man who was extremely ill at Edinburgh. In the case
of cheap detective stories and cheap novelettes, we can most of us feel, whatever
our degree of education, that it might be possible to read them if we gave full
indulgence to a lower and more facile part of our natures; at the worst we feel that
we might enjoy them as we might enjoy bull-baiting or getting drunk. But the
literature of information is absolutely mysterious to us. We can no more think of
amusing ourselves with it than of reading whole pages of a Surbiton local directory.
To read such things would not be a piece of vulgar indulgence; it would be a highly
arduous and meritorious enterprise. It is this fact which constitutes a profound
and almost unfathomable interest in this particular branch of popular literature.

Primarily, at least, there is one rather peculiar thing which must in justice be
said about it. The readers of this strange science must be allowed to be, upon the
whole, as disinterested as a prophet seeing visions or a child reading fairy-tales.
Here, again, we find, as we so often do, that whatever view of this matter of popular
literature we can trust, we can trust least of all the comment and censure current
among the vulgar educated. The ordinary version of the ground of this popularity
for information, which would be given by a person of greater cultivation, would
be that common men are chiefly interested in those sordid facts that surround
them on every side. A very small degree of examination will show us that whatever

ground there is for the popularity of these insane encyclopaedias, it cannot be the ground of utility. The version of life given by a penny novelette may be very moonstruck and unreliable, but it is at least more likely to contain facts relevant to daily life than compilations on the subject of the number of cows' tails that would reach the North Pole. There are many more people who are in love than there are people who have any intention of counting or collecting cows' tails. It is evident to me that the grounds of this widespread madness of information for information's sake must be sought in other and deeper parts of human nature than those daily needs which lie so near the surface that even social philosophers have discovered them somewhere in that profound and eternal instinct for enthusiasm and minding other people's business which made great popular movements like the Crusades or the Gordon Riots.

I once had the pleasure of knowing a man who actually talked in private life after the manner of these papers. His conversation consisted of fragmentary statements about height and weight and depth and time and population, and his conversation was a nightmare of dulness. During the shortest pause he would ask whether his interlocutors were aware how many tons of rust were scraped every year off the Menai Bridge, and how many rival shops Mr. Whiteley had bought up since he opened his business. The attitude of his acquaintances towards this inexhaustible entertainer varied according to his presence or absence between indifference and terror. It was frightful to think of a man's brain being stocked with such inexpressibly profitless treasures. It was like visiting some imposing British Museum and finding its galleries and glass cases filled with specimens of London mud, of common mortar, of broken walking-sticks and cheap tobacco. Years afterwards I discovered that this intolerable prosaic bore had been, in fact, a poet. I learnt that every item of this multitudinous information was totally and unblushingly untrue, that for all I knew he had made it up as he went along; that no tons of rust are scraped off the Menai Bridge, and that the rival tradesmen and Mr. Whiteley were creatures of the poet's brain. Instantly I conceived consuming respect for the man who was so circumstantial, so monotonous, so entirely purposeless a liar. With him it must have been a case of art for art's sake. The joke sustained so gravely through a respected lifetime was of that order of joke which is shared with omniscience. But what struck me more cogently upon reflection was the fact that these immeasurable trivialities, which had struck me as utterly vulgar and arid when I thought they were true, immediately became picturesque and almost brilliant when I thought they were inventions of the human fancy. And here, as it seems to me, I laid my finger upon a fundamental quality of the cultivated class which prevents it, and will, perhaps, always prevent it from seeing with the eyes of popular imagination. The merely educated can scarcely ever be brought to believe that this world is itself an interesting place. When they look at a work of art, good or bad, they expect to be interested, but when they look at a newspaper advertisement or a group in the street, they do not, properly and literally speaking, expect to be interested. But to common and simple people this world is a work of art, though it is, like many great works of art, anonymous. They look to life for interest with the same kind of cheerful and uneradicable assurance with which we look for interest at a comedy for which we have paid money at the door. To the eyes of the ultimate school of contemporary fastidiousness, the universe is indeed an ill-drawn and over-coloured picture, the scrawlings in circles of a baby upon the slate of night; its starry skies are a vulgar pattern which they would not have for a wallpaper, its flowers and fruits have a cockney brilliancy, like the holiday hat of a flower-girl. Hence, degraded by art to its own level, they have lost altogether that primitive and typical taste of man—the taste for news. By this essential taste for news, I mean the pleasure in hearing the mere fact that a man has died at the age of 110 in South Wales, or that the horses ran away at a funeral in San Francisco. Large masses of the early faiths and politics of the world, numbers of the miracles and heroic anecdotes, are based primarily upon this love of something that has just happened, this divine institution of gossip. When Christianity was named the good news, it spread rapidly, not only because it was good, but also because it was news. So it is that if any of us have ever spoken to a navvy in a train about the daily paper, we have generally found the navvy interested, not in those struggles of Parliaments and trades unions which sometimes are, and are always supposed to be, for his benefit; but in the fact that an unusually large whale has been washed up on the coast of Orkney, or that some leading millionaire like Mr. Harmsworth is reported to break a hundred pipes a year. The educated classes, cloyed and demoralized with the mere indulgence of art and mood, can no longer understand the idle and splendid disinterestedness of the reader of *Pearson's Weekly*. He still keeps something of that feeling which should be the birthright of men—the feeling that this planet is like a new house into which we have just moved our baggage. Any detail of it has a value, and, with a truly sportsmanlike instinct, the average man takes most pleasure in the details which are most complicated, irrelevant, and at once difficult and useless to discover. Those parts of the newspaper which announce the giant gooseberry and the raining frogs are really the modern representatives of the popular tendency which produced the hydra and the werewolf and the dog-headed men. Folk in the Middle Ages were not interested in a dragon or a glimpse of the devil because they thought that it was a beautiful prose idyll, but because they thought that it had really just been seen. It was not like so much artistic literature, a refuge indicating the dulness of the world: it was an incident pointedly illustrating the fecund poetry of the world.

That much can be said, and is said, against the literature of information, I do not for a moment deny. It is shapeless, it is trivial, it may give an unreal air of knowledge, it unquestionably lies along with the rest of popular literature under the general indictment that it may spoil the chance of better work, certainly by wasting time, possibly by ruining taste. But these obvious objections are the objections which we hear so persistently from everyone that one cannot help wondering where the papers in question procure their myriads of readers. The natural necessity and natural good underlying such crude institutions is far less often a subject of speculation; yet the healthy hungers which lie at the back of the habits of modern democracy are surely worthy of the same sympathetic study that we give to the dogmas of the fanatics long dethroned and the intrigues of commonwealths long obliterated from the earth. And this is the base and consideration which I have to offer: that perhaps the taste for shreds and patches of journalistic science and history is not, as is continually asserted, the vulgar and senile curiosity of a people that has grown old, but simply the babyish and indiscriminate curiosity of a people still young and entering history for the first time. In other words, I suggest that they only tell each other in magazines the same kind of stories of commonplace portents and conventional eccentricities which, in any case, they would tell each other in taverns. Science itself is only the exaggeration and specialization of this thirst for useless fact, which is the mark of the youth of man. But science has become strangely separated from the mere news and scandal of flowers and birds; men have ceased to see that a pterodactyl was as fresh and natural as a flower, that a flower is as monstrous as a pterodactyl. The rebuilding of this bridge between science and human nature is one of the greatest needs of mankind. We have all to show that before we go on to any visions or creations we can be contented with a planet of miracles.

Chapter 10
A Defence of Heraldry

he modern view of heraldry is pretty accurately represented by the words of the famous barrister who, after cross-examining for some time a venerable dignitary of Heralds' College, summed up his results in the remark that 'the silly old man didn't even understand his own silly old trade.'

Heraldry properly so called was, of course, a wholly limited and aristocratic thing, but the remark needs a kind of qualification not commonly realized. In a sense there was a plebeian heraldry, since every shop was, like every castle, distinguished not by a name, but a sign. The whole system dates from a time when picture-writing still really ruled the world. In those days few could read or write; they signed their names with a pictorial symbol, a cross—and a cross is a great improvement on most men's names.

Now, there is something to be said for the peculiar influence of pictorial symbols on men's minds. All letters, we learn, were originally pictorial and heraldic: thus the letter A is the portrait of an ox, but the portrait is now reproduced in so impressionist a manner that but little of the rural atmosphere can be absorbed by contemplating it. But as long as some pictorial and poetic quality remains in the symbol, the constant use of it must do something for the aesthetic education of those employing it. Public-houses are now almost the only shops that use the ancient signs, and the mysterious attraction which they exercise may be (by the optimistic) explained in this manner. There are taverns with names so dreamlike and exquisite that even Sir Wilfrid Lawson might waver on the threshold for a moment, suffering the poet to struggle with the moralist. So it was with the heraldic images. It is impossible to believe that the red lion of Scotland acted upon those employing it merely as a naked convenience like a number or a letter; it is impossible to believe that the Kings of Scotland would have cheerfully accepted the substitute of a pig or a frog. There are, as we say, certain real advantages in pictorial symbols, and one of them is that everything that is pictorial suggests, without naming or defining. There is a road from the eye to the heart that does not go through the intellect. Men do not quarrel about the meaning of sunsets; they never dispute that the hawthorn says the best and wittiest thing about the spring.

Thus in the old aristocratic days there existed this vast pictorial symbolism of all the colours and degrees of aristocracy. When the great trumpet of equality was blown, almost immediately afterwards was made one of the greatest blunders in the history of mankind. For all this pride and vivacity, all these towering symbols and flamboyant colours, should have been extended to mankind. The tobacconist should have had a crest, and the cheesemonger a war-cry. The grocer who sold margarine as butter should have felt that there was a stain on the escutcheon of the Higginses. Instead of doing this, the democrats made the appalling mistake—a mistake at the root of the whole modern malady—of decreasing the human magnificence of the past instead of increasing it. They did not say, as they should have done, to the common citizen, 'You are as good as the Duke of Norfolk,' but used that meaner democratic formula, 'The Duke of Norfolk is no better than you are.'

For it cannot be denied that the world lost something finally and most unfortunately about the beginning of the nineteenth century. In former times the mass of the people was conceived as mean and commonplace, but only as comparatively mean and commonplace; they were dwarfed and eclipsed by certain high stations and splendid callings. But with the Victorian era came a principle which conceived men not as comparatively, but as positively, mean and commonplace. A man of any station was represented as being by nature a dingy and trivial person—a person born, as it were, in a black hat. It began to be thought that it was ridiculous for a man to wear beautiful garments, instead of it being—as, of course, it is—ridiculous for him to deliberately wear ugly ones. It was considered affected for a man to speak bold and heroic words, whereas, of course, it is emotional speech which is natural, and ordinary civil speech which is affected. The whole relations of beauty and ugliness, of dignity and ignominy were turned upside down. Beauty became an extravagance, as if top-hats and umbrellas were not the real extravagance—a landscape from the land of the goblins. Dignity became a form of foolery and shamelessness, as if the very essence of a fool were not a lack of dignity. And the consequence is that it is practically most difficult to propose any decoration or public dignity for modern men without making them laugh. They laugh at the idea of carrying crests and coats-of-arms instead of laughing at their own boots and neckties. We are forbidden to say that tradesmen should have a poetry of their own, although there is nothing so poetical as trade. A grocer should have a coat-of-arms worthy of his strange merchandise gathered from distant and fantastic lands; a postman should have a coat-of-arms capable of expressing the strange honour and responsibility of the man who carries men's souls in a bag; the chemist should have a coat-of-arms symbolizing something of the mysteries of the house of healing, the cavern of a merciful witchcraft.

There were in the French Revolution a class of people at whom everybody laughed, and at whom it was probably difficult, as a practical matter, to refrain from laughing. They attempted to erect, by means of huge wooden statues and brand-new festivals, the most extraordinary new religions. They adored the Goddess of Reason, who would appear, even when the fullest allowance has been made for their many virtues, to be the deity who had least smiled upon them. But these capering maniacs, disowned alike by the old world and the new, were men who had seen a great truth unknown alike to the new world and the old. They had seen the thing that was hidden from the wise and understanding, from the whole modern democratic civilization down to the present time. They realized that democracy must have a heraldry, that it must have a proud and high-coloured pageantry, if it is to keep always before its own mind its own sublime mission. Unfortunately for this ideal, the world has in this matter followed English democracy rather than French; and those who look back to the nineteenth century will assuredly look back to it as we look back to the reign of the Puritans, as the time of black coats and black tempers. From the strange life the men of that time led, they might be assisting at the funeral of liberty instead of at its christening. The moment we really believe in democracy, it will begin to blossom, as aristocracy blossomed, into symbolic colours and shapes. We shall never make anything of democracy until we make fools of ourselves. For if a man really cannot make a fool of himself, we may be quite certain that the effort is superfluous.

Chapter 11
A Defence of Ugly Things

here are some people who state that the exterior, sex, or physique of another person is indifferent to them, that they care only for the communion of mind with mind; but these people need not detain us. There are some statements that no one ever thinks of believing, however often they are made.

But while nothing in this world would persuade us that a great friend of Mr. Forbes Robertson, let us say, would experience no surprise or discomfort at seeing him enter the room in the bodily form of Mr. Chaplin, there is a confusion constantly made between being attracted by exterior, which is natural and universal, and being attracted by what is called physical beauty, which is not entirely natural and not in the least universal. Or rather, to speak more strictly, the conception of physical beauty has been narrowed to mean a certain kind of physical beauty which no more exhausts the possibilities of external attractiveness than the respectability of a Clapham builder exhausts the possibilities of moral attractiveness.

The tyrants and deceivers of mankind in this matter have been the Greeks. All their splendid work for civilization ought not to have wholly blinded us to the fact of their great and terrible sin against the variety of life. It is a remarkable fact that while the Jews have long ago been rebelled against and accused of blighting the world with a stringent and one-sided ethical standard, nobody has noticed that the Greeks have committed us to an infinitely more horrible asceticism—an asceticism of the fancy, a worship of one aesthetic type alone. Jewish severity had at least common-sense as its basis; it recognised that men lived in a world of fact, and that if a man married within the degrees of blood certain consequences might follow. But they did not starve their instinct for contrasts and combinations; their prophets gave two wings to the ox and any number of eyes to the cherubim with all the riotous ingenuity of Lewis Carroll. But the Greeks carried their police regulation into elfland; they vetoed not the actual adulteries of the earth but the wild weddings of ideas, and forbade the banns of thought.

It is extraordinary to watch the gradual emasculation of the monsters of Greek myth under the pestilent influence of the Apollo Belvedere. The chimaera was a creature of whom any healthy-minded people would have been proud; but when we see it in Greek pictures we feel inclined to tie a ribbon round its neck and give it a saucer of milk. Who ever feels that the giants in Greek art and poetry were really big—big as some folk-lore giants have been? In some Scandinavian story a hero walks for miles along a mountain ridge, which eventually turns out to be the bridge of the giant's nose. That is what we should call, with a calm conscience, a large giant. But this earthquake fancy terrified the Greeks, and their terror has terrified all mankind out of their natural love of size, vitality, variety, energy, ugliness. Nature intended every human face, so long as it was forcible, individual, and expressive, to be regarded as distinct from all others, as a poplar is distinct from an oak, and an apple-tree from a willow. But what the Dutch gardeners did for trees the Greeks did for the human form; they lopped away its living and sprawling features to give it a certain academic shape; they hacked off noses and pared down chins with a ghastly horticultural calm. And they have really succeeded so far as to make us call some of the most powerful and endearing faces ugly, and some of the most silly and repulsive faces beautiful. This disgraceful *via media*, this pitiful sense of dignity, has bitten far deeper into the soul of modern civilization than the external and practical Puritanism of Israel. The Jew at the worst told a man to dance in fetters; the Greek put an exquisite vase upon his head and told him not to move.

Scripture says that one star differeth from another in glory, and the same conception applies to noses. To insist that one type of face is ugly because it differs from that of the Venus of Milo is to look at it entirely in a misleading light. It is strange that we should resent people differing from ourselves; we should resent much more violently their resembling ourselves. This principle has made a sufficient hash of literary criticism, in which it is always the custom to complain of the lack of sound logic in a fairy tale, and the entire absence of true oratorical power in a three-act farce. But to call another man's face ugly because it powerfully expresses another man's soul is like complaining that a cabbage has not two legs. If we did so, the only course for the cabbage would be to point out with severity, but with some show of truth, that we were not a beautiful green all over.

But this frigid theory of the beautiful has not succeeded in conquering the art of the world, except in name. In some quarters, indeed, it has never held sway. A glance at Chinese dragons or Japanese gods will show how independent are Orientals of the conventional idea of facial and bodily regularity, and how keen and fiery is their enjoyment of real beauty, of goggle eyes, of sprawling claws, of gaping mouths and writhing coils. In the Middle Ages men broke away from the Greek standard of beauty, and lifted up in adoration to heaven great towers, which seemed alive with dancing apes and devils. In the full summer of technical artistic perfection the revolt was carried to its real consummation in the study of the faces of men. Rembrandt declared the sane and manly gospel that a man was dignified, not when he was like a Greek god, but when he had a strong, square nose like a cudgel, a boldly-blocked head like a helmet, and a jaw like a steel trap.

This branch of art is commonly dismissed as the grotesque. We have never been able to understand why it should be humiliating to be laughable, since it is giving an elevated artistic pleasure to others. If a gentleman who saw us in the street were suddenly to burst into tears at the mere thought of our existence, it might be considered disquieting and uncomplimentary; but laughter is not uncomplimentary. In truth, however, the phrase 'grotesque' is a misleading description of ugliness in art. It does not follow that either the Chinese dragons or the Gothic gargoyles or the goblinish old women of Rembrandt were in the least intended to be comic. Their extravagance was not the extravagance of satire, but simply the extravagance of vitality; and here lies the whole key of the place of ugliness in aesthetics. We like to see a crag jut out in shameless decision from the cliff, we like to see the red pines stand up hardily upon a high cliff, we like to see a chasm cloven from end to end of a mountain. With equally noble enthusiasm we like to see a nose jut out decisively, we like to see the red hair of a friend stand up hardily in bristles upon his head, we like to see his mouth broad and clean cut like the mountain crevasse. At least some of us like all this; it is not a question of humour. We do not burst with amusement at the first sight of the pines or the chasm; but we like them because they are expressive of the dramatic stillness of Nature, her bold experiments, her definite departures, her fearlessness and savage pride in her children. The moment we have snapped the spell of conventional beauty, there are a million beautiful faces waiting for us everywhere, just as there are a million beautiful spirits.

Chapter 12
A Defence of Farce

have never been able to understand why certain forms of art should be marked off as something debased and trivial. A comedy is spoken of as 'degenerating into farce'; it would be fair criticism to speak of it 'changing into farce'; but as for degenerating into farce, we might equally reasonably speak of it as degenerating into tragedy. Again, a story is spoken of as 'melodramatic,' and the phrase, queerly enough, is not meant as a compliment. To speak of something as 'pantomimic' or 'sensational' is innocently supposed to be biting, Heaven knows why, for all works of art are sensations, and a good pantomime (now extinct) is one of the pleasantest sensations of all. 'This stuff is fit for a detective story,' is often said, as who should say, 'This stuff is fit for an epic.'

Whatever may be the rights and wrongs of this mode of classification, there can be no doubt about one most practical and disastrous effect of it. These lighter or wilder forms of art, having no standard set up for them, no gust of generous artistic pride to lift them up, do actually tend to become as bad as they are supposed to be. Neglected children of the great mother, they grow up in darkness, dirty and unlettered, and when they are right they are right almost by accident, because of the blood in their veins. The common detective story of mystery and murder seems to the intelligent reader to be little except a strange glimpse of a planet peopled by congenital idiots, who cannot find the end of their own noses or the character of their own wives. The common pantomime seems like some horrible satiric picture of a world without cause or effect, a mass of 'jarring atoms,' a prolonged mental torture of irrelevancy. The ordinary farce seems a world of almost piteous vulgarity, where a half-witted and stunted creature is afraid when his wife comes home, and amused when she sits down on the doorstep. All this is, in a sense, true, but it is the fault of nothing in heaven or earth except the attitude and the phrases quoted at the beginning of this article. We have no doubt in the world that, if the other forms of art had been equally despised, they would have been equally despicable. If people had spoken of 'sonnets' with the same accent with which they speak of 'music-hall songs,' a sonnet would have been a thing so fearful and wonderful that we almost regret we cannot have a specimen; a rowdy sonnet is a thing to dream about. If people had said that epics were only fit for children and nursemaids, 'Paradise Lost' might have been an average pantomime: it might have been called 'Harlequin Satan, or How Adam 'Ad 'em.' For who would trouble to bring to perfection a work in which even perfection is grotesque? Why should Shakespeare write 'Othello' if even his triumph consisted in the eulogy, 'Mr. Shakespeare is fit for something better than writing tragedies'?

The case of farce, and its wilder embodiment in harlequinade, is especially important. That these high and legitimate forms of art, glorified by Aristophanes and Molière, have sunk into such contempt may be due to many causes: I myself have little doubt that it is due to the astonishing and ludicrous lack of belief in hope and hilarity which marks modern aesthetics, to such an extent that it has spread even to the revolutionists (once the hopeful section of men), so that even those who ask us to fling the stars into the sea are not quite sure that they will be any better there than they were before. Every form of literary art must be a symbol of some phase of the human spirit; but whereas the phase is, in human life, sufficiently convincing in itself, in art it must have a certain pungency and neatness of form, to compensate for its lack of reality. Thus any set of young people round a tea-table may have all the comedy emotions of 'Much Ado about Nothing' or 'Northanger Abbey,' but if their actual conversation were reported, it would possibly not be a worthy addition to literature. An old man sitting by his fire may have all the desolate grandeur of Lear or Père Goriot, but if he comes into literature he must do something besides sit by the fire. The artistic justification, then, of farce and pantomime must consist in the emotions of life which correspond to them. And these emotions are to an incredible extent crushed out by the modern insistence on the painful side of life only. Pain, it is said, is the dominant element of life; but this is true only in a very special sense. If pain were for one single instant literally the dominant element in life, every man would be found hanging dead from his own bed-post by the morning. Pain, as the black and catastrophic thing, attracts the youthful artist, just as the schoolboy draws devils and skeletons and men hanging. But joy is a far more elusive and elvish matter, since it is our reason for existing, and a very feminine reason; it mingles with every breath we draw and every cup of tea we drink. The literature of joy is infinitely more difficult, more rare and more triumphant than the black and white literature of pain. And of all the varied forms of the literature of joy, the form most truly worthy of moral reverence and artistic ambition is the form called 'farce'—or its wilder shape in pantomime. To the quietest human being, seated in the quietest house, there will sometimes come a sudden and unmeaning hunger for the possibilities or impossibilities of things; he will abruptly wonder whether the teapot may not suddenly begin to pour out honey or sea-water, the clock to point to all hours of the day at once, the candle to burn green or crimson, the door to open upon a lake or a potato-field instead of a London street. Upon anyone who feels this nameless anarchism there rests for the time being the abiding spirit of pantomime. Of the clown who cuts the policeman in two it may be said (with no darker meaning) that he realizes one of our visions. And it may be noted here that this internal quality in pantomime is perfectly symbolized and preserved by that commonplace or cockney landscape and architecture which characterizes pantomime and farce. If the whole affair happened in some alien atmosphere, if a pear-tree began to grow apples or a river to run with wine in some strange fairyland, the effect would be quite different. The streets and shops and door-knockers of the harlequinade, which to the vulgar aesthete make it seem commonplace, are in truth the very essence of the aesthetic departure. It must be an actual modern door which opens and shuts, constantly disclosing different interiors; it must be a real baker whose loaves fly up into the air without his touching them, or else the whole internal excitement of this elvish invasion of civilization, this abrupt entrance of Puck into Pimlico, is lost. Some day, perhaps, when the present narrow phase of aesthetics has ceased to monopolize the name, the glory of a farcical art may become fashionable. Long after men have ceased to drape their houses in green and gray and to adorn them with Japanese vases, an aesthete may build a house on pantomime principles, in which all the doors shall have their bells and knockers on the inside, all the staircases be constructed to vanish on the pressing of a button, and all the dinners (humorous dinners in themselves) come up cooked through a trapdoor. We are very sure, at least, that it is as reasonable to regulate one's life and lodgings by this kind of art as by any other.

The whole of this view of farce and pantomime may seem insane to us; but we fear that it is we who are insane. Nothing in this strange age of transition is so depressing as its merriment. All the most brilliant men of the day when they set about the writing of comic literature do it under one destructive fallacy and disadvantage: the notion that comic literature is in some sort of way superficial. They give us little knick-knacks of the brittleness of which they positively boast, although two thousand years have beaten as vainly upon the follies of the 'Frogs' as on the wisdom of the 'Republic.' It is all a mean shame of joy. When we come out from a performance of the 'Midsummer Night's Dream' we feel as near to the stars as when we come out from 'King Lear.' For the joy of these works is older than sorrow, their extravagance is saner than wisdom, their love is stronger than death.

The old masters of a healthy madness, Aristophanes or Rabelais or Shakespeare, doubtless had many brushes with the precisians or ascetics of their day, but we cannot but feel that for honest severity and consistent self-maceration they would always have had respect. But what abysses of scorn, inconceivable to any modern, would they have reserved for an aesthetic type and movement which violated morality and did not even find pleasure, which outraged sanity and could not attain to exuberance, which contented itself with the fool's cap without the bells!

Chapter 13
A Defence of Humility

he act of defending any of the cardinal virtues has to-day all the exhilaration of a vice. Moral truisms have been so much disputed that they have begun to sparkle like so many brilliant paradoxes. And especially (in this age of egoistic idealism) there is about one who defends humility something inexpressibly rakish.

It is no part of my intention to defend humility on practical grounds. Practical grounds are uninteresting, and, moreover, on practical grounds the case for humility is overwhelming. We all know that the 'divine glory of the ego' is socially a great nuisance; we all do actually value our friends for modesty, freshness, and simplicity of heart. Whatever may be the reason, we all do warmly respect humility—in other people.

But the matter must go deeper than this. If the grounds of humility are found only in social convenience, they may be quite trivial and temporary. The egoists may be the martyrs of a nobler dispensation, agonizing for a more arduous ideal. To judge from the comparative lack of ease in their social manner, this seems a reasonable suggestion.

There is one thing that must be seen at the outset of the study of humility from an intrinsic and eternal point of view. The new philosophy of self-esteem and self-assertion declares that humility is a vice. If it be so, it is quite clear that it is one of those vices which are an integral part of original sin. It follows with the precision of clockwork every one of the great joys of life. No one, for example, was ever in love without indulging in a positive debauch of humility. All full-blooded and natural people, such as schoolboys, enjoy humility the moment they attain hero-worship. Humility, again, is said both by its upholders and opponents to be the peculiar growth of Christianity. The real and obvious reason of this is often missed. The pagans insisted upon self-assertion because it was the essence of their creed that the gods, though strong and just, were mystic, capricious, and even indifferent. But the essence of Christianity was in a literal sense the New Testament—a covenant with God which opened to men a clear deliverance. They thought themselves secure; they claimed palaces of pearl and silver under the oath and seal of the Omnipotent; they believed themselves rich with an irrevocable benediction which set them above the stars; and immediately they discovered humility. It was only another example of the same immutable paradox. It is always the secure who are humble.

This particular instance survives in the evangelical revivalists of the street. They are irritating enough, but no one who has really studied them can deny that the irritation is occasioned by these two things, an irritating hilarity and an irritating humility. This combination of joy and self-prostration is a great deal too universal to be ignored. If humility has been discredited as a virtue at the present day, it is not wholly irrelevant to remark that this discredit has arisen at the same time as a great collapse of joy in current literature and philosophy. Men have revived the splendour of Greek self-assertion at the same time that they have revived the bitterness of Greek pessimism. A literature has arisen which commands us all to arrogate to ourselves the liberty of self-sufficing deities at the same time that it exhibits us to ourselves as dingy maniacs who ought to be chained up like dogs. It is certainly a curious state of things altogether. When we are genuinely happy, we think we are unworthy of happiness. But when we are demanding a divine emancipation we seem to be perfectly certain that we are unworthy of anything.

The only explanation of the matter must be found in the conviction that humility has infinitely deeper roots than any modern men suppose; that it is a metaphysical and, one might almost say, a mathematical virtue. Probably this can best be tested by a study of those who frankly disregard humility and assert the supreme duty of perfecting and expressing one's self. These people tend, by a perfectly natural process, to bring their own great human gifts of culture, intellect, or moral power to a great perfection, successively shutting out everything that they feel to be lower than themselves. Now shutting out things is all very well, but it has one simple corollary—that from everything that we shut out we are ourselves shut out. When we shut our door on the wind, it would be equally true to say that the wind shuts its door on us. Whatever virtues a triumphant egoism really leads to, no one can reasonably pretend that it leads to knowledge. Turning a beggar from the door may be right enough, but pretending to know all the stories the beggar might have narrated is pure nonsense; and this is practically the claim of the egoism which thinks that self-assertion can obtain knowledge. A beetle may or may not be inferior to a man—the matter awaits demonstration; but if he were inferior by ten thousand fathoms, the fact remains that there is probably a beetle view of things of which a man is entirely ignorant. If he wishes to conceive that point of view, he will scarcely reach it by persistently revelling in the fact that he is not a beetle. The most brilliant exponent of the egoistic school, Nietszche, with deadly and honourable logic, admitted that the philosophy of self-satisfaction led to looking down upon the weak, the cowardly, and the ignorant. Looking down on things may be a delightful experience, only there is nothing, from a mountain to a cabbage, that is really *seen* when it is seen from a balloon. The philosopher of the ego sees everything, no doubt, from a high and rarified heaven; only he sees everything foreshortened or deformed.

Now if we imagine that a man wished truly, as far as possible, to see everything as it was, he would certainly proceed on a different principle. He would seek to divest himself for a time of those personal peculiarities which tend to divide him from the thing he studies. It is as difficult, for example, for a man to examine a fish without developing a certain vanity in possessing a pair of legs, as if they were the latest article of personal adornment. But if a fish is to be approximately understood, this physiological dandyism must be overcome. The earnest student of fish morality will, spiritually speaking, chop off his legs. And similarly the student of birds will eliminate his arms; the frog-lover will with one stroke of the imagination remove all his teeth, and the spirit wishing to enter into all the hopes and fears of jelly-fish will simplify his personal appearance to a really alarming extent. It would appear, therefore, that this great body of ours and all its natural instincts, of which we are proud, and justly proud, is rather an encumbrance at the moment when we attempt to appreciate things as they should be appreciated. We do actually go through a process of mental asceticism, a castration of the entire being, when we wish to feel the abounding good in all things. It is good for us at certain times that ourselves should be like a mere window—as clear, as luminous, and as invisible.

In a very entertaining work, over which we have roared in childhood, it is stated that a point has no parts and no magnitude. Humility is the luxurious art of reducing ourselves to a point, not to a small thing or a large one, but to a thing with no size at all, so that to it all the cosmic things are what they really are—of immeasurable stature. That the trees are high and the grasses short is a mere accident of our own foot-rules and our own stature. But to the spirit which has stripped off for a moment its own idle temporal standards the grass is an everlasting forest, with dragons for denizens; the stones of the road are as incredible mountains piled one upon the other; the dandelions are like gigantic bonfires illuminating the lands around; and the heath-bells on their stalks are like planets hung in heaven each higher than the other. Between one stake of a paling and another there are new and terrible landscapes; here a desert, with nothing but one misshapen rock; here a miraculous forest, of which all the trees flower above the head with the hues of sunset; here, again, a sea full of monsters that Dante would not have dared to dream. These are the visions of him who, like the child in the fairy tales, is not afraid to become small. Meanwhile, the sage whose faith is in magnitude and ambition is, like a giant, becoming larger and larger, which only means that the stars are becoming smaller and smaller. World after world falls from him into insignificance; the whole passionate and intricate life of common things becomes as lost to him as is the life of the infusoria to a man without a microscope. He rises always through desolate eternities. He may find new systems, and forget them; he may discover fresh universes, and learn to despise them. But the towering and tropical vision of things as they really are—the gigantic daisies, the heaven-consuming dandelions, the great Odyssey of strange-coloured oceans and strange-shaped trees, of dust like the wreck of temples, and thistledown like the ruin of stars—all this colossal vision shall perish with the last of the humble.

Chapter 14
A Defence of Slang

he aristocrats of the nineteenth century have destroyed entirely their one solitary utility. It is their business to be flaunting and arrogant; but they flaunt unobtrusively, and their attempts at arrogance are depressing. Their chief duty hitherto has been the development of variety, vivacity, and fulness of life; oligarchy was the world's first experiment in liberty. But now they have adopted the opposite ideal of 'good form,' which may be defined as Puritanism without religion. Good form has sent them all into black like the stroke of a funeral bell. They engage, like Mr. Gilbert's curates, in a war of mildness, a positive competition of obscurity. In old times the lords of the earth sought above all things to be distinguished from each other; with that object they erected outrageous images on their helmets and painted preposterous colours on their shields. They wished to make it entirely clear that a Norfolk was as different, say, from an Argyll as a white lion from a black pig. But to-day their ideal is precisely the opposite one, and if a Norfolk and an Argyll were dressed so much alike that they were mistaken for each other they would both go home dancing with joy.

The consequences of this are inevitable. The aristocracy must lose their function of standing to the world for the idea of variety, experiment, and colour, and we must find these things in some other class. To ask whether we shall find them in the middle class would be to jest upon sacred matters. The only conclusion, therefore, is that it is to certain sections of the lower class, chiefly, for example, to omnibus-conductors, with their rich and rococo mode of thought, that we must look for guidance towards liberty and light.

The one stream of poetry which is continually flowing is slang. Every day a nameless poet weaves some fairy tracery of popular language. It may be said that the fashionable world talks slang as much as the democratic; this is true, and it strongly supports the view under consideration. Nothing is more startling than the contrast between the heavy, formal, lifeless slang of the man-about-town and the light, living, and flexible slang of the coster. The talk of the upper strata of the educated classes is about the most shapeless, aimless, and hopeless literary product that the world has ever seen. Clearly in this, again, the upper classes have degenerated. We have ample evidence that the old leaders of feudal war could speak on occasion with a certain natural symbolism and eloquence that they had not gained from books. When Cyrano de Bergerac, in Rostand's play, throws doubts on the reality of Christian's dulness and lack of culture, the latter replies:

'Bah! on trouve des mots quand on monte à l'assaut;
Oui, j'ai un certain esprit facile et militaire;'

and these two lines sum up a truth about the old oligarchs. They could not write three legible letters, but they could sometimes speak literature. Douglas, when he hurled the heart of Bruce in front of him in his last battle, cried out, 'Pass first, great heart, as thou wert ever wont.' A Spanish nobleman, when commanded by the King to receive a high-placed and notorious traitor, said: 'I will receive him in all obedience, and burn down my house afterwards.' This is literature without culture; it is the speech of men convinced that they have to assert proudly the poetry of life.

Anyone, however, who should seek for such pearls in the conversation of a young man of modern Belgravia would have much sorrow in his life. It is not only impossible for aristocrats to assert proudly the poetry of life; it is more impossible for them than for anyone else. It is positively considered vulgar for a nobleman to boast of his ancient name, which is, when one comes to think of it, the only rational object of his existence. If a man in the street proclaimed, with rude feudal rhetoric, that he was the Earl of Doncaster, he would be arrested as a lunatic; but if it were discovered that he really was the Earl of Doncaster, he would simply be cut as a cad. No poetical prose must be expected from Earls as a class. The fashionable slang is hardly even a language; it is like the formless cries of animals, dimly indicating certain broad, well-understood states of mind. 'Bored,' 'cut up,' 'jolly,' 'rotten,' and so on, are like the words of some tribe of savages whose vocabulary has only twenty of them. If a man of fashion wished to protest against some solecism in another man of fashion, his utterance would be a mere string of set phrases, as lifeless as a string of dead fish. But an omnibus conductor (being filled with the Muse) would burst out into a solid literary effort: 'You're a gen'leman, aren't yer ... yer boots is a lot brighter than yer 'ed ... there's precious little of yer, and that's clothes ... that's right, put yer cigar in yer mouth 'cos I can't see yer be'ind it ... take it out again, do yer! you're young for smokin', but I've sent for yer mother ... Goin'? oh, don't run away: I won't 'arm yer. I've got a good 'art, I 'ave ... "Down with croolty to animals," I say,' and so on. It is evident that this mode of speech is not only literary, but literary in a very ornate and almost artificial sense. Keats never put into a sonnet so many remote metaphors as a coster puts into a curse; his speech is one long allegory, like Spenser's 'Faerie Queen.'

I do not imagine that it is necessary to demonstrate that this poetic allusiveness is the characteristic of true slang. Such an expression as 'Keep your hair on' is positively Meredithian in its perverse and mysterious manner of expressing an idea. The Americans have a well-known expression about 'swelled-head' as a description of self-approval, and the other day I heard a remarkable fantasia upon this air. An American said that after the Chinese War the Japanese wanted 'to put on their hats with a shoe-horn.' This is a monument of the true nature of slang, which consists in getting further and further away from the original conception, in treating it more and more as an assumption. It is rather like the literary doctrine of the Symbolists.

The real reason of this great development of eloquence among the lower orders again brings us back to the case of the aristocracy in earlier times. The lower classes live in a state of war, a war of words. Their readiness is the product of the same fiery individualism as the readiness of the old fighting oligarchs. Any cabman has to be ready with his tongue, as any gentleman of the last century had to be ready with his sword. It is unfortunate that the poetry which is developed by this process should be purely a grotesque poetry. But as the higher orders of society have entirely abdicated their right to speak with a heroic eloquence, it is no wonder that the language should develop by itself in the direction of a rowdy eloquence. The essential point is that somebody must be at work adding new symbols and new circumlocutions to a language.

All slang is metaphor, and all metaphor is poetry. If we paused for a moment to examine the cheapest cant phrases that pass our lips every day, we should find that they were as rich and suggestive as so many sonnets. To take a single instance: we speak of a man in English social relations 'breaking the ice.' If this were expanded into a sonnet, we should have before us a dark and sublime picture of an ocean of everlasting ice, the sombre and baffling mirror of the Northern nature, over which men walked and danced and skated easily, but under which the living waters roared and toiled fathoms below. The world of slang is a kind of topsy-turveydom of poetry, full of blue moons and white elephants, of men losing their heads, and men whose tongues run away with them—a whole chaos of fairy tales.

Chapter 15
A Defence of Baby-Worship

he two facts which attract almost every normal person to children are, first, that they are very serious, and, secondly, that they are in consequence very happy. They are jolly with the completeness which is possible only in the absence of humour. The most un-fathomable schools and sages have never attained to the gravity which dwells in the eyes of a baby of three months old. It is the gravity of aston-ishment at the universe, and astonishment at the universe is not mysticism, but a transcendent common-sense. The fascination of children lies in this: that with each of them all things are remade, and the universe is put again upon its trial. As we walk the streets and see below us those delightful bulbous heads, three times too big for the body, which mark these human mushrooms, we ought always primarily to remember that within every one of these heads there is a new universe, as new as it was on the seventh day of creation. In each of those orbs there is a new system of stars, new grass, new cities, a new sea.

There is always in the healthy mind an obscure prompting that religion teaches us rather to dig than to climb; that if we could once understand the common clay of earth we should understand everything. Similarly, we have the sentiment that if we could destroy custom at a blow and see the stars as a child sees them, we should need no other apocalypse. This is the great truth which has always lain at the back of baby-worship, and which will support it to the end. Maturity, with its endless energies and aspirations, may easily be convinced that it will find new things to appreciate; but it will never be convinced, at bottom, that it has properly appreciated what it has got. We may scale the heavens and find new stars innumerable, but there is still the new star we have not found—that on which we were born.

But the influence of children goes further than its first trifling effort of remak-ing heaven and earth. It forces us actually to remodel our conduct in accordance with this revolutionary theory of the marvellousness of all things. We do (even when we are perfectly simple or ignorant)—we do actually treat talking in children as marvellous, walking in children as marvellous, common intelligence in children as marvellous. The cynical philosopher fancies he has a victory in this matter—that he can laugh when he shows that the words or antics of the child, so much admired by its worshippers, are common enough. The fact is that this is precisely where baby-worship is so profoundly right. Any words and any antics in a lump of clay are wonderful, the child's words and antics are wonderful, and it is only fair to say that the philosopher's words and antics are equally wonderful.

The truth is that it is our attitude towards children that is right, and our atti-tude towards grown-up people that is wrong. Our attitude towards our equals in age consists in a servile solemnity, overlying a considerable degree of indifference or disdain. Our attitude towards children consists in a condescending indulgence, overlying an unfathomable respect. We bow to grown people, take off our hats to them, refrain from contradicting them flatly, but we do not appreciate them properly. We make puppets of children, lecture them, pull their hair, and reverence, love, and fear them. When we reverence anything in the mature, it is their virtues or their wisdom, and this is an easy matter. But we reverence the faults and follies of children.

We should probably come considerably nearer to the true conception of things if we treated all grown-up persons, of all titles and types, with precisely that dark affection and dazed respect with which we treat the infantile limitations. A child has a difficulty in achieving the miracle of speech, consequently we find his blunders almost as marvellous as his accuracy. If we only adopted the same attitude towards Premiers and Chancellors of the Exchequer, if we genially encouraged their stammering and delightful attempts at human speech, we should be in a far more wise and tolerant temper. A child has a knack of making experiments in life, generally healthy in motive, but often intolerable in a domestic commonwealth. If we only treated all commercial buccaneers and bumptious tyrants on the same terms, if we gently chided their brutalities as rather quaint mistakes in the conduct of life, if we simply told them that they would 'understand when they were older,' we should probably be adopting the best and most crushing attitude towards the weaknesses of humanity. In our relations to children we prove that the paradox is entirely true, that it is possible to combine an amnesty that verges on contempt with a worship that verges upon terror. We forgive children with the same kind of blasphemous gentleness with which Omar Khayyam forgave the Omnipotent.

The essential rectitude of our view of children lies in the fact that we feel them and their ways to be supernatural while, for some mysterious reason, we do not feel ourselves or our own ways to be supernatural. The very smallness of children makes it possible to regard them as marvels; we seem to be dealing with a new race, only to be seen through a microscope. I doubt if anyone of any tenderness or imagination can see the hand of a child and not be a little frightened of it. It is awful to think of the essential human energy moving so tiny a thing; it is like imagining that human nature could live in the wing of a butterfly or the leaf of a tree. When we look upon lives so human and yet so small, we feel as if we ourselves were enlarged to an embarrassing bigness of stature. We feel the same kind of obligation to these creatures that a deity might feel if he had created something that he could not understand.

But the humorous look of children is perhaps the most endearing of all the bonds that hold the Cosmos together. Their top-heavy dignity is more touching than any humility; their solemnity gives us more hope for all things than a thousand carnivals of optimism; their large and lustrous eyes seem to hold all the stars in their astonishment; their fascinating absence of nose seems to give to us the most perfect hint of the humour that awaits us in the kingdom of heaven.

Chapter 16
A Defence of Detective Stories

In attempting to reach the genuine psychological reason for the popularity of detective stories, it is necessary to rid ourselves of many mere phrases. It is not true, for example, that the populace prefer bad literature to good, and accept detective stories because they are bad literature. The mere absence of artistic subtlety does not make a book popular. Bradshaw's Railway Guide contains few gleams of psychological comedy, yet it is not read aloud uproariously on winter evenings. If detective stories are read with more exuberance than railway guides, it is certainly because they are more artistic. Many good books have fortunately been popular; many bad books, still more fortunately, have been unpopular. A good detective story would probably be even more popular than a bad one. The trouble in this matter is that many people do not realize that there is such a thing as a good detective story; it is to them like speaking of a good devil. To write a story about a burglary is, in their eyes, a sort of spiritual manner of committing it. To persons of somewhat weak sensibility this is natural enough; it must be confessed that many detective stories are as full of sensational crime as one of Shakespeare's plays.

There is, however, between a good detective story and a bad detective story as much, or, rather more, difference than there is between a good epic and a bad one. Not only is a detective story a perfectly legitimate form of art, but it has certain definite and real advantages as an agent of the public weal.

The first essential value of the detective story lies in this, that it is the earliest and only form of popular literature in which is expressed some sense of the poetry of modern life. Men lived among mighty mountains and eternal forests for ages before they realized that they were poetical; it may reasonably be inferred that some of our descendants may see the chimney-pots as rich a purple as the mountain-peaks, and find the lamp-posts as old and natural as the trees. Of this realization of a great city itself as something wild and obvious the detective story is certainly the 'Iliad.' No one can have failed to notice that in these stories the hero or the investigator crosses London with something of the loneliness and liberty of a prince in a tale of elfland, that in the course of that incalculable journey the casual omnibus assumes the primal colours of a fairy ship. The lights of the city begin to glow like innumerable goblin eyes, since they are the guardians of some secret, however crude, which the writer knows and the reader does not. Every twist of the road is like a finger pointing to it; every fantastic skyline of chimney-pots seems wildly and derisively signalling the meaning of the mystery.

This realization of the poetry of London is not a small thing. A city is, properly speaking, more poetic even than a countryside, for while Nature is a chaos of

unconscious forces, a city is a chaos of conscious ones. The crest of the flower
or the pattern of the lichen may or may not be significant symbols. But there
is no stone in the street and no brick in the wall that is not actually a deliberate
symbol—a message from some man, as much as if it were a telegram or a post-card.
The narrowest street possesses, in every crook and twist of its intention, the soul
of the man who built it, perhaps long in his grave. Every brick has as human a
hieroglyph as if it were a graven brick of Babylon; every slate on the roof is as
educational a document as if it were a slate covered with addition and subtraction
sums. Anything which tends, even under the fantastic form of the minutiae of
Sherlock Holmes, to assert this romance of detail in civilization, to emphasize this
unfathomably human character in flints and tiles, is a good thing. It is good that
the average man should fall into the habit of looking imaginatively at ten men in
the street even if it is only on the chance that the eleventh might be a notorious
thief. We may dream, perhaps, that it might be possible to have another and
higher romance of London, that men's souls have stranger adventures than their
bodies, and that it would be harder and more exciting to hunt their virtues than
to hunt their crimes. But since our great authors (with the admirable exception of
Stevenson) decline to write of that thrilling mood and moment when the eyes of
the great city, like the eyes of a cat, begin to flame in the dark, we must give fair
credit to the popular literature which, amid a babble of pedantry and preciosity,
declines to regard the present as prosaic or the common as commonplace. Popular
art in all ages has been interested in contemporary manners and costume; it dressed
the groups around the Crucifixion in the garb of Florentine gentlefolk or Flemish
burghers. In the last century it was the custom for distinguished actors to present
Macbeth in a powdered wig and ruffles. How far we are ourselves in this age from
such conviction of the poetry of our own life and manners may easily be conceived
by anyone who chooses to imagine a picture of Alfred the Great toasting the cakes
dressed in tourist's knickerbockers, or a performance of 'Hamlet' in which the
Prince appeared in a frock-coat, with a crape band round his hat. But this instinct
of the age to look back, like Lot's wife, could not go on for ever. A rude, popular
literature of the romantic possibilities of the modern city was bound to arise. It
has arisen in the popular detective stories, as rough and refreshing as the ballads
of Robin Hood.

There is, however, another good work that is done by detective stories. While
it is the constant tendency of the Old Adam to rebel against so universal and
automatic a thing as civilization, to preach departure and rebellion, the romance
of police activity keeps in some sense before the mind the fact that civilization
itself is the most sensational of departures and the most romantic of rebellions.
By dealing with the unsleeping sentinels who guard the outposts of society, it
tends to remind us that we live in an armed camp, making war with a chaotic world,
and that the criminals, the children of chaos, are nothing but the traitors within
our gates. When the detective in a police romance stands alone, and somewhat

fatuously fearless amid the knives and fists of a thieves' kitchen, it does certainly serve to make us remember that it is the agent of social justice who is the original and poetic figure, while the burglars and footpads are merely placid old cosmic conservatives, happy in the immemorial respectability of apes and wolves. The romance of the police force is thus the whole romance of man. It is based on the fact that morality is the most dark and daring of conspiracies. It reminds us that the whole noiseless and unnoticeable police management by which we are ruled and protected is only a successful knight-errantry.

Chapter 17
A Defence of Patriotism

he decay of patriotism in England during the last year or two is a serious and distressing matter. Only in consequence of such a decay could the current lust of territory be confounded with the ancient love of country. We may imagine that if there were no such thing as a pair of lovers left in the world, all the vocabulary of love might without rebuke be transferred to the lowest and most automatic desire. If no type of chivalrous and purifying passion remained, there would be no one left to say that lust bore none of the marks of love, that lust was rapacious and love pitiful, that lust was blind and love vigilant, that lust sated itself and love was insatiable. So it is with the 'love of the city,' that high and ancient intellectual passion which has been written in red blood on the same table with the primal passions of our being. On all sides we hear to-day of the love of our country, and yet anyone who has literally such a love must be bewildered at the talk, like a man hearing all men say that the moon shines by day and the sun by night. The conviction must come to him at last that these men do not realize what the word 'love' means, that they mean by the love of country, not what a mystic might mean by the love of God, but something of what a child might mean by the love of jam. To one who loves his fatherland, for instance, our boasted indifference to the ethics of a national war is mere mysterious gibberism. It is like telling a man that a boy has committed murder, but that he need not mind because it is only his son. Here clearly the word 'love' is used unmeaningly. It is the essence of love to be sensitive, it is a part of its doom; and anyone who objects to the one must certainly get rid of the other. This sensitiveness, rising sometimes to an almost morbid sensitiveness, was the mark of all great lovers like Dante and all great patriots like Chatham. 'My country, right or wrong,' is a thing that no patriot would think of saying except in a desperate case. It is like saying, 'My mother, drunk or sober.' No doubt if a decent man's mother took to drink he would share her troubles to the last; but to talk as if he would be in a state of gay indifference as to whether his mother took to drink or not is certainly not the language of men who know the great mystery.

What we really need for the frustration and overthrow of a deaf and raucous Jingoism is a renascence of the love of the native land. When that comes, all shrill cries will cease suddenly. For the first of all the marks of love is seriousness: love will not accept sham bulletins or the empty victory of words. It will always esteem the most candid counsellor the best. Love is drawn to truth by the unerring magnetism of agony; it gives no pleasure to the lover to see ten doctors dancing with vociferous optimism round a death-bed.

We have to ask, then, Why is it that this recent movement in England, which has honestly appeared to many a renascence of patriotism, seems to us to have none of the marks of patriotism—at least, of patriotism in its highest form? Why has the adoration of our patriots been given wholly to qualities and circumstances good in themselves, but comparatively material and trivial:—trade, physical force, a skirmish at a remote frontier, a squabble in a remote continent? Colonies are things to be proud of, but for a country to be only proud of its extremities is like a man being only proud of his legs. Why is there not a high central intellectual patriotism, a patriotism of the head and heart of the Empire, and not merely of its fists and its boots? A rude Athenian sailor may very likely have thought that the glory of Athens lay in rowing with the right kind of oars, or having a good supply of garlic; but Pericles did not think that this was the glory of Athens. With us, on the other hand, there is no difference at all between the patriotism preached by Mr. Chamberlain and that preached by Mr. Pat Rafferty, who sings 'What do you think of the Irish now?' They are both honest, simple-minded, vulgar eulogies upon trivialities and truisms.

I have, rightly or wrongly, a notion of the chief cause of this pettiness in English patriotism of to-day, and I will attempt to expound it. It may be taken generally that a man loves his own stock and environment, and that he will find something to praise in it; but whether it is the most praiseworthy thing or no will depend upon the man's enlightenment as to the facts. If the son of Thackeray, let us say, were brought up in ignorance of his father's fame and genius, it is not improbable that he would be proud of the fact that his father was over six feet high. It seems to me that we, as a nation, are precisely in the position of this hypothetical child of Thackeray's. We fall back upon gross and frivolous things for our patriotism, for a simple reason. We are the only people in the world who are not taught in childhood our own literature and our own history.

We are, as a nation, in the truly extraordinary condition of not knowing our own merits. We have played a great and splendid part in the history of universal thought and sentiment; we have been among the foremost in that eternal and bloodless battle in which the blows do not slay, but create. In painting and music we are inferior to many other nations; but in literature, science, philosophy, and political eloquence, if history be taken as a whole, we can hold our own with any. But all this vast heritage of intellectual glory is kept from our schoolboys like a heresy; and they are left to live and die in the dull and infantile type of patriotism which they learnt from a box of tin soldiers. There is no harm in the box of tin soldiers; we do not expect children to be equally delighted with a beautiful box of tin philanthropists. But there is great harm in the fact that the subtler and more civilized honour of England is not presented so as to keep pace with the expanding mind. A French boy is taught the glory of Molière as well as that of Turenne; a German boy is taught his own great national philosophy before he learns the philosophy of antiquity. The result is that, though French patriotism is often crazy and boastful, though German patriotism is often isolated and pedantic, they are neither of them merely dull, common, and brutal, as is so often the strange fate of the nation of Bacon and Locke. It is natural enough, and even righteous enough, under the circumstances. An Englishman must love England for something; consequently, he tends to exalt commerce or prize-fighting, just as a German might tend to exalt music, or a Flamand to exalt painting, because he really believes it is the chief merit of his fatherland. It would not be in the least extraordinary if a claim of eating up provinces and pulling down princes were the chief boast of a Zulu. The extraordinary thing is, that it is the chief boast of a people who have Shakespeare, Newton, Burke, and Darwin to boast of.

The peculiar lack of any generosity or delicacy in the current English nationalism appears to have no other possible origin but in this fact of our unique neglect in education of the study of the national literature. An Englishman could not be silly enough to despise other nations if he once knew how much England had done for them. Great men of letters cannot avoid being humane and universal. The absence of the teaching of English literature in our schools is, when we come to think of it, an almost amazing phenomenon. It is even more amazing when we listen to the arguments urged by headmasters and other educational conservatives against the direct teaching of English. It is said, for example, that a vast amount of English grammar and literature is picked up in the course of learning Latin and Greek. This is perfectly true, but the topsy-turviness of the idea never seems to strike them. It is like saying that a baby picks up the art of walking in the course of learning to hop, or that a Frenchman may successfully be taught German by helping a Prussian to learn Ashanti. Surely the obvious foundation of all education is the language in which that education is conveyed; if a boy has only time to learn one thing, he had better learn that.

We have deliberately neglected this great heritage of high national sentiment. We have made our public schools the strongest walls against a whisper of the honour of England. And we have had our punishment in this strange and perverted fact that, while a unifying vision of patriotism can ennoble bands of brutal savages or dingy burghers, and be the best thing in their lives, we, who are—the world being judge—humane, honest, and serious individually, have a patriotism that is the worst thing in ours. What have we done, and where have we wandered, we that have produced sages who could have spoken with Socrates and poets who could walk with Dante, that we should talk as if we have never done anything more intelligent than found colonies and kick niggers? We are the children of light, and it is we that sit in darkness. If we are judged, it will not be for the merely intellectual transgression of failing to appreciate other nations, but for the supreme spiritual transgression of failing to appreciate ourselves.

Varied Types

Chapter 1
Charlotte Brontë

bjection is often raised against realistic biography because it reveals so much that is important and even sacred about a man's life. The real objection to it will rather be found in the fact that it reveals about a man the precise points which are unimportant. It reveals and asserts and insists on exactly those things in a man's life of which the man himself is wholly unconscious; his exact class in society, the circumstances of his ancestry, the place of his present location. These are things which do not, properly speaking, ever arise before the human vision. They do not occur to a man's mind; it may be said, with almost equal truth, that they do not occur in a man's life. A man no more thinks about himself as the inhabitant of the third house in a row of Brixton villas than he thinks about himself as a strange animal with two legs. What a man's name was, what his income was, whom he married, where he lived, these are not sanctities; they are irrelevancies.

A very strong case of this is the case of the Brontës. The Brontë is in the position of the mad lady in a country village; her eccentricities form an endless source of innocent conversation to that exceedingly mild and bucolic circle, the literary world. The truly glorious gossips of literature, like Mr. Augustine Birrell and Mr. Andrew Lang, never tire of collecting all the glimpses and anecdotes and sermons and side-lights and sticks and straws which will go to make a Brontë museum. They are the most personally discussed of all Victorian authors, and the limelight of biography has left few darkened corners in the dark old Yorkshire house. And yet the whole of this biographical investigation, though natural and picturesque, is not wholly suitable to the Brontës. For the Brontë genius was above all things deputed to assert the supreme unimportance of externals. Up to that point truth had always been conceived as existing more or less in the novel of manners. Charlotte Brontë electrified the world by showing that an infinitely older and more elemental truth could be conveyed by a novel in which no person, good or bad, had any manners at all. Her work represents the first great assertion that the humdrum life of modern civilisation is a disguise as tawdry and deceptive as the costume of a *bal masqué*. She showed that abysses may exist inside a governess and eternities inside a manufacturer; her heroine is the commonplace spinster, with the dress of merino and the soul of flame. It is significant to notice that Charlotte Brontë, following consciously or unconsciously the great trend of her genius, was the first to take away from the heroine not only the artificial gold and diamonds of wealth and fashion, but even the natural gold and diamonds of physical beauty and grace. Instinctively she felt that the whole of the exterior must be made ugly that the whole of the interior might be made sublime. She chose the ugliest of women in the ugliest of centuries, and revealed within them all the hells and heavens of Dante.

It may, therefore, I think, be legitimately said that the externals of the Brontës' life, though singularly picturesque in themselves, matter less than the externals of almost any other writers. It is interesting to know whether Jane Austen had any knowledge of the lives of the officers and women of fashion whom she introduced into her masterpieces. It is interesting to know whether Dickens had ever seen a shipwreck or been inside a workhouse. For in these authors much of the conviction is conveyed, not always by adherence to facts, but always by grasp of them. But the whole aim and purport and meaning of the work of the Brontës is that the most futile thing in the whole universe is fact. Such a story as "Jane Eyre" is in itself so monstrous a fable that it ought to be excluded from a book of fairy tales. The characters do not do what they ought to do, nor what they would do, nor it might be said, such is the insanity of the atmosphere, not even what they intend to do. The conduct of Rochester is so primevally and superhumanly caddish that Bret Harte in his admirable travesty scarcely exaggerated it. "Then, resuming his usual manner, he threw his boots at my head and withdrew," does perhaps reach to something resembling caricature. The scene in which Rochester dresses up as an old gipsy has something in it which is really not to be found in any other branch of art, except in the end of the pantomime, where the Emperor turns into a pantaloon. Yet, despite this vast nightmare of illusion and morbidity and ignorance of the world, "Jane Eyre" is perhaps the truest book that was ever written. Its essential truth to life sometimes makes one catch one's breath. For it is not true to manners, which are constantly false, or to facts, which are almost always false; it is true to the only existing thing which is true, emotion, the irreducible minimum, the indestructible germ. It would not matter a single straw if a Brontë story were a hundred times more moonstruck and improbable than "Jane Eyre," or a hundred times more moonstruck and improbable than "Wuthering Heights." It would not matter if George Read stood on his head, and Mrs. Read rode on a dragon, if Fairfax Rochester had four eyes and St. John Rivers three legs, the story would still remain the truest story in the world. The typical Brontë character is, indeed, a kind of monster. Everything in him except the essential is dislocated. His hands are on his legs and his feet on his arms, his nose is above his eyes, but his heart is in the right place.

The great and abiding truth for which the Brontë cycle of fiction stands is a certain most important truth about the enduring spirit of youth, the truth of the near kinship between terror and joy. The Brontë heroine, dingily dressed, badly educated, hampered by a humiliating inexperience, a kind of ugly innocence, is yet, by the very fact of her solitude and her gaucherie, full of the greatest delight that is possible to a human being, the delight of expectation, the delight of an ardent and flamboyant ignorance. She serves to show how futile it is of humanity to suppose that pleasure can be attained chiefly by putting on evening dress every evening, and having a box at the theatre every first night. It is not the man of

pleasure who has pleasure; it is not the man of the world who appreciates the
world. The man who has learnt to do all conventional things perfectly has at the
same time learnt to do them prosaically. It is the awkward man, whose evening
dress does not fit him, whose gloves will not go on, whose compliments will not
come off, who is really full of the ancient ecstasies of youth. He is frightened
enough of society actually to enjoy his triumphs. He has that element of fear
which is one of the eternal ingredients of joy. This spirit is the central spirit of
the Brontë novel. It is the epic of the exhilaration of the shy man. As such it is
of incalculable value in our time, of which the curse is that it does not take joy
reverently because it does not take it fearfully. The shabby and inconspicuous
governess of Charlotte Brontë, with the small outlook and the small creed, had
more commerce with the awful and elemental forces which drive the world than a
legion of lawless minor poets. She approached the universe with real simplicity,
and, consequently, with real fear and delight. She was, so to speak, shy before
the multitude of the stars, and in this she had possessed herself of the only force
which can prevent enjoyment being as black and barren as routine. The faculty of
being shy is the first and the most delicate of the powers of enjoyment. The fear
of the Lord is the beginning of pleasure.

Upon the whole, therefore, I think it may justifiably be said that the dark
wild youth of the Brontës in their dark wild Yorkshire home has been somewhat
exaggerated as a necessary factor in their work and their conception. The emotions with which they dealt were universal emotions, emotions of the morning of
existence, the springtide joy and the springtide terror. Every one of us as a boy or
girl has had some midnight dream of nameless obstacle and unutterable menace, in
which there was, under whatever imbecile forms, all the deadly stress and panic of
"Wuthering Heights." Every one of us has had a day-dream of our own potential
destiny not one atom more reasonable than "Jane Eyre." And the truth which the
Brontës came to tell us is the truth that many waters cannot quench love, and that
suburban respectability cannot touch or damp a secret enthusiasm. Clapham, like
every other earthly city, is built upon a volcano. Thousands of people go to and
fro in the wilderness of bricks and mortar, earning mean wages, professing a mean
religion, wearing a mean attire, thousands of women who have never found any
expression for their exaltation or their tragedy but to go on working harder and
yet harder at dull and automatic employments, at scolding children or stitching
shirts. But out of all these silent ones one suddenly became articulate, and spoke
a resonant testimony, and her name was Charlotte Brontë. Spreading around
us upon every side to-day like a huge and radiating geometrical figure are the
endless branches of the great city. There are times when we are almost stricken
crazy, as well we may be, by the multiplicity of those appalling perspectives, the
frantic arithmetic of that unthinkable population. But this thought of ours is in
truth nothing but a fancy. There are no chains of houses; there are no crowds of
men. The colossal diagram of streets and houses is an illusion, the opium dream

of a speculative builder. Each of these men is supremely solitary and supremely important to himself. Each of these houses stands in the centre of the world. There is no single house of all those millions which has not seemed to someone at some time the heart of all things and the end of travel.

Chapter 2
William Morris and His School

t is proper enough that the unveiling of the bust of William Morris should approximate to a public festival, for while there have been many men of genius in the Victorian era more despotic than he, there have been none so representative. He represents not only that rapacious hunger for beauty which has now for the first time become a serious problem in the healthy life of humanity, but he represents also that honourable instinct for finding beauty in common necessities of workmanship which gives it a stronger and more bony structure. The time has passed when William Morris was conceived to be irrelevant to be described as a designer of wall-papers. If Morris had been a hatter instead of a decorator, we should have become gradually and painfully conscious of an improvement in our hats. If he had been a tailor, we should have suddenly found our frock-coats trailing on the ground with the grandeur of mediæval raiment. If he had been a shoemaker, we should have found, with no little consternation, our shoes gradually approximating to the antique sandal. As a hairdresser, he would have invented some massing of the hair worthy to be the crown of Venus; as an ironmonger, his nails would have had some noble pattern, fit to be the nails of the Cross.

The limitations of William Morris, whatever they were, were not the limitations of common decoration. It is true that all his work, even his literary work, was in some sense decorative, had in some degree the qualities of a splendid wall-paper. His characters, his stories, his religious and political views, had, in the most emphatic sense, length and breadth without thickness. He seemed really to believe that men could enjoy a perfectly flat felicity. He made no account of the unexplored and explosive possibilities of human nature, of the unnameable terrors, and the yet more unnameable hopes. So long as a man was graceful in every circumstance, so long as he had the inspiring consciousness that the chestnut colour of his hair was relieved against the blue forest a mile behind, he would be serenely happy. So he would be, no doubt, if he were really fitted for a decorative existence; if he were a piece of exquisitely coloured card-board.

But although Morris took little account of the terrible solidity of human nature—took little account, so to speak, of human figures in the round, it is altogether unfair to represent him as a mere æsthete. He perceived a great public necessity and fulfilled it heroically. The difficulty with which he grappled was one so immense that we shall have to be separated from it by many centuries before we can really judge of it. It was the problem of the elaborate and deliberate ugliness of the most self-conscious of centuries. Morris at least saw the absurdity of the thing. He felt it was monstrous that the modern man, who was pre-eminently capable of realising the strangest and most contradictory beauties, who could feel at once the fiery aureole of the ascetic and the colossal calm of the Hellenic god, should himself, by a farcical bathos, be buried in a black coat, and hidden under a chimney-pot hat. He could not see why the harmless man who desired to be an artist in raiment should be condemned to be, at best, a black and white artist. It is indeed difficult to account for the clinging curse of ugliness which blights everything brought forth by the most prosperous of centuries. In all created nature there is not, perhaps, anything so completely ugly as a pillar-box. Its shape is the most unmeaning of shapes, its height and thickness just neutralising each other; its colour is the most repulsive of colours—a fat and soulless red, a red without a touch of blood or fire, like the scarlet of dead men's sins. Yet there is no reason whatever why such hideousness should possess an object full of civic dignity, the treasure-house of a thousand secrets, the fortress of a thousand souls. If the old Greeks had had such an institution, we may be sure that it would have been surmounted by the severe, but graceful, figure of the god of letter-writing. If the mediæval Christians has possessed it, it would have had a niche filled with the golden aureole of St. Rowland of the Postage Stamps. As it is, there it stands at all our street-corners, disguising one of the most beautiful of ideas under one of the most preposterous of forms. It is useless to deny that the miracles of science have not been such an incentive to art and imagination as were the miracles of religion. If men in the twelfth century had been told that the lightning had been driven for leagues underground, and had dragged at its destroying tail loads of laughing human beings, and if they had then been told that the people alluded to this pulverising portent chirpily as "The Twopenny Tube," they would have called down the fire of Heaven on us as a race of half-witted atheists. Probably they would have been quite right.

This clear and fine perception of what may be called the anæsthetic element in the Victorian era was, undoubtedly, the work of a great reformer: it requires a fine effort of the imagination to see an evil that surrounds us on every side. The manner in which Morris carried out his crusade may, considering the circumstances, be called triumphant. Our carpets began to bloom under our feet like the meadows in spring, and our hitherto prosaic stools and sofas seemed growing legs and arms at their own wild will. An element of freedom and rugged dignity came in with plain and strong ornaments of copper and iron. So delicate and universal has been the revolution in domestic art that almost every family in England has had its taste cunningly and treacherously improved, and if we look back at the early Victorian drawing-rooms it is only to realise the strange but essential truth that art, or human decoration, has, nine times out of ten in history, made things uglier than they were before, from the "coiffure" of a Papuan savage to the wall-paper of a British merchant in 1830.

But great and beneficent as was the æsthetic revolution of Morris, there was a very definite limit to it. It did not lie only in the fact that his revolution was in truth a reaction, though this was a partial explanation of his partial failure. When he was denouncing the dresses of modern ladies, "upholstered like arm-chairs instead of being draped like women," as he forcibly expressed it, he would hold up for practical imitation the costumes and handicrafts of the Middle Ages. Further than this retrogressive and imitative movement he never seemed to go. Now, the men of the time of Chaucer had many evil qualities, but there was at least one exhibition of moral weakness they did not give. They would have laughed at the idea of dressing themselves in the manner of the bowmen at the battle of Senlac, or painting themselves an æsthetic blue, after the custom of the ancient Britons. They would not have called that a movement at all. Whatever was beautiful in their dress or manners sprang honestly and naturally out of the life they led and preferred to lead. And it may surely be maintained that any real advance in the beauty of modern dress must spring honestly and naturally out of the life we lead and prefer to lead. We are not altogether without hints and hopes of such a change, in the growing orthodoxy of rough and athletic costumes. But if this cannot be, it will be no substitute or satisfaction to turn life into an interminable historical fancy-dress ball.

But the limitation of Morris's work lay deeper than this. We may best suggest it by a method after his own heart. Of all the various works he performed, none, perhaps, was so splendidly and solidly valuable as his great protest for the fables and superstitions of mankind. He has the supreme credit of showing that the fairy tales contain the deepest truth of the earth, the real record of men's feeling for things. Trifling details may be inaccurate, Jack may not have climbed up so tall a beanstalk, or killed so tall a giant; but it is not such things that make a story false; it is a far different class of things that makes every modern book of history as false as the father of lies; ingenuity, self-consciousness, hypocritical impartiality. It appears to us that of all the fairy-tales none contains so vital a moral truth as the old story, existing in many forms, of Beauty and the Beast. There is written, with all the authority of a human scripture, the eternal and essential truth that until we love a thing in all its ugliness we cannot make it beautiful. This was the weak point in William Morris as a reformer: that he sought to reform modern life, and that he hated modern life instead of loving it. Modern London is indeed a beast, big enough and black enough to be the beast in Apocalypse, blazing with a million eyes, and roaring with a million voices. But unless the poet can love this fabulous monster as he is, can feel with some generous excitement his massive and mysterious *joie-de-vivre*, the vast scale of his iron anatomy and the beating of his thunderous heart, he cannot and will not change the beast into the fairy prince. Morris's disadvantage was that he was not honestly a child of the nineteenth century: he could not understand its fascination, and consequently he could not really develop it. An abiding testimony to his tremendous personal influence in the æsthetic world is the vitality and recurrence of the Arts and Crafts Exhibitions, which are steeped in his personality like a chapel in that of a saint. If we look round at the exhibits in one of these æsthetic shows, we shall be struck by the large mass of modern objects that the decorative school leaves untouched. There is a noble instinct for giving the right touch of beauty to common and necessary things, but the things that are so touched are the ancient things, the things that always to some extent commended themselves to the lover of beauty. There are beautiful gates, beautiful fountains, beautiful cups, beautiful chairs, beautiful reading-desks. But there are no modern things made beautiful. There are no beautiful lamp-posts, beautiful letter-boxes, beautiful engines, beautiful bicycles. The spirit of William Morris has not seized hold of the century and made its humblest necessities beautiful. And this was because, with all his healthiness and energy, he had not the supreme courage to face the ugliness of things; Beauty shrank from the Beast and the fairy-tale had a different ending.

But herein, indeed, lay Morris's deepest claim to the name of a great reformer: that he left his work incomplete. There is, perhaps, no better proof that a man is a mere meteor, merely barren and brilliant, than that his work is done perfectly. A man like Morris draws attention to needs he cannot supply. In after-years we may have perhaps a newer and more daring Arts and Crafts Exhibition. In it we shall not decorate the armour of the twelfth century, but the machinery of the twentieth. A lamp-post shall be wrought nobly in twisted iron, fit to hold the sanctity of fire. A pillar-box shall be carved with figures emblematical of the secrets of comradeship and the silence and honour of the State. Railway signals, of all earthly things the most poetical, the coloured stars of life and death, shall be lamps of green and crimson worthy of their terrible and faithful service. But if ever this gradual and genuine movement of our time towards beauty—not backwards, but forwards—does truly come about, Morris will be the first prophet of it. Poet of the childhood of nations, craftsman in the new honesties of art, prophet of a merrier and wiser life, his full-blooded enthusiasm will be remembered when human life has once more assumed flamboyant colours and proved that this painful greenish grey of the æsthetic twilight in which we now live is, in spite of all the pessimists, not of the greyness of death, but the greyness of dawn.

Chapter 3
Optimism of Byron

verything is against our appreciating the spirit and the age of Byron. The age that has just passed from us is always like a dream when we wake in the morning, a thing incredible and centuries away. And the world of Byron seems a sad and faded world, a weird and inhuman world, where men were romantic in whiskers, ladies lived, apparently, in bowers, and the very word has the sound of a piece of stage scenery. Roses and nightingales recur in their poetry with the monotonous elegance of a wall-paper pattern. The whole is like a revel of dead men, a revel with splendid vesture and half-witted faces.

But the more shrewdly and earnestly we study the histories of men, the less ready shall we be to make use of the word "artificial." Nothing in the world has ever been artificial. Many customs, many dresses, many works of art are branded with artificiality because they exhibit vanity and self-consciousness: as if vanity were not a deep and elemental thing, like love and hate and the fear of death. Vanity may be found in darkling deserts, in the hermit and in the wild beasts that crawl around him. It may be good or evil, but assuredly it is not artificial: vanity is a voice out of the abyss.

The remarkable fact is, however, and it bears strongly on the present position of Byron, that when a thing is unfamiliar to us, when it is remote and the product of some other age or spirit, we think it not savage or terrible, but merely artificial. There are many instances of this: a fair one is the case of tropical plants and birds. When we see some of the monstrous and flamboyant blossoms that enrich the equatorial woods, we do not feel that they are conflagrations of nature; silent explosions of her frightful energy. We simply find it hard to believe that they are not wax flowers grown under a glass case. When we see some of the tropic birds, with their tiny bodies attached to gigantic beaks, we do not feel that they are freaks of the fierce humour of Creation. We almost believe that they are toys out of a child's play-box, artificially carved and artificially coloured. So it is with the great convulsion of Nature which was known as Byronism. The volcano is not an extinct volcano now; it is the dead stick of a rocket. It is the remains not of a natural but of an artificial fire.

But Byron and Byronism were something immeasurably greater than anything that is represented by such a view as this: their real value and meaning are indeed little understood. The first of the mistakes about Byron lies in the fact that he is treated as a pessimist. True, he treated himself as such, but a critic can hardly have even a slight knowledge of Byron without knowing that he had the smallest amount of knowledge of himself that ever fell to the lot of an intelligent man. The real character of what is known as Byron's pessimism is better worth study than any real pessimism could ever be.

It is the standing peculiarity of this curious world of ours that almost everything in it has been extolled enthusiastically and invariably extolled to the disadvantage of everything else.

One after another almost every one of the phenomena of the universe has been declared to be alone capable of making life worth living. Books, love, business, religion, alcohol, abstract truth, private emotion, money, simplicity, mysticism, hard work, a life close to nature, a life close to Belgrave Square are every one of them passionately maintained by somebody to be so good that they redeem the evil of an otherwise indefensible world. Thus, while the world is almost always condemned in summary, it is always justified, and indeed extolled, in detail after detail.

Existence has been praised and absolved by a chorus of pessimists. The work of giving thanks to Heaven is, as it were, divided ingeniously among them. Schopenhauer is told off as a kind of librarian in the House of God, to sing the praises of the austere pleasures of the mind. Carlyle, as steward, undertakes the working department and eulogises a life of labour in the fields. Omar Khayyam is established in the cellar, and swears that it is the only room in the house. Even the blackest of pessimistic artists enjoys his art. At the precise moment that he has written some shameless and terrible indictment of Creation, his one pang of joy in the achievement joins the universal chorus of gratitude, with the scent of the wild flower and the song of the bird.

Now Byron had a sensational popularity, and that popularity was, as far as words and explanations go, founded upon his pessimism. He was adored by an overwhelming majority, almost every individual of which despised the majority of mankind. But when we come to regard the matter a little more deeply we tend in some degree to cease to believe in this popularity of the pessimist. The popularity of pure and unadulterated pessimism is an oddity; it is almost a contradiction in terms. Men would no more receive the news of the failure of existence or of the harmonious hostility of the stars with ardour or popular rejoicing than they would light bonfires for the arrival of cholera or dance a breakdown when they were condemned to be hanged. When the pessimist is popular it must always be not because he shows all things to be bad, but because he shows some things to be good.

Men can only join in a chorus of praise, even if it is the praise of denunciation. The man who is popular must be optimistic about something, even if he is only optimistic about pessimism. And this was emphatically the case with Byron and the Byronists. Their real popularity was founded not upon the fact that they blamed everything, but upon the fact that they praised something. They heaped curses upon man, but they used man merely as a foil. The things they wished to praise by comparison were the energies of Nature. Man was to them what talk and fashion were to Carlyle, what philosophical and religious quarrels were to

Omar, what the whole race after practical happiness was to Schopenhauer, the thing which must be censured in order that somebody else may be exalted. It was merely a recognition of the fact that one cannot write in white chalk except on a black-board.

Surely it is ridiculous to maintain seriously that Byron's love of the desolate and inhuman in nature was the mark of vital scepticism and depression. When a young man can elect deliberately to walk alone in winter by the side of the shattering sea, when he takes pleasure in storms and stricken peaks, and the lawless melancholy of the older earth, we may deduce with the certainty of logic that he is very young and very happy. There is a certain darkness which we see in wine when seen in shadow; we see it again in the night that has just buried a gorgeous sunset. The wine seems black, and yet at the same time powerfully and almost impossibly red; the sky seems black, and yet at the same time to be only too dense a blend of purple and green. Such was the darkness which lay around the Byronic school. Darkness with them was only too dense a purple. They would prefer the sullen hostility of the earth because amid all the cold and darkness their own hearts were flaming like their own firesides.

Matters are very different with the more modern school of doubt and lamentation. The last movement of pessimism is perhaps expressed in Mr. Aubrey Beardsley's allegorical designs. Here we have to deal with a pessimism which tends naturally not towards the oldest elements of the cosmos, but towards the last and most fantastic fripperies of artificial life. Byronism tended towards the desert; the new pessimism towards the restaurant. Byronism was a revolt against artificiality; the new pessimism is a revolt in its favour.

The Byronic young man had an affectation of sincerity; the decadent, going a step deeper into the avenues of the unreal, has positively an affectation of affectation. And it is by their fopperies and their frivolities that we know that their sinister philosophy is sincere; in their lights and garlands and ribbons we read their indwelling despair. It was so, indeed, with Byron himself; his really bitter moments were his frivolous moments. He went on year after year calling down fire upon mankind, summoning the deluge and the destructive sea and all the ultimate energies of nature to sweep away the cities of the spawn of man. But through all this his subconscious mind was not that of a despairer; on the contrary, there is something of a kind of lawless faith in thus parleying with such immense and immemorial brutalities. It was not until the time in which he wrote "Don Juan" that he really lost this inward warmth and geniality, and a sudden shout of hilarious laughter announced to the world that Lord Byron had really become a pessimist.

One of the best tests in the world of what a poet really means is his metre. He may be a hypocrite in his metaphysics, but he cannot be a hypocrite in his prosody. And all the time that Byron's language is of horror and emptiness, his metre is a bounding *pas de quatre*. He may arraign existence on the most deadly charges, he may condemn it with the most desolating verdict, but he cannot alter the fact that on some walk in a spring morning when all the limbs are swinging and all the blood alive in the body, the lips may be caught repeating:

> "Oh, there's not a joy the world can give like that it takes away,
> When the glow of early youth declines in beauty's dull decay;
> 'Tis not upon the cheek of youth the blush that fades so fast,
> But the tender bloom of heart is gone ere youth itself be past."

That automatic recitation is the answer to the whole pessimism of Byron.

The truth is that Byron was one of a class who may be called the unconscious optimists, who are very often, indeed, the most uncompromising conscious pessimists, because the exuberance of their nature demands for an adversary a dragon as big as the world. But the whole of his essential and unconscious being was spirited and confident, and that unconscious being, long disguised and buried under emotional artifices, suddenly sprang into prominence in the face of a cold, hard, political necessity. In Greece he heard the cry of reality, and at the time that he was dying, he began to live. He heard suddenly the call of that buried and subconscious happiness which is in all of us, and which may emerge suddenly at the sight of the grass of a meadow or the spears of the enemy.

Chapter 4
Pope and the Art of Satire

he general critical theory common in this and the last century is that it was very easy for the imitators of Pope to write English poetry. The classical couplet was a thing that anyone could do. So far as that goes, one may justifiably answer by asking anyone to try. It may be easier really to have wit, than really, in the boldest and most enduring sense, to have imagination. But it is immeasurably easier to pretend to have imagination than to pretend to have wit. A man may indulge in a sham rhapsody, because it may be the triumph of a rhapsody to be unintelligible. But a man cannot indulge in a sham joke, because it is the ruin of a joke to be unintelligible. A man may pretend to be a poet: he can no more pretend to be a wit than he can pretend to bring rabbits out of a hat without having learnt to be a conjuror. Therefore, it may be submitted, there was a certain discipline in the old antithetical couplet of Pope and his followers. If it did not permit of the great liberty of wisdom used by the minority of great geniuses, neither did it permit of the great liberty of folly which is used by the majority of small writers. A prophet could not be a poet in those days, perhaps, but at least a fool could not be a poet. If we take, for the sake of example, such a line as Pope's:

"Damn with faint praise, assent with civil leer,"

the test is comparatively simple. A great poet would not have written such a line, perhaps. But a minor poet could not.

Supposing that a lyric poet of the new school really had to deal with such an idea as that expressed in Pope's line about Man:

"A being darkly wise and rudely great,"

Is it really so certain that he would go deeper into the matter than that old antithetical jingle goes? I venture to doubt whether he would really be any wiser or weirder or more imaginative or more profound. The one thing that he would really be, would be longer. Instead of writing,

"A being darkly wise and rudely great,"

the contemporary poet, in his elaborately ornamented book of verses, would produce something like the following:

"A creature
Of feature
More dark, more dark, more dark than skies,

Yea, darkly wise, yea, darkly wise:
Darkly wise as a formless fate.
And if he be great,
If he be great, then rudely great,
Rudely great as a plough that plies,
And darkly wise, and darkly wise."

Have we really learnt to think more broadly? Or have we only learnt to spread our thoughts thinner? I have a dark suspicion that a modern poet might manufacture an admirable lyric out of almost every line of Pope.

There is, of course, an idea in our time that the very antithesis of the typical line of Pope is a mark of artificiality. I shall have occasion more than once to point out that nothing in the world has ever been artificial. But certainly antithesis is not artificial. An element of paradox runs through the whole of existence itself. It begins in the realm of ultimate physics and metaphysics, in the two facts that we cannot imagine a space that is infinite, and that we cannot imagine a space that is finite. It runs through the inmost complications of divinity, in that we cannot conceive that Christ in the wilderness was truly pure, unless we also conceive that he desired to sin. It runs, in the same manner, through all the minor matters of morals, so that we cannot imagine courage existing except in conjunction with fear, or magnanimity existing except in conjunction with some temptation to meanness. If Pope and his followers caught this echo of natural irrationality, they were not any the more artificial. Their antitheses were fully in harmony with existence, which is itself a contradiction in terms.

Pope was really a great poet; he was the last great poet of civilisation. Immediately after the fall of him and his school come Burns and Byron, and the reaction towards the savage and the elemental. But to Pope civilisation was still an exciting experiment. Its perruques and ruffles were to him what feathers and bangles are to a South Sea Islander—the real romance of civilisation. And in all the forms of art which peculiarly belong to civilisation, he was supreme. In one especially he was supreme—the great and civilised art of satire. And in this we have fallen away utterly.

We have had a great revival in our time of the cult of violence and hostility. Mr. Henley and his young men have an infinite number of furious epithets with which to overwhelm anyone who differs from them. It is not a placid or untroubled position to be Mr. Henley's enemy, though we know that it is certainly safer than to be his friend. And yet, despite all this, these people produce no satire. Political and social satire is a lost art, like pottery and stained glass. It may be worth while to make some attempt to point out a reason for this.

It may seem a singular observation to say that we are not generous enough to write great satire. This, however, is approximately a very accurate way of describing the case. To write great satire, to attack a man so that he feels the attack and half acknowledges its justice, it is necessary to have a certain intellectual

magnanimity which realises the merits of the opponent as well as his defects. This
is, indeed, only another way of putting the simple truth that in order to attack an
army we must know not only its weak points, but also its strong points. England
in the present season and spirit fails in satire for the same simple reason that it fails
in war: it despises the enemy. In matters of battle and conquest we have got firmly
rooted in our minds the idea (an idea fit for the philosophers of Bedlam) that we
can best trample on a people by ignoring all the particular merits which give them
a chance of trampling upon us. It has become a breach of etiquette to praise the
enemy; whereas, when the enemy is strong, every honest scout ought to praise
the enemy. It is impossible to vanquish an army without having a full account of
its strength. It is impossible to satirise a man without having a full account of his
virtues. It is too much the custom in politics to describe a political opponent as
utterly inhuman, as utterly careless of his country, as utterly cynical, which no
man ever was since the beginning of the world. This kind of invective may often
have a great superficial success: it may hit the mood of the moment; it may raise
excitement and applause; it may impress millions. But there is one man among all
those millions whom it does not impress, whom it hardly ever touches; that is the
man against whom it is directed. The one person for whom the whole satire has
been written in vain is the man whom it is the whole object of the institution of
satire to reach. He knows that such a description of him is not true. He knows
that he is not utterly unpatriotic, or utterly self-seeking, or utterly barbarous
and revengeful. He knows that he is an ordinary man, and that he can count as
many kindly memories, as many humane instincts, as many hours of decent work
and responsibility as any other ordinary man. But behind all this he has his real
weaknesses, the real ironies of his soul: behind all these ordinary merits lie the
mean compromises, the craven silences, the sullen vanities, the secret brutalities,
the unmanly visions of revenge. It is to these that satire should reach if it is to
touch the man at whom it is aimed. And to reach these it must pass and salute a
whole army of virtues.

If we turn to the great English satirists of the seventeenth and eighteenth
centuries, for example, we find that they had this rough, but firm, grasp of the
size and strength, the value and the best points of their adversary. Dryden, before
hewing Ahitophel in pieces, gives a splendid and spirited account of the insane
valour and inspired cunning of the

"daring pilot in extremity,"

who was more untrustworthy in calm than in storm, and

"Steered too near the rocks to boast his wit."

The whole is, so far as it goes, a sound and picturesque version of the great
Shaftesbury. It would, in many ways, serve as a very sound and picturesque account
of Lord Randolph Churchill. But here comes in very pointedly the difference

between our modern attempts at satire and the ancient achievement of it. The opponents of Lord Randolph Churchill, both Liberal and Conservative, did not satirise him nobly and honestly, as one of those great wits to madness near allied. They represented him as a mere puppy, a silly and irreverent upstart whose impudence supplied the lack of policy and character. Churchill had grave and even gross faults, a certain coarseness, a certain hard boyish assertiveness, a certain lack of magnanimity, a certain peculiar patrician vulgarity. But he was a much larger man than satire depicted him, and therefore the satire could not and did not overwhelm him. And here we have the cause of the failure of contemporary satire, that it has no magnanimity, that is to say, no patience. It cannot endure to be told that its opponent has his strong points, just as Mr. Chamberlain could not endure to be told that the Boers had a regular army. It can be content with nothing except persuading itself that its opponent is utterly bad or utterly stupid—that is, that he is what he is not and what nobody else is. If we take any prominent politician of the day—such, for example, as Sir William Harcourt—we shall find that this is the point in which all party invective fails. The Tory satire at the expense of Sir William Harcourt is always desperately endeavouring to represent that he is inept, that he makes a fool of himself, that he is disagreeable and disgraceful and untrustworthy. The defect of all that is that we all know that it is untrue. Everyone knows that Sir William Harcourt is not inept, but is almost the ablest Parliamentarian now alive. Everyone knows that he is not disagreeable or disgraceful, but a gentleman of the old school who is on excellent social terms with his antagonists. Everyone knows that he is not untrustworthy, but a man of unimpeachable honour who is much trusted. Above all, he knows it himself, and is therefore affected by the satire exactly as any one of us would be if we were accused of being black or of keeping a shop for the receiving of stolen goods. We might be angry at the libel, but not at the satire: for a man is angry at a libel because it is false, but at a satire because it is true.

Mr. Henley and his young men are very fond of invective and satire; if they wish to know the reason of their failure in these things, they need only turn to the opening of Pope's superb attack upon Addison. The Henleyite's idea of satirising a man is to express a violent contempt for him, and by the heat of this to persuade others and himself that the man is contemptible. I remember reading a satiric attack on Mr. Gladstone by one of the young anarchic Tories, which began by asserting that Mr. Gladstone was a bad public speaker. If these people would, as I have said, go quietly and read Pope's "Atticus," they would see how a great satirist approaches a great enemy:

> "Peace to all such! But were there one whose fires
> True genius kindles, and fair fame inspires,
> Blest with each talent, and each art to please,
> And born to write, converse, and live with ease.
> Should such a man—"

And then follows the torrent of that terrible criticism. Pope was not such a fool as to try to make out that Addison was a fool. He knew that Addison was not a fool, and he knew that Addison knew it. But hatred, in Pope's case, had become so great and, I was almost going to say, so pure, that it illuminated all things, as love illuminates all things. He said what was really wrong with Addison; and in calm and clear and everlasting colours he painted the picture of the evil of the literary temperament:

> "Bear, like the Turk, no brother near the throne,
> View him with scornful, yet with jealous eyes,
> And hate for arts that caused himself to rise.
> Like Cato give his little Senate laws,
> And sit attentive to his own applause.
> While wits and templars every sentence raise,
> And wonder with a foolish face of praise."

This is the kind of thing which really goes to the mark at which it aims. It is penetrated with sorrow and a kind of reverence, and it is addressed directly to a man. This is no mock-tournament to gain the applause of the crowd. It is a deadly duel by the lonely seashore.

In current political materialism there is everywhere the assumption that, without understanding anything of his case or his merits, we can benefit a man practically. Without understanding his case and his merits, we cannot even hurt him.

Chapter 5
Francis

sceticism is a thing which, in its very nature, we tend in these days to misunderstand. Asceticism, in the religious sense, is the repudiation of the great mass of human joys because of the supreme joyfulness of the one joy, the religious joy. But asceticism is not in the least confined to religious asceticism: there is scientific asceticism which asserts that truth is alone satisfying: there is æsthetic asceticism which asserts that art is alone satisfying: there is amatory asceticism which asserts that love is alone satisfying. There is even epicurean asceticism, which asserts that beer and skittles are alone satisfying. Wherever the manner of praising anything involves the statement that the speaker could live with that thing alone, there lies the germ and essence of asceticism. When William Morris, for example, says that "love is enough," it is obvious that he asserts in those words that art, science, politics, ambition, money, houses, carriages, concerts, gloves, walking-sticks, door-knockers, railway-stations, cathedrals, and any other things one may choose to tabulate are unnecessary. When Omar Khayyam says:

"A book of verses underneath the bough,
A loaf of bread, a jug of wine, and thou
Beside me singing in the wilderness—
O wilderness were Paradise enow."

It is clear that he speaks fully as much ascetically as he does æsthetically. He makes a list of things and says that he wants no more. The same thing was done by a mediæval monk. Examples might, of course, be multiplied a hundred-fold. One of the most genuinely poetical of our younger poets says, as the one thing certain, that

"From quiet home and first beginning
Out to the undiscovered ends—
There's nothing worth the wear of winning
But laughter and the love of friends."

Here we have a perfect example of the main important fact, that all true joy expresses itself in terms of asceticism.

But if, in any case, it should happen that a class or a generation lose the sense of the peculiar kind of joy which is being celebrated, they immediately begin to call the enjoyers of that joy gloomy and self-destroying. The most formidable liberal philosophers have called the monks melancholy because they denied themselves the pleasures of liberty and marriage. They might as well call the trippers on a

Bank Holiday melancholy because they deny themselves, as a rule, the pleasures of silence and meditation. A simpler and stronger example is, however, to hand. If ever it should happen that the system of English athletics should vanish from the public schools and the universities, if science should supply some new and non-competitive manner of perfecting the physique, if public ethics swung round to an attitude of absolute contempt and indifference towards the feeling called sport, then it is easy to see what would happen. Future historians would simply state that in the dark days of Queen Victoria young men at Oxford and Cambridge were subjected to a horrible sort of religious torture. They were forbidden, by fantastic monastic rules, to indulge in wine or tobacco during certain arbitrarily fixed periods of time, before certain brutal fights and festivals. Bigots insisted on their rising at unearthly hours and running violently around fields for no object. Many men ruined their health in these dens of superstition, many died there. All this is perfectly true and irrefutable. Athleticism in England is an asceticism, as much as the monastic rules. Men have overstrained themselves and killed themselves through English athleticism. There is one difference and one only: we do feel the love of sport; we do not feel the love of religious offices. We see only the price in the one case and only the purchase in the other.

The only question that remains is what was the joy of the old Christian ascetics of which their asceticism was merely the purchasing price? The mere possibility of the query is an extraordinary example of the way in which we miss the main points of human history. We are looking at humanity too close, and see only the details and not the vast and dominant features. We look at the rise of Christianity, and conceive it as a rise of self-abnegation and almost of pessimism. It does not occur to us that the mere assertion that this raging and confounding universe is governed by justice and mercy is a piece of staggering optimism fit to set all men capering. The detail over which these monks went mad with joy was the universe itself; the only thing really worthy of enjoyment. The white daylight shone over all the world, the endless forests stood up in their order. The lightning awoke and the tree fell and the sea gathered into mountains and the ship went down, and all these disconnected and meaningless and terrible objects were all part of one dark and fearful conspiracy of goodness, one merciless scheme of mercy. That this scheme of Nature was not accurate or well founded is perfectly tenable, but surely it is not tenable that it was not optimistic. We insist, however, upon treating this matter tail foremost. We insist that the ascetics were pessimists because they gave up threescore years and ten for an eternity of happiness. We forget that the bare proposition of an eternity of happiness is by its very nature ten thousand times more optimistic than ten thousand pagan saturnalias.

Mr. Adderley's life of Francis of Assisi does not, of course, bring this out; nor does it fully bring out the character of Francis. It has rather the tone of a devotional book. A devotional book is an excellent thing, but we do not look in it for the portrait of a man, for the same reason that we do not look in a love-sonnet for the portrait of a woman, because men in such conditions of mind not only apply all virtues to their idol, but all virtues in equal quantities. There is no outline, because the artist cannot bear to put in a black line. This blaze of benediction, this conflict between lights, has its place in poetry, not in biography. The successful examples of it may be found, for instance, in the more idealistic odes of Spenser. The design is sometimes almost indecipherable, for the poet draws in silver upon white.

It is natural, of course, that Mr. Adderley should see Francis primarily as the founder of the Franciscan Order. We suspect this was only one, perhaps a minor one, of the things that he was; we suspect that one of the minor things that Christ did was to found Christianity. But the vast practical work of Francis is assuredly not to be ignored, for this amazingly unworldly and almost maddeningly simple-minded infant was one of the most consistently successful men that ever fought with this bitter world. It is the custom to say that the secret of such men is their profound belief in themselves, and this is true, but not all the truth. Workhouses and lunatic asylums are thronged with men who believe in themselves. Of Francis it is far truer to say that the secret of his success was his profound belief in other people, and it is the lack of this that has commonly been the curse of these obscure Napoleons. Francis always assumed that everyone must be just as anxious about their common relative, the water-rat, as he was. He planned a visit to the Emperor to draw his attention to the needs of "his little sisters the larks." He used to talk to any thieves and robbers he met about their misfortune in being unable to give rein to their desire for holiness. It was an innocent habit, and doubtless the robbers often "got round him," as the phrase goes. Quite as often, however, they discovered that he had "got round" them, and discovered the other side, the side of secret nobility.

Conceiving of St. Francis as primarily the founder of the Franciscan Order, Mr. Adderley opens his narrative with an admirable sketch of the history of Monasticism in Europe, which is certainly the best thing in the book. He distinguishes clearly and fairly between the Manichæan ideal that underlies so much of Eastern Monasticism and the ideal of self-discipline which never wholly vanished from the Christian form. But he does not throw any light on what must be for the outsider the absorbing problem of this Catholic asceticism, for the excellent reason that, not being an outsider, he does not find it a problem at all.

To most people, however, there is a fascinating inconsistency in the position of St. Francis. He expressed in loftier and bolder language than any earthly thinker the conception that laughter is as divine as tears. He called his monks the mountebanks of God. He never forgot to take pleasure in a bird as it flashed past him, or a drop of water, as it fell from his finger: he was, perhaps, the happiest of the sons of men. Yet this man undoubtedly founded his whole polity on the negation of what we think the most imperious necessities; in his three vows of poverty, chastity, and obedience, he denied to himself and those he loved most, property, love, and liberty. Why was it that the most large-hearted and poetic spirits in that age found their most congenial atmosphere in these awful renunciations? Why did he who loved where all men were blind, seek to blind himself where all men loved? Why was he a monk, and not a troubadour? These questions are far too large to be answered fully here, but in any life of Francis they ought at least to have been asked; we have a suspicion that if they were answered, we should suddenly find that much of the enigma of this sullen time of ours was answered also. So it was with the monks. The two great parties in human affairs are only the party which sees life black against white, and the party which sees it white against black, the party which macerates and blackens itself with sacrifice because the background is full of the blaze of an universal mercy, and the party which crowns itself with flowers and lights itself with bridal torches because it stands against a black curtain of incalculable night. The revellers are old, and the monks are young. It was the monks who were the spendthrifts of happiness, and we who are its misers.

Doubtless, as is apparent from Mr. Adderley's book, the clear and tranquil life of the Three Vows had a fine and delicate effect on the genius of Francis. He was primarily a poet. The perfection of his literary instinct is shown in his naming the fire "brother," and the water "sister," in the quaint demagogic dexterity of the appeal in the sermon to the fishes "that they alone were saved in the Flood." In the amazingly minute and graphic dramatisation of the life, disappointments, and excuses of any shrub or beast that he happened to be addressing, his genius has a curious resemblance to that of Burns. But if he avoided the weakness of Burns' verses to animals, the occasional morbidity, bombast, and moralisation on himself, the credit is surely due to a cleaner and more transparent life.

The general attitude of St. Francis, like that of his Master, embodied a kind of terrible common sense. The famous remark of the Caterpillar in "Alice in Wonderland"—"Why not?" impresses us as his general motto. He could not see why he should not be on good terms with all things. The pomp of war and ambition, the great empire of the Middle Ages, and all its fellows begin to look tawdry and top-heavy, under the rationality of that innocent stare. His questions were blasting and devastating, like the questions of a child. He would not have been afraid even of the nightmares of cosmogony, for he had no fear in him. To him the world was small, not because he had any views as to its size, but for the reason that gossiping ladies find it small, because so many relatives were to be found in it. If you had taken him to the loneliest star that the madness of an astronomer can conceive, he would have only beheld in it the features of a new friend.

Chapter 6
Rostand

hen "Cyrano de Bergerac" was published, it bore the subordinate title of a heroic comedy. We have no tradition in English literature which would justify us in calling a comedy heroic, though there was once a poet who called a comedy divine. By the current modern conception, the hero has his place in a tragedy, and the one kind of strength which is systematically denied to him is the strength to succeed. That the power of a man's spirit might possibly go to the length of turning a tragedy into a comedy is not admitted; nevertheless, almost all the primitive legends of the world are comedies, not only in the sense that they have a happy ending, but in the sense that they are based upon a certain optimistic assumption that the hero is destined to be the destroyer of the monster. Singularly enough, this modern idea of the essential disastrous character of life, when seriously considered, connects itself with a hyper-æsthetic view of tragedy and comedy which is largely due to the influence of modern France, from which the great heroic comedies of Monsieur Rostand have come. The French genius has an instinct for remedying its own evil work, and France gives always the best cure for "Frenchiness." The idea of comedy which is held in England by the school which pays most attention to the technical niceties of art is a view which renders such an idea as that of heroic comedy quite impossible. The fundamental conception in the minds of the majority of our younger writers is that comedy is, *par excellence*, a fragile thing. It is conceived to be a conventional world of the most absolutely delicate and gimcrack description. Such stories as Mr. Max Beerbohm's "Happy Hypocrite" are conceptions which would vanish or fall into utter nonsense if viewed by one single degree too seriously. But great comedy, the comedy of Shakespeare or Sterne, not only can be, but must be, taken seriously. There is nothing to which a man must give himself up with more faith and self-abandonment than to genuine laughter. In such comedies one laughs with the heroes, and not at them. The humour which steeps the stories of Falstaff and Uncle Toby is a cosmic and philosophic humour, a geniality which goes down to the depths. It is not superficial reading, it is not even, strictly speaking, light reading. Our sympathies are as much committed to the characters as if they were the predestined victims in a Greek tragedy. The modern writer of comedies may be said to boast of the brittleness of his characters. He seems always on the eve of knocking his puppets to pieces. When John Oliver Hobbes wrote for the first time a comedy of serious emotions, she named it, with a thinly-disguised contempt for her own work, "A Sentimental Comedy." The ground of this conception of the artificiality of comedy is a profound pessimism. Life in the eyes of these mournful buffoons is itself an utterly tragic thing; comedy must be as hollow as a grinning mask. It is a refuge from the world, and not even, properly speaking, a part of it. Their wit is a thin sheet of shining ice over the eternal waters of bitterness.

"Cyrano de Bergerac" came to us as the new decoration of an old truth, that merriment was one of the world's natural flowers, and not one of its exotics. The gigantesque levity, the flamboyant eloquence, the Rabelaisian puns and digressions were seen to be once more what they had been in Rabelais, the mere outbursts of a human sympathy and bravado as old and solid as the stars. The human spirit demanded wit as headlong and haughty as its will. All was expressed in the words of Cyrano at his highest moment of happiness, *Il me faut des géants*. An essential aspect of this question of heroic comedy is the question of drama in rhyme. There is nothing that affords so easy a point of attack for the dramatic realist as the conduct of a play in verse. According to his canons, it is indeed absurd to represent a number of characters facing some terrible crisis in their lives by capping rhymes like a party playing *bouts rimés*. In his eyes it must appear somewhat ridiculous that two enemies taunting each other with insupportable insults should obligingly provide each other with metrical spacing and neat and convenient rhymes. But the whole of this view rests finally upon the fact that few persons, if any, to-day understand what is meant by a poetical play. It is a singular thing that those poetical plays which are now written in England by the most advanced students of the drama follow exclusively the lines of Maeterlinck, and use verse and rhyme for the adornment of a profoundly tragic theme. But rhyme has a supreme appropriateness for the treatment of the higher comedy. The land of heroic comedy is, as it were, a paradise of lovers, in which it is not difficult to imagine that men could talk poetry all day long. It is far more conceivable that men's speech should flower naturally into these harmonious forms, when they are filled with the essential spirit of youth, than when they are sitting gloomily in the presence of immemorial destiny. The great error consists in supposing that poetry is an unnatural form of language. We should all like to speak poetry at the moment when we truly live, and if we do not speak, it is because we have an impediment in our speech. It is not song that is the narrow or artificial thing, it is conversation that is a broken and stammering attempt at song. When we see men in a spiritual extravaganza, like "Cyrano de Bergerac," speaking in rhyme, it is not our language disguised or distorted, but our language rounded and made whole. Rhymes answer each other as the sexes in flowers and in humanity answer each other. Men do not speak so, it is true. Even when they are inspired or in love they talk inanities. But the poetic comedy does not misrepresent the speech one half so much as the speech misrepresents the soul. Monsieur Rostand showed even more than his usual insight when he called "Cyrano de Bergerac" a comedy, despite the fact that, strictly speaking, it ends with disappointment and death. The essence of tragedy is a spiritual breakdown or decline, and in the great French play the spiritual sentiment mounts unceasingly until the last line. It is not the facts themselves, but our feeling about them, that makes tragedy and comedy, and death is more joyful in Rostand than life in Maeterlinck. The same apparent contradiction holds good in the case of the drama of "L'Aiglon," now being performed with so much success. Although the hero is a weakling, the subject a fiasco, the end a premature death and a personal disillusionment, yet, in spite of this theme, which might have been chosen for its depressing qualities, the unconquerable pæan of the praise of things, the ungovernable gaiety of the poet's song swells so high that at the end it seems to drown all the weak voices of the characters in one crashing chorus of great things and great men. A multitude of mottoes might be taken from the play to indicate and illustrate, not only its own spirit, but much of the spirit of modern life. When in the vision of the field of Wagram the horrible voices of the wounded cry out, *Les corbeaux, les corbeaux,* the Duke, overwhelmed with a nightmare of hideous trivialities, cries out, *Où, où, sont les aigles?* That antithesis might stand alone as an invocation at the beginning of the twentieth century to the spirit of heroic comedy. When an ex-General of Napoleon is asked his reason for having betrayed the Emperor, he replies, *La fatigue,* and at that a veteran private of the Great Army rushes forward, and crying passionately, *Et nous?* pours out a terrible description of the life lived by the commoner soldier. To-day, when pessimism is almost as much a symbol of wealth and fashion as jewels or cigars, when the pampered heirs of the ages can sum up life in few other words but *la fatigue,* there might surely come a cry from the vast mass of common humanity from the beginning—*et nous?* It is this potentiality for enthusiasm among the mass of men that makes the function of comedy at once common and sublime. Shakespeare's "Much Ado About Nothing" is a great comedy, because behind it is the whole pressure of that love of love which is the youth of the world, which is common to all the young, especially to those who swear they will die bachelors and old maids. "Love's Labour's Lost" is filled with the same energy, and there it falls even more definitely into the scope of our subject, since it is a comedy in rhyme in which all men speak lyrically as naturally as the birds sing in pairing time. What the love of love is to the Shakespearean comedies, that other and more mysterious human passion, the love of death, is to "L'Aiglon." Whether we shall ever have in England a new tradition of poetic comedy it is difficult at present to say, but we shall assuredly never have it until we realise that comedy is built upon everlasting foundations in the nature of things, that it is not a thing too light to capture, but too deep to plumb. Monsieur Rostand, in his description of the Battle of Wagram, does not shrink from bringing about the Duke's ears the frightful voices of actual battle, of men torn by crows, and suffocated with blood, but when the Duke, terrified at these dreadful appeals, asks them for their final word, they all cry together *Vive l'Empereur!* Monsieur Rostand, perhaps, did not know that he was writing an allegory. To me that field of Wagram is the field of the modern war of literature. We hear nothing but the voices of pain; the whole is one phonograph of horror. It is right that we should hear these things, it is right that not one of them should be silenced; but these cries of distress are not in life, as they are in modern art, the only voices; they are the voices of men, but not the voice of man. When questioned finally and seriously as to their conception of their destiny, men have from the beginning of time answered in a thousand philosophies and religions with a single voice and in a sense most sacred and tremendous, *Vive l'Empereur.*

Chapter 7
Charles II

here are a great many bonds which still connect us with Charles II., one of the idlest men of one of the idlest epochs. Among other things Charles II. represented one thing which is very rare and very satisfying; he was a real and consistent sceptic. Scepticism, both in its advantages and disadvantages, is greatly misunderstood in our time. There is a curious idea abroad that scepticism has some connection with such theories as materialism and atheism and secularism. This is of course a mistake; the true sceptic has nothing to do with these theories simply because they are theories. The true sceptic is as much a spiritualist as he is a materialist. He thinks that the savage dancing round an African idol stands quite as good a chance of being right as Darwin. He thinks that mysticism is every bit as rational as rationalism. He has indeed the most profound doubts as to whether St. Matthew wrote his own gospel. But he has quite equally profound doubts as to whether the tree he is looking at is a tree and not a rhinoceros.

This is the real meaning of that mystery which appears so prominently in the lives of great sceptics, which appears with especial prominence in the life of Charles II. I mean their constant oscillation between atheism and Roman Catholicism. Roman Catholicism is indeed a great and fixed and formidable system, but so is atheism. Atheism is indeed the most daring of all dogmas, more daring than the vision of a palpable day of judgment. For it is the assertion of a universal negative; for a man to say that there is no God in the universe is like saying that there are no insects in any of the stars.

Thus it was with that wholesome and systematic sceptic, Charles II. When he took the Sacrament according to the forms of the Roman Church in his last hour he was acting consistently as a philosopher. The wafer might not be God; similarly it might not be a wafer. To the genuine and poetical sceptic the whole world is incredible, with its bulbous mountains and its fantastic trees. The whole order of things is as outrageous as any miracle which could presume to violate it. Transubstantiation might be a dream, but if it was, it was assuredly a dream within a dream. Charles II. sought to guard himself against hell fire because he could not think hell itself more fantastic than the world as it was revealed by science. The priest crept up the staircase, the doors were closed, the few of the faithful who were present hushed themselves respectfully, and so, with every circumstance of secrecy and sanctity, with the cross uplifted and the prayers poured out, was consummated the last great act of logical unbelief.

The problem of Charles II. consists in this, that he has scarcely a moral virtue to his name, and yet he attracts us morally. We feel that some of the virtues have been dropped out in the lists made by all the saints and sages, and that Charles II.

was pre-eminently successful in these wild and unmentionable virtues. The real truth of this matter and the real relation of Charles II. to the moral ideal is worth somewhat more exhaustive study.

It is a commonplace that the Restoration movement can only be understood when considered as a reaction against Puritanism. But it is insufficiently realised that the tyranny which half frustrated all the good work of Puritanism was of a very peculiar kind. It was not the fire of Puritanism, the exultation in sobriety, the frenzy of a restraint, which passed away; that still burns in the heart of England, only to be quenched by the final overwhelming sea. But it is seldom remembered that the Puritans were in their day emphatically intellectual bullies, that they relied swaggeringly on the logical necessity of Calvinism, that they bound omnipotence itself in the chains of syllogism. The Puritans fell, through the damning fact that they had a complete theory of life, through the eternal paradox that a satisfactory explanation can never satisfy. Like Brutus and the logical Romans, like the logical French Jacobins, like the logical English utilitarians, they taught the lesson that men's wants have always been right and their arguments always wrong. Reason is always a kind of brute force; those who appeal to the head rather than the heart, however pallid and polite, are necessarily men of violence. We speak of "touching" a man's heart, but we can do nothing to his head but hit it. The tyranny of the Puritans over the bodies of men was comparatively a trifle; pikes, bullets, and conflagrations are comparatively a trifle. Their real tyranny was the tyranny of aggressive reason over the cowed and demoralised human spirit. Their brooding and raving can be forgiven, can in truth be loved and reverenced, for it is humanity on fire; hatred can be genial, madness can be homely. The Puritans fell, not because they were fanatics, but because they were rationalists.

When we consider these things, when we remember that Puritanism, which means in our day a moral and almost temperamental attitude, meant in that day a singularly arrogant logical attitude, we shall comprehend a little more the grain of good that lay in the vulgarity and triviality of the Restoration. The Restoration, of which Charles II. was a pre-eminent type, was in part a revolt of all the chaotic and unclassed parts of human nature, the parts that are left over, and will always be left over, by every rationalistic system of life. This does not merely account for the revolt of the vices and of that empty recklessness and horseplay which is sometimes more irritating than any vice. It accounts also for the return of the virtue of politeness, for that also is a nameless thing ignored by logical codes. Politeness has indeed about it something mystical; like religion, it is everywhere understood and nowhere defined. Charles is not entirely to be despised because, as the type of this movement, he let himself float upon this new tide of politeness. There was some moral and social value in his perfection in little things. He could not keep the Ten Commandments, but he kept the ten thousand commandments. His name is unconnected with any great acts of duty or sacrifice, but it is connected with a great many of those acts of magnanimous politeness, of a kind of dramatic delicacy, which lie on the dim borderland between morality and art. "Charles II.," said Thackeray, with unerring brevity, "was a rascal, but not a snob." Unlike George IV. he was a gentleman, and a gentleman is a man who obeys strange statutes, not to be found in any moral text-book, and practises strange virtues nameless from the beginning of the world.

So much may be said and should be said for the Restoration, that it was the revolt of something human, if only the debris of human nature. But more cannot be said. It was emphatically a fall and not an ascent, a recoil and not an advance, a sudden weakness and not a sudden strength. That the bow of human nature was by Puritanism bent immeasurably too far, that it overstrained the soul by stretching it to the height of an almost horrible idealism, makes the collapse of the Restoration infinitely more excusable, but it does not make it any the less a collapse. Nothing can efface the essential distinction that Puritanism was one of the world's great efforts after the discovery of the true order, whereas it was the essence of the Restoration that it involved no effort at all. It is true that the Restoration was not, as has been widely assumed, the most immoral epoch of our history. Its vices cannot compare for a moment in this respect with the monstrous tragedies and almost suffocating secrecies and villainies of the Court of James I. But the dram-drinking and nose-slitting of the saturnalia of Charles II. seem at once more human and more detestable than the passions and poisons of the Renaissance, much in the same way that a monkey appears inevitably more human and more detestable than a tiger. Compared with the Renaissance, there is something Cockney about the Restoration. Not only was it too indolent for great morality, it was too indolent even for great art. It lacked that seriousness which is needed even for the pursuit of pleasure, that discipline which is essential even to a game of lawn tennis. It would have appeared to Charles II.'s poets quite as arduous to write "Paradise Lost" as to regain Paradise.

All old and vigorous languages abound in images and metaphors, which, though lightly and casually used, are in truth poems in themselves, and poems of a high and striking order. Perhaps no phrase is so terribly significant as the phrase "killing time." It is a tremendous and poetical image, the image of a kind of cosmic parricide. There are on the earth a race of revellers who do, under all their exuberance, fundamentally regard time as an enemy. Of these were Charles II. and the men of the Restoration. Whatever may have been their merits, and as we have said we think that they had merits, they can never have a place among the great representatives of the joy of life, for they belonged to those lower epicureans who kill time, as opposed to those higher epicureans who make time live.

Of a people in this temper Charles II. was the natural and rightful head. He may have been a pantomime King, but he was a King, and with all his geniality he let nobody forget it. He was not, indeed, the aimless flaneur that he has been represented. He was a patient and cunning politician, who disguised his wisdom under so perfect a mask of folly that he not only deceived his allies and opponents, but has deceived almost all the historians that have come after him. But if Charles was, as he emphatically was, the only Stuart who really achieved despotism, it was greatly due to the temper of the nation and the age. Despotism is the easiest of all governments, at any rate for the governed.

It is indeed a form of slavery, and it is the despot who is the slave. Men in a state of decadence employ professionals to fight for them, professionals to dance for them, and a professional to rule them.

Almost all the faces in the portraits of that time look, as it were, like masks put on artificially with the perruque. A strange unreality broods over the period. Distracted as we are with civic mysteries and problems we can afford to rejoice. Our tears are less desolate than their laughter, our restraints are larger than their liberty.

Chapter 8
Stevenson

recent incident has finally convinced us that Stevenson was, as we suspected, a great man. We knew from recent books that we have noticed, from the scorn of "Ephemera Critica" and Mr. George Moore, that Stevenson had the first essential qualification of a great man: that of being misunderstood by his opponents. But from the book which Messrs. Chatto & Windus have issued, in the same binding as Stevenson's works, "Robert Louis Stevenson," by Mr. H. Bellyse Baildon,[1] we learn that he has the other essential qualification, that of being misunderstood by his admirers. Mr. Baildon has many interesting things to tell us about Stevenson himself, whom he knew at college. Nor are his criticisms by any means valueless. That upon the plays, especially "Beau Austin," is remarkably thoughtful and true. But it is a very singular fact, and goes far, as we say, to prove that Stevenson had that unfathomable quality which belongs to the great, that this admiring student of Stevenson can number and marshal all the master's work and distribute praise and blame with decision and even severity, without ever thinking for a moment of the principles of art and ethics which would have struck us as the very things that Stevenson nearly killed himself to express.

Mr. Baildon, for example, is perpetually lecturing Stevenson for his "pessimism"; surely a strange charge against a man who has done more than any modern artist to make men ashamed of their shame of life. But he complains that, in "The Master of Ballantrae" and "Dr. Jekyll and Mr. Hyde," Stevenson gives evil a final victory over good. Now if there was one point that Stevenson more constantly and passionately emphasised than any other it was that we must worship good for its own value and beauty, without any reference whatever to victory or failure in space and time. "Whatever we are intended to do," he said, "we are not intended to succeed." That the stars in their courses fight against virtue, that humanity is in its nature a forlorn hope, this was the very spirit that through the whole of Stevenson's work sounded a trumpet to all the brave. The story of Henry Durie is dark enough, but could anyone stand beside the grave of that sodden monomaniac and not respect him? It is strange that men should see sublime inspiration in the ruins of an old church and see none in the ruins of a man.

The author has most extraordinary ideas about Stevenson's tales of blood and spoil; he appears to think that they prove Stevenson to have had (we use Mr. Baildon's own phrase) a kind of "homicidal mania." "He [Stevenson] arrives pretty much at the paradox that one can hardly be better employed than in taking life." Mr. Baildon might as well say that Dr. Conan Doyle delights in committing

---

[1] "Robert Louis Stevenson: A Life Study in Criticism." By H. Bellyse Baildon. Chatto & Windus.

inexplicable crimes, that Mr. Clark Russell is a notorious pirate, and that Mr. Wilkie Collins thought that one could hardly be better employed than in stealing moonstones and falsifying marriage registers. But Mr. Baildon is scarcely alone in this error: few people have understood properly the goriness of Stevenson. Stevenson was essentially the robust schoolboy who draws skeletons and gibbets in his Latin grammar. It was not that he took pleasure in death, but that he took pleasure in life, in every muscular and emphatic action of life, even if it were an action that took the life of another.

Let us suppose that one gentleman throws a knife at another gentleman and pins him to the wall. It is scarcely necessary to remark that there are in this transaction two somewhat varying personal points of view. The point of view of the man pinned is the tragic and moral point of view, and this Stevenson showed clearly that he understood in such stories as "The Master of Ballantrae" and "Weir of Hermiston." But there is another view of the matter—that in which the whole act is an abrupt and brilliant explosion of bodily vitality, like breaking a rock with a blow of a hammer, or just clearing a five-barred gate. This is the standpoint of romance, and it is the soul of "Treasure Island" and "The Wrecker." It was not, indeed, that Stevenson loved men less, but that he loved clubs and pistols more. He had, in truth, in the devouring universalism of his soul, a positive love for inanimate objects such as has not been known since St. Francis called the sun brother and the well sister. We feel that he was actually in love with the wooden crutch that Silver sent hurtling in the sunlight, with the box that Billy Bones left at the "Admiral Benbow," with the knife that Wicks drove through his own hand and the table. There is always in his work a certain clean-cut angularity which makes us remember that he was fond of cutting wood with an axe.

Stevenson's new biographer, however, cannot make any allowance for this deep-rooted poetry of mere sight and touch. He is always imputing something to Stevenson as a crime which Stevenson really professed as an object. He says of that glorious riot of horror, "The Destroying Angel," in "The Dynamiter," that it is "highly fantastic and putting a strain on our credulity." This is rather like describing the travels of Baron Munchausen as "unconvincing." The whole story of "The Dynamiter" is a kind of humorous nightmare, and even in that story "The Destroying Angel" is supposed to be an extravagant lie made up on the spur of the moment. It is a dream within a dream, and to accuse it of improbability is like accusing the sky of being blue. But Mr. Baildon, whether from hasty reading or natural difference of taste, cannot in the least comprehend that rich and romantic irony of Stevenson's London stories. He actually says of that portentous monument of humour, Prince Florizel of Bohemia, that, "though evidently admired by his creator, he is to me on the whole rather an irritating presence." From this we are almost driven to believe (though desperately and against our will) that Mr. Baildon thinks that Prince Florizel is to be taken seriously, as if he were a man in real life. For ourselves. Prince Florizel is almost our favourite character in fiction;

but we willingly add the proviso that if we met him in real life we should kill him.

The fact is, that the whole mass of Stevenson's spiritual and intellectual virtues have been partly frustrated by one additional virtue—that of artistic dexterity. If he had chalked up his great message on a wall, like Walt Whitman, in large and straggling letters, it would have startled men like a blasphemy. But he wrote his light-headed paradoxes in so flowing a copy-book hand that everyone supposed they must be copy-book sentiments. He suffered from his versatility, not, as is loosely said, by not doing every department well enough, but by doing every department too well. As child, cockney, pirate, or Puritan, his disguises were so good that most people could not see the same man under all. It is an unjust fact that if a man can play the fiddle, give legal opinions, and black boots just tolerably, he is called an Admirable Crichton, but if he does all three thoroughly well, he is apt to be regarded, in the several departments, as a common fiddler, a common lawyer, and a common boot-black. This is what has happened in the case of Stevenson. If "Dr. Jekyll," "The Master of Ballantrae," "The Child's Garden of Verses," and "Across the Plains" had been each of them one shade less perfectly done than they were, everyone would have seen that they were all parts of the same message; but by succeeding in the proverbial miracle of being in five places at once, he has naturally convinced others that he was five different people. But the real message of Stevenson was as simple as that of Mohamet, as moral as that of Dante, as confident as that of Whitman, and as practical as that of James Watt. The conception which unites the whole varied work of Stevenson was that romance, or the vision of the possibilities of things, was far more important than mere occurrences: that one was the soul of our life, the other the body, and that the soul was the precious thing. The germ of all his stories lies in the idea that every landscape or scrap of scenery has a soul: and that soul is a story. Standing before a stunted orchard with a broken stone wall, we may know as a mere fact that no one has been through it but an elderly female cook. But everything exists in the human soul: that orchard grows in our own brain, and there it is the shrine and theatre of some strange chance between a girl and a ragged poet and a mad farmer. Stevenson stands for the conception that ideas are the real incidents: that our fancies are our adventures. To think of a cow with wings is essentially to have met one. And this is the reason for his wide diversities of narrative: he had to make one story as rich as a ruby sunset, another as grey as a hoary monolith: for the story was the soul, or rather the meaning, of the bodily vision. It is quite inappropriate to judge "The Teller of Tales" (as the Samoans called him) by the particular novels he wrote, as one would judge Mr. George Moore by "Esther Waters." These novels were only the two or three of his soul's adventures that he happened to tell. But he died with a thousand stories in his heart.

Chapter 9
Thomas Carlyle

here are two main moral necessities for the work of a great man: the first is that he should believe in the truth of his message; the second is that he should believe in the acceptability of his message. It was the whole tragedy of Carlyle that he had the first and not the second.

The ordinary capital, however, which is made out of Carlyle's alleged gloom is a very paltry matter. Carlyle had his faults, both as a man and as a writer, but the attempt to explain his gospel in terms of his "liver" is merely pitiful. If indigestion invariably resulted in a "Sartor Resartus," it would be a vastly more tolerable thing than it is. Diseases do not turn into poems; even the decadent really writes with the healthy part of his organism. If Carlyle's private faults and literary virtues ran somewhat in the same line, he is only in the situation of every man; for every one of us it is surely very difficult to say precisely where our honest opinions end and our personal predilections begin. But to attempt to denounce Carlyle as a mere savage egotist cannot arise from anything but a pure inability to grasp Carlyle's gospel. "Ruskin," says a critic, "did, all the same, verily believe in God; Carlyle believed only in himself." This is certainly a distinction between the author he has understood and the author he has not understood. Carlyle believed in himself, but he could not have believed in himself more than Ruskin did; they both believed in God, because they felt that if everything else fell into wrack and ruin, themselves were permanent witnesses to God. Where they both failed was not in belief in God or in belief in themselves; they failed in belief in other people. It is not enough for a prophet to believe in his message; he must believe in its acceptability. Christ, St. Francis, Bunyan, Wesley, Mr. Gladstone, Walt Whitman, men of indescribable variety, were all alike in a certain faculty of treating the average man as their equal, of trusting to his reason and good feeling without fear and without condescension. It was this simplicity of confidence, not only in God, but in the image of God, that was lacking in Carlyle.

But the attempts to discredit Carlyle's religious sentiment must absolutely fall to the ground. The profound security of Carlyle's sense of the unity of the Cosmos is like that of a Hebrew prophet; and it has the same expression that it had in the Hebrew prophets—humour. A man must be very full of faith to jest about his divinity. No Neo-Pagan delicately suggesting a revival of Dionysus, no vague, half-converted Theosophist groping towards a recognition of Buddha, would ever think of cracking jokes on the matter. But to the Hebrew prophets their religion was so solid a thing, like a mountain or a mammoth, that the irony of its contact with trivial and fleeting matters struck them like a blow. So it was with Carlyle. His supreme contribution, both to philosophy and literature, was his sense of the sarcasm of eternity. Other writers had seen the hope or the terror of the heavens, he alone saw the humour of them. Other writers had seen that there could be something elemental and eternal in a song or statute, he alone saw that there could be something elemental and eternal in a joke. No one who ever read it will forget the passage, full of dark and agnostic gratification, in which he narrates that some Court chronicler described Louis XV. as "falling asleep in the Lord." "Enough for us that he did fall asleep; that, curtained in thick night, under what keeping we ask not, he at least will never, through unending ages, insult the face of the sun any more ... and we go on, if not to better forms of beastliness, at least to fresher ones."

The supreme value of Carlyle to English literature was that he was the founder of modern irrationalism; a movement fully as important as modern rationalism. A great deal is said in these days about the value or valuelessness of logic. In the main, indeed, logic is not a productive tool so much as a weapon of defence. A man building up an intellectual system has to build like Nehemiah, with the sword in one hand and the trowel in the other. The imagination, the constructive quality, is the trowel, and argument is the sword. A wide experience of actual intellectual affairs will lead most people to the conclusion that logic is mainly valuable as a weapon wherewith to exterminate logicians.

But though this may be true enough in practice, it scarcely clears up the position of logic in human affairs. Logic is a machine of the mind, and if it is used honestly it ought to bring out an honest conclusion. When people say that you can prove anything by logic, they are not using words in a fair sense. What they mean is that you can prove anything by bad logic. Deep in the mystic ingratitude of the soul of man there is an extraordinary tendency to use the name for an organ, when what is meant is the abuse or decay of that organ. Thus we speak of a man suffering from "nerves," which is about as sensible as talking about a man suffering from ten fingers. We speak of "liver" and "digestion" when we mean the failure of liver and the absence of digestion. And in the same manner we speak of the dangers of logic, when what we really mean is the danger of fallacy.

But the real point about the limitation of logic and the partial overthrow of logic by writers like Carlyle is deeper and somewhat different. The fault of the great mass of logicians is not that they bring out a false result, or, in other words, are not logicians at all. Their fault is that by an inevitable psychological habit they tend to forget that there are two parts of a logical process, the first the choosing of an assumption, and the second the arguing upon it, and humanity, if it devotes itself too persistently to the study of sound reasoning, has a certain tendency to lose the faculty of sound assumption. It is astonishing how constantly one may hear from rational and even rationalistic persons such a phrase as "He did not prove the very thing with which he started," or, "The whole of his case rested upon a pure assumption," two peculiarities which may be found by the curious in the works of Euclid. It is astonishing, again, how constantly one hears rationalists arguing upon some deep topic, apparently without troubling about the deep assumptions involved, having lost their sense, as it were, of the real colour and character of a man's assumption. For instance, two men will argue about whether patriotism is a good thing and never discover until the end, if at all, that the cosmopolitan is basing his whole case upon the idea that man should, if he can, become as God, with equal sympathies and no prejudices, while the nationalist denies any such duty at the very start, and regards man as an animal who has preferences, as a bird has feathers.

Thus it was with Carlyle: he startled men by attacking not arguments, but assumptions. He simply brushed aside all the matters which the men of the nineteenth century held to be incontrovertible, and appealed directly to the very different class of matters which they knew to be true. He induced men to study less the truth of their reasoning, and more the truth of the assumptions upon which they reasoned. Even where his view was not the highest truth, it was always a refreshing and beneficent heresy. He denied every one of the postulates upon which the age of reason based itself. He denied the theory of progress which assumed that we must be better off than the people of the twelfth century. Whether we were better than the people of the twelfth century, according to him, depended entirely upon whether we chose or deserved to be.

He denied every type and species of prop or association or support which threw the responsibility upon civilisation or society, or anything but the individual conscience. He has often been called a prophet. The real ground of the truth of this phrase is often neglected. Since the last era of purely religious literature, the era of English Puritanism, there has been no writer in whose eyes the soul stood so much alone.

Carlyle was, as we have suggested, a mystic, and mysticism was with him, as with all its genuine professors, only a transcendent form of common sense. Mysticism and common sense alike consist in a sense of the dominance of certain truths and tendencies which cannot be formally demonstrated or even formally named. Mysticism and common sense are alike appeals to realities that we all know to be real, but which have no place in argument except as postulates. Carlyle's work did consist in breaking through formulæ, old and new, to these old and silent and ironical sanities. Philosophers might abolish kings a hundred times over, he maintained, they could not alter the fact that every man and woman does choose a king and repudiate all the pride of citizenship for the exultation of humility. If inequality of this kind was a weakness, it was a weakness bound up with the very strength of the universe. About hero worship, indeed, few critics have done the smallest justice to Carlyle. Misled by those hasty and choleric passages in which he sometimes expressed a preference for mere violence, passages which were a great deal more connected with his temperament than with his philosophy, they have finally imbibed the notion that Carlyle's theory of hero worship was a theory of terrified submission to stern and arrogant men. As a matter of fact, Carlyle is really inhumane about some questions, but he is never inhumane about hero worship. His view is not that human nature is so vulgar and silly a thing that it must be guided and driven; it is, on the contrary, that human nature is so chivalrous and fundamentally magnanimous a thing that even the meanest have it in them to love a leader more than themselves, and to prefer loyalty to rebellion. When he speaks of this trait in human nature Carlyle's tone invariably softens. We feel that for the moment he is kindled with admiration of mankind, and almost reaches the verge of Christianity. Whatever else was acid and captious about Carlyle's utterances, his hero worship was not only humane, it was almost optimistic. He admired great men primarily, and perhaps correctly, because he thought that they were more human than other men. The evil side of the influence of Carlyle and his religion of hero worship did not consist in the emotional worship of valour and success; that was a part of him, as, indeed, it is a part of all healthy children. Where Carlyle really did harm was in the fact that he, more than any modern man, is responsible for the increase of that modern habit of what is vulgarly called "Going the whole hog." Often in matters of passion and conquest it is a singularly hoggish hog. This remarkable modern craze for making one's philosophy, religion, politics, and temper all of a piece, of seeking in all incidents for opportunities to assert and reassert some favourite mental attitude, is a thing which existed comparatively little in other centuries. Solomon and Horace, Petrarch and Shakespeare were pessimists when they were melancholy, and optimists when they were happy. But the optimist of to-day seems obliged to prove that gout and unrequited love make him dance with joy, and the pessimist of to-day to prove that sunshine and a good supper convulse him with inconsolable anguish. Carlyle was strongly possessed with this mania for spiritual consistency. He wished to take the same view of the wars of the angels and of the paltriest riot at Donnybrook Fair. It was this species of insane logic which led him into his chief errors, never his natural enthusiasms. Let us take an example. Carlyle's defence of slavery is a thoroughly ridiculous thing, weak alike in argument and in moral instinct. The truth is, that he only took it up from the passion for applying everywhere his paradoxical defence of aristocracy. He blundered, of course, because he did not see that slavery has nothing in the world to do with aristocracy, that it is, indeed, almost its opposite. The defence which Carlyle and all its thoughtful defenders have made for aristocracy was that a few persons could more rapidly and firmly decide public affairs in the interests of the people. But slavery is not even supposed to be a government for the good of the governed. It is a possession of the governed avowedly for the good of the governors. Aristocracy uses the strong for the service of the weak; slavery uses the weak for the service of the strong. It is no derogation to man as a spiritual being, as Carlyle firmly believed he was, that he should be ruled and guided for his own good like a child—for a child who is always ruled and guided we regard as the very type of spiritual existence. But it is a derogation and an absolute contradiction to that human spirituality in which Carlyle believed that a man should be owned like a tool for someone else's good, as if he had no personal destiny in the Cosmos. We draw attention to this particular error of Carlyle's because we think that it is a curious example of the waste and unclean places into which that remarkable animal, "the whole hog," more than once led him.

In this respect Carlyle has had unquestionably long and an unquestionably bad influence. The whole of that recent political ethic which conceives that if we only go far enough we may finish a thing for once and all, that being strong consists chiefly in being deliberately deaf and blind, owes a great deal of its complete sway to his example. Out of him flows most of the philosophy of Nietzsche, who is in modern times the supreme maniac of this moonstruck consistency. Though Nietzsche and Carlyle were in reality profoundly different, Carlyle being a stiff-necked peasant and Nietzsche a very fragile aristocrat, they were alike in this one quality of which we speak, the strange and pitiful audacity with which they applied their single ethical test to everything in heaven and earth. The disciple of Nietzsche, indeed, embraces immorality like an austere and difficult faith. He urges himself to lust and cruelty with the same tremulous enthusiasm with which a Christian urges himself to purity and patience; he struggles as a monk struggles with bestial visions and temptations with the ancient necessities of honour and justice and compassion. To this madhouse, it can hardly be denied, has Carlyle's intellectual courage brought many at last.

Chapter 10
Tolstoy and the Cult of Simplicity

he whole world is certainly heading for a great simplicity, not deliberately, but rather inevitably. It is not a mere fashion of false innocence, like that of the French aristocrats before the Revolution, who built an altar to Pan, and who taxed the peasantry for the enormous expenditure which is needed in order to live the simple life of peasants. The simplicity towards which the world is driving is the necessary outcome of all our systems and speculations and of our deep and continuous contemplation of things. For the universe is like everything in it; we have to look at it repeatedly and habitually before we see it. It is only when we have seen it for the hundredth time that we see it for the first time. The more consistently things are contemplated, the more they tend to unify themselves and therefore to simplify themselves. The simplification of anything is always sensational. Thus monotheism is the most sensational of things: it is as if we gazed long at a design full of disconnected objects, and, suddenly, with a stunning thrill, they came together into a huge and staring face.

Few people will dispute that all the typical movements of our time are upon this road towards simplification. Each system seeks to be more fundamental than the other; each seeks, in the literal sense, to undermine the other. In art, for example, the old conception of man, classic as the Apollo Belvedere, has first been attacked by the realist, who asserts that man, as a fact of natural history, is a creature with colourless hair and a freckled face. Then comes the Impressionist, going yet deeper, who asserts that to his physical eye, which alone is certain, man is a creature with purple hair and a grey face. Then comes the Symbolist, and says that to his soul, which alone is certain, man is a creature with green hair and a blue face. And all the great writers of our time represent in one form or another this attempt to reestablish communication with the elemental, or, as it is sometimes more roughly and fallaciously expressed, to return to nature. Some think that the return to nature consists in drinking no wine; some think that it consists in drinking a great deal more than is good for them. Some think that the return to nature is achieved by beating swords into ploughshares; some think it is achieved by turning ploughshares into very ineffectual British War Office bayonets. It is natural, according to the Jingo, for a man to kill other people with gunpowder and himself with gin. It is natural, according to the humanitarian revolutionist, to kill other people with dynamite and himself with vegetarianism. It would be too obviously Philistine a sentiment, perhaps, to suggest that the claim of either of these persons to be obeying the voice of nature is interesting when we consider that they require huge volumes of paradoxical argument to persuade themselves or anyone else of the truth of their conclusions. But the giants of our time are undoubtedly alike in that they approach by very different roads this conception of the return to simplicity. Ibsen returns to nature by the angular exterior of fact, Maeterlinck by the eternal tendencies of fable. Whitman returns to nature by seeing how much he can accept, Tolstoy by seeing how much he can reject.

Now, this heroic desire to return to nature, is, of course, in some respects, rather like the heroic desire of a kitten to return to its own tail. A tail is a simple and beautiful object, rhythmic in curve and soothing in texture; but it is certainly one of the minor but characteristic qualities of a tail that it should hang behind. It is impossible to deny that it would in some degree lose its character if attached to any other part of the anatomy. Now, nature is like a tail in the sense that it vitally important, if it is to discharge its real duty, that it should be always behind. To imagine that we can see nature, especially our own nature, face to face, is a folly; it is even a blasphemy. It is like the conduct of a cat in some mad fairy-tale, who should set out on his travels with the firm conviction that he would find his tail growing like a tree in the meadows at the end of the world. And the actual effect of the travels of the philosopher in search of nature, when seen from the outside, looks very like the gyrations of the tail-pursuing kitten, exhibiting much enthusiasm but little dignity, much cry and very little tail. The grandeur of nature is that she is omnipotent and unseen, that she is perhaps ruling us most when we think that she is heeding us least. "Thou art a God that hidest Thyself," said the Hebrew poet. It may be said with all reverence that it is behind a man's back that the spirit of nature hides.

It is this consideration that lends a certain air of futility even to all the inspired simplicities and thunderous veracities of Tolstoy. We feel that a man cannot make himself simple merely by warring on complexity; we feel, indeed, in our saner moments, that a man cannot make himself simple at all. A self-conscious simplicity may well be far more intrinsically ornate than luxury itself. Indeed, a great deal of the pomp and sumptuousness of the world's history was simple in the truest sense. It was born of an almost babyish receptiveness; it was the work of men who had eyes to wonder and men who had ears to hear.

> "King Solomon brought merchant men
> Because of his desire
> With peacocks, apes, and ivory,
> From Tarshish unto Tyre."

But this proceeding was not a part of the wisdom of Solomon; it was a part of his folly—I had almost said of his innocence. Tolstoy, we feel, would not be content with hurling satire and denunciation at "Solomon in all his glory." With fierce and unimpeachable logic he would go a step further. He would spend days and nights in the meadows stripping the shameless crimson coronals off the lilies of the field.

The new collection of "Tales from Tolstoy," translated and edited by Mr. R. Nisbet Bain, is calculated to draw particular attention to this ethical and ascetic side of Tolstoy's work. In one sense, and that the deepest sense, the work of Tolstoy is, of course, a genuine and noble appeal to simplicity. The narrow notion that an artist may not teach is pretty well exploded by now. But the truth of the matter is, that an artist teaches far more by his mere background and properties, his landscape, his costume, his idiom and technique—all the part of his work, in short, of which he is probably entirely unconscious, than by the elaborate and pompous moral dicta which he fondly imagines to be his opinions. The real distinction between the ethics of high art and the ethics of manufactured and didactic art lies in the simple fact that the bad fable has a moral, while the good fable is a moral. And the real moral of Tolstoy comes out constantly in these stories, the great moral which lies at the heart of all his work, of which he is probably unconscious, and of which it is quite likely that he would vehemently disapprove. The curious cold white light of morning that shines over all the tales, the folklore simplicity with which "a man or a woman" are spoken of without further identification, the love—one might almost say the lust—for the qualities of brute materials, the hardness of wood, and the softness of mud, the ingrained belief in a certain ancient kindliness sitting beside the very cradle of the race of man—these influences are truly moral. When we put beside them the trumpeting and tearing nonsense of the didactic Tolstoy, screaming for an obscene purity, shouting for an inhuman peace, hacking up human life into small sins with a chopper, sneering at men, women, and children out of respect to humanity, combining in one chaos of contradictions an unmanly Puritan and an uncivilised prig, then, indeed, we scarcely know whither Tolstoy has vanished. We know not what to do with this small and noisy moralist who is inhabiting one corner of a great and good man.

It is difficult in every case to reconcile Tolstoy the great artist with Tolstoy the almost venomous reformer. It is difficult to believe that a man who draws in such noble outlines the dignity of the daily life of humanity regards as evil that divine act of procreation by which that dignity is renewed from age to age. It is difficult to believe that a man who has painted with so frightful an honesty the heartrending emptiness of the life of the poor can really grudge them every one of their pitiful pleasures, from courtship to tobacco. It is difficult to believe that a poet in prose who has so powerfully exhibited the earth-born air of man, the essential kinship of a human being, with the landscape in which he lives, can deny so elemental a virtue as that which attaches a man to his own ancestors and his own land. It is difficult to believe that the man who feels so poignantly the detestable insolence of oppression would not actually, if he had the chance, lay the oppressor flat with his fist. All, however, arises from the search after a false simplicity, the aim of being, if I may so express it, more natural than it is natural to be. It would not only be more human, it would be more humble of us to be content to be complex. The truest kinship with humanity would lie in doing as humanity has always done, accepting with a sportsmanlike relish the estate to which we are called, the star of our happiness, and the fortunes of the land of our birth.

The work of Tolstoy has another and more special significance. It represents the re-assertion of a certain awful common sense which characterised the most extreme utterances of Christ. It is true that we cannot turn the cheek to the smiter; it is true that we cannot give our cloak to the robber; civilisation is too complicated, too vain-glorious, too emotional. The robber would brag, and we should blush; in other words, the robber and we are alike sentimentalists. The command of Christ is impossible, but it is not insane; it is rather sanity preached to a planet of lunatics. If the whole world was suddenly stricken with a sense of humour it would find itself mechanically fulfilling the Sermon on the Mount. It is not the plain facts of the world which stand in the way of that consummation, but its passions of vanity and self-advertisement and morbid sensibility. It is true that we cannot turn the cheek to the smiter, and the sole and sufficient reason is that we have not the pluck. Tolstoy and his followers have shown that they have the pluck, and even if we think they are mistaken, by this sign they conquer. Their theory has the strength of an utterly consistent thing. It represents that doctrine of mildness and non-resistance which is the last and most audacious of all the forms of resistance to every existing authority. It is the great strike of the Quakers which is more formidable than many sanguinary revolutions. If human beings could only succeed in achieving a real passive resistance they would be strong with the appalling strength of inanimate things, they would be calm with the maddening calm of oak or iron, which conquer without vengeance and are conquered without humiliation. The theory of Christian duty enunciated by them is that we should never conquer by force, but always, if we can, conquer by persuasion. In their mythology St. George did not conquer the dragon: he tied a pink ribbon round its neck and gave it a saucer of milk. According to them, a course of consistent kindness to Nero would have turned him into something only faintly represented by Alfred the Great. In fact, the policy recommended by this school for dealing with the bovine stupidity and bovine fury of this world is accurately summed up in the celebrated verse of Mr. Edward Lear:

> "There was an old man who said, 'How
> Shall I flee from this terrible cow?
> I will sit on a stile and continue to smile
> Till I soften the heart of this cow.' "

Their confidence in human nature is really honourable and magnificent; it takes the form of refusing to believe the overwhelming majority of mankind, even when they set out to explain their own motives. But although most of us would in all probability tend at first sight to consider this new sect of Christians as little less outrageous than some brawling and absurd sect in the Reformation, yet we should fall into a singular error in doing so. The Christianity of Tolstoy is, when we come to consider it, one of the most thrilling and dramatic incidents in our modern civilisation. It represents a tribute to the Christian religion more sensational than the breaking of seals or the falling of stars.

From the point of view of a rationalist, the whole world is rendered almost irrational by the single phenomenon of Christian Socialism. It turns the scientific universe topsy-turvy, and makes it essentially possible that the key of all social evolution may be found in the dusty casket of some discredited creed. It cannot be amiss to consider this phenomenon as it realty is.

The religion of Christ has, like many true things, been disproved an extraordinary number of times. It was disproved by the Neo-Platonist philosophers at the very moment when it was first starting forth upon its startling and universal career. It was disproved again by many of the sceptics of the Renaissance only a few years before its second and supremely striking embodiment, the religion of Puritanism, was about to triumph over many kings and civilise many continents. We all agree that these schools of negation were only interludes in its history; but we all believe naturally and inevitably that the negation of our own day is really a breaking up of the theological cosmos, an Armageddon, a Ragnorak, a twilight of the gods. The man of the nineteenth century, like a schoolboy of sixteen, believes that his doubt and depression are symbols of the end of the world. In our day the great irreligionists who did nothing but dethrone God and drive angels before them have been outstripped, distanced, and made to look orthodox and humdrum. A newer race of sceptics has found something infinitely more exciting to do than nailing down the lids upon a million coffins, and the body upon a single cross. They have disputed not only the elementary creeds, but the elementary laws of mankind, property, patriotism, civil obedience. They have arraigned civilisation as openly as the materialists have arraigned theology; they have damned all the philosophers even lower than they have damned the saints. Thousands of modern men move quietly and conventionally among their fellows while holding views of national limitation or landed property that would have made Voltaire shudder like a nun listening to blasphemies. And the last and wildest phase of this saturnalia of scepticism, the school that goes furthest among thousands who go so far, the school that denies the moral validity of those ideals of courage or obedience which are recognised even among pirates, this school bases itself upon the literal words of Christ, like Dr. Watts or Messrs. Moody and Sankey. Never in the whole history of the world was such a tremendous tribute paid to the vitality of an ancient creed. Compared with this, it would be a small thing if the Red Sea were cloven asunder, or the sun did stand still at midday. We are faced with the phenomenon that a set of revolutionists whose contempt for all the ideals of family and nation would evoke horror in a thieves' kitchen, who can rid themselves of those elementary instincts of the man and the gentleman which cling to the very bones of our civilisation, cannot rid themselves of the influence of two or three remote Oriental anecdotes written in corrupt Greek. The fact, when realised, has about it something stunning and hypnotic. The most convinced rationalist is in its presence suddenly stricken with a strange and ancient vision, sees the immense sceptical cosmogonies of this age as dreams going the way of a thousand forgotten heresies, and believes for a moment that the dark sayings handed down through eighteen centuries may, indeed, contain in themselves the revolutions of which we have only begun to dream.

This value which we have above suggested unquestionably belongs to the Tolstoians, who may roughly be described as the new Quakers. With their strange optimism, and their almost appalling logical courage, they offer a tribute to Christianity which no orthodoxies could offer. It cannot but be remarkable to watch a revolution in which both the rulers and the rebels march under the same symbol. But the actual theory of non-resistance itself, with all its kindred theories, is not, I think, characterised by that intellectual obviousness and necessity which its supporters claim for it. A pamphlet before us shows us an extraordinary number of statements about the new Testament, of which the accuracy is by no means so striking as the confidence. To begin with, we must protest against a habit of quoting and paraphrasing at the same time. When a man is discussing what Jesus meant, let him state first of all what He said, not what the man thinks He would have said if he had expressed Himself more clearly. Here is an instance of question and answer:

Q. "How did our Master Himself sum up the law in a few words?"

A. "Be ye merciful, be ye perfect even as your Father; your Father in the spirit world is merciful, is perfect."

There is nothing in this, perhaps, which Christ might not have said except the abominable metaphysical modernism of "the spirit world"; but to say that it is recorded that He did say it, is like saying it is recorded that He preferred palm trees to sycamores. It is a simple and unadulterated untruth. The author should know that these words have meant a thousand things to a thousand people, and that if more ancient sects had paraphrased them as cheerfully as he, he would never have had the text upon which he founds his theory. In a pamphlet in which plain printed words cannot be left alone, it is not surprising if there are mis-statements upon larger matters. Here is a statement clearly and philosophically laid down which we can only content ourselves with flatly denying: "The fifth rule of our Lord is that we should take special pains to cultivate the same kind of regard for people of foreign countries, and for those generally who do not belong to us, or even have an antipathy to us, which we already entertain towards our own people, and those who are in sympathy with us." I should very much like to know where in the whole of the New Testament the author finds this violent, unnatural, and immoral proposition. Christ did not have the same kind of regard for one person as for another. We are specifically told that there were certain persons whom He specially loved. It is most improbable that He thought of other nations as He thought of His own. The sight of His national city moved Him to tears, and the highest compliment He paid was, "Behold an Israelite indeed." The author has simply confused two entirely distinct things. Christ commanded us to have love for all men, but even if we had equal love for all men, to speak of having the same love for all men is merely bewildering nonsense. If we love a man at all, the impression he produces on us must be vitally different to the impression produced by another man whom we love. To speak of having the same kind of regard for both is about as sensible as asking a man whether he prefers chrysanthemums or billiards. Christ did not love humanity; He never said He loved humanity; He loved men. Neither He nor anyone else can love humanity; it is like loving a gigantic centipede. And the reason that the Tolstoians can even endure to think of an equally distributed affection is that their love of humanity is a logical love, a love into which they are coerced by their own theories, a love which would be an insult to a tom-cat.

But the greatest error of all lies in the mere act of cutting up the teaching of the New Testament into five rules. It precisely and ingeniously misses the most dominant characteristic of the teaching—its absolute spontaneity. The abyss between Christ and all His modern interpreters is that we have no record that He ever wrote a word, except with His finger in the sand. The whole is the history of one continuous and sublime conversation. Thousands of rules have been deduced from it before these Tolstoian rules were made, and thousands will be deduced afterwards. It was not for any pompous proclamation, it was not for any elaborate output of printed volumes; it was for a few splendid and idle words that the cross was set up on Calvary, and the earth gaped, and the sun was darkened at noonday.

Chapter 11
Savonarola

avonarola is a man whom we shall probably never understand until we know what horror may lie at the heart of civilisation. This we shall not know until we are civilised. It may be hoped, in one sense, that we may never understand Savonarola.

The great deliverers of men have, for the most part, saved them from calamities which we all recognise as evil, from calamities which are the ancient enemies of humanity. The great law-givers saved us from anarchy: the great physicians saved us from pestilence: the great reformers saved us from starvation. But there is a huge and bottomless evil compared with which all these are fleabites, the most desolating curse that can fall upon men or nations, and it has no name except we call it satisfaction. Savonarola did not save men from anarchy, but from order; not from pestilence, but from paralysis; not from starvation, but from luxury. Men like Savonarola are the witnesses to the tremendous psychological fact at the back of all our brains, but for which no name has ever been found, that ease is the worst enemy of happiness, and civilisation potentially the end of man.

For I fancy that Savonarola's thrilling challenge to the luxury of his day went far deeper than the mere question of sin. The modern rationalistic admirers of Savonarola, from George Eliot downwards, dwell, truly enough, upon the sound ethical justification of Savonarola's anger, upon the hideous and extravagant character of the crimes which polluted the palaces of the Renaissance. But they need not be so anxious to show that Savonarola was no ascetic, that he merely picked out the black specks of wickedness with the priggish enlightenment of a member of an Ethical Society. Probably he did hate the civilisation of his time, and not merely its sins; and that is precisely where he was infinitely more profound than a modern moralist. He saw, that the actual crimes were not the only evils: that stolen jewels and poisoned wine and obscene pictures were merely the symptoms; that the disease was the complete dependence upon jewels and wine and pictures. This is a thing constantly forgotten in judging of ascetics and Puritans in old times. A denunciation of harmless sports did not always mean an ignorant hatred of what no one but a narrow moralist would call harmful. Sometimes it meant an exceedingly enlightened hatred of what no one but a narrow moralist would call harmless. Ascetics are sometimes more advanced than the average man, as well as less.

Such, at least, was the hatred in the heart of Savonarola. He was making war against no trivial human sins, but against godless and thankless quiescence, against getting used to happiness, the mystic sin by which all creation fell. He was preaching that severity which is the sign-manual of youth and hope. He was preaching that alertness, that clean agility and vigilance, which is as necessary to gain pleasure as to gain holiness, as indispensable in a lover as in a monk. A critic has truly pointed out that Savonarola could not have been fundamentally anti-æsthetic, since he had such friends as Michael Angelo, Botticelli, and Luca della Robbia. The fact is that this purification and austerity are even more necessary for the appreciation of life and laughter than for anything else. To let no bird fly past unnoticed, to spell patiently the stones and weeds, to have the mind a storehouse of sunset, requires a discipline in pleasure, and an education in gratitude.

The civilisation which surrounded Savonarola on every side was a civilisation which had already taken the wrong turn, the turn that leads to endless inventions and no discoveries, in which new things grow old with confounding rapidity, but in which no old things ever grow new. The monstrosity of the crimes of the Renaissance was not a mark of imagination; it was a mark, as all monstrosity is, of the loss of imagination. It is only when a man has really ceased to see a horse as it is, that he invents a centaur, only when he can no longer be surprised at an ox, that he worships the devil. Diablerie is the stimulant of the jaded fancy; it is the dram-drinking of the artist. Savonarola addressed himself to the hardest of all earthly tasks, that of making men turn back and wonder at the simplicities they had learnt to ignore. It is strange that the most unpopular of all doctrines is the doctrine which declares the common life divine. Democracy, of which Savonarola was so fiery an exponent, is the hardest of gospels; there is nothing that so terrifies men as the decree that they are all kings. Christianity, in Savonarola's mind, identical with democracy, is the hardest of gospels; there is nothing that so strikes men with fear as the saying that they are all the sons of God.

Savonarola and his republic fell. The drug of despotism was administered to the people, and they forgot what they had been. There are some at the present day who have so strange a respect for art and letters, and for mere men of genius, that they conceive the reign of the Medici to be an improvement on that of the great Florentine republican. It is such men as these and their civilisation that we have at the present day to fear. We are surrounded on many sides by the same symptoms as those which awoke the unquenchable wrath of Savonarola—a hedonism that is more sick of happiness than an invalid is sick of pain, an art sense that seeks the assistance of crime since it has exhausted nature. In many modern works we find veiled and horrible hints of a truly Renaissance sense of the beauty of blood, the poetry of murder. The bankrupt and depraved imagination does not see that a living man is far more dramatic than a dead one. Along with this, as in the time of the Medici, goes the falling back into the arms of despotism, the hunger for the strong man which is unknown among strong men. The masterful hero is worshipped as he is worshipped by the readers of the "Bow Bells Novelettes," and for the same reason—a profound sense of personal weakness. That tendency to devolve our duties descends on us, which is the soul of slavery, alike whether for its menial tasks it employs serfs or emperors. Against all this the great clerical republican stands in everlasting protest, preferring his failure to his rival's success. The issue is still between him and Lorenzo, between the responsibilities of liberty and the license of slavery, between the perils of truth and the security of silence, between the pleasure of toil and the toil of pleasure. The supporters of Lorenzo the Magnificent are assuredly among us, men for whom even nations and empires only exist to satisfy the moment, men to whom the last hot hour of summer is better than a sharp and wintry spring. They have an art, a literature, a political philosophy, which are all alike valued for their immediate effect upon the taste, not for what they promise of the destiny of the spirit. Their statuettes and sonnets are rounded and perfect, while "Macbeth" is in comparison a fragment, and the Moses of Michael Angelo a hint. Their campaigns and battles are always called triumphant, while Cæsar and Cromwell wept for many humiliations. And the end of it all is the hell of no resistance, the hell of an unfathomable softness, until the whole nature recoils into madness and the chamber of civilisation is no longer merely a cushioned apartment, but a padded cell.

This last and worst of human miseries Savonarola saw afar off, and bent his whole gigantic energies to turning the chariot into another course. Few men understood his object; some called him a madman, some a charlatan, some an enemy of human joy. They would not even have understood if he had told them, if he had said that he was saving them from a calamity of contentment which should be the end of joys and sorrows alike. But there are those to-day who feel the same silent danger, and who bend themselves to the same silent resistance. They also are supposed to be contending for some trivial political scruple.

Mr. M'Hardy says, in defending Savonarola, that the number of fine works of art destroyed in the Burning of the Vanities has been much exaggerated. I confess that I hope the pile contained stacks of incomparable masterpieces if the sacrifice made that one real moment more real. Of one thing I am sure, that Savonarola's friend Michael Angelo would have piled all his own statues one on top of the other, and burnt them to ashes, if only he had been certain that the glow transfiguring the sky was the dawn of a younger and wiser world.

Chapter 12
The Position of Sir Walter Scott

alter Scott is a writer who should just now be re-emerging into his own high place in letters, for unquestionably the recent, though now dwindling, schools of severely technical and æsthetic criticism have been unfavourable to him. He was a chaotic and unequal writer, and if there is one thing in which artists have improved since his time, it is in consistency and equality. It would perhaps be unkind to inquire whether the level of the modern man of letters, as compared with Scott, is due to the absence of valleys or the absence of mountains. But in any case, we have learnt in our day to arrange our literary effects carefully, and the only point in which we fall short of Scott is in the incidental misfortune that we have nothing particular to arrange.

It is said that Scott is neglected by modern readers; if so, the matter could be more appropriately described by saying that modern readers are neglected by Providence. The ground of this neglect, in so far as it exists, must be found, I suppose, in the general sentiment that, like the beard of Polonius, he is too long. Yet it is surely a peculiar thing that in literature alone a house should be despised because it is too large, or a host impugned because he is too generous. If romance be really a pleasure, it is difficult to understand the modern reader's consuming desire to get it over, and if it be not a pleasure, it is difficult to understand his desire to have it at all. Mere size, it seems to me, cannot be a fault. The fault must lie in some disproportion. If some of Scott's stories are dull and dilatory, it is not because they are giants, but because they are hunchbacks or cripples. Scott was very far indeed from being a perfect writer, but I do not think that it can be shown that the large and elaborate plan on which his stories are built was by any means an imperfection. He arranged his endless prefaces and his colossal introductions just as an architect plans great gates and long approaches to a really large house. He did not share the latter-day desire to get quickly through a story. He enjoyed narrative as a sensation; he did not wish to swallow a story like a pill, that it should do him good afterwards. He desired to taste it like a glass of port, that it might do him good at the time. The reader sits late at his banquets. His characters have that air of immortality which belongs to those of Dumas and Dickens. We should not be surprised to meet them in any number of sequels. Scott, in his heart of hearts, probably would have liked to write an endless story without either beginning or close.

Walter Scott is a great, and, therefore, mysterious man. He will never be understood until Romance is understood, and that will be only when Time, Man, and Eternity are understood. To say that Scott had more than any other man that ever lived a sense of the romantic seems, in these days, a slight and superficial tribute. The whole modern theory arises from one fundamental mistake—the idea that romance is in some way a plaything with life, a figment, a conventionality, a thing upon the outside. No genuine criticism of romance will ever arise until we have grasped the fact that romance lies not upon the outside of life, but absolutely in the centre of it. The centre of every man's existence is a dream. Death, disease, insanity, are merely material accidents, like toothache or a twisted ankle. That these brutal forces always besiege and often capture the citadel does not prove that they are the citadel. The boast of the realist (applying what the reviewers call his scalpel) is that he cuts into the heart of life; but he makes a very shallow incision, if he only reaches as deep as habits and calamities and sins. Deeper than all these lies a man's vision of himself, as swaggering and sentimental as a penny novelette. The literature of can-dour unearths innumerable weaknesses and elements of lawlessness which is called romance. It perceives superficial habits like murder and dipsomania, but it does not perceive the deepest of sins—the sin of vanity—vanity which is the mother of all day-dreams and adventures, the one sin that is not shared with any boon companion, or whispered to any priest.

In estimating, therefore, the ground of Scott's pre-eminence in romance we must absolutely rid ourselves of the notion that romance or adventure are merely materialistic things involved in the tangle of a plot or the multiplicity of drawn swords. We must remember that it is, like tragedy or farce, a state of the soul, and that, for some dark and elemental reason which we can never understand, this state of the soul is evoked in us by the sight of certain places or the contemplation of certain human crises, by a stream rushing under a heavy and covered wooden bridge, or by a man plunging a knife or sword into tough timber. In the selection of these situations which catch the spirit of romance as in a net, Scott has never been equalled or even approached. His finest scenes affect us like fragments of a hilarious dream. They have the same quality which is often possessed by those nocturnal comedies—that of seeming more human than our waking life—even while they are less possible. Sir Arthur Wardour, with his daughter and the old beggar crouching in a cranny of the cliff as night falls and the tide closes around them, are actually in the coldest and bitterest of practical situations. Yet the whole incident has a quality that can only be called boyish. It is warmed with all the colours of an incredible sunset. Rob Roy trapped in the Tolbooth, and confronted with Bailie Nicol Jarvie, draws no sword, leaps from no window, affects none of the dazzling external acts upon which contemporary romance depends, yet that plain and humourous dialogue is full of the essential philosophy of romance which is an almost equal betting upon man and destiny. Perhaps the most profoundly thrilling of all Scott's situations is that in which the family of Colonel Mannering are waiting for the carriage which may or may not arrive by night to bring an unknown man into a princely possession. Yet almost the whole of that thrilling scene consists of a ridiculous conversation about food, and flirtation between a frivolous old lawyer and a fashionable girl. We can say nothing about what makes these scenes, except that the wind bloweth where it listeth, and that here the wind blows strong.

It is in this quality of what may be called spiritual adventurousness that Scott stands at so different an elevation to the whole of the contemporary crop of romancers who have followed the leadership of Dumas. There has, indeed, been a great and inspiriting revival of romance in our time, but it is partly frustrated in almost every case by this rooted conception that romance consists in the vast multiplication of incidents and the violent acceleration of narrative. The heroes of Mr. Stanley Weyman scarcely ever have their swords out of their hands; the deeper presence of romance is far better felt when the sword is at the hip ready for innumerable adventures too terrible to be pictured. The Stanley Weyman hero has scarcely time to eat his supper except in the act of leaping from a window or whilst his other hand is employed in lunging with a rapier. In Scott's heroes, on the other hand, there is no characteristic so typical or so worthy of humour as their disposition to linger over their meals. The conviviality of the Clerk of Copmanhurst or of Mr. Pleydell, and the thoroughly solid things they are described as eating, is one of the most perfect of Scott's poetic touches. In short, Mr. Stanley Weyman is filled with the conviction that the sole essence of romance is to move with insatiable rapidity from incident to incident. In the truer romance of Scott there is more of the sentiment of "Oh! still delay, thou art so fair"! more of a certain patriarchal enjoyment of things as they are—of the sword by the side and the wine-cup in the hand. Romance, indeed, does not consist by any means so much in experiencing adventures as in being ready for them. How little the actual boy cares for incidents in comparison to tools and weapons may be tested by the fact that the most popular story of adventure is concerned with a man who lived for years on a desert island with two guns and a sword, which he never had to use on an enemy.

Closely connected with this is one of the charges most commonly brought against Scott, particularly in his own day—the charge of a fanciful and monotonous insistence upon the details of armour and costume. The critic in the *Edinburgh Review* said indignantly that he could tolerate a somewhat detailed description of the apparel of Marmion, but when it came to an equally detailed account of the apparel of his pages and yeomen the mind could bear it no longer. The only thing to be said about that critic is that he had never been a little boy. He foolishly imagined that Scott valued the plume and dagger of Marmion for Marmion's sake. Not being himself romantic, he could not understand that Scott valued the plume because it was a plume, and the dagger because it was a dagger. Like a child, he loved weapons with a manual materialistic love, as one loves the softness of fur or the coolness of marble. One of the profound philosophical truths which are almost confined to infants is this love of things, not for their use or origin, but for their own inherent characteristics, the child's love of the toughness of wood, the wetness of water, the magnificent soapiness of soap. So it was with

Scott, who had so much of the child in him. Human beings were perhaps the principal characters in his stories, but they were certainly not the only characters. A battle-axe was a person of importance, a castle had a character and ways of its own. A church bell had a word to say in the matter. Like a true child, he almost ignored the distinction between the animate and inanimate. A two-handed sword might be carried only by a menial in a procession, but it was something important and immeasurably fascinating—it was a two-handed sword.

There is one quality which is supreme and continuous in Scott which is little appreciated at present. One of the values we have really lost in recent fiction is the value of eloquence. The modern literary artist is compounded of almost every man except the orator. Yet Shakespeare and Scott are certainly alike in this, that they could both, if literature had failed, have earned a living as professional demagogues. The feudal heroes in the "Waverley Novels" retort upon each other with a passionate dignity, haughty and yet singularly human, which can hardly be paralleled in political eloquence except in "Julius Cæsar." With a certain fiery impartiality which stirs the blood, Scott distributes his noble orations equally among saints and villains. He may deny a villain every virtue or triumph, but he cannot endure to deny him a telling word; he will ruin a man, but he will not silence him. In truth, one of Scott's most splendid traits is his difficulty, or rather incapacity, for despising any of his characters. He did not scorn the most revolting miscreant as the realist of to-day commonly scorns his own hero. Though his soul may be in rags, every man of Scott can speak like a king.

This quality, as I have said, is sadly to seek in the fiction of the passing hour. The realist would, of course, repudiate the bare idea of putting a bold and brilliant tongue in every man's head, but even where the moment of the story naturally demands eloquence the eloquence seems frozen in the tap. Take any contemporary work of fiction and turn to the scene where the young Socialist denounces the millionaire, and then compare the stilted sociological lecture given by that self-sacrificing bore with the surging joy of words in Rob Roy's declaration of himself, or Athelstane's defiance of De Bracy. That ancient sea of human passion upon which high words and great phrases are the resplendent foam is just now at a low ebb. We have even gone the length of congratulating ourselves because we can see the mud and the monsters at the bottom.

In politics there is not a single man whose position is due to eloquence in the first degree; its place is taken by repartees and rejoinders purely intellectual, like those of an omnibus conductor. In discussing questions like the farm-burning in South Africa no critic of the war uses his material as Burke or Grattan (perhaps exaggeratively) would have used it—the speaker is content with facts and expositions of facts. In another age he might have risen and hurled that great song in prose, perfect as prose and yet rising into a chant, which Meg Merrilies hurled at Ellangowan, at the rulers of Britain: "Ride your ways. Laird of Ellangowan; ride your ways, Godfrey Bertram—this day have ye quenched seven smoking hearths.

See if the fire in your ain parlour burns the blyther for that. Ye have riven the thack of seven cottar houses. Look if your ain roof-tree stands the faster for that. Ye may stable your stirks in the sheilings of Dern-cleugh. See that the hare does not couch on the hearthstane of Ellangowan. Ride your ways, Godfrey Bertram."

The reason is, of course, that these men are afraid of bombast and Scott was not. A man will not reach eloquence if he is afraid of bombast, just as a man will not jump a hedge if he is afraid of a ditch. As the object of all eloquence is to find the least common denominator of men's souls, to fall just within the natural comprehension, it cannot obviously have any chance with a literary ambition which aims at falling just outside it. It is quite right to invent subtle analyses and detached criticisms, but it is unreasonable to expect them to be punctuated with roars of popular applause. It is possible to conceive of a mob shouting any central and simple sentiment, good or bad, but it is impossible to think of a mob shouting a distinction in terms. In the matter of eloquence, the whole question is one of the immediate effect of greatness, such as is produced even by fine bombast. It is absurd to call it merely superficial; here there is no question of superficiality; we might as well call a stone that strikes us between the eyes merely superficial. The very word "superficial" is founded on a fundamental mistake about life, the idea that second thoughts are best. The superficial impression of the world is by far the deepest. What we really feel, naturally and casually, about the look of skies and trees and the face of friends, that and that alone will almost certainly remain our vital philosophy to our dying day.

Scott's bombast, therefore, will always be stirring to anyone who approaches it, as he should approach all literature, as a little child. We could easily excuse the contemporary critic for not admiring melodramas and adventure stories, and Punch and Judy, if he would admit that it was a slight deficiency in his artistic sensibilities. Beyond all question, it marks a lack of literary instinct to be unable to simplify one's mind at the first signal of the advance of romance. "You do me wrong," said Brian de Bois-Guilbert to Rebecca. "Many a law, many a commandment have I broken, but my word, never." "Die," cries Balfour of Burley to the villain in "Old Mortality." "Die, hoping nothing, believing nothing—" "And fearing nothing," replies the other. This is the old and honourable fine art of bragging, as it was practised by the great worthies of antiquity. The man who cannot appreciate it goes along with the man who cannot appreciate beef or claret or a game with children or a brass band. They are afraid of making fools of themselves, and are unaware that that transformation has already been triumphantly effected.

Scott is separated, then, from much of the later conception of fiction by this quality of eloquence. The whole of the best and finest work of the modern novelist (such as the work of Mr. Henry James) is primarily concerned with that delicate and fascinating speech which burrows deeper and deeper like a mole; but we have wholly forgotten that speech which mounts higher and higher like a wave and falls in a crashing peroration. Perhaps the most thoroughly brilliant and typical man of this decade is Mr. Bernard Shaw. In his admirable play of "Candida" it is clearly a part of the character of the Socialist clergyman that he should be eloquent, but he is not eloquent because the whole "G.B.S." condition of mind renders impossible that poetic simplicity which eloquence requires. Scott takes his heroes and villains seriously, which is, after all, the way that heroes and villains take themselves—especially villains. It is the custom to call these old romantic poses artificial; but the word artificial is the last and silliest evasion of criticism. There was never anything in the world that was really artificial. It had some motive or ideal behind it, and generally a much better one than we think.

Of the faults of Scott as an artist it is not very necessary to speak, for faults are generally and easily pointed out, while there is yet no adequate valuation of the varieties and contrasts of virtue. We have compiled a complete botanical classification of the weeds in the poetical garden, but the flowers still flourish, neglected and nameless. It is true, for example, that Scott had an incomparably stiff and pedantic way of dealing with his heroines: he made a lively girl of eighteen refuse an offer in the language of Dr. Johnson. To him, as to most men of his time, woman was not an individual, but an institution—a toast that was drunk some time after that of Church and King. But it is far better to consider the difference rather as a special merit, in that he stood for all those clean and bracing shocks of incident which are untouched by passion or weakness, for a certain breezy bachelorhood, which is almost essential to the literature of adventure. With all his faults, and all his triumphs, he stands for the great mass of natural manliness which must be absorbed into art unless art is to be a mere luxury and freak. An appreciation of Scott might be made almost a test of decadence. If ever we lose touch with this one most reckless and defective writer, it will be a proof to us that we have erected round ourselves a false cosmos, a world of lying and horrible perfection, leaving outside of it Walter Scott and that strange old world which is as confused and as indefensible and as inspiring and as healthy as he.

Chapter 13
Bret Harte

here are more than nine hundred and ninety-nine excellent reasons which we could all have for admiring the work of Bret Harte. But one supreme reason stands not in a certain general superiority to them all—a reason which may be stated in three propositions united in a common conclusion: first, that he was a genuine American; second, that he was a genuine humourist; and, third, that he was not an American humourist. Bret Harte had his own peculiar humour, but it had nothing in particular to do with American humour. American humour has its own peculiar excellence, but it has nothing in particular to do with Bret Harte. American humour is purely exaggerative; Bret Harte's humour was sympathetic and analytical.

In order fully to understand this, it is necessary to realise, genuinely and thoroughly, that there is such a thing as an international difference in humour. If we take the crudest joke in the world—the joke, let us say, of a man sitting down on his hat—we shall yet find that all the nations would differ in their way of treating it humourously, and that if American humour treated it at all, it would be in a purely American manner. For example, there was a case of an orator in the House of Commons, who, after denouncing all the public abuses he could think of, did sit down on his hat. An Irishman immediately rose, full of the whole wealth of Irish humour, and said, "Should I be in order, Sir, in congratulating the honourable gentleman on the fact that when he sat down on his hat his head was not in it?" Here is a glorious example of Irish humour—the bull not unconscious, not entirely conscious, but rather an idea so absurd that even the utterer of it can hardly realise how abysmally absurd it is. But every other nation would have treated the idea in a manner slightly different. The Frenchman's humour would have been logical: he would have said, "The orator denounces modern abuses and destroys to himself the top-hat: behold a good example!" What the Scotchman's humour would have said I am not so certain, but it would probably have dealt with the serious advisability of making such speeches on top of someone else's hat. But American humour on such a general theme would be the humour of exaggeration. The American humourist would say that the English politicians so often sat down on their hats that the noise of the House of Commons was one crackle of silk. He would say that when an important orator rose to speak in the House of Commons, long rows of hatters waited outside the House with note-books to take down orders from the participants in the debate. He would say that the whole hat trade of London was disorganised by the news that a clever remark had been made by a young M. P. on the subject of the imports of Jamaica. In short, American humour, neither unfathomably absurd like the Irish, nor transfiguringly lucid and appropriate like the French, nor sharp and sensible and full of realities of life like the Scotch, is simply the humour of imagination. It consists in piling towers on towers and mountains on mountains; of heaping a joke up to the stars and extending it to the end of the world.

With this distinctively American humour Bret Harte had little or nothing in common. The wild, sky-breaking humour of America has its fine qualities, but it must in the nature of things be deficient in two qualities, not only of supreme importance to life and letters, but of supreme importance to humour—reverence and sympathy. And these two qualities were knit into the closest texture of Bret Harte's humour. Everyone who has read and enjoyed Mark Twain as he ought to be read and enjoyed will remember a very funny and irreverent story about an organist who was asked to play appropriate music to an address upon the parable of the Prodigal Son, and who proceeded to play with great spirit, "We'll all get blind drunk, when Johnny comes marching home." The best way of distinguishing Bret Harte from the rest of American humour is to say that if Bret Harte had described that scene, it would in some subtle way have combined a sense of the absurdity of the incident with some sense of the sublimity and pathos of the theme. You would have felt that the organist's tune was funny, but not that the Prodigal Son was funny. But America is under a kind of despotism of humour. Everyone is afraid of humour: the meanest of human nightmares. Bret Harte had, to express the matter briefly but more or less essentially, the power of laughing not only at things, but also with them. America has laughed at things magnificently, with Gargantuan reverberations of laughter. But she has not even begun to learn the richer lesson of laughing with them.

The supreme proof of the fact that Bret Harte had the instinct of reverence may be found in the fact that he was a really great parodist. This may have the appearance of being a paradox, but, as in the case of many other paradoxes, it is not so important whether it is a paradox as whether it is not obviously true. Mere derision, mere contempt, never produced or could produce parody. A man who simply despises Paderewski for having long hair is not necessarily fitted to give an admirable imitation of his particular touch on the piano. If a man wishes to parody Paderewski's style of execution, he must emphatically go through one process first: he must admire it, and even reverence it. Bret Harte had a real power of imitating great authors, as in his parodies on Dumas, on Victor Hugo, on Charlotte Brontë. This means, and can only mean, that he had perceived the real beauty, the real ambition of Dumas and Victor Hugo and Charlotte Brontë. To take an example, Bret Harte has in his imitation of Hugo a passage like this:

"M. Madeline was, if possible, better than M. Myriel. M. Myriel was an angel. M. Madeline was a good man." I do not know whether Victor Hugo ever used this antithesis; but I am certain that he would have used it and thanked his stars if he had thought of it. This is real parody, inseparable from admiration. It is the same in the parody of Dumas, which is arranged on the system of "Aramis killed three of them. Porthos three. Athos three." You cannot write that kind of thing unless you have first exulted in the arithmetical ingenuity of the plots of Dumas. It is the same in the parody of Charlotte Brontë, which opens with a dream of a storm-beaten cliff, containing jewels and pelicans. Bret Harte could not have written it unless he had really understood the triumph of the Brontës, the triumph of asserting that great mysteries lie under the surface of the most sullen life, and that the most real part of a man is in his dreams.

This kind of parody is for ever removed from the purview of ordinary American humour. Can anyone imagine Mark Twain, that admirable author, writing even a tolerable imitation of authors so intellectually individual as Hugo or Charlotte Brontë? Mark Twain would yield to the spirit of contempt which destroys parody. All those who hate authors fail to satirise them, for they always accuse them of the wrong faults. The enemies of Thackeray call him a worldling, instead of what he was, a man too ready to believe in the goodness of the unworldly. The enemies of Meredith call his gospel too subtle, instead of what it is, a gospel, if anything, too robust. And it is this vulgar misunderstanding which we find in most parody—which we find in all American parody—but which we never find in the parodies of Bret Harte.

"The skies they were ashen and sober,
The streets they were dirty and drear,
It was the dark month of October,
In that most immemorial year.
Like the skies, I was perfectly sober,
But my thoughts they were palsied and sear,
Yes, my thoughts were decidedly queer."

This could only be written by a genuine admirer of Edgar Allan Poe, who permitted himself for a moment to see the fun of the thing. Parody might indeed be defined as the worshipper's half-holiday.

The same general characteristic of sympathy amounting to reverence marks Bret Harte's humour in his better-known class of works, the short stories. He does not make his characters absurd in order to make them contemptible: it might almost be said that he makes them absurd in order to make them dignified. For example, the greatest creation of Bret Harte, greater even than Colonel Starbottle (and how terrible it is to speak of anyone greater than Colonel Starbottle!) is that unutterable being who goes by the name of Yuba Bill. He is, of course, the coach-driver in the Bret Harte district. Some ingenious person, whose remarks I read the other day, had compared him on this ground with old Mr. Weller. It would be difficult to find a comparison indicating a more completely futile instinct for literature. Tony Weller and Yuba Bill were both coach-drivers, and this fact establishes a resemblance just about as much as the fact that Jobson in "Rob Roy" and George Warrington in "Pendennis" were both lawyers; or that Antonio and

Mr. Pickwick were both merchants; or that Sir Galahad and Sir Willoughby Patten were both knights. Tony Weller is a magnificent grotesque. He is a gargoyle, and his mouth, like the mouths of so many gargoyles, is always open. He is garrulous, exuberant, flowery, preposterously sociable. He holds that great creed of the convivial, the creed which is at the back of so much that is greatest in Dickens, the creed that eternity begins at ten o'clock at night, and that nights last forever. But Yuba Bill is a figure of a widely different character. He is not convivial; it might almost be said that he is too great ever to be sociable. A circle of quiescence and solitude such as that which might ring a saint or a hermit rings this majestic and profound humourist. His jokes do not flow upon him like those of Mr. Weller, sparkling, continual, and deliberate, like the play of a fountain in a pleasure garden; they fall suddenly and capriciously, like a crash of avalanches from a great mountain. Tony Weller has the noisy humour of London, Yuba Bill has the silent humour of the earth.

One of the worst of the disadvantages of the rich and random fertility of Bret Harte is the fact that it is very difficult to trace or recover all the stories that he has written. I have not within reach at the moment the story in which the character of Yuba Bill is exhibited in its most solemn grandeur, but I remember that it concerned a ride on the San Francisco stage coach, a difficulty arising from storm and darkness, and an intelligent young man who suggested to Yuba Bill that a certain manner of driving the coach in a certain direction might minimise the dangers of the journey. A profound silence followed the intelligent young man's suggestion, and then (I quote from memory) Yuba Bill observed at last:

"Air you settin' any value on that remark?"

The young man professed not fully to comprehend him, and Yuba Bill continued reflectively:

" 'Cos there's a comic paper in 'Frisco pays for them things, and I've seen worse in it."

To be rebuked thus is like being rebuked by the Pyramids or by the starry heavens. There is about Yuba Bill this air of a pugnacious calm, a stepping back to get his distance for a shattering blow, which is like that of Dr. Johnson at his best. And the effect is inexpressively increased by the background and the whole picture which Bret Harte paints so powerfully; the stormy skies, the sombre gorge, the rocking and spinning coach, and high above the feverish passengers the huge dark form of Yuba Bill, a silent mountain of humour.

Another unrecovered and possibly irrecoverable fragment about Yuba Bill, I recall in a story about his visiting a lad who had once been his protége in the Wild West, and who had since become a distinguished literary man in Boston. Yuba Bill visits him, and on finding him in evening dress lifts up his voice in a superb lamentation over the tragedy of finding his old friend at last "a 'otel waiter." Then, vindictively pursuing the satire, he calls fiercely to his young friend, "Hi, Alphonse! bring me a patty de foy gras, damme." These are the things that make us love the eminent Bill. He is one of those who achieve the noblest and most difficult of all the triumphs of a fictitious character—the triumph of giving us the impression of having a great deal more in him than appears between the two boards of the story. Smaller characters give us the impression that the author has told the whole truth about them, greater characters give the impression that the author has given of them, not the truth, but merely a few hints and samples. In some mysterious way we seem to feel that even if Shakespeare was wrong about Falstaff, Falstaff existed and was real; that even if Dickens was wrong about Micawber, Micawber existed and was real. So we feel that there is in the great salt-sea of Yuba Bill's humour as good fish as ever came out of it. The fleeting jests which Yuba Bill throws to the coach passengers only give us the opportunity of fancying and deducing the vast mass of jests which Yuba Bill shares with his creator.

Bret Harte had to deal with countries and communities of an almost unex-ampled laxity, a laxity passing the laxity of savages, the laxity of civilised men grown savage. He dealt with a life which we in a venerable and historic society may find it somewhat difficult to realise. It was the life of an entirely new people, a people who, having no certain past, could have no certain future. The strangest of all the sardonic jests that history has ever played may be found in this fact: that there is a city which is of all cities the most typical of innovation and dissipation, and a certain almost splendid vulgarity, and that this city bears the name in a quaint old European language of the most perfect exponent of the simplicity and holiness of the Christian tradition; the city is called San Francisco. San Francisco, the capital of the Bret Harte country, is a city typifying novelty in a manner in which it is typified by few modern localities. San Francisco has in all probability its cathedrals, but it may well be that its cathedrals are less old and less traditional than many of our hotels. If its inhabitants built a temple to the most primal and forgotten god of whose worship we can find a trace, that temple would still be a modern thing compared with many taverns in Suffolk round which there lingers a faint tradition of Mr. Pickwick. And everything in that new gold country was new, even to the individual inhabitants. Good, bad, and indifferent, heroes and dastards, they were all men from nowhere.

Most of us have come across the practical problem of London landladies, the problem of the doubtful foreign gentleman in a street of respectable English people. Those who have done so can form some idea of what it would be to live in a street full of doubtful foreign gentlemen, in a parish, in a city, in a nation composed entirely of doubtful foreign gentlemen. Old California, at the time of the first rush after gold, was actually this paradox of the nation of foreigners. It was a republic of incognitos: no one knew who anyone else was, and only the more ill-mannered and uneasy even desired to know. In such a country as this, gentlemen took more trouble to conceal their gentility than thieves living in South Kensington would take to conceal their blackguardism. In such a country everyone is an equal, because everyone is a stranger. In such a country it is not strange if men in moral matters feel something of the irresponsibility of a dream. To plan plans which are continually miscarrying against men who are continually disappearing by the assistance of you know not whom, to crush you know not whom, this must be a demoralising life for any man; it must be beyond description demoralising for those who have been trained in no lofty or orderly scheme of right. Small blame to them indeed if they become callous and supercilious and cynical. And the great glory and achievement of Bret Harte consists in this, that he realised that they do not become callous, supercilious, and cynical, but that they do become sentimental and romantic, and profoundly affectionate. He discovered the intense sensibility of the primitive man. To him we owe the realisation of the fact that while modern barbarians of genius like Mr. Henley, and in his weaker moments Mr. Rudyard Kipling, delight in describing the coarseness and crude cynicism and fierce humour of the unlettered classes, the unlettered classes are in reality highly sentimental and religious, and not in the least like the creations of Mr. Henley and Mr. Kipling. Bret Harte tells the truth about the wildest, the grossest, the most rapacious of all the districts of the earth—the truth that, while it is very rare indeed in the world to find a thoroughly good man, it is rarer still, rare to the point of monstrosity, to find a man who does not either desire to be one, or imagine that he is one already.

Chapter 14
Alfred the Great

he celebrations in connection with the millenary of King Alfred struck a note of sympathy in the midst of much that was unsympathetic, because, altogether apart from any peculiar historical opinions, all men feel the sanctifying character of that which is at once strong and remote; the ancient thing is always the most homely, and the distant thing the most near. The only possible peacemaker is a dead man, ever since by the sublime religious story a dead man only could reconcile heaven and earth. In a certain sense we always feel the past ages as human, and our own age as strangely and even weirdly dehumanised. In our own time the details overpower us; men's badges and buttons seem to grow larger and larger as in a horrible dream. To study humanity in the present is like studying a mountain with a magnifying glass; to study it in the past is like studying it through a telescope.

For this reason England, like every other great and historic nation, has sought its typical hero in remote and ill-recorded times. The personal and moral greatness of Alfred is, indeed, beyond question. It does not depend any more than the greatness of any other human hero upon the accuracy of any or all of the stories that are told about him. Alfred may not have done one of the things which are reported of him, but it is immeasurably easier to do every one of those things than to be the man of whom such things are reported falsely. Fable is, generally speaking, far more accurate than fact, for fable describes a man as he was to his own age, fact describes him as he is to a handful of inconsiderable antiquarians many centuries after. Whether Alfred watched the cakes for the neat-herd's wife, whether he sang songs in the Danish camp, is of no interest to anyone except those who set out to prove under considerable disadvantages that they are genealogically descended from him. But the man is better pictured in these stories than in any number of modern realistic trivialities about his favourite breakfast and his favourite musical composer. Fable is more historical than fact, because fact tells us about one man and fable tells us about a million men. If we read of a man who could make green grass red and turn the sun into the moon, we may not believe these particular details about him, but we learn something infinitely more important than such trivialities, the fact that men could look into his face and believe it possible. The glory and greatness of Alfred, therefore, is like that of all the heroes of the morning of the world, set far beyond the chance of that strange and sudden dethronement which may arise from the unsealing of a manuscript or the turning over of a stone. Men may have told lies when they said that he first entrapped the Danes with his song and then overcame them with his armies, but we know very well that it is not of us that such lies are told. There may be myths clustering about each of our personalities; local saga-men and chroniclers have very likely circulated the story that we are addicted to drink, or that we ferociously ill-use our wives. But they do not commonly lie to the effect that we have shed our blood to save all the inhabitants of the street. A story grows easily, but a heroic story is not a very easy thing to evoke. Wherever that exists we may be pretty certain that we are in the presence of a dark but powerful historic personality. We are in the presence of a thousand lies all pointing with their fantastic fingers to one undiscovered truth.

Upon this ground alone every encouragement is due to the cult of Alfred. Every nation requires to have behind it some historic personality, the validity of which is proved, as the validity of a gun is proved, by its long range. It is wonderful and splendid that we treasure, not the truth, but the very gossip about a man who died a thousand years ago. We may say to him, as M. Rostand says to the Austrian Prince:

> *"Dors, ce n'est pas toujours la Légende qui ment:*
> *Une rêve est parfois moins trompeur qu'un document."*

To have a man so simple and so honourable to represent us in the darkness of primeval history, binds all the intervening centuries together, and mollifies all their monstrosities. It makes all history more comforting and intelligible; it makes the desolate temple of the ages as human as an inn parlour.

But whether it come through reliable facts or through more reliable false-hoods the personality of Alfred has its own unmistakable colour and stature. Lord Rosebery uttered a profound truth when he said that that personality was pe-culiarly English. The great magnificence of the English character is expressed in the word "service." There is, perhaps, no nation so vitally theocratical as the English; no nation in which the strong men have so consistently preferred the instrumental to the despotic attitude, the pleasures of the loyal to the pleasures of the royal position. We have had tyrants like Edward I. and Queen Elizabeth, but even our tyrants have had the worried and responsible air of stewards of a great estate. Our typical hero is such a man as the Duke of Wellington, who had every kind of traditional and external arrogance, but at the back of all that the strange humility which made it physically possible for him without a gleam of humour or discomfort to go on his knees to a preposterous bounder like George IV. Across the infinite wastes of time and through all the mists of legend we still feel the presence in Alfred of this strange and unconscious self-effacement. After the fullest estimate of our misdeeds we can still say that our very despots have been less self-assertive than many popular patriots. As we consider these things we grow more and more impatient of any modern tendencies towards the enthronement of a more self-conscious and theatrical ideal. Lord Rosebery called up before our imaginations the picture of what Alfred would have thought of the vast modern developments of his nation, its immense fleet, its widespread Empire, its enormous contribution to the mechanical civilisation of the world. It cannot be anything but profitable to conceive Alfred as full of astonishment and admiration at these things; it cannot be anything but good for us that we should realise that to the childlike eyes of a great man of old time our inventions and appliances have not the vulgarity and ugliness that we see in them. To Alfred a steamboat would be a new and sensational sea-dragon, and the penny postage a miracle achieved by the despotism of a demi-god.

But when we have realised all this there is something more to be said in connection with Lord Rosebery's vision. What would King Alfred have said if he had been asked to expend the money which he devoted to the health and education of his people upon a struggle with some race of Visigoths or Parthians inhabiting a small section of a distant continent? What would he have said if he had known that that science of letters which he taught to England would eventually be used not to spread truth, but to drug the people with political assurances as imbecile in themselves as the assurance that fire does not burn and water does not drown? What would he have said if the same people who, in obedience to that ideal of service and sanity of which he was the example, had borne every privation in order to defeat Napoleon, should come at last to find no better compliment to one of their heroes than to call him the Napoleon of South Africa? What would he have said if that nation for which he had inaugurated a long line of incomparable men of principle should forget all its traditions and coquette with the immoral mysticism of the man of destiny?

Let us follow these things by all means if we find them good, and can see nothing better. But to pretend that Alfred would have admired them is like pretending that St. Dominic would have seen eye to eye with Mr. Bradlaugh, or that Fra Angelico would have revelled in the posters of Mr. Aubrey Beardsley. Let us follow them if we will, but let us take honestly all the disadvantages of our change; in the wildest moment of triumph let us feel the shadow upon our glories of the shame of the great king.

Chapter 15
Maeterlinck

he selection of "Thoughts from Maeterlinck" is a very creditable and also a very useful compilation. Many modern critics object to the hacking and hewing of a consistent writer which is necessary for this kind of work, but upon more serious consideration, the view is not altogether adequate. Maeterlinck is a very great man; and in the long run this process of mutilation has happened to all great men. It was the mark of a great patriot to be drawn and quartered and his head set on one spike in one city and his left leg on another spike in another city. It was the mark of a saint that even these fragments began to work miracles. So it has been with all the very great men of the world. However careless, however botchy, may be the version of Maeterlinck or of anyone else given in such a selection as this, it is assuredly far less careless and far less botchy than the version, the parody, the wild misrepresentation of Maeterlinck which future ages will hear and distant critics be called upon to consider.

No one can feel any reasonable doubt that we have heard about Christ and Socrates and Buddha and St. Francis a mere chaos of excerpts, a mere book of quotations. But from those fragmentary epigrams we can deduce greatness as clearly as we can deduce Venus from the torso of Venus or Hercules *ex pede Herculem*. If we knew nothing else about the Founder of Christianity, for example, beyond the fact that a religious teacher lived in a remote country, and in the course of his peregrinations and proclamations consistently called Himself "the Son of Man," we should know by that alone that he was a man of almost immeasurable greatness. If future ages happened to record nothing else about Socrates except that he owned his title to be the wisest of men because he knew that he knew nothing, they would be able to deduce from that the height and energy of his civilisation, the glory that was Greece. The credit of such random compilations as that which "E.S.S." and Mr. George Allen have just effected is quite secure. It is the pure, pedantic, literal editions, the complete works of this author or that author which are forgotten. It is such books as this that have revolutionised the destiny of the world. Great things like Christianity or Platonism have never been founded upon consistent editions; all of them have been founded upon scrap-books.

The position of Maeterlinck in modern life is a thing too obvious to be easily determined in words. It is, perhaps, best expressed by saying that it is the great glorification of the inside of things at the expense of the outside. There is one great evil in modern life for which nobody has found even approximately a tolerable description: I can only invent a word and call it "remotism." It is the tendency to think first of things which, as a matter of fact, lie far away from the actual centre of human experience. Thus people say, "All our knowledge of life begins with the amoeba." It is false; our knowledge of life begins with ourselves. Thus they say that the British Empire is glorious, and at the very word Empire they think at once of Australia and New Zealand, and Canada, and Polar bears, and parrots and kangaroos, and it never occurs to any one of them to think of the Surrey Hills. The one real struggle in modern life is the struggle between the man like Maeterlinck, who sees the inside as the truth, and the man like Zola, who sees the outside as the truth. A hundred cases might be given. We may take, for the sake of argument, the case of what is called falling in love. The sincere realist, the man who believes in a certain finality in physical science, says, "You may, if you like, describe this thing as a divine and sacred and incredible vision; that is your sentimental theory about it. But what it is, is an animal and sexual instinct designed for certain natural purposes." The man on the other side, the idealist, replies, with quite equal confidence, that this is the very reverse of the truth. I put it as it has always struck me; he replies, "Not at all. You may, if you like, describe this thing as an animal and sexual instinct, designed for certain natural purposes; that is your philosophical or zoölogical theory about it. What it is, beyond all doubt of any kind, is a divine and sacred and incredible vision." The fact that it is an animal necessity only comes to the naturalistic philosopher after looking abroad, studying its origins and results, constructing an explanation of its existence, more or less natural and conclusive. The fact that it is a spiritual triumph comes to the first errand boy who happens to feel it. If a lad of seventeen falls in love and is struck dead by a hansom cab an hour afterwards, he has known the thing as it is, a spiritual ecstasy; he has never come to trouble about the thing as it may be, a physical destiny. If anyone says that falling in love is an animal thing, the answer is very simple. The only way of testing the matter is to ask those who are experiencing it, and none of those would admit for a moment that it was an animal thing.

Maeterlinck's appearance in Europe means primarily this subjective intensity; by this the materialism is not overthrown: materialism is undermined. He brings, not something which is more poetic than realism, not something which is more spiritual than realism, not something which is more right than realism, but something which is more real than realism. He discovers the one indestructible thing. This material world on which such vast systems have been superimposed—this may mean anything. It may be a dream, it may be a joke, it may be a trap or temptation, it may be a charade, it may be the beatific vision: the only thing of which we are certain is this human soul. This human soul finds itself alone in a terrible world, afraid of the grass. It has brought forth poetry and religion in order to explain matters; it will bring them forth again. It matters not one atom how often the lulls of materialism and scepticism occur; they are always broken by the reappearance of a fanatic. They have come in our time: they have been broken by Maeterlinck.

Chapter 16
Ruskin

do not think anyone could find any fault with the way in which Mr. Collingwood has discharged his task,[2] except, of course, Mr. Ruskin himself, who would certainly have scored through all the eulogies in passionate red ink and declared that his dear friend had selected for admiration the very parts of his work which were vile, brainless, and revolting. That, however, was merely Ruskin's humour, and one of the deepest disappointments with Mr. Collingwood is that he, like everyone else, fails to appreciate Ruskin as a humourist. Yet he was a great humourist: half the explosions which are solemnly scolded as "one-sided" were simply meant to be one-sided, were mere laughing experiments in language. Like a woman, he saw the humour of his own prejudices, did not sophisticate them by logic, but deliberately exaggerated them by rhetoric. One tenth of his paradoxes would have made the fortune of a modern young man with gloves of an art yellow. He was as fond of nonsense as Mr. Max Beerbohm. Only ... he was fond of other things too. He did not ask humanity to dine on pickles.

But while his kaleidoscope of fancy and epigram gives him some kinship with the present day, he was essentially of an earlier type: he was the last of the prophets. With him vanishes the secret of that early Victorian simplicity which gave a man the courage to mount a pulpit above the head of his fellows. Many elements, good and bad, have destroyed it; humility as well as fear, camaraderie as well as scepticism, have bred in us a desire to give our advice lightly and persuasively, to mask our morality, to whisper a word and glide away. The contrast was in some degree typified in the House of Commons under the last leadership of Mr. Gladstone: the old order with its fist on the box, and the new order with its feet on the table. Doubtless the wine of that prophecy was too strong even for the strong heads that carried it. It made Ruskin capricious and despotic, Tennyson lonely and whimsical, Carlyle harsh to the point of hatred, and Kingsley often rabid to the ruin of logic and charity. One alone of that race of giants, the greatest and most neglected, was sober after the cup. No mission, no frustration could touch with hysteria the humanity of Robert Browning.

But though Ruskin seems to close the roll of the militant prophets, we feel how needful are such figures when we consider with what pathetic eagerness men pay prophetic honours even to those who disclaim the prophetic character. Ibsen declares that he only depicts life, that as far as he is concerned there is nothing to be done, and still armies of "Ibsenites" rally to the flag and enthusiastically do nothing. I have found traces of a school which avowedly follows Mr. Henry James: an idea full of humour. I like to think of a crowd with pikes and torches shouting

[2] "The Life of John Ruskin." By W.G. Collingwood. London: Methuen.

passages from "The Awkward Age." It is right and proper for a multitude to declare its readiness to follow a prophet to the end of the world, but if he himself explains, with pathetic gesticulations, that he is only going for a walk in the park, there is not much for the multitude to do. But the disciple of Ruskin had plenty to do. He made roads; in his spare moments he studied the whole of geology and botany. He lifted up paving stones and got down into early Florentine cellars, where, by hanging upside down, he could catch a glimpse of a Cimabue unpraisable but by divine silence. He rushed from one end of a city to the other comparing ceilings. His limbs were weary, his clothes were torn, and in his eyes was that unfathomable joy of life which man will never know again until once more he takes himself seriously.

Mr. Collingwood's excellent chapters on the art criticism of Ruskin would be better, in my opinion, if they showed more consciousness of the after revolutions that have reversed, at least in detail, much of Ruskin's teaching. We no longer think that art became valueless when it was first corrupted with anatomical accuracy. But if we return to that Raphaelism to which he was so unjust, let us not fall into the old error of intelligent reactionaries, that of ignoring our own debt to revolutions. Ruskin could not destroy the market of Raphaelism, but he could and did destroy its monopoly. We may go back to the Renaissance, but let us remember that we go back free. We can picnic now in the ruins of our dungeon and deride our deliverer.

But neither in Mr. Collingwood's book nor in Ruskin's own delightful "Præterita" shall we ever get to the heart of the matter. The work of Ruskin and his peers remains incomprehensible by the very completeness of their victory. Fallen forever is that vast brick temple of Utilitarianism, of which we may find the fragments but never renew the spell. Liberal Unionists howl in its high places, and in its ruins Mr. Lecky builds his nest. Its records read with something of the mysterious arrogance of Chinese: hardly a generation away from us, we read of a race who believed in the present with the same sort of servile optimism with which the Oriental believes in the past. It may be that banging his head against that roof for twenty years did not improve the temper of the prophet. But he made what he praised in the old Italian pictures—"an opening into eternity."

Chapter 17
Queen Victoria

nyone who possesses spiritual or political courage has made up his mind to a prospect of immutable mutability; but even in a "transformation" there is something catastrophic in the removal of the back scene. It is a truism to say of the wise and noble lady who is gone from us that we shall always remember her; but there is a subtler and higher compliment still in confessing that we often forgot her. We forgot her as we forget the sunshine, as we forget the postulates of an argument, as we commonly forget our own existence. Mr. Gladstone is the only figure whose loss prepared us for such earthquakes altering the landscape. But Mr. Gladstone seemed a fixed and stationary object in our age for the same reason that one railway train looks stationary from another; because he and the age of progress were both travelling at the same impetuous rate of speed. In the end, indeed, it was probably the age that dropped behind. For a symbol of the Queen's position we must rather recur to the image of a stretch of scenery, in which she was as a mountain so huge and familiar that its disappearance would make the landscape round our own door seem like a land of strangers. She had an inspired genius for the familiarising virtues; her sympathy and sanity made us feel at home even in an age of revolutions. That indestructible sense of security which for good and evil is so typical of our nation, that almost scornful optimism which, in the matter of ourselves, cannot take peril or even decadence seriously, reached by far its highest and healthiest form in the sense that we were watched over by one so thoroughly English in her silence and self-control, in her shrewd trustfulness and her brilliant inaction. Over and above those sublime laws of labour and pity by which she ordered her life, there are a very large number of minor intellectual matters in which we might learn a lesson from the Queen. There is one especially which is increasingly needed in an age when moral claims become complicated and hysterical. That Queen Victoria was a model of political unselfishness is well known; it is less often remarked that few modern people have an unselfishness so completely free from morbidity, so fully capable of deciding a moral question without exaggerating its importance. No eminent person of our time has been so utterly devoid of that disease of self-assertion which is often rampant among the unselfish. She had one most rare and valuable faculty, the faculty of letting things pass—Acts of Parliament and other things. Her predecessors, whether honest men or knaves, were attacked every now and then with a nightmare of despotic responsibility; they suddenly conceived that it rested with them to save the world and the Protestant Constitution. Queen Victoria had far too much faith in the world to try to save it. She knew that Acts of Parliament, even bad Acts of Parliament, do not destroy nations. But she knew that ignorance, ill-temper, tyranny, and officiousness do destroy nations, and not upon any provocation would she set an example in these things. We fancy that this sense of proportion, this largeness and coolness of intellectual magnanimity is the one of the thousand virtues of Queen Victoria of which the near future will stand most in need. We are gaining many new mental powers, and with them new mental responsibilities. In psychology, in sociology, above all in education, we are learning to do a great many clever things. Unless we are much mistaken the next great task will be to learn not to do them. If that time comes, assuredly we cannot do better than turn once more to the memory of the great Queen who for seventy years followed through every possible tangle and distraction the fairy thread of common sense.

We are suffering just now from an outbreak of the imagination which exhibits itself in politics and the most unlikely places. The German Emperor, for example, is neither a tyrant nor a lunatic, as used to be absurdly represented; he is simply a minor poet; and he feels just as any minor poet would feel if he found himself on the throne of Barbarossa. The revival of militarism and ecclesiasticism is an invasion of politics by the artistic sense; it is heraldry rather than chivalry that is lusted after. Amid all this waving of wands and flaunting of uniforms, all this hedonistic desire to make the most of everything, there is something altogether quiet and splendid about the sober disdain with which this simple and courteous lady in a black dress left idle beside her the sceptre of a hundred tyrants. The heart of the whole nation warmed as it had never warmed for centuries at the thought of having in their midst a woman who cared nothing for her rights, and nothing for those fantastic duties which are more egotistical than rights themselves.

The work of the Queen for progressive politics has surely been greatly underrated. She invented democratic monarchy as much as James Watt invented the steam engine. William IV., from whom we think of her as inheriting her Constitutional position, held in fact a position entirely different to that which she now hands on to Edward VII. William IV. was a limited monarch; that is to say, he had a definite, open, and admitted power in politics, but it was a limited power. Queen Victoria was not a limited monarch; in the only way in which she cared to be a monarch at all she was as unlimited as Haroun Alraschid. She had unlimited willing obedience, and unlimited social supremacy. To her belongs the credit of inventing a new kind of monarchy; in which the Crown, by relinquishing the whole of that political and legal department of life which is concerned with coercion, regimentation, and punishment, was enabled to rise above it and become the symbol of the sweeter and purer relations of humanity, the social intercourse which leads and does not drive. Too much cannot be said for the wise audacity and confident completeness with which the Queen cut away all those cords of political supremacy to which her predecessors had clung madly as the only stays of the monarchy. She had her reward. For while William IV.'s supremacy may be called a survival, it is not too much to say that the Queen's supremacy might be called a prophecy. By lifting a figure purely human over the heads of judges and warriors, we uttered in some symbolic fashion the abiding, if unreasoning, hope which dwells in all human hearts, that some day we may find a simpler solution of the woes of nations than the summons and the treadmill, that we may find in some such influence as the social influence of a woman, what was called in the noble old language of mediæval monarchy, "a fountain of mercy and a fountain of honour."

In the universal reverence paid to the Queen there was hardly anywhere a touch of snobbishness. Snobbishness, in so far as it went out towards former sovereigns, went out to them as aristocrats rather than as kings, as heads of that higher order of men, who were almost angels or demons in their admitted superiority to common lines of conduct. This kind of reverence was always a curse: nothing can be conceived as worse for the mass of the people than that they should think the morality for which they have to struggle an inferior morality, a thing unfitted for a haughtier class. But of this patrician element there was hardly a trace in the dignity of the Queen. Indeed, the degree to which the middle and lower classes took her troubles and problems to their hearts was almost grotesque in its familiarity. No one thought of the Queen as an aristocrat like the Duke of Devonshire, or even as a member of the governing classes like Mr. Chamberlain. Men thought of her as something nearer to them even in being further off; as one who was a good queen, and who would have been, had her fate demanded, with equal cheerfulness, a good washerwoman. Herein lay her unexampled triumph, the greatest and perhaps the last triumph of monarchy. Monarchy in its healthiest days had the same basis as democracy: the belief in human nature when entrusted with power. A king was only the first citizen who received the franchise.

Both royalty and religion have been accused of despising humanity, and in practice it has been too often true; but after all both the conception of the prophet and that of the king were formed by paying humanity the supreme compliment of selecting from it almost at random. This daring idea that a healthy human being, when thrilled by all the trumpets of a great trust, would rise to the situation, has often been tested, but never with such complete success as in the case of our dead Queen. On her was piled the crushing load of a vast and mystical tradition, and she stood up straight under it. Heralds proclaimed her as the anointed of God, and it did not seem presumptuous. Brave men died in thousands shouting her name, and it did not seem unnatural. No mere intellect, no mere worldly success could, in this age of bold inquiry, have sustained that tremendous claim; long ago we should have stricken Cæsar and dethroned Napoleon. But these glories and these sacrifices did not seem too much to celebrate a hardworking human nature; they were possible because at the heart of our Empire was nothing but a defiant humility. If the Queen had stood for any novel or fantastic imperial claims, the whole would have seemed a nightmare; the whole was successful because she stood, and no one could deny that she stood, for the humblest, the shortest and the most indestructible of human gospels, that when all troubles and troublemongers have had their say, our work can be done till sunset, our life can be lived till death.

Chapter 18
The German Emperor

he list of the really serious, the really convinced, the really important and comprehensible people now alive includes, as most Englishmen would now be prepared to admit, the German Emperor. He is a practical man and a poet. I do not know whether there are still people in existence who think there is some kind of faint antithesis between these two characters; but I incline to think there must be, because of the surprise which the career of the German Emperor has generally evoked. When he came to the throne it became at once apparent that he was poetical; people assumed in consequence that he was unpractical; that he would plunge Europe into war, that he would try to annex France, that he would say he was the Emperor of Russia, that he would stand on his head in the Reichstag, that he would become a pirate on the Spanish Main. Years upon years have passed; he has gone on making speeches, he has gone on talking about God and his sword, he has poured out an ever increased rhetoric and æstheticism. And yet all the time people have slowly and surely realised that he knows what he is about, that he is one of the best friends of peace, that his influence on Europe is not only successful, but in many ways good, that he knows what world he is living in better than a score of materialists.

The explanation never comes to them—he is a poet; therefore, a practical man. The affinity of the two words, merely as words, is much nearer than many people suppose, for the matter of that. There is one Greek word for "I do" from which we get the word practical, and another Greek word for "I do" from which we get the word poet. I was doubtless once informed of a profound difference between the two, but I have forgotten it. The two words practical and poetical may mean two subtly different things in that old and subtle language, but they mean the same in English and the same in the long run. It is ridiculous to suppose that the man who can understand the inmost intricacies of a human being who has never existed at all cannot make a guess at the conduct of man who lives next door. It is idle to say that a man who has himself felt the mad longing under the mad moon for a vagabond life cannot know why his son runs away to sea. It is idle to say that a man who has himself felt the hunger for any kind of exhilaration, from angel or devil, cannot know why his butler takes to drink. It is idle to say that a man who has been fascinated with the wild fastidiousness of destiny does not know why stockbrokers gamble, to say that a man who has been knocked into the middle of eternal life by a face in a crowd does not know why the poor marry young; that a man who found his path to all things kindly and pleasant blackened and barred suddenly by the body of a man does not know what it is to desire murder. It is idle, in short, for a man who has created men to say that he does not understand them.

A man who is a poet may, of course, easily make mistakes in these personal and practical relations; such mistakes and similar ones have been made by poets; such mistakes and greater ones have been made by soldiers and statesmen and men of business. But in so far as a poet is in these things less of a practical man he is also less of a poet.

If Shakespeare really married a bad wife when he had conceived the character of Beatrice he ought to have been ashamed of himself: he had failed not only in his life, he had failed in his art. If Balzac got into rows with his publishers he ought to be rebuked and not commiserated, having evolved so many consistent business men from his own inside. The German Emperor is a poet, and therefore he succeeds, because poetry is so much nearer to reality than all the other human occupations. He is a poet, and succeeds because the majority of men are poets. It is true, if that matter is at all important, that the German Emperor is not a good poet. The majority of men are poets, only they happen to be bad poets. The German Emperor fails ridiculously, if that is all that is in question, in almost every one of the artistic occupations to which he addresses himself: he is neither a first-rate critic, nor a first-rate musician, nor a first-rate painter, nor a first-rate poet. He is a twelfth-rate poet, but because he is a poet at all he knocks to pieces all the first-rate politicians in the war of politics.

Having made clear my position so far, I discover with a certain amount of interest that I have not yet got to the subject of these remarks. The German Emperor is a poet, and although, as far as I know, every line he ever wrote may be nonsense, he is a poet in this real sense, that he has realised the meaning of every function he has performed. Why should we jeer at him because he has a great many uniforms, for instance? The very essence of the really imaginative man is that he realises the various types or capacities in which he can appear. Every one of us, or almost every one of us, does in reality fulfil almost as many offices as Pooh-Bah. Almost every one of us is a ratepayer, an immortal soul, an Englishman, a baptised person, a mammal, a minor poet, a juryman, a married man, a bicyclist, a Christian, a purchaser of newspapers, and a critic of Mr. Alfred Austin. We ought to have uniforms for all these things. How beautiful it would be if we appeared to-morrow in the uniform of a ratepayer, in brown and green, with buttons made in the shape of coins, and a blue income-tax paper tastefully arranged as a favour; or, again, if we appeared dressed as immortal souls, in a blue uniform with stars. It would be very exciting to dress up as Englishmen, or to go to a fancy dress ball as Christians.

Some of the costumes I have suggested might appear a little more difficult to carry out. The dress of a person who purchases newspapers (though it mostly consists of coloured evening editions arranged in a stiff skirt, like that of a saltatrice, round the waist of the wearer) has many mysterious points. The attire of a person prepared to criticise the Poet Laureate is something so awful and striking that I dare not even begin to describe it; the one fact which I am willing to reveal, and to state seriously and responsibly, is that it buttons up behind.

But most assuredly we ought not to abuse the Kaiser because he is fond of putting on all his uniforms; he does so because he has a large number of established and involuntary incarnations. He tries to do his duty in that state of life to which it shall please God to call him; and it so happens that he has been called to as many different estates as there are regiments in the German Army. He is a huntsman and proud of being a huntsman, an engineer and proud of being an engineer, an infantry soldier and proud of being so, a light horseman and proud of being so. There is nothing wrong in all this; the only wrong thing is that it should be confined to the merely destructive arts of war. The sight of the German Kaiser in the most magnificent of the uniforms in which he had led armies to victory is not in itself so splendid or delightful as that of many other sights which might come before us without a whisper of the alarms of war. It is not so splendid or delightful as the sight of an ordinary householder showing himself in that magnificent uniform of purple and silver which should signalise the father of three children. It is not so splendid or delightful as the appearance of a young clerk in an insurance office decorated with those three long crimson plumes which are the well-known insignia of a gentleman who is just engaged to be married. Nor can it compare with the look of a man wearing the magnificent green and silver armour by which we know one who has induced an acquaintance to give up getting drunk, or the blue and gold which is only accorded to persons who have prevented fights in the street. We belong to quite as many regiments as the German Kaiser. Our regiments are regiments that are embattled everywhere; they fight an unending fight against all that is hopeless and rapacious and of evil report. The only difference is that we have the regiments, but not the uniforms.

Only one obvious point occurs to me to add. If the Kaiser has more than any other man the sense of the poetry of the ancient things, the sword, the crown, the ship, the nation, he has the sense of the poetry of modern things also. He has one sense, and it is even a joke against him. He feels the poetry of one thing that is more poetic than sword or crown or ship or nation, the poetry of the telegram. No one ever sent a telegram who did not feel like a god. He is a god, for he is a minor poet; a minor poet, but a poet still.

Chapter 19
Tennyson

r. Morton Luce has written a short study of Tennyson which has considerable cultivation and suggestiveness, which will be sufficient to serve as a notebook for Tennyson's admirers, but scarcely sufficient, perhaps, to serve as a pamphlet against his opponents. If a critic has, as he ought to have, any of the functions anciently attributed to a prophet, it ought not to be difficult for him to prophesy that Tennyson will pass through a period of facile condemnation and neglect before we arrive at the true appreciation of his work. The same thing has happened to the most vigorous of essayists, Macaulay, and the most vigorous of romancers, Dickens, because we live in a time when mere vigour is considered a vulgar thing. The same idle and frigid reaction will almost certainly discredit the stateliness and care of Tennyson, as it has discredited the recklessness and inventiveness of Dickens. It is only necessary to remember that no action can be discredited by a reaction.

The attempts which have been made to discredit the poetical position of Tennyson are in the main dictated by an entire misunderstanding of the nature of poetry. When critics like Matthew Arnold, for example, suggest that his poetry is deficient in elaborate thought, they only prove, as Matthew Arnold proved, that they themselves could never be great poets. It is no valid accusation against a poet that the sentiment he expresses is commonplace. Poetry is always commonplace; it is vulgar in the noblest sense of that noble word. Unless a man can make the same kind of ringing appeal to absolute and admitted sentiments that is made by a popular orator, he has lost touch with emotional literature. Unless he is to some extent a demagogue, he cannot be a poet. A man who expresses in poetry new and strange and undiscovered emotions is not a poet; he is a brain specialist. Tennyson can never be discredited before any serious tribunal of criticism because the sentiments and thoughts to which he dedicates himself are those sentiments and thoughts which occur to anyone. These are the peculiar province of poetry; poetry, like religion, is always a democratic thing, even if it pretends the contrary. The faults of Tennyson, so far as they existed, were not half so much in the common character of his sentiments as in the arrogant perfection of his workmanship. He was not by any means so wrong in his faults as he was in his perfections.

Men are very much too ready to speak of men's work being ordinary, when we consider that, properly considered, every man is extraordinary. The average man is a tribal fable, like the Man-Wolf or the Wise Man of the Stoics. In every man's heart there is a revolution; how much more in every poet's? The supreme business of criticism is to discover that part of a man's work which is his and to ignore that part which belongs to others. Why should any critic of poetry spend time and attention on that part of a man's work which is unpoetical? Why should any man be interested in aspects which are uninteresting? The business of a critic is to discover the importance of men and not their crimes. It is true that the Greek word critic carries with it the meaning of a judge, and up to this point of history judges have had to do with the valuation of men's sins, and not with the valuation of their virtues.

Tennyson's work, disencumbered of all that uninteresting accretion which he had inherited or copied, resolves itself, like that of any other man of genius, into those things which he really inaugurated. Underneath all his exterior of polished and polite rectitude there was in him a genuine fire of novelty; only that, like all the able men of his period, he disguised revolution under the name of evolution. He is only a very shallow critic who cannot see an eternal rebel in the heart of the Conservative.

Tennyson had certain absolutely personal ideas, as much his own as the ideas of Browning or Meredith, though they were fewer in number. One of these, for example, was the fact that he was the first of all poets (and perhaps the last) to attempt to treat poetically that vast and monstrous vision of fact which science had recently revealed to mankind. Scientific discoveries seem commonly fables as fantastic in the ears of poets as poems in the ears of men of science. The poet is always a Ptolemaist; for him the sun still rises and the earth stands still. Tennyson really worked the essence of modern science into his poetical constitution, so that its appalling birds and frightful flowers were really part of his literary imagery. To him blind and brutal monsters, the products of the wild babyhood of the Universe, were as the daisies and the nightingales were to Keats; he absolutely realised the great literary paradox mentioned in the Book of Job: "He saw Behemoth, and he played with him as with a bird."

Instances of this would not be difficult to find. But the tests of poetry are those instances in which this outrageous scientific phraseology becomes natural and unconscious. Tennyson wrote one of his own exquisite lyrics describing the exultation of a lover on the evening before his bridal day. This would be an occasion, if ever there was one, for falling back on those ancient and assured falsehoods of the domed heaven and the flat earth in which generations of poets have made us feel at home. We can imagine the poet in such a lyric saluting the setting sun and prophesying the sun's resurrection. There is something extraordinarily typical of Tennyson's scientific faith in the fact that this, one of the most sentimental and elemental of his poems, opens with the two lines:

> "Move eastward, happy earth, and leave
> Yon orange sunset waning slow."

Rivers had often been commanded to flow by poets, and flowers to blossom in their season, and both were doubtless grateful for the permission. But the terrestrial globe of science has only twice, so far as we know, been encouraged in poetry to continue its course, one instance being that of this poem, and the other the incomparable "Address to the Terrestrial Globe" in the "Bab Ballads."

There was, again, another poetic element entirely peculiar to Tennyson, which his critics have, in many cases, ridiculously confused with a fault. This was the fact that Tennyson stood alone among modern poets in the attempt to give a poetic character to the conception of Liberal Conservatism, of splendid compromise. The carping critics who have abused Tennyson for this do not see that it was far more daring and original for a poet to defend conventionality than to defend a cart-load of revolutions. His really sound and essential conception of Liberty,

> "Turning to scorn with lips divine
> The falsehood of extremes,"

is as good a definition of Liberalism as has been uttered in poetry in the Liberal century. Moderation is *not* a compromise; moderation is a passion; the passion of great judges. That Tennyson felt that lyrical enthusiasm could be devoted to established customs, to indefensible and ineradicable national constitutions, to the dignity of time and the empire of unutterable common sense, all this did not make him a tamer poet, but an infinitely more original one. Any poetaster can describe a thunderstorm; it requires a poet to describe the ancient and quiet sky.

I cannot, indeed, fall in with Mr. Morton Luce in his somewhat frigid and patrician theory of poetry. "Dialect," he says, "mostly falls below the dignity of art." I cannot feel myself that art has any dignity higher than the indwelling and divine dignity of human nature. Great poets like Burns were far more undignified when they clothed their thoughts in what Mr. Morton Luce calls "the seemly raiment of cultured speech" than when they clothed them in the headlong and flexible patois in which they thought and prayed and quarrelled and made love. If Tennyson failed (which I do not admit) in such poems as "The Northern Farmer," it was not because he used too much of the spirit of the dialect, but because he used too little.

Tennyson belonged undoubtedly to a period from which we are divided; the period in which men had queer ideas of the antagonism of science and religion; the period in which the Missing Link was really missing. But his hold upon the old realities of existence never wavered; he was the apostle of the sanctity of laws, of the sanctity of customs; above all, like every poet, he was the apostle of the sanctity of words.

Chapter 20
Elizabeth Barrett Browning

he delightful new edition of Mrs. Browning's "Casa Guidi Windows" which Mr. John Lane has just issued ought certainly to serve as an opportunity for the serious criticism and inevitable admiration to which a great poet is entitled. For Mrs. Browning was a great poet, and not, as is idly and vulgarly supposed, only a great poetess. The word poetess is bad English, and it conveys a particularly bad compliment. Nothing is more remarkable about Mrs. Browning's work than the absence of that trite and namby-pamby elegance which the last two centuries demanded from lady writers. Wherever her verse is bad it is bad from some extravagance of imagery, some violence of comparison, some kind of debauch of cleverness. Her nonsense never arises from weakness, but from a confusion of powers. If the phrase explain itself, she is far more a great poet than she is a good one.

Mrs. Browning often appears more luscious and sentimental than many other literary women, but this was because she was stronger. It requires a certain amount of internal force to break down. A complete self-humiliation requires enormous strength, more strength than most of us possess. When she was writing the poetry of self-abandonment she really abandoned herself with the valour and decision of an anchorite abandoning the world. Such a couplet as:

> "Our Euripides, the human,
> With his dropping of warm tears,"

gives to most of us a sickly and nauseous sensation. Nothing can be well conceived more ridiculous than Euripides going about dropping tears with a loud splash, and Mrs. Browning coming after him with a thermometer. But the one emphatic point about this idiotic couplet is that Mrs. Hemans would never have written it. She would have written something perfectly dignified, perfectly harmless, perfectly inconsiderable. Mrs. Browning was in a great and serious difficulty. She really meant something. She aimed at a vivid and curious image, and she missed it. She had that catastrophic and public failure which is, as much as a medal or a testimonial, the badge of the brave.

In spite of the tiresome half-truth that art is unmoral, the arts require a certain considerable number of moral qualities, and more especially all the arts require courage. The art of drawing, for example, requires even a kind of physical courage. Anyone who has tried to draw a straight line and failed knows that he fails chiefly in nerve, as he might fail to jump off a cliff. And similarly all great literary art involves the element of risk, and the greatest literary artists have commonly been those who have run the greatest risk of talking nonsense. Almost all great poets rant, from Shakespeare downwards. Mrs. Browning was Elizabethan in her luxuriance and her audacity, and the gigantic scale of her wit. We often feel with her as we feel with Shakespeare, that she would have done better with half as much talent. The great curse of the Elizabethans is upon her, that she cannot leave anything alone, she cannot write a single line without a conceit:

> "And the eyes of the peacock fans
> Winked at the alien glory,"

she said of the Papal fans in the presence of the Italian tricolour:

> "And a royal blood sends glances up her princely eye to trouble,
> And the shadow of a monarch's crown is softened in her hair,"

is her description of a beautiful and aristocratic lady. The notion of peacock feathers winking like so many London urchins is perhaps one of her rather aggressive and outrageous figures of speech. The image of a woman's hair as the softened shadow of a crown is a singularly vivid and perfect one. But both have the same quality of intellectual fancy and intellectual concentration. They are both instances of a sort of ethereal epigram. This is the great and dominant characteristic of Mrs. Browning, that she was significant alike in failure and success. Just as every marriage in the world, good or bad, is a marriage, dramatic, irrevocable, and big with coming events, so every one of her wild weddings between alien ideas is an accomplished fact which produces a certain effect on the imagination, which has for good or evil become part and parcel of our mental vision forever. She gives the reader the impression that she never declined a fancy, just as some gentlemen of the eighteenth century never declined a duel. When she fell it was always because she missed the foothold, never because she funked the leap.

"Casa Guidi Windows" is, in one aspect, a poem very typical of its author. Mrs. Browning may fairly be called the peculiar poet of Liberalism, of that great movement of the first half of the nineteenth century towards the emancipation of men from ancient institutions which had gradually changed their nature, from the houses of refuge which had turned into dungeons, and the mystic jewels which remained only as fetters. It was not what we ordinarily understand by revolt. It had no hatred in its heart for ancient and essentially human institutions. It had that deeply conservative belief in the most ancient of institutions, the average man, which goes by the name of democracy. It had none of the spirit of modern Imperialism which is kicking a man because he is down. But, on the other hand, it had none of the spirit of modern Anarchism and scepticism which is kicking a man merely because he is up. It was based fundamentally on a belief in the destiny of humanity, whether that belief took an irreligious form, as in Swinburne, or a religious form, as in Mrs. Browning. It had that rooted and natural conviction that the Millennium was coming to-morrow which has been the conviction of all iconoclasts and reformers, and for which some rationalists have been absurd enough to blame the early Christians. But they had none of that disposition to pin their whole faith to some black-and-white scientific system which afterwards became the curse of philosophical Radicalism. They were not like the sociologists who lay down a final rectification of things, amounting to nothing except an end of the world, a great deal more depressing than would be the case if it were knocked to pieces by a comet. Their ideal, like the ideal of all sensible people, was a chaotic and confused notion of goodness made up of English primroses and Greek statues, birds singing in April, and regiments being cut to pieces for a flag. They were neither Radicals nor Socialists, but Liberals, and a Liberal is a noble and indispensable lunatic who tries to make a cosmos of his own head.

Mrs. Browning and her husband were more liberal than most Liberals. Theirs was the hospitality of the intellect and the hospitality of the heart, which is the best definition of the term. They never fell into the habit of the idle revolutionists of supposing that the past was bad because the future was good, which amounted to asserting that because humanity had never made anything but mistakes it was now quite certain to be right. Browning possessed in a greater degree than any other man the power of realising that all conventions were only victorious revolutions. He could follow the mediæval logicians in all their sowing of the wind and reaping of the whirlwind with all that generous ardour which is due to abstract ideas. He could study the ancients with the young eyes of the Renaissance and read a Greek grammar like a book of love lyrics. This immense and almost confounding Liberalism of Browning doubtless had some effect upon his wife. In her vision of New Italy she went back to the image of Ancient Italy like an honest and true revolutionist; for does not the very word "revolution" mean a rolling backward. All true revolutions are reversions to the natural and the normal. A revolutionist who breaks with the past is a notion fit for an idiot. For how could a man even wish for something which he had never heard of? Mrs. Browning's inexhaustible sympathy with all the ancient and essential passions of humanity was nowhere more in evidence than in her conception of patriotism. For some dark reason, which it is difficult indeed to fathom, belief in patriotism in our day is held to mean principally a belief in every other nation abandoning its patriotic feelings. In the case of no other passion does this weird contradiction exist. Men whose lives are mainly based upon friendship sympathise with the friendships of others. The interest of engaged couples in each other is a proverb, and like many other proverbs sometimes a nuisance. In patriotism alone it is considered correct just now to assume that the sentiment does not exist in other people. It was not so with the great Liberals of Mrs. Browning's time. The Brownings had, so to speak, a disembodied talent for patriotism. They loved England and they loved Italy; yet they were the very reverse of cosmopolitans. They loved the two countries as countries, not as arbitrary divisions of the globe. They had hold of the root and essence of patriotism. They knew how certain flowers and birds and rivers pass into the mills of the brain and come out as wars and discoveries, and how some triumphant adventure or some staggering crime wrought in a remote continent may bear about it the colour of an Italian city or the soul of a silent village of Surrey.

Heretics

Chapter 1
Introductory Remarks on the Importance of Orthodoxy

othing more strangely indicates an enormous and silent evil of modern society than the extraordinary use which is made nowadays of the word "orthodox." In former days the heretic was proud of not being a heretic. It was the kingdoms of the world and the police and the judges who were heretics. He was orthodox. He had no pride in having rebelled against them; they had rebelled against him. The armies with their cruel security, the kings with their cold faces, the decorous processes of State, the reasonable processes of law—all these like sheep had gone astray. The man was proud of being orthodox, was proud of being right. If he stood alone in a howling wilderness he was more than a man; he was a church. He was the centre of the universe; it was round him that the stars swung. All the tortures torn out of forgotten hells could not make him admit that he was heretical. But a few modern phrases have made him boast of it. He says, with a conscious laugh, "I suppose I am very heretical," and looks round for applause. The word "heresy" not only means no longer being wrong; it practically means being clear-headed and courageous. The word "orthodoxy" not only no longer means being right; it practically means being wrong. All this can mean one thing, and one thing only. It means that people care less for whether they are philosophically right. For obviously a man ought to confess himself crazy before he confesses himself heretical. The Bohemian, with a red tie, ought to pique himself on his orthodoxy. The dynamiter, laying a bomb, ought to feel that, whatever else he is, at least he is orthodox.

It is foolish, generally speaking, for a philosopher to set fire to another philosopher in Smithfield Market because they do not agree in their theory of the universe. That was done very frequently in the last decadence of the Middle Ages, and it failed altogether in its object. But there is one thing that is infinitely more absurd and unpractical than burning a man for his philosophy. This is the habit of saying that his philosophy does not matter, and this is done universally in the twentieth century, in the decadence of the great revolutionary period. General theories are everywhere contemned; the doctrine of the Rights of Man is dismissed with the doctrine of the Fall of Man. Atheism itself is too theological for us to-day. Revolution itself is too much of a system; liberty itself is too much of a restraint. We will have no generalizations. Mr. Bernard Shaw has put the view in a perfect epigram: "The golden rule is that there is no golden rule." We are more and more to discuss details in art, politics, literature. A man's opinion on tramcars matters; his opinion on Botticelli matters; his opinion on all things does not matter. He may turn over and explore a million objects, but he must not find that strange object, the universe; for if he does he will have a religion, and be lost. Everything matters—except everything.

Examples are scarcely needed of this total levity on the subject of cosmic philosophy. Examples are scarcely needed to show that, whatever else we think of as affecting practical affairs, we do not think it matters whether a man is a pessimist or an optimist, a Cartesian or a Hegelian, a materialist or a spiritualist. Let me, however, take a random instance. At any innocent tea-table we may easily hear a man say, "Life is not worth living." We regard it as we regard the statement that it is a fine day; nobody thinks that it can possibly have any serious effect on the man or on the world. And yet if that utterance were really believed, the world would stand on its head. Murderers would be given medals for saving men from life; firemen would be denounced for keeping men from death; poisons would be used as medicines; doctors would be called in when people were well; the Royal Humane Society would be rooted out like a horde of assassins. Yet we never speculate as to whether the conversational pessimist will strengthen or disorganize society; for we are convinced that theories do not matter.

This was certainly not the idea of those who introduced our freedom. When the old Liberals removed the gags from all the heresies, their idea was that religious and philosophical discoveries might thus be made. Their view was that cosmic truth was so important that every one ought to bear independent testimony. The modern idea is that cosmic truth is so unimportant that it cannot matter what any one says. The former freed inquiry as men loose a noble hound; the latter frees inquiry as men fling back into the sea a fish unfit for eating. Never has there been so little discussion about the nature of men as now, when, for the first time, any one can discuss it. The old restriction meant that only the orthodox were allowed to discuss religion. Modern liberty means that nobody is allowed to discuss it. Good taste, the last and vilest of human superstitions, has succeeded in silencing us where all the rest have failed. Sixty years ago it was bad taste to be an avowed atheist. Then came the Bradlaughites, the last religious men, the last men who cared about God; but they could not alter it. It is still bad taste to be an avowed atheist. But their agony has achieved just this—that now it is equally bad taste to be an avowed Christian. Emancipation has only locked the saint in the same tower of silence as the heresiarch. Then we talk about Lord Anglesey and the weather, and call it the complete liberty of all the creeds.

But there are some people, nevertheless—and I am one of them—who think that the most practical and important thing about a man is still his view of the universe. We think that for a landlady considering a lodger, it is important to know his income, but still more important to know his philosophy. We think that for a general about to fight an enemy, it is important to know the enemy's numbers, but still more important to know the enemy's philosophy. We think the question is not whether the theory of the cosmos affects matters, but whether in the long run, anything else affects them. In the fifteenth century men cross-examined and tormented a man because he preached some immoral attitude; in the nineteenth century we feted and flattered Oscar Wilde because he preached such an attitude, and then broke his heart in penal servitude because he carried it out. It may be a question which of the two methods was the more cruel; there can be no kind of question which was the more ludicrous. The age of the Inquisition has not at least the disgrace of having produced a society which made an idol of the very same man for preaching the very same things which it made him a convict for practising.

Now, in our time, philosophy or religion, our theory, that is, about ultimate things, has been driven out, more or less simultaneously, from two fields which it used to occupy. General ideals used to dominate literature. They have been driven out by the cry of "art for art's sake." General ideals used to dominate politics. They have been driven out by the cry of "efficiency," which may roughly be translated as "politics for politics' sake." Persistently for the last twenty years the ideals of order or liberty have dwindled in our books; the ambitions of wit and eloquence have dwindled in our parliaments. Literature has purposely become less political; politics have purposely become less literary. General theories of the relation of things have thus been extruded from both; and we are in a position to ask, "What have we gained or lost by this extrusion? Is literature better, is politics better, for having discarded the moralist and the philosopher?"

When everything about a people is for the time growing weak and ineffective, it begins to talk about efficiency. So it is that when a man's body is a wreck he begins, for the first time, to talk about health. Vigorous organisms talk not about their processes, but about their aims. There cannot be any better proof of the physical efficiency of a man than that he talks cheerfully of a journey to the end of the world. And there cannot be any better proof of the practical efficiency of a nation than that it talks constantly of a journey to the end of the world, a journey to the Judgment Day and the New Jerusalem. There can be no stronger sign of a coarse material health than the tendency to run after high and wild ideals; it is in the first exuberance of infancy that we cry for the moon. None of the strong men in the strong ages would have understood what you meant by working for efficiency. Hildebrand would have said that he was working not for efficiency, but for the Catholic Church. Danton would have said that he was working not for efficiency, but for liberty, equality, and fraternity. Even if the ideal of such men were simply the ideal of kicking a man downstairs, they thought of the end like men, not of the process like paralytics. They did not say, "Efficiently elevating my right leg, using, you will notice, the muscles of the thigh and calf, which are in excellent order, I—" Their feeling was quite different. They were so filled with the beautiful vision of the man lying flat at the foot of the staircase that in that ecstasy the rest followed in a flash. In practice, the habit of generalizing and idealizing did not by any means mean worldly weakness. The time of big theories was the time of big results. In the era of sentiment and fine words, at the end of the eighteenth century, men were really robust and effective. The sentimentalists conquered Napoleon. The cynics could not catch De Wet. A hundred years ago our affairs for good or evil were wielded triumphantly by rhetoricians. Now our affairs are hopelessly muddled by strong, silent men. And just as this repudiation of big words and big visions has brought forth a race of small men in politics, so it has brought forth a race of small men in the arts. Our modern politicians claim the colossal license of Caesar and the Superman, claim that they are too practical to be pure and too patriotic to be moral; but the upshot of it all is that a mediocrity is Chancellor of the Exchequer. Our new artistic philosophers call for the same moral license, for a freedom to wreck heaven and earth with their energy; but the upshot of it all is that a mediocrity is Poet Laureate. I do not say that there are no stronger men than these; but will any one say that there are any men stronger than those men of old who were dominated by their philosophy and steeped in their religion? Whether bondage be better than freedom may be discussed. But that their bondage came to more than our freedom it will be difficult for any one to deny.

The theory of the unmorality of art has established itself firmly in the strictly artistic classes. They are free to produce anything they like. They are free to write a "Paradise Lost" in which Satan shall conquer God. They are free to write a "Divine Comedy" in which heaven shall be under the floor of hell. And what have they done? Have they produced in their universality anything grander or more beautiful than the things uttered by the fierce Ghibbeline Catholic, by the rigid Puritan schoolmaster? We know that they have produced only a few roundels. Milton does not merely beat them at his piety, he beats them at their own irreverence. In all their little books of verse you will not find a finer defiance of God than Satan's. Nor will you find the grandeur of paganism felt as that fiery Christian felt it who described Faranata lifting his head as in disdain of hell. And the reason is very obvious. Blasphemy is an artistic effect, because blasphemy depends upon a philosophical conviction. Blasphemy depends upon belief and is fading with it. If any one doubts this, let him sit down seriously and try to think blasphemous thoughts about Thor. I think his family will find him at the end of the day in a state of some exhaustion.

Neither in the world of politics nor that of literature, then, has the rejection of general theories proved a success. It may be that there have been many moonstruck and misleading ideals that have from time to time perplexed mankind. But assuredly there has been no ideal in practice so moonstruck and misleading as the ideal of practicality. Nothing has lost so many opportunities as the opportunism of Lord Rosebery. He is, indeed, a standing symbol of this epoch—the man who is theoretically a practical man, and practically more unpractical than any theorist. Nothing in this universe is so unwise as that kind of worship of worldly wisdom. A man who is perpetually thinking of whether this race or that race is strong, of whether this cause or that cause is promising, is the man who will never believe in anything long enough to make it succeed. The opportunist politician is like a man who should abandon billiards because he was beaten at billiards, and abandon golf because he was beaten at golf. There is nothing which is so weak for working purposes as this enormous importance attached to immediate victory. There is nothing that fails like success.

And having discovered that opportunism does fail, I have been induced to look at it more largely, and in consequence to see that it must fail. I perceive that it is far more practical to begin at the beginning and discuss theories. I see that the men who killed each other about the orthodoxy of the Homoousion were far more sensible than the people who are quarrelling about the Education Act. For the Christian dogmatists were trying to establish a reign of holiness, and trying to get defined, first of all, what was really holy. But our modern educationists are trying to bring about a religious liberty without attempting to settle what is religion or what is liberty. If the old priests forced a statement on mankind, at least they previously took some trouble to make it lucid. It has been left for the modern mobs of Anglicans and Nonconformists to persecute for a doctrine without even stating it.

For these reasons, and for many more, I for one have come to believe in going back to fundamentals. Such is the general idea of this book. I wish to deal with my most distinguished contemporaries, not personally or in a merely literary manner, but in relation to the real body of doctrine which they teach. I am not concerned with Mr. Rudyard Kipling as a vivid artist or a vigorous personality; I am concerned with him as a Heretic—that is to say, a man whose view of things has the hardihood to differ from mine. I am not concerned with Mr. Bernard Shaw as one of the most brilliant and one of the most honest men alive; I am concerned with him as a Heretic—that is to say, a man whose philosophy is quite solid, quite coherent, and quite wrong. I revert to the doctrinal methods of the thirteenth century, inspired by the general hope of getting something done.

Suppose that a great commotion arises in the street about something, let us say a lamp-post, which many influential persons desire to pull down. A grey-clad monk, who is the spirit of the Middle Ages, is approached upon the matter, and begins to say, in the arid manner of the Schoolmen, "Let us first of all consider, my brethren, the value of Light. If Light be in itself good—" At this point he is somewhat excusably knocked down. All the people make a rush for the lamp-post, the lamp-post is down in ten minutes, and they go about congratulating each other on their unmediaeval practicality. But as things go on they do not work out so easily. Some people have pulled the lamp-post down because they wanted the electric light; some because they wanted old iron; some because they wanted darkness, because their deeds were evil. Some thought it not enough of a lamp-post, some too much; some acted because they wanted to smash municipal machinery; some because they wanted to smash something. And there is war in the night, no man knowing whom he strikes. So, gradually and inevitably, to-day, to-morrow, or the next day, there comes back the conviction that the monk was right after all, and that all depends on what is the philosophy of Light. Only what we might have discussed under the gas-lamp, we now must discuss in the dark.

Chapter 2
On the Negative Spirit

uch has been said, and said truly, of the monkish morbidity, of the hysteria which as often gone with the visions of hermits or nuns. But let us never forget that this visionary religion is, in one sense, necessarily more wholesome than our modern and reasonable morality. It is more wholesome for this reason, that it can contemplate the idea of success or triumph in the hopeless fight towards the ethical ideal, in what Stevenson called, with his usual startling felicity, "the lost fight of virtue." A modern morality, on the other hand, can only point with absolute conviction to the horrors that follow breaches of law; its only certainty is a certainty of ill. It can only point to imperfection. It has no perfection to point to. But the monk meditating upon Christ or Buddha has in his mind an image of perfect health, a thing of clear colours and clean air. He may contemplate this ideal wholeness and happiness far more than he ought; he may contemplate it to the neglect of exclusion of essential THINGS; he may contemplate it until he has become a dreamer or a driveller; but still it is wholeness and happiness that he is contemplating. He may even go mad; but he is going mad for the love of sanity. But the modern student of ethics, even if he remains sane, remains sane from an insane dread of insanity.

The anchorite rolling on the stones in a frenzy of submission is a healthier person fundamentally than many a sober man in a silk hat who is walking down Cheapside. For many such are good only through a withering knowledge of evil. I am not at this moment claiming for the devotee anything more than this primary advantage, that though he may be making himself personally weak and miserable, he is still fixing his thoughts largely on gigantic strength and happiness, on a strength that has no limits, and a happiness that has no end. Doubtless there are other objections which can be urged without unreason against the influence of gods and visions in morality, whether in the cell or street. But this advantage the mystic morality must always have—it is always jollier. A young man may keep himself from vice by continually thinking of disease. He may keep himself from it also by continually thinking of the Virgin Mary. There may be question about which method is the more reasonable, or even about which is the more efficient. But surely there can be no question about which is the more wholesome.

I remember a pamphlet by that able and sincere secularist, Mr. G. W. Foote, which contained a phrase sharply symbolizing and dividing these two methods. The pamphlet was called BEER AND BIBLE, those two very noble things, all the nobler for a conjunction which Mr. Foote, in his stern old Puritan way, seemed to think sardonic, but which I confess to thinking appropriate and charming. I have not the work by me, but I remember that Mr. Foote dismissed very contemptuously any attempts to deal with the problem of strong drink by religious offices or intercessions, and said that a picture of a drunkard's liver would be more efficacious in the matter of temperance than any prayer or praise. In that picturesque expression, it seems to me, is perfectly embodied the incurable morbidity of modern ethics. In that temple the lights are low, the crowds kneel, the solemn anthems are uplifted. But that upon the altar to which all men kneel is no longer the perfect flesh, the body and substance of the perfect man; it is still flesh, but it is diseased. It is the drunkard's liver of the New Testament that is marred for us, which we take in remembrance of him.

Now, it is this great gap in modern ethics, the absence of vivid pictures of purity and spiritual triumph, which lies at the back of the real objection felt by so many sane men to the realistic literature of the nineteenth century. If any ordinary man ever said that he was horrified by the subjects discussed in Ibsen or Maupassant, or by the plain language in which they are spoken of, that ordinary man was lying. The average conversation of average men throughout the whole of modern civilization in every class or trade is such as Zola would never dream of printing. Nor is the habit of writing thus of these things a new habit. On the contrary, it is the Victorian prudery and silence which is new still, though it is already dying. The tradition of calling a spade a spade starts very early in our literature and comes down very late. But the truth is that the ordinary honest man, whatever vague account he may have given of his feelings, was not either disgusted or even annoyed at the candour of the moderns. What disgusted him, and very justly, was not the presence of a clear realism, but the absence of a clear idealism. Strong and genuine religious sentiment has never had any objection to realism; on the contrary, religion was the realistic thing, the brutal thing, the thing that called names. This is the great difference between some recent developments of Nonconformity and the great Puritanism of the seventeenth century. It was the whole point of the Puritans that they cared nothing for decency. Modern Nonconformist newspapers distinguish themselves by suppressing precisely those nouns and adjectives which the founders of Nonconformity distinguished themselves by flinging at kings and queens. But if it was a chief claim of religion that it spoke plainly about evil, it was the chief claim of all that it spoke plainly about good. The thing which is resented, and, as I think, rightly resented, in that great modern literature of which Ibsen is typical, is that while the eye that can perceive what are the wrong things increases in an uncanny and devouring clarity, the eye which sees what things are right is growing mistier and mistier every moment, till it goes almost blind with doubt. If we compare, let us say, the morality of the DIVINE COMEDY with the morality of Ibsen's GHOSTS, we shall see all that modern ethics have really done. No one, I imagine, will accuse the author of the INFERNO of an Early Victorian prudishness or a Podsnapian optimism. But Dante describes three moral instruments—Heaven, Purgatory, and Hell, the vision of perfection, the vision of improvement, and the vision of failure. Ibsen has only one—Hell. It is often said, and with perfect truth, that no one could read a play like GHOSTS and remain indifferent to the necessity of an ethical self-command. That is quite true, and the same is to be said of the most monstrous and material descriptions of the eternal fire. It is quite certain the realists like Zola do in one sense promote morality—they promote it in the sense in which the hangman promotes it, in the sense in which the devil promotes it. But they only affect that small minority which will accept any virtue of courage. Most healthy people dismiss these moral dangers as they dismiss the possibility of bombs or microbes. Modern realists are indeed Terrorists, like the dynamiters; and they fail just as much in their effort to create a thrill. Both realists and dynamiters are well-meaning people engaged in the task, so obviously ultimately hopeless, of using science to promote morality.

I do not wish the reader to confuse me for a moment with those vague persons who imagine that Ibsen is what they call a pessimist. There are plenty of wholesome people in Ibsen, plenty of good people, plenty of happy people, plenty of examples of men acting wisely and things ending well. That is not my meaning. My meaning is that Ibsen has throughout, and does not disguise, a certain vagueness and a changing attitude as well as a doubting attitude towards what is really wisdom and virtue in this life—a vagueness which contrasts very remarkably with the decisiveness with which he pounces on something which he perceives to be a root of evil, some convention, some deception, some ignorance. We know that the hero of GHOSTS is mad, and we know why he is mad. We do also know that Dr. Stockman is sane; but we do not know why he is sane. Ibsen does not profess to know how virtue and happiness are brought about, in the sense that he professes to know how our modern sexual tragedies are brought about. Falsehood works ruin in THE PILLARS OF SOCIETY, but truth works equal ruin in THE WILD DUCK. There are no cardinal virtues of Ibsenism. There is no ideal man of Ibsen. All this is not only admitted, but vaunted in the most valuable and thoughtful of all the eulogies upon Ibsen, Mr. Bernard Shaw's QUINTESSENCE OF IBSENISM. Mr. Shaw sums up Ibsen's teaching in the phrase, "The golden rule is that there is no golden rule." In his eyes this absence of an enduring and positive ideal, this absence of a permanent key to virtue, is the one great Ibsen merit. I am not discussing now with any fulness whether this is so or not. All I venture to point out, with an increased firmness, is that this omission, good or bad, does leave us face to face with the problem of a human consciousness filled with very definite images of evil, and with no definite image of good. To us light must be henceforward the dark thing—the thing of which we cannot speak. To us, as to Milton's devils in Pandemonium, it is darkness that is visible. The human race, according to religion, fell once, and in falling gained knowledge of good and of evil. Now we have fallen a second time, and only the knowledge of evil remains to us.

A great silent collapse, an enormous unspoken disappointment, has in our time fallen on our Northern civilization. All previous ages have sweated and been crucified in an attempt to realize what is really the right life, what was really the good man. A definite part of the modern world has come beyond question to the conclusion that there is no answer to these questions, that the most that we can do is to set up a few notice-boards at places of obvious danger, to warn men, for instance, against drinking themselves to death, or ignoring the mere existence of their neighbours. Ibsen is the first to return from the baffled hunt to bring us the tidings of great failure.

Every one of the popular modern phrases and ideals is a dodge in order to shirk the problem of what is good. We are fond of talking about "liberty"; that, as we talk of it, is a dodge to avoid discussing what is good. We are fond of talking about "progress"; that is a dodge to avoid discussing what is good. We are fond of talking about "education"; that is a dodge to avoid discussing what is good. The modern man says, "Let us leave all these arbitrary standards and embrace liberty." This is, logically rendered, "Let us not decide what is good, but let it be considered good not to decide it." He says, "Away with your old moral formulae; I am for progress." This, logically stated, means, "Let us not settle what is good; but let us settle whether we are getting more of it." He says, "Neither in religion nor morality, my friend, lie the hopes of the race, but in education." This, clearly expressed, means, "We cannot decide what is good, but let us give it to our children."

Mr. H.G. Wells, that exceedingly clear-sighted man, has pointed out in a recent work that this has happened in connection with economic questions. The old economists, he says, made generalizations, and they were (in Mr. Wells's view) mostly wrong. But the new economists, he says, seem to have lost the power of making any generalizations at all. And they cover this incapacity with a general claim to be, in specific cases, regarded as "experts", a claim "proper enough in a hairdresser or a fashionable physician, but indecent in a philosopher or a man of science." But in spite of the refreshing rationality with which Mr. Wells has indicated this, it must also be said that he himself has fallen into the same enormous modern error. In the opening pages of that excellent book MANKIND IN THE MAKING, he dismisses the ideals of art, religion, abstract morality, and the rest, and says that he is going to consider men in their chief function, the function of parenthood. He is going to discuss life as a "tissue of births." He is not going to ask what will produce satisfactory saints or satisfactory heroes, but what will produce satisfactory fathers and mothers. The whole is set forward so sensibly that it is a few moments at least before the reader realises that it is another example of unconscious shirking. What is the good of begetting a man until we have settled what is the good of being a man? You are merely handing on to him a problem you dare not settle yourself. It is as if a man were asked, "What is the use of a hammer?" and answered, "To make hammers"; and when asked, "And of those hammers, what is the use?" answered, "To make hammers again". Just as such a man would be perpetually putting off the question of the ultimate use of carpentry, so Mr. Wells and all the rest of us are by these phrases successfully putting off the question of the ultimate value of the human life.

The case of the general talk of "progress" is, indeed, an extreme one. As enunciated to-day, "progress" is simply a comparative of which we have not settled the superlative. We meet every ideal of religion, patriotism, beauty, or brute pleasure with the alternative ideal of progress—that is to say, we meet every proposal of getting something that we know about, with an alternative proposal of getting a great deal more of nobody knows what. Progress, properly understood, has, indeed, a most dignified and legitimate meaning. But as used in opposition to precise moral ideals, it is ludicrous. So far from it being the truth that the ideal of progress is to be set against that of ethical or religious finality, the reverse is the truth. Nobody has any business to use the word "progress" unless he has a definite creed and a cast-iron code of morals. Nobody can be progressive without being doctrinal; I might almost say that nobody can be progressive without being infallible—at any rate, without believing in some infallibility. For progress by its very name indicates a direction; and the moment we are in the least doubtful about the direction, we become in the same degree doubtful about the progress. Never perhaps since the beginning of the world has there been an age that had less right to use the word "progress" than we. In the Catholic twelfth century, in the philosophic eighteenth century, the direction may have been a good or a bad one, men may have differed more or less about how far they went, and in what direction, but about the direction they did in the main agree, and consequently they had the genuine sensation of progress. But it is precisely about the direction that we disagree. Whether the future excellence lies in more law or less law, in more liberty or less liberty; whether property will be finally concentrated or finally cut up; whether sexual passion will reach its sanest in an almost virgin intellectualism or in a full animal freedom; whether we should love everybody with Tolstoy, or spare nobody with Nietzsche;—these are the things about which we are actually fighting most. It is not merely true that the age which has settled least what is progress is this "progressive" age. It is, moreover, true that the people who have settled least what is progress are the most "progressive" people in it. The ordinary mass, the men who have never troubled about progress, might be trusted perhaps to progress. The particular individuals who talk about progress would certainly fly to the four winds of heaven when the pistol-shot started the race. I do not, therefore, say that the word "progress" is unmeaning; I say it is unmeaning without the previous definition of a moral doctrine, and that it can only be applied to groups of persons who hold that doctrine in common. Progress is not an illegitimate word, but it is logically evident that it is illegitimate for us. It is a sacred word, a word which could only rightly be used by rigid believers and in the ages of faith.

Chapter 3
On Mr. Rudyard Kipling and Making the World Small

here is no such thing on earth as an uninteresting subject; the only thing that can exist is an uninterested person. Nothing is more keenly required than a defence of bores. When Byron divided humanity into the bores and bored, he omitted to notice that the higher qualities exist entirely in the bores, the lower qualities in the bored, among whom he counted himself. The bore, by his starry enthusiasm, his solemn happiness, may, in some sense, have proved himself poetical. The bored has certainly proved himself prosaic.

We might, no doubt, find it a nuisance to count all the blades of grass or all the leaves of the trees; but this would not be because of our boldness or gaiety, but because of our lack of boldness and gaiety. The bore would go onward, bold and gay, and find the blades of grass as splendid as the swords of an army. The bore is stronger and more joyous than we are; he is a demigod—nay, he is a god. For it is the gods who do not tire of the iteration of things; to them the nightfall is always new, and the last rose as red as the first.

The sense that everything is poetical is a thing solid and absolute; it is not a mere matter of phraseology or persuasion. It is not merely true, it is ascertainable. Men may be challenged to deny it; men may be challenged to mention anything that is not a matter of poetry. I remember a long time ago a sensible sub-editor coming up to me with a book in his hand, called "Mr. Smith," or "The Smith Family," or some such thing. He said, "Well, you won't get any of your damned mysticism out of this," or words to that effect. I am happy to say that I undeceived him; but the victory was too obvious and easy. In most cases the name is unpoetical, although the fact is poetical. In the case of Smith, the name is so poetical that it must be an arduous and heroic matter for the man to live up to it. The name of Smith is the name of the one trade that even kings respected, it could claim half the glory of that *arma virumque* which all epics acclaimed. The spirit of the smithy is so close to the spirit of song that it has mixed in a million poems, and every blacksmith is a harmonious blacksmith.

Even the village children feel that in some dim way the smith is poetic, as the grocer and the cobbler are not poetic, when they feast on the dancing sparks and deafening blows in the cavern of that creative violence. The brute repose of Nature, the passionate cunning of man, the strongest of earthly metals, the weirdest of earthly elements, the unconquerable iron subdued by its only conqueror, the wheel and the ploughshare, the sword and the steam-hammer, the arraying of armies and the whole legend of arms, all these things are written, briefly indeed, but quite legibly, on the visiting-card of Mr. Smith. Yet our novelists call their hero "Aylmer Valence," which means nothing, or "Vernon Raymond," which means nothing, when it is in their power to give him this sacred name of Smith—this name made of iron and flame. It would be very natural if a certain hauteur, a certain carriage of the head, a certain curl of the lip, distinguished every one whose name is Smith. Perhaps it does; I trust so. Whoever else are parvenus, the Smiths are not parvenus. From the darkest dawn of history this clan has gone forth to battle; its trophies are on every hand; its name is everywhere; it is older than the nations, and its sign is the Hammer of Thor. But as I also remarked, it is not quite the usual case. It is common enough that common things should be poetical; it is not so common that common names should be poetical. In most cases it is the name that is the obstacle. A great many people talk as if this claim of ours, that all things are poetical, were a mere literary ingenuity, a play on words. Precisely the contrary is true. It is the idea that some things are not poetical which is literary, which is a mere product of words. The word "signal-box" is unpoetical. But the thing signal-box is not unpoetical; it is a place where men, in an agony of vigilance, light blood-red and sea-green fires to keep other men from death. That is the plain, genuine description of what it is; the prose only comes in with what it is called. The word "pillar-box" is unpoetical. But the thing pillar-box is not unpoetical; it is the place to which friends and lovers commit their messages, conscious that when they have done so they are sacred, and not to be touched, not only by others, but even (religious touch!) by themselves. That red turret is one of the last of the temples. Posting a letter and getting married are among the few things left that are entirely romantic; for to be entirely romantic a thing must be irrevocable. We think a pillar-box prosaic, because there is no rhyme to it. We think a pillar-box unpoetical, because we have never seen it in a poem. But the bold fact is entirely on the side of poetry. A signal-box is only called a signal-box; it is a house of life and death. A pillar-box is only called a pillar-box; it is a sanctuary of human words. If you think the name of "Smith" prosaic, it is not because you are practical and sensible; it is because you are too much affected with literary refinements. The name shouts poetry at you. If you think of it otherwise, it is because you are steeped and sodden with verbal reminiscences, because you remember everything in Punch or Comic Cuts about Mr. Smith being drunk or Mr. Smith being henpecked. All these things were given to you poetical. It is only by a long and elaborate process of literary effort that you have made them prosaic.

Now, the first and fairest thing to say about Rudyard Kipling is that he has borne a brilliant part in thus recovering the lost provinces of poetry. He has not been frightened by that brutal materialistic air which clings only to words; he has pierced through to the romantic, imaginative matter of the things themselves. He has perceived the significance and philosophy of steam and of slang. Steam may be, if you like, a dirty by-product of science. Slang may be, if you like, a dirty by-product of language. But at least he has been among the few who saw the divine parentage of these things, and knew that where there is smoke there is fire—that is, that wherever there is the foulest of things, there also is the purest. Above all, he has had something to say, a definite view of things to utter, and that always means that a man is fearless and faces everything. For the moment we have a view of the universe, we possess it.

Now, the message of Rudyard Kipling, that upon which he has really concentrated, is the only thing worth worrying about in him or in any other man. He has often written bad poetry, like Wordsworth. He has often said silly things, like Plato. He has often given way to mere political hysteria, like Gladstone. But no one can reasonably doubt that he means steadily and sincerely to say something, and the only serious question is, What is that which he has tried to say? Perhaps the best way of stating this fairly will be to begin with that element which has been most insisted by himself and by his opponents—I mean his interest in militarism. But when we are seeking for the real merits of a man it is unwise to go to his enemies, and much more foolish to go to himself.

Now, Mr. Kipling is certainly wrong in his worship of militarism, but his opponents are, generally speaking, quite as wrong as he. The evil of militarism is not that it shows certain men to be fierce and haughty and excessively warlike. The evil of militarism is that it shows most men to be tame and timid and excessively peaceable. The professional soldier gains more and more power as the general courage of a community declines. Thus the Praetorian guard became more and more important in Rome as Rome became more and more luxurious and feeble. The military man gains the civil power in proportion as the civilian loses the military virtues. And as it was in ancient Rome so it is in contemporary Europe. There never was a time when nations were more militarist. There never was a time when men were less brave. All ages and all epics have sung of arms and the man; but we have effected simultaneously the deterioration of the man and the fantastic perfection of the arms. Militarism demonstrated the decadence of Rome, and it demonstrates the decadence of Prussia.

And unconsciously Mr. Kipling has proved this, and proved it admirably. For in so far as his work is earnestly understood the military trade does not by any means emerge as the most important or attractive. He has not written so well about soldiers as he has about railway men or bridge builders, or even journalists. The fact is that what attracts Mr. Kipling to militarism is not the idea of courage, but the idea of discipline. There was far more courage to the square mile in the Middle Ages, when no king had a standing army, but every man had a bow or sword. But the fascination of the standing army upon Mr. Kipling is not courage, which scarcely interests him, but discipline, which is, when all is said and done, his primary theme. The modern army is not a miracle of courage; it has not enough opportunities, owing to the cowardice of everybody else. But it is really a miracle of organization, and that is the truly Kiplingite ideal. Kipling's subject is not that valour which properly belongs to war, but that interdependence and efficiency which belongs quite as much to engineers, or sailors, or mules, or railway engines. And thus it is that when he writes of engineers, or sailors, or mules, or steam-engines, he writes at his best. The real poetry, the "true romance" which Mr. Kipling has taught, is the romance of the division of labour and the discipline of all the trades. He sings the arts of peace much more accurately than the arts of war. And his main contention is vital and valuable. Every thing is military in the sense that everything depends upon obedience. There is no perfectly epicurean corner; there is no perfectly irresponsible place. Everywhere men have made the way for us with sweat and submission. We may fling ourselves into a hammock in a fit of divine carelessness. But we are glad that the net-maker did not make the hammock in a fit of divine carelessness. We may jump upon a child's rocking-horse for a joke. But we are glad that the carpenter did not leave the legs of it unglued for a joke. So far from having merely preached that a soldier cleaning his side-arm is to be adored because he is military, Kipling at his best and clearest has preached that the baker baking loaves and the tailor cutting coats is as military as anybody.

Being devoted to this multitudinous vision of duty, Mr. Kipling is naturally a cosmopolitan. He happens to find his examples in the British Empire, but almost any other empire would do as well, or, indeed, any other highly civilized country. That which he admires in the British army he would find even more apparent in the German army; that which he desires in the British police he would find flourishing, in the French police. The ideal of discipline is not the whole of life, but it is spread over the whole of the world. And the worship of it tends to confirm in Mr. Kipling a certain note of worldly wisdom, of the experience of the wanderer, which is one of the genuine charms of his best work.

The great gap in his mind is what may be roughly called the lack of patriotism—that is to say, he lacks altogether the faculty of attaching himself to any cause or community finally and tragically; for all finality must be tragic. He admires England, but he does not love her; for we admire things with reasons, but love them without reasons. He admires England because she is strong, not because she is English. There is no harshness in saying this, for, to do him justice, he avows it with his usual picturesque candour. In a very interesting poem, he says that—

"If England was what England seems"

—that is, weak and inefficient; if England were not what (as he believes) she is—that is, powerful and practical—

"How quick we'd chuck 'er! But she ain't!"

He admits, that is, that his devotion is the result of a criticism, and this is quite enough to put it in another category altogether from the patriotism of the Boers, whom he hounded down in South Africa. In speaking of the really patriotic peoples, such as the Irish, he has some difficulty in keeping a shrill irritation out of his language. The frame of mind which he really describes with beauty and

nobility is the frame of mind of the cosmopolitan man who has seen men and
cities.

"For to admire and for to see,
For to be'old this world so wide."

He is a perfect master of that light melancholy with which a man looks back on
having been the citizen of many communities, of that light melancholy with which
a man looks back on having been the lover of many women. He is the philanderer
of the nations. But a man may have learnt much about women in flirtations, and
still be ignorant of first love; a man may have known as many lands as Ulysses, and
still be ignorant of patriotism.

Mr. Rudyard Kipling has asked in a celebrated epigram what they can know
of England who know England only. It is a far deeper and sharper question to
ask, "What can they know of England who know only the world?" for the world
does not include England any more than it includes the Church. The moment we
care for anything deeply, the world—that is, all the other miscellaneous interests—
becomes our enemy. Christians showed it when they talked of keeping one's self
"unspotted from the world;" but lovers talk of it just as much when they talk of
the "world well lost." Astronomically speaking, I understand that England is
situated on the world; similarly, I suppose that the Church was a part of the world,
and even the lovers inhabitants of that orb. But they all felt a certain truth—the
truth that the moment you love anything the world becomes your foe. Thus Mr.
Kipling does certainly know the world; he is a man of the world, with all the
narrowness that belongs to those imprisoned in that planet. He knows England as
an intelligent English gentleman knows Venice. He has been to England a great
many times; he has stopped there for long visits. But he does not belong to it, or
to any place; and the proof of it is this, that he thinks of England as a place. The
moment we are rooted in a place, the place vanishes. We live like a tree with the
whole strength of the universe.

The globe-trotter lives in a smaller world than the peasant. He is always
breathing, an air of locality. London is a place, to be compared to Chicago;
Chicago is a place, to be compared to Timbuctoo. But Timbuctoo is not a place,
since there, at least, live men who regard it as the universe, and breathe, not an
air of locality, but the winds of the world. The man in the saloon steamer has
seen all the races of men, and he is thinking of the things that divide men—diet,
dress, decorum, rings in the nose as in Africa, or in the ears as in Europe, blue
paint among the ancients, or red paint among the modern Britons. The man in
the cabbage field has seen nothing at all; but he is thinking of the things that
unite men—hunger and babies, and the beauty of women, and the promise or
menace of the sky. Mr. Kipling, with all his merits, is the globe-trotter; he has
not the patience to become part of anything. So great and genuine a man is not to
be accused of a merely cynical cosmopolitanism; still, his cosmopolitanism is his

weakness. That weakness is splendidly expressed in one of his finest poems, "The Sestina of the Tramp Royal," in which a man declares that he can endure anything in the way of hunger or horror, but not permanent presence in one place. In this there is certainly danger. The more dead and dry and dusty a thing is the more it travels about; dust is like this and the thistle-down and the High Commissioner in South Africa. Fertile things are somewhat heavier, like the heavy fruit trees on the pregnant mud of the Nile. In the heated idleness of youth we were all rather inclined to quarrel with the implication of that proverb which says that a rolling stone gathers no moss. We were inclined to ask, "Who wants to gather moss, except silly old ladies?" But for all that we begin to perceive that the proverb is right. The rolling stone rolls echoing from rock to rock; but the rolling stone is dead. The moss is silent because the moss is alive.

The truth is that exploration and enlargement make the world smaller. The telegraph and the steamboat make the world smaller. The telescope makes the world smaller; it is only the microscope that makes it larger. Before long the world will be cloven with a war between the telescopists and the microscopists. The first study large things and live in a small world; the second study small things and live in a large world. It is inspiriting without doubt to whizz in a motor-car round the earth, to feel Arabia as a whirl of sand or China as a flash of rice-fields. But Arabia is not a whirl of sand and China is not a flash of rice-fields. They are ancient civilizations with strange virtues buried like treasures. If we wish to understand them it must not be as tourists or inquirers, it must be with the loyalty of children and the great patience of poets. To conquer these places is to lose them. The man standing in his own kitchen-garden, with fairyland opening at the gate, is the man with large ideas. His mind creates distance; the motor-car stupidly destroys it. Moderns think of the earth as a globe, as something one can easily get round, the spirit of a schoolmistress. This is shown in the odd mistake perpetually made about Cecil Rhodes. His enemies say that he may have had large ideas, but he was a bad man. His friends say that he may have been a bad man, but he certainly had large ideas. The truth is that he was not a man essentially bad, he was a man of much geniality and many good intentions, but a man with singularly small views. There is nothing large about painting the map red; it is an innocent game for children. It is just as easy to think in continents as to think in cobble-stones. The difficulty comes in when we seek to know the substance of either of them. Rhodes' prophecies about the Boer resistance are an admirable comment on how the "large ideas" prosper when it is not a question of thinking in continents but of understanding a few two-legged men. And under all this vast illusion of the cosmopolitan planet, with its empires and its Reuter's agency, the real life of man goes on concerned with this tree or that temple, with this harvest or that drinking-song, totally uncomprehended, totally untouched. And it watches from its splendid parochialism, possibly with a smile of amusement, motor-car civilization going its triumphant way, outstripping time, consuming space, seeing all and seeing nothing, roaring on at last to the capture of the solar system, only to find the sun cockney and the stars suburban.

Chapter 4
Mr. Bernard Shaw

n the glad old days, before the rise of modern morbidities, when genial old Ibsen filled the world with wholesome joy, and the kindly tales of the forgotten Emile Zola kept our firesides merry and pure, it used to be thought a disadvantage to be misunderstood. It may be doubted whether it is always or even generally a disadvantage. The man who is misunderstood has always this advantage over his enemies, that they do not know his weak point or his plan of campaign. They go out against a bird with nets and against a fish with arrows. There are several modern examples of this situation. Mr. Chamberlain, for instance, is a very good one. He constantly eludes or vanquishes his opponents because his real powers and deficiencies are quite different to those with which he is credited, both by friends and foes. His friends depict him as a strenuous man of action; his opponents depict him as a coarse man of business; when, as a fact, he is neither one nor the other, but an admirable romantic orator and romantic actor. He has one power which is the soul of melodrama—the power of pretending, even when backed by a huge majority, that he has his back to the wall. For all mobs are so far chivalrous that their heroes must make some show of misfortune—that sort of hypocrisy is the homage that strength pays to weakness. He talks foolishly and yet very finely about his own city that has never deserted him. He wears a flaming and fantastic flower, like a decadent minor poet. As for his bluffness and toughness and appeals to common sense, all that is, of course, simply the first trick of rhetoric. He fronts his audiences with the venerable affectation of Mark Antony—

> "I am no orator, as Brutus is;
> But as you know me all, a plain blunt man."

It is the whole difference between the aim of the orator and the aim of any other artist, such as the poet or the sculptor. The aim of the sculptor is to convince us that he is a sculptor; the aim of the orator, is to convince us that he is not an orator. Once let Mr. Chamberlain be mistaken for a practical man, and his game is won. He has only to compose a theme on empire, and people will say that these plain men say great things on great occasions. He has only to drift in the large loose notions common to all artists of the second rank, and people will say that business men have the biggest ideals after all. All his schemes have ended in smoke; he has touched nothing that he did not confuse. About his figure there is a Celtic pathos; like the Gaels in Matthew Arnold's quotation, "he went forth to battle, but he always fell." He is a mountain of proposals, a mountain of failures; but still a mountain. And a mountain is always romantic.

There is another man in the modern world who might be called the antithesis of Mr. Chamberlain in every point, who is also a standing monument of the advantage of being misunderstood. Mr. Bernard Shaw is always represented by those who disagree with him, and, I fear, also (if such exist) by those who agree with him, as a capering humorist, a dazzling acrobat, a quick-change artist. It is said that he cannot be taken seriously, that he will defend anything or attack anything, that he will do anything to startle and amuse. All this is not only untrue, but it is, glaringly, the opposite of the truth; it is as wild as to say that Dickens had not the boisterous masculinity of Jane Austen. The whole force and triumph of Mr. Bernard Shaw lie in the fact that he is a thoroughly consistent man. So far from his power consisting in jumping through hoops or standing on his head, his power consists in holding his own fortress night and day. He puts the Shaw test rapidly and rigorously to everything that happens in heaven or earth. His standard never varies. The thing which weak-minded revolutionists and weak-minded Conservatives really hate (and fear) in him, is exactly this, that his scales, such as they are, are held even, and that his law, such as it is, is justly enforced. You may attack his principles, as I do; but I do not know of any instance in which you can attack their application. If he dislikes lawlessness, he dislikes the lawlessness of Socialists as much as that of Individualists. If he dislikes the fever of patriotism, he dislikes it in Boers and Irishmen as well as in Englishmen. If he dislikes the vows and bonds of marriage, he dislikes still more the fiercer bonds and wilder vows that are made by lawless love. If he laughs at the authority of priests, he laughs louder at the pomposity of men of science. If he condemns the irresponsibility of faith, he condemns with a sane consistency the equal irresponsibility of art. He has pleased all the bohemians by saying that women are equal to men; but he has infuriated them by suggesting that men are equal to women. He is almost mechanically just; he has something of the terrible quality of a machine. The man who is really wild and whirling, the man who is really fantastic and incalculable, is not Mr. Shaw, but the average Cabinet Minister. It is Sir Michael Hicks-Beach who jumps through hoops. It is Sir Henry Fowler who stands on his head. The solid and respectable statesman of that type does really leap from position to position; he is really ready to defend anything or nothing; he is really not to be taken seriously. I know perfectly well what Mr. Bernard Shaw will be saying thirty years hence; he will be saying what he has always said. If thirty years hence I meet Mr. Shaw, a reverent being with a silver beard sweeping the earth, and say to him, "One can never, of course, make a verbal attack upon a lady," the patriarch will lift his aged hand and fell me to the earth. We know, I say, what Mr. Shaw will be, saying thirty years hence. But is there any one so darkly read in stars and oracles that he will dare to predict what Mr. Asquith will be saying thirty years hence?

The truth is, that it is quite an error to suppose that absence of definite convictions gives the mind freedom and agility. A man who believes something is ready and witty, because he has all his weapons about him. He can apply his test in an instant. The man engaged in conflict with a man like Mr. Bernard Shaw may fancy he has ten faces; similarly a man engaged against a brilliant duellist may fancy that the sword of his foe has turned to ten swords in his hand. But this is not really because the man is playing with ten swords, it is because he is aiming very straight with one. Moreover, a man with a definite belief always appears bizarre, because he does not change with the world; he has climbed into a fixed star, and the earth whizzes below him like a zoetrope. Millions of mild black-coated men call themselves sane and sensible merely because they always catch the fashionable insanity, because they are hurried into madness after madness by the maelstrom of the world.

People accuse Mr. Shaw and many much sillier persons of "proving that black is white." But they never ask whether the current colour-language is always correct. Ordinary sensible phraseology sometimes calls black white, it certainly calls yellow white and green white and reddish-brown white. We call wine "white wine" which is as yellow as a Blue-coat boy's legs. We call grapes "white grapes" which are manifestly pale green. We give to the European, whose complexion is a sort of pink drab, the horrible title of a "white man"—a picture more blood-curdling than any spectre in Poe.

Now, it is undoubtedly true that if a man asked a waiter in a restaurant for a bottle of yellow wine and some greenish-yellow grapes, the waiter would think him mad. It is undoubtedly true that if a Government official, reporting on the Europeans in Burmah, said, "There are only two thousand pinkish men here" he would be accused of cracking jokes, and kicked out of his post. But it is equally obvious that both men would have come to grief through telling the strict truth. That too truthful man in the restaurant; that too truthful man in Burmah, is Mr. Bernard Shaw. He appears eccentric and grotesque because he will not accept the general belief that white is yellow. He has based all his brilliancy and solidity upon the hackneyed, but yet forgotten, fact that truth is stranger than fiction. Truth, of course, must of necessity be stranger than fiction, for we have made fiction to suit ourselves.

So much then a reasonable appreciation will find in Mr. Shaw to be bracing and excellent. He claims to see things as they are; and some things, at any rate, he does see as they are, which the whole of our civilization does not see at all. But in Mr. Shaw's realism there is something lacking, and that thing which is lacking is serious.

Mr. Shaw's old and recognized philosophy was that powerfully presented in "The Quintessence of Ibsenism." It was, in brief, that conservative ideals were bad, not because they were conservative, but because they were ideals. Every ideal prevented men from judging justly the particular case; every moral generalization oppressed the individual; the golden rule was there was no golden rule. And the objection to this is simply that it pretends to free men, but really restrains them from doing the only thing that men want to do. What is the good of telling a community that it has every liberty except the liberty to make laws? The liberty to make laws is what constitutes a free people. And what is the good of telling a man (or a philosopher) that he has every liberty except the liberty to make generalizations. Making generalizations is what makes him a man. In short, when Mr. Shaw forbids men to have strict moral ideals, he is acting like one who should forbid them to have children. The saying that "the golden rule is that there is no golden rule," can, indeed, be simply answered by being turned round. That there is no golden rule is itself a golden rule, or rather it is much worse than a golden rule. It is an iron rule; a fetter on the first movement of a man.

But the sensation connected with Mr. Shaw in recent years has been his sudden development of the religion of the Superman. He who had to all appearance mocked at the faiths in the forgotten past discovered a new god in the unimaginable future. He who had laid all the blame on ideals set up the most impossible of all ideals, the ideal of a new creature. But the truth, nevertheless, is that any one who knows Mr. Shaw's mind adequately, and admires it properly, must have guessed all this long ago.

For the truth is that Mr. Shaw has never seen things as they really are. If he had he would have fallen on his knees before them. He has always had a secret ideal that has withered all the things of this world. He has all the time been silently comparing humanity with something that was not human, with a monster from Mars, with the Wise Man of the Stoics, with the Economic Man of the Fabians, with Julius Caesar, with Siegfried, with the Superman. Now, to have this inner and merciless standard may be a very good thing, or a very bad one, it may be excellent or unfortunate, but it is not seeing things as they are. It is not seeing things as they are to think first of a Briareus with a hundred hands, and then call every man a cripple for only having two. It is not seeing things as they are to start with a vision of Argus with his hundred eyes, and then jeer at every man with two eyes as if he had only one. And it is not seeing things as they are to imagine a demigod of infinite mental clarity, who may or may not appear in the latter days of the earth, and then to see all men as idiots. And this is what Mr. Shaw has always in some degree done. When we really see men as they are, we do not criticise, but worship; and very rightly. For a monster with mysterious eyes and miraculous thumbs, with strange dreams in his skull, and a queer tenderness for this place or that baby, is truly a wonderful and unnerving matter. It is only the quite arbitrary and priggish habit of comparison with something else which makes it possible to be at our ease in front of him. A sentiment of superiority keeps us cool and practical; the mere facts would make our knees knock under as with religious fear. It is the fact that every instant of conscious life is an unimaginable prodigy. It is the fact that every face in the street has the incredible unexpectedness of a fairy-tale. The thing which prevents a man from realizing this is not any clear-sightedness or experience, it is simply a habit of pedantic and fastidious comparisons between one thing and another. Mr. Shaw, on the practical side perhaps the most humane man alive, is in this sense inhumane. He has even been infected to some extent with the primary intellectual weakness of his new master, Nietzsche, the strange notion that the greater and stronger a man was the more he would despise other things. The greater and stronger a man is the more he would be inclined to prostrate himself before a periwinkle. That Mr. Shaw keeps a lifted head and a contemptuous face before the colossal panorama of empires and civilizations, this does not in itself convince one that he sees things as they are. I should be most effectively convinced that he did if I found him staring with religious astonishment at his own feet. "What are those two beautiful and industrious beings," I can imagine him murmuring to himself, "whom I see everywhere, serving me I know not why? What fairy godmother bade them come trotting out of elfland when I was born? What god of the borderland, what barbaric god of legs, must I propitiate with fire and wine, lest they run away with me?"

The truth is, that all genuine appreciation rests on a certain mystery of humility and almost of darkness. The man who said, "Blessed is he that expecteth nothing, for he shall not be disappointed," put the eulogy quite inadequately and even falsely. The truth "Blessed is he that expecteth nothing, for he shall be gloriously surprised." The man who expects nothing sees redder roses than common men can see, and greener grass, and a more startling sun. Blessed is he that expecteth nothing, for he shall possess the cities and the mountains; blessed is the meek, for he shall inherit the earth. Until we realize that things might not be we cannot realize that things are. Until we see the background of darkness we cannot admire the light as a single and created thing. As soon as we have seen that darkness, all light is lightening, sudden, blinding, and divine. Until we picture nonentity we underrate the victory of God, and can realize none of the trophies of His ancient war. It is one of the million wild jests of truth that we know nothing until we know nothing.

Now this is, I say deliberately, the only defect in the greatness of Mr. Shaw, the only answer to his claim to be a great man, that he is not easily pleased. He is an almost solitary exception to the general and essential maxim, that little things please great minds. And from this absence of that most uproarious of all things, humility, comes incidentally the peculiar insistence on the Superman. After be-labouring a great many people for a great many years for being unprogressive, Mr. Shaw has discovered, with characteristic sense, that it is very doubtful whether any existing human being with two legs can be progressive at all. Having come to doubt whether humanity can be combined with progress, most people, easily pleased, would have elected to abandon progress and remain with humanity. Mr. Shaw, not being easily pleased, decides to throw over humanity with all its limitations and go in for progress for its own sake. If man, as we know him, is incapable of the philosophy of progress, Mr. Shaw asks, not for a new kind of philosophy, but for a new kind of man. It is rather as if a nurse had tried a rather bitter food for some years on a baby, and on discovering that it was not suitable, should not throw away the food and ask for a new food, but throw the baby out of window, and ask for a new baby. Mr. Shaw cannot understand that the thing which is valuable and lovable in our eyes is man—the old beer-drinking, creed-making, fighting, failing, sensual, respectable man. And the things that have been founded on this creature immortally remain; the things that have been founded on the fancy of the Superman have died with the dying civilizations which alone have given them birth. When Christ at a symbolic moment was establishing His great society, He chose for its corner-stone neither the brilliant Paul nor the mystic John, but a shuffler, a snob a coward—in a word, a man. And upon this rock He has built His Church, and the gates of Hell have not prevailed against it. All the empires and the kingdoms have failed, because of this inherent and continual weakness, that they were founded by strong men and upon strong men. But this one thing, the historic Christian Church, was founded on a weak man, and for that reason it is indestructible. For no chain is stronger than its weakest link.

Chapter 5
Mr. H. G. Wells and the Giants

e ought to see far enough into a hypocrite to see even his sincerity. We ought to be interested in that darkest and most real part of a man in which dwell not the vices that he does not display, but the virtues that he cannot. And the more we approach the problems of human history with this keen and piercing charity, the smaller and smaller space we shall allow to pure hypocrisy of any kind. The hypocrites shall not deceive us into thinking them saints; but neither shall they deceive us into thinking them hypocrites. And an increasing number of cases will crowd into our field of inquiry, cases in which there is really no question of hypocrisy at all, cases in which people were so ingenuous that they seemed absurd, and so absurd that they seemed disingenuous.

There is one striking instance of an unfair charge of hypocrisy. It is always urged against the religious in the past, as a point of inconsistency and duplicity, that they combined a profession of almost crawling humility with a keen struggle for earthly success and considerable triumph in attaining it. It is felt as a piece of humbug, that a man should be very punctilious in calling himself a miserable sinner, and also very punctilious in calling himself King of France. But the truth is that there is no more conscious inconsistency between the humility of a Christian and the rapacity of a Christian than there is between the humility of a lover and the rapacity of a lover. The truth is that there are no things for which men will make such herculean efforts as the things of which they know they are unworthy. There never was a man in love who did not declare that, if he strained every nerve to breaking, he was going to have his desire. And there never was a man in love who did not declare also that he ought not to have it. The whole secret of the practical success of Christendom lies in the Christian humility, however imperfectly fulfilled. For with the removal of all question of merit or payment, the soul is suddenly released for incredible voyages. If we ask a sane man how much he merits, his mind shrinks instinctively and instantaneously. It is doubtful whether he merits six feet of earth. But if you ask him what he can conquer—he can conquer the stars. Thus comes the thing called Romance, a purely Christian product. A man cannot deserve adventures; he cannot earn dragons and hippogriffs. The mediaeval Europe which asserted humility gained Romance; the civilization which gained Romance has gained the habitable globe. How different the Pagan and Stoical feeling was from this has been admirably expressed in a famous quotation. Addison makes the great Stoic say—

> " 'Tis not in mortals to command success;
> But we'll do more, Sempronius, we'll deserve it."

But the spirit of Romance and Christendom, the spirit which is in every lover, the spirit which has bestridden the earth with European adventure, is quite opposite. 'Tis not in mortals to deserve success. But we'll do more, Sempronius; we'll obtain it.

And this gay humility, this holding of ourselves lightly and yet ready for an infinity of unmerited triumphs, this secret is so simple that every one has supposed that it must be something quite sinister and mysterious. Humility is so practical a virtue that men think it must be a vice. Humility is so successful that it is mistaken for pride. It is mistaken for it all the more easily because it generally goes with a certain simple love of splendour which amounts to vanity. Humility will always, by preference, go clad in scarlet and gold; pride is that which refuses to let gold and scarlet impress it or please it too much. In a word, the failure of this virtue actually lies in its success; it is too successful as an investment to be believed in as a virtue. Humility is not merely too good for this world; it is too practical for this world; I had almost said it is too worldly for this world.

The instance most quoted in our day is the thing called the humility of the man of science; and certainly it is a good instance as well as a modern one. Men find it extremely difficult to believe that a man who is obviously uprooting mountains and dividing seas, tearing down temples and stretching out hands to the stars, is really a quiet old gentleman who only asks to be allowed to indulge his harmless old hobby and follow his harmless old nose. When a man splits a grain of sand and the universe is turned upside down in consequence, it is difficult to realize that to the man who did it, the splitting of the grain is the great affair, and the capsizing of the cosmos quite a small one. It is hard to enter into the feelings of a man who regards a new heaven and a new earth in the light of a by-product. But undoubtedly it was to this almost eerie innocence of the intellect that the great men of the great scientific period, which now appears to be closing, owed their enormous power and triumph. If they had brought the heavens down like a house of cards their plea was not even that they had done it on principle; their quite unanswerable plea was that they had done it by accident. Whenever there was in them the least touch of pride in what they had done, there was a good ground for attacking them; but so long as they were wholly humble, they were wholly victorious. There were possible answers to Huxley; there was no answer possible to Darwin. He was convincing because of his unconsciousness; one might almost say because of his dulness. This childlike and prosaic mind is beginning to wane in the world of science. Men of science are beginning to see themselves, as the fine phrase is, in the part; they are beginning to be proud of their humility. They are beginning to be aesthetic, like the rest of the world, beginning to spell truth with a capital T, beginning to talk of the creeds they imagine themselves to have destroyed, of the discoveries that their forbears made. Like the modern English, they are beginning to be soft about their own hardness. They are becoming conscious of their own strength—that is, they are growing weaker. But one purely modern man has emerged in the strictly modern decades who does carry into our world the clear personal simplicity of the old world of science. One man of genius we have who is an artist, but who was a man of science, and who seems to be marked above all things with this great scientific humility. I mean Mr. H. G. Wells. And in his case, as in the others above spoken of, there must be a great preliminary difficulty in convincing the ordinary person that such a virtue is predicable of such a man. Mr. Wells began his literary work with violent visions—visions of the last pangs of this planet; can it be that a man who begins with violent visions is humble? He went on to wilder and wilder stories about carving beasts into men and shooting angels like birds. Is the man who shoots angels and carves beasts into men humble? Since then he has done something bolder than either of these blasphemies; he has prophesied the political future of all men; prophesied it with aggressive authority and a ringing decision of detail. Is the prophet of the future of all men humble? It will indeed be difficult, in the present condition of current thought about such things as pride and humility, to answer the query of how a man can be humble who does such big things and such bold things. For the only answer is the answer which I gave at the beginning of this essay. It is the humble man who does the big things. It is the humble man who does the bold things. It is the humble man who has the sensational sights vouchsafed to him, and this for three obvious reasons: first, that he strains his eyes more than any other men to see them; second, that he is more overwhelmed and uplifted with them when they come; third, that he records them more exactly and sincerely and with less adulteration from his more commonplace and more conceited everyday self. Adventures are to those to whom they are most unexpected—that is, most romantic. Adventures are to the shy: in this sense adventures are to the unadventurous.

Now, this arresting, mental humility in Mr. H. G. Wells may be, like a great many other things that are vital and vivid, difficult to illustrate by examples, but if I were asked for an example of it, I should have no difficulty about which example to begin with. The most interesting thing about Mr. H. G. Wells is that he is the only one of his many brilliant contemporaries who has not stopped growing. One can lie awake at night and hear him grow. Of this growth the most evident manifestation is indeed a gradual change of opinions; but it is no mere change of opinions. It is not a perpetual leaping from one position to another like that of Mr. George Moore. It is a quite continuous advance along a quite solid road in a quite definable direction. But the chief proof that it is not a piece of fickleness and vanity is the fact that it has been upon the whole an advance from more startling opinions to more humdrum opinions. It has been even in some sense an advance from unconventional opinions to conventional opinions. This fact fixes Mr. Wells's honesty and proves him to be no poseur. Mr. Wells once held that the upper classes and the lower classes would be so much differentiated in the future that one class would eat the other. Certainly no paradoxical charlatan who had once found arguments for so startling a view would ever have deserted it except for something yet more startling. Mr. Wells has deserted it in favour of the blameless belief that both classes will be ultimately subordinated or assimilated to a sort of scientific middle class, a class of engineers. He has abandoned the sensational theory with the same honourable gravity and simplicity with which he adopted it. Then he thought it was true; now he thinks it is not true. He has come to the most dreadful conclusion a literary man can come to, the conclusion that the ordinary view is the right one. It is only the last and wildest kind of courage that can stand on a tower before ten thousand people and tell them that twice two is four.

Mr. H. G. Wells exists at present in a gay and exhilarating progress of conservativism. He is finding out more and more that conventions, though silent, are alive. As good an example as any of this humility and sanity of his may be found in his change of view on the subject of science and marriage. He once held, I believe, the opinion which some singular sociologists still hold, that human creatures could successfully be paired and bred after the manner of dogs or horses. He no longer holds that view. Not only does he no longer hold that view, but he has written about it in "Mankind in the Making" with such smashing sense and humour, that I find it difficult to believe that anybody else can hold it either. It is true that his chief objection to the proposal is that it is physically impossible, which seems to me a very slight objection, and almost negligible compared with the others. The one objection to scientific marriage which is worthy of final attention is simply that such a thing could only be imposed on unthinkable slaves and cowards. I do not know whether the scientific marriage-mongers are right (as they say) or wrong (as Mr. Wells says) in saying that medical supervision would produce strong and healthy men. I am only certain that if it did, the first act of the strong and healthy men would be to smash the medical supervision.

The mistake of all that medical talk lies in the very fact that it connects the idea of health with the idea of care. What has health to do with care? Health has to do with carelessness. In special and abnormal cases it is necessary to have care. When we are peculiarly unhealthy it may be necessary to be careful in order to be healthy. But even then we are only trying to be healthy in order to be careless. If we are doctors we are speaking to exceptionally sick men, and they ought to be told to be careful. But when we are sociologists we are addressing the normal man, we are addressing humanity. And humanity ought to be told to be recklessness itself. For all the fundamental functions of a healthy man ought emphatically to be performed with pleasure and for pleasure; they emphatically ought not to be performed with precaution or for precaution. A man ought to eat because he has a good appetite to satisfy, and emphatically not because he has a body to sustain. A man ought to take exercise not because he is too fat, but because he loves foils or horses or high mountains, and loves them for their own sake. And a man ought to marry because he has fallen in love, and emphatically not because the world requires to be populated. The food will really renovate his tissues as long as he is not thinking about his tissues. The exercise will really get him into training so long as he is thinking about something else. And the marriage will really stand some chance of producing a generous-blooded generation if it had its origin in its own natural and generous excitement. It is the first law of health that our necessities should not be accepted as necessities; they should be accepted as luxuries. Let us, then, be careful about the small things, such as a scratch or a slight illness, or anything that can be managed with care. But in the name of all sanity, let us be careless about the important things, such as marriage, or the fountain of our very life will fail.

Mr. Wells, however, is not quite clear enough of the narrower scientific outlook to see that there are some things which actually ought not to be scientific. He is still slightly affected with the great scientific fallacy; I mean the habit of beginning not with the human soul, which is the first thing a man learns about, but with some such thing as protoplasm, which is about the last. The one defect in his splendid mental equipment is that he does not sufficiently allow for the stuff or material of men. In his new Utopia he says, for instance, that a chief point of the Utopia will be a disbelief in original sin. If he had begun with the human soul—that is, if he had begun on himself—he would have found original sin almost the first thing to be believed in. He would have found, to put the matter shortly, that a permanent possibility of selfishness arises from the mere fact of having a self, and not from any accidents of education or ill-treatment. And the weakness of all Utopias is this, that they take the greatest difficulty of man and assume it to be overcome, and then give an elaborate account of the overcoming of the smaller ones. They first assume that no man will want more than his share, and then are very ingenious in explaining whether his share will be delivered by motor-car or balloon. And an even stronger example of Mr. Wells's indifference to the human psychology can be found in his cosmopolitanism, the abolition in his Utopia of all patriotic boundaries. He says in his innocent way that Utopia must be a world-state, or else people might make war on it. It does not seem to occur to him that, for a good many of us, if it were a world-state we should still make war on it to the end of the world. For if we admit that there must be varieties in art or opinion what sense is there in thinking there will not be varieties in government? The fact is very simple. Unless you are going deliberately to prevent a thing being good, you cannot prevent it being worth fighting for. It is impossible to prevent a possible conflict of civilizations, because it is impossible to prevent a possible conflict between ideals. If there were no longer our modern strife between nations, there would only be a strife between Utopias. For the highest thing does not tend to union only; the highest thing, tends also to differentiation. You can often get men to fight for the union; but you can never prevent them from fighting also for the differentiation. This variety in the highest thing is the meaning of the fierce patriotism, the fierce nationalism of the great European civilization. It is also, incidentally, the meaning of the doctrine of the Trinity.

But I think the main mistake of Mr. Wells's philosophy is a somewhat deeper one, one that he expresses in a very entertaining manner in the introductory part of the new Utopia. His philosophy in some sense amounts to a denial of the possibility of philosophy itself. At least, he maintains that there are no secure and reliable ideas upon which we can rest with a final mental satisfaction. It will be both clearer, however, and more amusing to quote Mr. Wells himself.

He says, "Nothing endures, nothing is precise and certain (except the mind of a pedant) ... Being indeed!—there is no being, but a universal becoming of individualities, and Plato turned his back on truth when he turned towards his museum of specific ideals." Mr. Wells says, again, "There is no abiding thing in what we know. We change from weaker to stronger lights, and each more powerful light pierces our hitherto opaque foundations and reveals fresh and different opacities below." Now, when Mr. Wells says things like this, I speak with all respect when I say that he does not observe an evident mental distinction. It cannot be true that there is nothing abiding in what we know. For if that were so we should not know it all and should not call it knowledge. Our mental state may be very different from that of somebody else some thousands of years back; but it cannot be entirely different, or else we should not be conscious of a difference. Mr. Wells must surely realize the first and simplest of the paradoxes that sit by the springs of truth. He must surely see that the fact of two things being different implies that they are similar. The hare and the tortoise may differ in the quality of swiftness, but they must agree in the quality of motion. The swiftest hare cannot be swifter than an isosceles triangle or the idea of pinkness. When we say the hare moves faster, we say that the tortoise moves. And when we say of a thing that it moves, we say, without need of other words, that there are things that do not move. And even in the act of saying that things change, we say that there is something unchangeable.

But certainly the best example of Mr. Wells's fallacy can be found in the example which he himself chooses. It is quite true that we see a dim light which, compared with a darker thing, is light, but which, compared with a stronger light, is darkness. But the quality of light remains the same thing, or else we should not call it a stronger light or recognize it as such. If the character of light were not fixed in the mind, we should be quite as likely to call a denser shadow a stronger light, or vice versa If the character of light became even for an instant unfixed, if it became even by a hair's-breadth doubtful, if, for example, there crept into our idea of light some vague idea of blueness, then in that flash we have become doubtful whether the new light has more light or less. In brief, the progress may be as varying as a cloud, but the direction must be as rigid as a French road. North and South are relative in the sense that I am North of Bournemouth and South of Spitzbergen. But if there be any doubt of the position of the North Pole, there is in equal degree a doubt of whether I am South of Spitzbergen at all. The absolute idea of light may be practically unattainable. We may not be able to procure pure light. We may not be able to get to the North Pole. But because the North Pole is unattainable, it does not follow that it is indefinable. And it is only because the North Pole is not indefinable that we can make a satisfactory map of Brighton and Worthing.

In other words, Plato turned his face to truth but his back on Mr. H. G. Wells, when he turned to his museum of specified ideals. It is precisely here that Plato shows his sense. It is not true that everything changes; the things that change are all the manifest and material things. There is something that does not change; and that is precisely the abstract quality, the invisible idea. Mr. Wells says truly enough, that a thing which we have seen in one connection as dark we may see in another connection as light. But the thing common to both incidents is the mere idea of light—which we have not seen at all. Mr. Wells might grow taller and taller for unending aeons till his head was higher than the loneliest star. I can imagine his writing a good novel about it. In that case he would see the trees first as tall things and then as short things; he would see the clouds first as high and then as low. But there would remain with him through the ages in that starry loneliness the idea of tallness; he would have in the awful spaces for companion and comfort the definite conception that he was growing taller and not (for instance) growing fatter.

And now it comes to my mind that Mr. H. G. Wells actually has written a very delightful romance about men growing as tall as trees; and that here, again, he seems to me to have been a victim of this vague relativism. "The Food of the Gods" is, like Mr. Bernard Shaw's play, in essence a study of the Superman idea. And it lies, I think, even through the veil of a half-pantomimic allegory, open to the same intellectual attack. We cannot be expected to have any regard for a great creature if he does not in any manner conform to our standards. For unless he passes our standard of greatness we cannot even call him great. Nietzsche summed up all that is interesting in the Superman idea when he said, "Man is a thing which has to be surpassed." But the very word "surpass" implies the existence of a standard common to us and the thing surpassing us. If the Superman is more manly than men are, of course they will ultimately deify him, even if they happen to kill him first. But if he is simply more supermanly, they may be quite indifferent to him as they would be to another seemingly aimless monstrosity. He must submit to our test even in order to overawe us. Mere force or size even is a standard; but that alone will never make men think a man their superior. Giants, as in the wise old fairy-tales, are vermin. Supermen, if not good men, are vermin.

"The Food of the Gods" is the tale of "Jack the Giant-Killer" told from the point of view of the giant. This has not, I think, been done before in literature; but I have little doubt that the psychological substance of it existed in fact. I have little doubt that the giant whom Jack killed did regard himself as the Superman. It is likely enough that he considered Jack a narrow and parochial person who wished to frustrate a great forward movement of the life-force. If (as not unfrequently was the case) he happened to have two heads, he would point out the elementary maxim which declares them to be better than one. He would enlarge on the subtle modernity of such an equipment, enabling a giant to look at a subject from two points of view, or to correct himself with promptitude. But Jack was the champion of the enduring human standards, of the principle of one man one head and one man one conscience, of the single head and the single heart and the single eye. Jack was quite unimpressed by the question of whether the giant was a particularly gigantic giant. All he wished to know was whether he was a good giant—that is, a giant who was any good to us. What were the giant's religious views; what his views on politics and the duties of the citizen? Was he fond of children—or fond of them only in a dark and sinister sense? To use a fine phrase for emotional sanity, was his heart in the right place? Jack had sometimes to cut him up with a sword in order to find out. The old and correct story of Jack the Giant-Killer is simply the whole story of man; if it were understood we should need no Bibles or histories. But the modern world in particular does not seem to understand it at all. The modern world, like Mr. Wells is on the side of the giants; the safest place, and therefore the meanest and the most prosaic. The modern world, when it praises its little Caesars, talks of being strong and brave: but it does not seem to see the eternal paradox involved in the conjunction of these ideas. The strong cannot be brave. Only the weak can be brave; and yet again, in practice, only those who can be brave can be trusted, in time of doubt, to be strong. The only way in which a giant could really keep himself in training against the inevitable Jack would be by continually fighting other giants ten times as big as himself. That is by ceasing to be a giant and becoming a Jack. Thus that sympathy with the small or the defeated as such, with which we Liberals and Nationalists have been often reproached, is not a useless sentimentalism at all, as Mr. Wells and his friends fancy. It is the first law of practical courage. To be in the weakest camp is to be in the strongest school. Nor can I imagine anything that would do humanity more good than the advent of a race of Supermen, for them to fight like dragons. If the Superman is better than we, of course we need not fight him; but in that case, why not call him the Saint? But if he is merely stronger (whether physically, mentally, or morally stronger, I do not care a farthing), then he ought to have to reckon with us at least for all the strength we have. If we are weaker than he, that is no reason why we should be weaker than ourselves. If we are not tall enough to touch the giant's knees, that is no reason why we should become shorter by falling on our own. But that is at bottom the meaning of all modern hero-worship and celebration of the Strong Man, the Caesar the Superman. That he may be something more than man, we must be something less.

Doubtless there is an older and better hero-worship than this. But the old hero was a being who, like Achilles, was more human than humanity itself. Nietzsche's Superman is cold and friendless. Achilles is so foolishly fond of his friend that he slaughters armies in the agony of his bereavement. Mr. Shaw's sad Caesar says in his desolate pride, "He who has never hoped can never despair." The Man-God of old answers from his awful hill, "Was ever sorrow like unto my sorrow?" A great man is not a man so strong that he feels less than other men; he is a man so strong that he feels more. And when Nietzsche says, "A new commandment I give to you, 'be hard,'" he is really saying, "A new commandment I give to you, 'be dead.'" Sensibility is the definition of life.

I recur for a last word to Jack the Giant-Killer. I have dwelt on this matter of Mr. Wells and the giants, not because it is specially prominent in his mind; I know that the Superman does not bulk so large in his cosmos as in that of Mr. Bernard Shaw. I have dwelt on it for the opposite reason; because this heresy of immoral hero-worship has taken, I think, a slighter hold of him, and may perhaps still be prevented from perverting one of the best thinkers of the day. In the course of "The New Utopia" Mr. Wells makes more than one admiring allusion to Mr. W. E. Henley. That clever and unhappy man lived in admiration of a vague violence, and was always going back to rude old tales and rude old ballads, to strong and primitive literatures, to find the praise of strength and the justification of tyranny. But he could not find it. It is not there. The primitive literature is shown in the tale of Jack the Giant-Killer. The strong old literature is all in praise of the weak. The rude old tales are as tender to minorities as any modern political idealist. The rude old ballads are as sentimentally concerned for the under-dog as the Aborigines Protection Society. When men were tough and raw, when they lived amid hard knocks and hard laws, when they knew what fighting really was, they had only two kinds of songs. The first was a rejoicing that the weak had conquered the strong, the second a lamentation that the strong had, for once in a way, conquered the weak. For this defiance of the statu quo, this constant effort to alter the existing balance, this premature challenge to the powerful, is the whole nature and inmost secret of the psychological adventure which is called man. It is his strength to disdain strength. The forlorn hope is not only a real hope, it is the only real hope of mankind. In the coarsest ballads of the greenwood men are admired most when they defy, not only the king, but what is more to the point, the hero. The moment Robin Hood becomes a sort of Superman, that moment the chivalrous chronicler shows us Robin thrashed by a poor tinker whom he thought to thrust aside. And the chivalrous chronicler makes Robin Hood receive the thrashing in a glow of admiration. This magnanimity is not a product of modern humanitarianism; it is not a product of anything to do with peace. This magnanimity is merely one of the lost arts of war. The Henleyites call for a sturdy and fighting England, and they go back to the fierce old stories of the sturdy and fighting English. And the thing that they find written across that fierce old literature everywhere, is "the policy of Majuba."

Chapter 6
Christmas and the Aesthetes

he world is round, so round that the schools of optimism and pessimism have been arguing from the beginning whether it is the right way up. The difficulty does not arise so much from the mere fact that good and evil are mingled in roughly equal proportions; it arises chiefly from the fact that men always differ about what parts are good and what evil. Hence the difficulty which besets "undenominational religions." They profess to include what is beautiful in all creeds, but they appear to many to have collected all that is dull in them. All the colours mixed together in purity ought to make a perfect white. Mixed together on any human paint-box, they make a thing like mud, and a thing very like many new religions. Such a blend is often something much worse than any one creed taken separately, even the creed of the Thugs. The error arises from the difficulty of detecting what is really the good part and what is really the bad part of any given religion. And this pathos falls rather heavily on those persons who have the misfortune to think of some religion or other, that the parts commonly counted good are bad, and the parts commonly counted bad are good.

It is tragic to admire and honestly admire a human group, but to admire it in a photographic negative. It is difficult to congratulate all their whites on being black and all their blacks on their whiteness. This will often happen to us in connection with human religions. Take two institutions which bear witness to the religious energy of the nineteenth century. Take the Salvation Army and the philosophy of Auguste Comte.

The usual verdict of educated people on the Salvation Army is expressed in some such words as these: "I have no doubt they do a great deal of good, but they do it in a vulgar and profane style; their aims are excellent, but their methods are wrong." To me, unfortunately, the precise reverse of this appears to be the truth. I do not know whether the aims of the Salvation Army are excellent, but I am quite sure their methods are admirable. Their methods are the methods of all intense and hearty religions; they are popular like all religion, military like all religion, public and sensational like all religion. They are not reverent any more than Roman Catholics are reverent, for reverence in the sad and delicate meaning of the term reverence is a thing only possible to infidels. That beautiful twilight you will find in Euripides, in Renan, in Matthew Arnold; but in men who believe you will not find it—you will find only laughter and war. A man cannot pay that kind of reverence to truth solid as marble; they can only be reverent towards a beautiful lie. And the Salvation Army, though their voice has broken out in a mean environment and an ugly shape, are really the old voice of glad and angry faith, hot as the riots of Dionysus, wild as the gargoyles of Catholicism, not to be mistaken for a philosophy. Professor Huxley, in one of his clever phrases, called the Salvation Army "corybantic Christianity." Huxley was the last and noblest of those Stoics who have never understood the Cross. If he had understood Christianity he would have known that there never has been, and never can be, any Christianity that is not corybantic.

And there is this difference between the matter of aims and the matter of methods, that to judge of the aims of a thing like the Salvation Army is very difficult, to judge of their ritual and atmosphere very easy. No one, perhaps, but a sociologist can see whether General Booth's housing scheme is right. But any healthy person can see that banging brass cymbals together must be right. A page of statistics, a plan of model dwellings, anything which is rational, is always difficult for the lay mind. But the thing which is irrational any one can understand. That is why religion came so early into the world and spread so far, while science came so late into the world and has not spread at all. History unanimously attests the fact that it is only mysticism which stands the smallest chance of being understanded of the people. Common sense has to be kept as an esoteric secret in the dark temple of culture. And so while the philanthropy of the Salvationists and its genuineness may be a reasonable matter for the discussion of the doctors, there can be no doubt about the genuineness of their brass bands, for a brass band is purely spiritual, and seeks only to quicken the internal life. The object of philanthropy is to do good; the object of religion is to be good, if only for a moment, amid a crash of brass.

And the same antithesis exists about another modern religion—I mean the religion of Comte, generally known as Positivism, or the worship of humanity. Such men as Mr. Frederic Harrison, that brilliant and chivalrous philosopher, who still, by his mere personality, speaks for the creed, would tell us that he offers us the philosophy of Comte, but not all Comte's fantastic proposals for pontiffs and ceremonials, the new calendar, the new holidays and saints' days. He does not mean that we should dress ourselves up as priests of humanity or let off fireworks because it is Milton's birthday. To the solid English Comtist all this appears, he confesses, to be a little absurd. To me it appears the only sensible part of Comtism. As a philosophy it is unsatisfactory. It is evidently impossible to worship humanity, just as it is impossible to worship the Savile Club; both are excellent institutions to which we may happen to belong. But we perceive clearly that the Savile Club did not make the stars and does not fill the universe. And it is surely unreasonable to attack the doctrine of the Trinity as a piece of bewildering mysticism, and then to ask men to worship a being who is ninety million persons in one God, neither confounding the persons nor dividing the substance.

But if the wisdom of Comte was insufficient, the folly of Comte was wisdom. In an age of dusty modernity, when beauty was thought of as something barbaric and ugliness as something sensible, he alone saw that men must always have the sacredness of mummery. He saw that while the brutes have all the useful things, the things that are truly human are the useless ones. He saw the falsehood of that almost universal notion of to-day, the notion that rites and forms are something artificial, additional, and corrupt. Ritual is really much older than thought; it is much simpler and much wilder than thought. A feeling touching the nature of things does not only make men feel that there are certain proper things to say; it makes them feel that there are certain proper things to do. The more agreeable of these consist of dancing, building temples, and shouting very loud; the less agreeable, of wearing green carnations and burning other philosophers alive. But everywhere the religious dance came before the religious hymn, and man was a ritualist before he could speak. If Comtism had spread the world would have been converted, not by the Comtist philosophy, but by the Comtist calendar. By discouraging what they conceive to be the weakness of their master, the English Positivists have broken the strength of their religion. A man who has faith must be prepared not only to be a martyr, but to be a fool. It is absurd to say that a man is ready to toil and die for his convictions when he is not even ready to wear a wreath round his head for them. I myself, to take a corpus vile, am very certain that I would not read the works of Comte through for any consideration whatever. But I can easily imagine myself with the greatest enthusiasm lighting a bonfire on Darwin Day.

That splendid effort failed, and nothing in the style of it has succeeded. There has been no rationalist festival, no rationalist ecstasy. Men are still in black for the death of God. When Christianity was heavily bombarded in the last century upon no point was it more persistently and brilliantly attacked than upon that of its alleged enmity to human joy. Shelley and Swinburne and all their armies have passed again and again over the ground, but they have not altered it. They have not set up a single new trophy or ensign for the world's merriment to rally to. They have not given a name or a new occasion of gaiety. Mr. Swinburne does not hang up his stocking on the eve of the birthday of Victor Hugo. Mr. William Archer does not sing carols descriptive of the infancy of Ibsen outside people's doors in the snow. In the round of our rational and mournful year one festival remains out of all those ancient gaieties that once covered the whole earth. Christmas remains to remind us of those ages, whether Pagan or Christian, when the many acted poetry instead of the few writing it. In all the winter in our woods there is no tree in glow but the holly.

The strange truth about the matter is told in the very word "holiday." A bank holiday means presumably a day which bankers regard as holy. A half-holiday means, I suppose, a day on which a schoolboy is only partially holy. It is hard to see at first sight why so human a thing as leisure and larkiness should always have a religious origin. Rationally there appears no reason why we should not sing and give each other presents in honour of anything—the birth of Michael Angelo or the opening of Euston Station. But it does not work. As a fact, men only become greedily and gloriously material about something spiritualistic. Take away the Nicene Creed and similar things, and you do some strange wrong to the sellers of sausages. Take away the strange beauty of the saints, and what has remained to us is the far stranger ugliness of Wandsworth. Take away the supernatural, and what remains is the unnatural.

And now I have to touch upon a very sad matter. There are in the modern world an admirable class of persons who really make protest on behalf of that *antiqua pulchritudo* of which Augustine spoke, who do long for the old feasts and formalities of the childhood of the world. William Morris and his followers showed how much brighter were the dark ages than the age of Manchester. Mr. W. B. Yeats frames his steps in prehistoric dances, but no man knows and joins his voice to forgotten choruses that no one but he can hear. Mr. George Moore collects every fragment of Irish paganism that the forgetfulness of the Catholic Church has left or possibly her wisdom preserved. There are innumerable persons with eye-glasses and green garments who pray for the return of the maypole or the Olympian games. But there is about these people a haunting and alarming something which suggests that it is just possible that they do not keep Christmas. It is painful to regard human nature in such a light, but it seems somehow possible that Mr. George Moore does not wave his spoon and shout when the pudding is set alight. It is even possible that Mr. W. B. Yeats never pulls crackers. If so, where is the sense of all their dreams of festive traditions? Here is a solid and ancient festive tradition still plying a roaring trade in the streets, and they think it vulgar. if this is so, let them be very certain of this, that they are the kind of people who in the time of the maypole would have thought the maypole vulgar; who in the time of the Canterbury pilgrimage would have thought the Canterbury pilgrimage vulgar; who in the time of the Olympian games would have thought the Olympian games vulgar. Nor can there be any reasonable doubt that they were vulgar. Let no man deceive himself; if by vulgarity we mean coarseness of speech, rowdiness of behaviour, gossip, horseplay, and some heavy drinking, vulgarity there always was wherever there was joy, wherever there was faith in the gods. Wherever you have belief you will have hilarity, wherever you have hilarity you will have some dangers. And as creed and mythology produce this gross and vigorous life, so in its turn this gross and vigorous life will always produce creed and mythology. If we ever get the English back on to the English land they will become again a religious people, if all goes well, a superstitious people. The absence from modern life of both the higher and lower forms of faith is largely due to a divorce from nature and the trees and clouds. If we have no more turnip ghosts it is chiefly from the lack of turnips.

Chapter 7
Omar and the Sacred Vine

new morality has burst upon us with some violence in connection with the problem of strong drink; and enthusiasts in the matter range from the man who is violently thrown out at 12.30, to the lady who smashes American bars with an axe. In these discussions it is almost always felt that one very wise and moderate position is to say that wine or such stuff should only be drunk as a medicine. With this I should venture to disagree with a peculiar ferocity. The one genuinely dangerous and immoral way of drinking wine is to drink it as a medicine. And for this reason, If a man drinks wine in order to obtain pleasure, he is trying to obtain something exceptional, something he does not expect every hour of the day, something which, unless he is a little insane, he will not try to get every hour of the day. But if a man drinks wine in order to obtain health, he is trying to get something natural; something, that is, that he ought not to be without; something that he may find it difficult to reconcile himself to being without. The man may not be seduced who has seen the ecstasy of being ecstatic; it is more dazzling to catch a glimpse of the ecstasy of being ordinary. If there were a magic ointment, and we took it to a strong man, and said, "This will enable you to jump off the Monument," doubtless he would jump off the Monument, but he would not jump off the Monument all day long to the delight of the City. But if we took it to a blind man, saying, "This will enable you to see," he would be under a heavier temptation. It would be hard for him not to rub it on his eyes whenever he heard the hoof of a noble horse or the birds singing at daybreak. It is easy to deny one's self festivity; it is difficult to deny one's self normality. Hence comes the fact which every doctor knows, that it is often perilous to give alcohol to the sick even when they need it. I need hardly say that I do not mean that I think the giving of alcohol to the sick for stimulus is necessarily unjustifiable. But I do mean that giving it to the healthy for fun is the proper use of it, and a great deal more consistent with health.

The sound rule in the matter would appear to be like many other sound rules—a paradox. Drink because you are happy, but never because you are miserable. Never drink when you are wretched without it, or you will be like the grey-faced gin-drinker in the slum; but drink when you would be happy without it, and you will be like the laughing peasant of Italy. Never drink because you need it, for this is rational drinking, and the way to death and hell. But drink because you do not need it, for this is irrational drinking, and the ancient health of the world.

For more than thirty years the shadow and glory of a great Eastern figure has lain upon our English literature. Fitzgerald's translation of Omar Khayyam concentrated into an immortal poignancy all the dark and drifting hedonism of our time. Of the literary splendour of that work it would be merely banal to speak;

in few other of the books of men has there been anything so combining the gay
pugnacity of an epigram with the vague sadness of a song. But of its philosophical,
ethical, and religious influence which has been almost as great as its brilliancy,
I should like to say a word, and that word, I confess, one of uncompromising
hostility. There are a great many things which might be said against the spirit of
the Rubaiyat, and against its prodigious influence. But one matter of indictment
towers ominously above the rest—a genuine disgrace to it, a genuine calamity to
us. This is the terrible blow that this great poem has struck against sociability and
the joy of life. Some one called Omar "the sad, glad old Persian." Sad he is; glad
he is not, in any sense of the word whatever. He has been a worse foe to gladness
than the Puritans.

A pensive and graceful Oriental lies under the rose-tree with his wine-pot
and his scroll of poems. It may seem strange that any one's thoughts should, at
the moment of regarding him, fly back to the dark bedside where the doctor
doles out brandy. It may seem stranger still that they should go back to the grey
wastrel shaking with gin in Houndsditch. But a great philosophical unity links
the three in an evil bond. Omar Khayyam's wine-bibbing is bad, not because it is
wine-bibbing. It is bad, and very bad, because it is medical wine-bibbing. It is the
drinking of a man who drinks because he is not happy. His is the wine that shuts
out the universe, not the wine that reveals it. It is not poetical drinking, which is
joyous and instinctive; it is rational drinking, which is as prosaic as an investment,
as unsavoury as a dose of camomile. Whole heavens above it, from the point of
view of sentiment, though not of style, rises the splendour of some old English
drinking-song—

> "Then pass the bowl, my comrades all,
> And let the zider vlow."

For this song was caught up by happy men to express the worth of truly
worthy things, of brotherhood and garrulity, and the brief and kindly leisure of
the poor. Of course, the great part of the more stolid reproaches directed against
the Omarite morality are as false and babyish as such reproaches usually are. One
critic, whose work I have read, had the incredible foolishness to call Omar an
atheist and a materialist. It is almost impossible for an Oriental to be either; the
East understands metaphysics too well for that. Of course, the real objection
which a philosophical Christian would bring against the religion of Omar, is not
that he gives no place to God, it is that he gives too much place to God. His is
that terrible theism which can imagine nothing else but deity, and which denies
altogether the outlines of human personality and human will.

> "The ball no question makes of Ayes or Noes,
> But Here or There as strikes the Player goes;
> And He that tossed you down into the field,
> He knows about it all—he knows—he knows."

A Christian thinker such as Augustine or Dante would object to this because it ignores freewill, which is the valour and dignity of the soul. The quarrel of the highest Christianity with this scepticism is not in the least that the scepticism denies the existence of God; it is that it denies the existence of man.

In this cult of the pessimistic pleasure-seeker the Rubaiyat stands first in our time; but it does not stand alone. Many of the most brilliant intellects of our time have urged us to the same self-conscious snatching at a rare delight. Walter Pater said that we were all under sentence of death, and the only course was to enjoy exquisite moments simply for those moments' sake. The same lesson was taught by the very powerful and very desolate philosophy of Oscar Wilde. It is the carpe diem religion; but the carpe diem religion is not the religion of happy people, but of very unhappy people. Great joy does, not gather the rosebuds while it may; its eyes are fixed on the immortal rose which Dante saw. Great joy has in it the sense of immortality; the very splendour of youth is the sense that it has all space to stretch its legs in. In all great comic literature, in "Tristram Shandy" or "Pickwick", there is this sense of space and incorruptibility; we feel the characters are deathless people in an endless tale.

It is true enough, of course, that a pungent happiness comes chiefly in certain passing moments; but it is not true that we should think of them as passing, or enjoy them simply "for those moments' sake." To do this is to rationalize the happiness, and therefore to destroy it. Happiness is a mystery like religion, and should never be rationalized. Suppose a man experiences a really splendid moment of pleasure. I do not mean something connected with a bit of enamel, I mean something with a violent happiness in it—an almost painful happiness. A man may have, for instance, a moment of ecstasy in first love, or a moment of victory in battle. The lover enjoys the moment, but precisely not for the moment's sake. He enjoys it for the woman's sake, or his own sake. The warrior enjoys the moment, but not for the sake of the moment; he enjoys it for the sake of the flag. The cause which the flag stands for may be foolish and fleeting; the love may be calf-love, and last a week. But the patriot thinks of the flag as eternal; the lover thinks of his love as something that cannot end. These moments are filled with eternity; these moments are joyful because they do not seem momentary. Once look at them as moments after Pater's manner, and they become as cold as Pater and his style. Man cannot love mortal things. He can only love immortal things for an instant.

Pater's mistake is revealed in his most famous phrase. He asks us to burn with a hard, gem-like flame. Flames are never hard and never gem-like—they cannot be handled or arranged. So human emotions are never hard and never gem-like; they are always dangerous, like flames, to touch or even to examine. There is only one way in which our passions can become hard and gem-like, and that is by becoming as cold as gems. No blow then has ever been struck at the natural loves and laughter of men so sterilizing as this *carpe diem* of the aesthetes. For any kind of pleasure a totally different spirit is required; a certain shyness, a

certain indeterminate hope, a certain boyish expectation. Purity and simplicity
are essential to passions—yes even to evil passions. Even vice demands a sort of
virginity.

Omar's (or Fitzgerald's) effect upon the other world we may let go, his hand
upon this world has been heavy and paralyzing. The Puritans, as I have said, are far
jollier than he. The new ascetics who follow Thoreau or Tolstoy are much livelier
company; for, though the surrender of strong drink and such luxuries may strike
us as an idle negation, it may leave a man with innumerable natural pleasures, and,
above all, with man's natural power of happiness. Thoreau could enjoy the sunrise
without a cup of coffee. If Tolstoy cannot admire marriage, at least he is healthy
enough to admire mud. Nature can be enjoyed without even the most natural
luxuries. A good bush needs no wine. But neither nature nor wine nor anything
else can be enjoyed if we have the wrong attitude towards happiness, and Omar
(or Fitzgerald) did have the wrong attitude towards happiness. He and those he
has influenced do not see that if we are to be truly gay, we must believe that there
is some eternal gaiety in the nature of things. We cannot enjoy thoroughly even a
pas-de-quatre at a subscription dance unless we believe that the stars are dancing
to the same tune. No one can be really hilarious but the serious man. "Wine,"
says the Scripture, "maketh glad the heart of man," but only of the man who has
a heart. The thing called high spirits is possible only to the spiritual. Ultimately a
man cannot rejoice in anything except the nature of things. Ultimately a man can
enjoy nothing except religion. Once in the world's history men did believe that
the stars were dancing to the tune of their temples, and they danced as men have
never danced since. With this old pagan eudaemonism the sage of the Rubaiyat has
quite as little to do as he has with any Christian variety. He is no more a Bacchanal
than he is a saint. Dionysus and his church was grounded on a serious *joie-de-vivre*
like that of Walt Whitman. Dionysus made wine, not a medicine, but a sacrament.
Jesus Christ also made wine, not a medicine, but a sacrament. But Omar makes
it, not a sacrament, but a medicine. He feasts because life is not joyful; he revels
because he is not glad. "Drink," he says, "for you know not whence you come
nor why. Drink, for you know not when you go nor where. Drink, because the
stars are cruel and the world as idle as a humming-top. Drink, because there is
nothing worth trusting, nothing worth fighting for. Drink, because all things are
lapsed in a base equality and an evil peace." So he stands offering us the cup in his
hand. And at the high altar of Christianity stands another figure, in whose hand
also is the cup of the vine. "Drink" he says "for the whole world is as red as this
wine, with the crimson of the love and wrath of God. Drink, for the trumpets are
blowing for battle and this is the stirrup-cup. Drink, for this my blood of the new
testament that is shed for you. Drink, for I know of whence you come and why.
Drink, for I know of when you go and where."

Chapter 8
The Mildness of the Yellow Press

here is a great deal of protest made from one quarter or another nowadays against the influence of that new journalism which is associated with the names of Sir Alfred Harmsworth and Mr. Pearson. But almost everybody who attacks it attacks on the ground that it is very sensational, very violent and vulgar and startling. I am speaking in no affected contrariety, but in the simplicity of a genuine personal impression, when I say that this journalism offends as being not sensational or violent enough. The real vice is not that it is startling, but that it is quite insupportably tame. The whole object is to keep carefully along a certain level of the expected and the commonplace; it may be low, but it must take care also to be flat. Never by any chance in it is there any of that real plebeian pungency which can be heard from the ordinary cabman in the ordinary street. We have heard of a certain standard of decorum which demands that things should be funny without being vulgar, but the standard of this decorum demands that if things are vulgar they shall be vulgar without being funny. This journalism does not merely fail to exaggerate life—it positively underrates it; and it has to do so because it is intended for the faint and languid recreation of men whom the fierceness of modern life has fatigued. This press is not the yellow press at all; it is the drab press. Sir Alfred Harmsworth must not address to the tired clerk any observation more witty than the tired clerk might be able to address to Sir Alfred Harmsworth. It must not expose anybody (anybody who is powerful, that is), it must not offend anybody, it must not even please anybody, too much. A general vague idea that in spite of all this, our yellow press is sensational, arises from such external accidents as large type or lurid headlines. It is quite true that these editors print everything they possibly can in large capital letters. But they do this, not because it is startling, but because it is soothing. To people wholly weary or partly drunk in a dimly lighted train, it is a simplification and a comfort to have things presented in this vast and obvious manner. The editors use this gigantic alphabet in dealing with their readers, for exactly the same reason that parents and governesses use a similar gigantic alphabet in teaching children to spell. The nursery authorities do not use an A as big as a horseshoe in order to make the child jump; on the contrary, they use it to put the child at his ease, to make things smoother and more evident. Of the same character is the dim and quiet dame school which Sir Alfred Harmsworth and Mr. Pearson keep. All their sentiments are spelling-book sentiments—that is to say, they are sentiments with which the pupil is already respectfully familiar. All their wildest posters are leaves torn from a copy-book.

Of real sensational journalism, as it exists in France, in Ireland, and in America, we have no trace in this country. When a journalist in Ireland wishes to create a thrill, he creates a thrill worth talking about. He denounces a leading Irish member for corruption, or he charges the whole police system with a wicked and definite conspiracy. When a French journalist desires a frisson there is a frisson; he discovers, let us say, that the President of the Republic has murdered three wives. Our yellow journalists invent quite as unscrupulously as this; their moral condition is, as regards careful veracity, about the same. But it is their mental calibre which happens to be such that they can only invent calm and even reassuring things. The fictitious version of the massacre of the envoys of Pekin was mendacious, but it was not interesting, except to those who had private reasons for terror or sorrow. It was not connected with any bold and suggestive view of the Chinese situation. It revealed only a vague idea that nothing could be impressive except a great deal of blood. Real sensationalism, of which I happen to be very fond, may be either moral or immoral. But even when it is most immoral, it requires moral courage. For it is one of the most dangerous things on earth genuinely to surprise anybody. If you make any sentient creature jump, you render it by no means improbable that it will jump on you. But the leaders of this movement have no moral courage or immoral courage; their whole method consists in saying, with large and elaborate emphasis, the things which everybody else says casually, and without remembering what they have said. When they brace themselves up to attack anything, they never reach the point of attacking anything which is large and real, and would resound with the shock. They do not attack the army as men do in France, or the judges as men do in Ireland, or the democracy itself as men did in England a hundred years ago. They attack something like the War Office—something, that is, which everybody attacks and nobody bothers to defend, something which is an old joke in fourth-rate comic papers. just as a man shows he has a weak voice by straining it to shout, so they show the hopelessly unsensational nature of their minds when they really try to be sensational. With the whole world full of big and dubious institutions, with the whole wickedness of civilization staring them in the face, their idea of being bold and bright is to attack the War Office. They might as well start a campaign against the weather, or form a secret society in order to make jokes about mothers-in-law. Nor is it only from the point of view of particular amateurs of the sensational such as myself, that it is permissible to say, in the words of Cowper's Alexander Selkirk, that "their tameness is shocking to me." The whole modern world is pining for a genuinely sensational journalism. This has been discovered by that very able and honest journalist, Mr. Blatchford, who started his campaign against Christianity, warned on all sides, I believe, that it would ruin his paper, but who continued from an honourable sense of intellectual responsibility. He discovered, however, that while he had undoubtedly shocked his readers, he had also greatly advanced his newspaper. It was bought—first, by all the people who agreed with him and wanted to read it; and secondly, by all the people who disagreed with him, and wanted to write him letters. Those letters were voluminous (I helped, I am glad to say, to swell their volume), and they were generally inserted with a generous fulness. Thus was accidentally discovered (like the steam-engine) the great journalistic maxim—that if an editor can only make people angry enough, they will write half his newspaper for him for nothing.

Some hold that such papers as these are scarcely the proper objects of so serious a consideration; but that can scarcely be maintained from a political or ethical point of view. In this problem of the mildness and tameness of the Harmsworth mind there is mirrored the outlines of a much larger problem which is akin to it.

The Harmsworthian journalist begins with a worship of success and violence, and ends in sheer timidity and mediocrity. But he is not alone in this, nor does he come by this fate merely because he happens personally to be stupid. Every man, however brave, who begins by worshipping violence, must end in mere timidity. Every man, however wise, who begins by worshipping success, must end in mere mediocrity. This strange and paradoxical fate is involved, not in the individual, but in the philosophy, in the point of view. It is not the folly of the man which brings about this necessary fall; it is his wisdom. The worship of success is the only one out of all possible worships of which this is true, that its followers are foredoomed to become slaves and cowards. A man may be a hero for the sake of Mrs. Gallup's ciphers or for the sake of human sacrifice, but not for the sake of success. For obviously a man may choose to fail because he loves Mrs. Gallup or human sacrifice; but he cannot choose to fail because he loves success. When the test of triumph is men's test of everything, they never endure long enough to triumph at all. As long as matters are really hopeful, hope is a mere flattery or platitude; it is only when everything is hopeless that hope begins to be a strength at all. Like all the Christian virtues, it is as unreasonable as it is indispensable.

It was through this fatal paradox in the nature of things that all these modern adventurers come at last to a sort of tedium and acquiescence. They desired strength; and to them to desire strength was to admire strength; to admire strength was simply to admire the statu quo. They thought that he who wished to be strong ought to respect the strong. They did not realize the obvious verity that he who wishes to be strong must despise the strong. They sought to be everything, to have the whole force of the cosmos behind them, to have an energy that would drive the stars. But they did not realize the two great facts—first, that in the attempt to be everything the first and most difficult step is to be something; second, that the moment a man is something, he is essentially defying everything. The lower animals, say the men of science, fought their way up with a blind selfishness. If this be so, the only real moral of it is that our unselfishness, if it is to triumph, must be equally blind. The mammoth did not put his head on one side and wonder whether mammoths were a little out of date. Mammoths were at least as much up to date as that individual mammoth could make them. The great elk did not say, "Cloven hoofs are very much worn now." He polished his own weapons for his own use. But in the reasoning animal there has arisen a more horrible danger, that he may fail through perceiving his own failure. When modern sociologists talk of the necessity of accommodating one's self to the trend of the time, they forget that the trend of the time at its best consists entirely of people who will not accommodate themselves to anything. At its worst it consists of many millions of frightened creatures all accommodating themselves to a trend that is not there. And that is becoming more and more the situation of modern England. Every man speaks of public opinion, and means by public opinion, public opinion minus his opinion. Every man makes his contribution negative under the erroneous impression that the next man's contribution is positive. Every man surrenders his fancy to a general tone which is itself a surrender. And over all the heartless and fatuous unity spreads this new and wearisome and platitudinous press, incapable of invention, incapable of audacity, capable only of a servility all the more contemptible because it is not even a servility to the strong. But all who begin with force and conquest will end in this.

The chief characteristic of the "New journalism" is simply that it is bad journalism. It is beyond all comparison the most shapeless, careless, and colourless work done in our day.

I read yesterday a sentence which should be written in letters of gold and adamant; it is the very motto of the new philosophy of Empire. I found it (as the reader has already eagerly guessed) in Pearson's Magazine, while I was communing (soul to soul) with Mr. C. Arthur Pearson, whose first and suppressed name I am afraid is Chilperic. It occurred in an article on the American Presidential Election. This is the sentence, and every one should read it carefully, and roll it on the tongue, till all the honey be tasted.

"A little sound common sense often goes further with an audience of American working-men than much high-flown argument. A speaker who, as he brought forward his points, hammered nails into a board, won hundreds of votes for his side at the last Presidential Election."

I do not wish to soil this perfect thing with comment; the words of Mercury are harsh after the songs of Apollo. But just think for a moment of the mind, the strange inscrutable mind, of the man who wrote that, of the editor who approved it, of the people who are probably impressed by it, of the incredible American working-man, of whom, for all I know, it may be true. Think what their notion of "common sense" must be! It is delightful to realize that you and I are now able to win thousands of votes should we ever be engaged in a Presidential Election, by doing something of this kind. For I suppose the nails and the board are not essential to the exhibition of "common sense;" there may be variations. We may read—

"A little common sense impresses American working-men more than high-flown argument. A speaker who, as he made his points, pulled buttons off his waistcoat, won thousands of votes for his side." Or, "Sound common sense tells better in America than high-flown argument. Thus Senator Budge, who threw his false teeth in the air every time he made an epigram, won the solid approval of American working-men." Or again, "The sound common sense of a gentleman from Earlswood, who stuck straws in his hair during the progress of his speech, assured the victory of Mr. Roosevelt."

There are many other elements in this article on which I should love to linger. But the matter which I wish to point out is that in that sentence is perfectly revealed the whole truth of what our Chamberlainites, hustlers, bustlers, Empire-builders, and strong, silent men, really mean by "commonsense." They mean knocking, with deafening noise and dramatic effect, meaningless bits of iron into a useless bit of wood. A man goes on to an American platform and behaves like a mountebank fool with a board and a hammer; well, I do not blame him; I might even admire him. He may be a dashing and quite decent strategist. He may be a fine romantic actor, like Burke flinging the dagger on the floor. He may even (for all I know) be a sublime mystic, profoundly impressed with the ancient meaning of the divine trade of the Carpenter, and offering to the people a parable in the form of a ceremony. All I wish to indicate is the abyss of mental confusion in which such wild ritualism can be called "sound common sense." And it is in that abyss of mental confusion, and in that alone, that the new Imperialism lives and moves and has its being. The whole glory and greatness of Mr. Chamberlain consists in this: that if a man hits the right nail on the head nobody cares where he hits it to or what it does. They care about the noise of the hammer, not about the silent drip of the nail. Before and throughout the African war, Mr. Chamberlain was always knocking in nails, with ringing decisiveness. But when we ask, "But what have these nails held together? Where is your carpentry? Where are your contented Outlanders? Where is your free South Africa? Where is your British prestige? What have your nails done?" then what answer is there? We must go back (with an affectionate sigh) to our Pearson for the answer to the question of what the nails have done: "The speaker who hammered nails into a board won thousands of votes."

Now the whole of this passage is admirably characteristic of the new journalism which Mr. Pearson represents, the new journalism which has just purchased the Standard. To take one instance out of hundreds, the incomparable man with the board and nails is described in the Pearson's article as calling out (as he smote the symbolic nail), "Lie number one. Nailed to the Mast! Nailed to the Mast!" In the whole office there was apparently no compositor or office-boy to point out that we speak of lies being nailed to the counter, and not to the mast. Nobody in the office knew that Pearson's Magazine was falling into a stale Irish bull, which must be as old as St. Patrick. This is the real and essential tragedy of the sale of the Standard. It is not merely that journalism is victorious over literature. It is that bad journalism is victorious over good journalism.

It is not that one article which we consider costly and beautiful is being ousted by another kind of article which we consider common or unclean. It is that of the same article a worse quality is preferred to a better. If you like popular journalism (as I do), you will know that Pearson's Magazine is poor and weak popular journalism. You will know it as certainly as you know bad butter. You will know as certainly that it is poor popular journalism as you know that the Strand, in the great days of Sherlock Holmes, was good popular journalism. Mr. Pearson has been a monument of this enormous banality. About everything he says and does there is something infinitely weak-minded. He clamours for home trades and employs foreign ones to print his paper. When this glaring fact is pointed out, he does not say that the thing was an oversight, like a sane man. He cuts it off with scissors, like a child of three. His very cunning is infantile. And like a child of three, he does not cut it quite off. In all human records I doubt if there is such an example of a profound simplicity in deception. This is the sort of intelligence which now sits in the seat of the sane and honourable old Tory journalism. If it were really the triumph of the tropical exuberance of the Yankee press, it would be vulgar, but still tropical. But it is not. We are delivered over to the bramble, and from the meanest of the shrubs comes the fire upon the cedars of Lebanon.

The only question now is how much longer the fiction will endure that journalists of this order represent public opinion. It may be doubted whether any honest and serious Tariff Reformer would for a moment maintain that there was any majority for Tariff Reform in the country comparable to the ludicrous preponderance which money has given it among the great dailies. The only inference is that for purposes of real public opinion the press is now a mere plutocratic oligarchy. Doubtless the public buys the wares of these men, for one reason or another. But there is no more reason to suppose that the public admires their politics than that the public admires the delicate philosophy of Mr. Crosse or the darker and sterner creed of Mr. Blackwell. If these men are merely tradesmen, there is nothing to say except that there are plenty like them in the Battersea Park Road, and many much better. But if they make any sort of attempt to be politicians, we can only point out to them that they are not as yet even good journalists.

Chapter 9
The Moods of Mr. George Moore

r. George Moore began his literary career by writing his personal confessions; nor is there any harm in this if he had not continued them for the remainder of his life. He is a man of genuinely forcible mind and of great command over a kind of rhetorical and fugitive conviction which excites and pleases. He is in a perpetual state of temporary honesty. He has admired all the most admirable modern eccentrics until they could stand it no longer. Everything he writes, it is to be fully admitted, has a genuine mental power. His account of his reason for leaving the Roman Catholic Church is possibly the most admirable tribute to that communion which has been written of late years. For the fact of the matter is, that the weakness which has rendered barren the many brilliancies of Mr. Moore is actually that weakness which the Roman Catholic Church is at its best in combating. Mr. Moore hates Catholicism because it breaks up the house of looking-glasses in which he lives. Mr. Moore does not dislike so much being asked to believe in the spiritual existence of miracles or sacraments, but he does fundamentally dislike being asked to believe in the actual existence of other people. Like his master Pater and all the aesthetes, his real quarrel with life is that it is not a dream that can be moulded by the dreamer. It is not the dogma of the reality of the other world that troubles him, but the dogma of the reality of this world.

The truth is that the tradition of Christianity (which is still the only coherent ethic of Europe) rests on two or three paradoxes or mysteries which can easily be impugned in argument and as easily justified in life. One of them, for instance, is the paradox of hope or faith—that the more hopeless is the situation the more hopeful must be the man. Stevenson understood this, and consequently Mr. Moore cannot understand Stevenson. Another is the paradox of charity or chivalry that the weaker a thing is the more it should be respected, that the more indefensible a thing is the more it should appeal to us for a certain kind of defence. Thackeray understood this, and therefore Mr. Moore does not understand Thackeray. Now, one of these very practical and working mysteries in the Christian tradition, and one which the Roman Catholic Church, as I say, has done her best work in singling out, is the conception of the sinfulness of pride. Pride is a weakness in the character; it dries up laughter, it dries up wonder, it dries up chivalry and energy. The Christian tradition understands this; therefore Mr. Moore does not understand the Christian tradition.

For the truth is much stranger even than it appears in the formal doctrine of the sin of pride. It is not only true that humility is a much wiser and more vigorous thing than pride. It is also true that vanity is a much wiser and more vigorous thing than pride. Vanity is social—it is almost a kind of comradeship;

pride is solitary and uncivilized. Vanity is active; it desires the applause of infinite multitudes; pride is passive, desiring only the applause of one person, which it already has. Vanity is humorous, and can enjoy the joke even of itself; pride is dull, and cannot even smile. And the whole of this difference is the difference between Stevenson and Mr. George Moore, who, as he informs us, has "brushed Stevenson aside." I do not know where he has been brushed to, but wherever it is I fancy he is having a good time, because he had the wisdom to be vain, and not proud. Stevenson had a windy vanity; Mr. Moore has a dusty egoism. Hence Stevenson could amuse himself as well as us with his vanity; while the richest effects of Mr. Moore's absurdity are hidden from his eyes.

If we compare this solemn folly with the happy folly with which Stevenson belauds his own books and berates his own critics, we shall not find it difficult to guess why it is that Stevenson at least found a final philosophy of some sort to live by, while Mr. Moore is always walking the world looking for a new one. Stevenson had found that the secret of life lies in laughter and humility. Self is the gorgon. Vanity sees it in the mirror of other men and lives. Pride studies it for itself and is turned to stone.

It is necessary to dwell on this defect in Mr. Moore, because it is really the weakness of work which is not without its strength. Mr. Moore's egoism is not merely a moral weakness, it is a very constant and influential aesthetic weakness as well. We should really be much more interested in Mr. Moore if he were not quite so interested in himself. We feel as if we were being shown through a gallery of really fine pictures, into each of which, by some useless and discordant convention, the artist had represented the same figure in the same attitude. "The Grand Canal with a distant view of Mr. Moore," "Effect of Mr. Moore through a Scotch Mist," "Mr. Moore by Firelight," "Ruins of Mr. Moore by Moonlight," and so on, seems to be the endless series. He would no doubt reply that in such a book as this he intended to reveal himself. But the answer is that in such a book as this he does not succeed. One of the thousand objections to the sin of pride lies precisely in this, that self-consciousness of necessity destroys self-revelation. A man who thinks a great deal about himself will try to be many-sided, attempt a theatrical excellence at all points, will try to be an encyclopaedia of culture, and his own real personality will be lost in that false universalism. Thinking about himself will lead to trying to be the universe; trying to be the universe will lead to ceasing to be anything. If, on the other hand, a man is sensible enough to think only about the universe; he will think about it in his own individual way. He will keep virgin the secret of God; he will see the grass as no other man can see it, and look at a sun that no man has ever known. This fact is very practically brought out in Mr. Moore's "Confessions." In reading them we do not feel the presence of a clean-cut personality like that of Thackeray and Matthew Arnold. We only read a number of quite clever and largely conflicting opinions which might be uttered by any clever person, but which we are called upon to admire specifically, because they are uttered by Mr. Moore. He is the only thread that connects Catholicism and Protestantism, realism and mysticism—he or rather his name. He is profoundly absorbed even in views he no longer holds, and he expects us to be. And he intrudes the capital "I" even where it need not be intruded—even where it weakens the force of a plain statement. Where another man would say, "It is a fine day," Mr. Moore says, "Seen through my temperament, the day appeared fine." Where another man would say "Milton has obviously a fine style," Mr. Moore would say, "As a stylist Milton had always impressed me." The Nemesis of this self-centred spirit is that of being totally ineffectual. Mr. Moore has started many interesting crusades, but he has abandoned them before his disciples could begin. Even when he is on the side of the truth he is as fickle as the children of falsehood. Even when he has found reality he cannot find rest. One Irish quality he has which no Irishman was ever without—pugnacity; and that is certainly a great virtue, especially in the present age. But he has not the tenacity of conviction which goes with the fighting spirit in a man like Bernard Shaw. His weakness of introspection and selfishness in all their glory cannot prevent him fighting; but they will always prevent him winning.

Chapter 10
On Sandals and Simplicity

he great misfortune of the modern English is not at all that they are more boastful than other people (they are not); it is that they are boastful about those particular things which nobody can boast of without losing them. A Frenchman can be proud of being bold and logical, and still remain bold and logical. A German can be proud of being reflective and orderly, and still remain reflective and orderly. But an Englishman cannot be proud of being simple and direct, and still remain simple and direct. In the matter of these strange virtues, to know them is to kill them. A man may be conscious of being heroic or conscious of being divine, but he cannot (in spite of all the Anglo-Saxon poets) be conscious of being unconscious.

Now, I do not think that it can be honestly denied that some portion of this impossibility attaches to a class very different in their own opinion, at least, to the school of Anglo-Saxonism. I mean that school of the simple life, commonly associated with Tolstoy. If a perpetual talk about one's own robustness leads to being less robust, it is even more true that a perpetual talking about one's own simplicity leads to being less simple. One great complaint, I think, must stand against the modern upholders of the simple life—the simple life in all its varied forms, from vegetarianism to the honourable consistency of the Doukhobors. This complaint against them stands, that they would make us simple in the unimportant things, but complex in the important things. They would make us simple in the things that do not matter—that is, in diet, in costume, in etiquette, in economic system. But they would make us complex in the things that do matter—in philosophy, in loyalty, in spiritual acceptance, and spiritual rejection. It does not so very much matter whether a man eats a grilled tomato or a plain tomato; it does very much matter whether he eats a plain tomato with a grilled mind. The only kind of simplicity worth preserving is the simplicity of the heart, the simplicity which accepts and enjoys. There may be a reasonable doubt as to what system preserves this; there can surely be no doubt that a system of simplicity destroys it. There is more simplicity in the man who eats caviar on impulse than in the man who eats grape-nuts on principle. The chief error of these people is to be found in the very phrase to which they are most attached—"plain living and high thinking." These people do not stand in need of, will not be improved by, plain living and high thinking. They stand in need of the contrary. They would be improved by high living and plain thinking. A little high living (I say, having a full sense of responsibility, a little high living) would teach them the force and meaning of the human festivities, of the banquet that has gone on from the beginning of the world. It would teach them the historic fact that the artificial is, if anything, older than the natural. It would teach them that the loving-cup is as old as any hunger.

It would teach them that ritualism is older than any religion. And a little plain thinking would teach them how harsh and fanciful are the mass of their own ethics, how very civilized and very complicated must be the brain of the Tolstoyan who really believes it to be evil to love one's country and wicked to strike a blow.

A man approaches, wearing sandals and simple raiment, a raw tomato held firmly in his right hand, and says, "The affections of family and country alike are hindrances to the fuller development of human love;" but the plain thinker will only answer him, with a wonder not untinged with admiration, "What a great deal of trouble you must have taken in order to feel like that." High living will reject the tomato. Plain thinking will equally decisively reject the idea of the invariable sinfulness of war. High living will convince us that nothing is more materialistic than to despise a pleasure as purely material. And plain thinking will convince us that nothing is more materialistic than to reserve our horror chiefly for material wounds.

The only simplicity that matters is the simplicity of the heart. If that be gone, it can be brought back by no turnips or cellular clothing; but only by tears and terror and the fires that are not quenched. If that remain, it matters very little if a few Early Victorian armchairs remain along with it. Let us put a complex entree into a simple old gentleman; let us not put a simple entree into a complex old gentleman. So long as human society will leave my spiritual inside alone, I will allow it, with a comparative submission, to work its wild will with my physical interior. I will submit to cigars. I will meekly embrace a bottle of Burgundy. I will humble myself to a hansom cab. If only by this means I may preserve to myself the virginity of the spirit, which enjoys with astonishment and fear. I do not say that these are the only methods of preserving it. I incline to the belief that there are others. But I will have nothing to do with simplicity which lacks the fear, the astonishment, and the joy alike. I will have nothing to do with the devilish vision of a child who is too simple to like toys.

The child is, indeed, in these, and many other matters, the best guide. And in nothing is the child so righteously childlike, in nothing does he exhibit more accurately the sounder order of simplicity, than in the fact that he sees everything with a simple pleasure, even the complex things. The false type of naturalness harps always on the distinction between the natural and the artificial. The higher kind of naturalness ignores that distinction. To the child the tree and the lamp-post are as natural and as artificial as each other; or rather, neither of them are natural but both supernatural. For both are splendid and unexplained. The flower with which God crowns the one, and the flame with which Sam the lamplighter crowns the other, are equally of the gold of fairy-tales. In the middle of the wildest fields the most rustic child is, ten to one, playing at steam-engines. And the only spiritual or philosophical objection to steam-engines is not that men pay for them or work at them, or make them very ugly, or even that men are killed by them; but merely that men do not play at them. The evil is that the childish poetry of clockwork does not remain. The wrong is not that engines are too much admired, but that they are not admired enough. The sin is not that engines are mechanical, but that men are mechanical.

In this matter, then, as in all the other matters treated in this book, our main conclusion is that it is a fundamental point of view, a philosophy or religion which is needed, and not any change in habit or social routine. The things we need most for immediate practical purposes are all abstractions. We need a right view of the human lot, a right view of the human society; and if we were living eagerly and angrily in the enthusiasm of those things, we should, ipso facto, be living simply in the genuine and spiritual sense. Desire and danger make every one simple. And to those who talk to us with interfering eloquence about Jaeger and the pores of the skin, and about Plasmon and the coats of the stomach, at them shall only be hurled the words that are hurled at fops and gluttons, "Take no thought what ye shall eat or what ye shall drink, or wherewithal ye shall be clothed. For after all these things do the Gentiles seek. But seek first the kingdom of God and His righteousness, and all these things shall be added unto you." Those amazing words are not only extraordinarily good, practical politics; they are also superlatively good hygiene. The one supreme way of making all those processes go right, the processes of health, and strength, and grace, and beauty, the one and only way of making certain of their accuracy, is to think about something else. If a man is bent on climbing into the seventh heaven, he may be quite easy about the pores of his skin. If he harnesses his waggon to a star, the process will have a most satisfactory effect upon the coats of his stomach. For the thing called "taking thought," the thing for which the best modern word is "rationalizing," is in its nature, inapplicable to all plain and urgent things. Men take thought and ponder rationalistically, touching remote things—things that only theoretically matter, such as the transit of Venus. But only at their peril can men rationalize about so practical a matter as health.

Chapter 11
Science and the Savages

permanent disadvantage of the study of folk-lore and kindred subjects is that the man of science can hardly be in the nature of things very frequently a man of the world. He is a student of nature; he is scarcely ever a student of human nature. And even where this difficulty is overcome, and he is in some sense a student of human nature, this is only a very faint beginning of the painful progress towards being human. For the study of primitive race and religion stands apart in one important respect from all, or nearly all, the ordinary scientific studies. A man can understand astronomy only by being an astronomer; he can understand entomology only by being an entomologist (or, perhaps, an insect); but he can understand a great deal of anthropology merely by being a man. He is himself the animal which he studies. Hence arises the fact which strikes the eye everywhere in the records of ethnology and folk-lore—the fact that the same frigid and detached spirit which leads to success in the study of astronomy or botany leads to disaster in the study of mythology or human origins. It is necessary to cease to be a man in order to do justice to a microbe; it is not necessary to cease to be a man in order to do justice to men. That same suppression of sympathies, that same waving away of intuitions or guess-work which make a man preternaturally clever in dealing with the stomach of a spider, will make him preternaturally stupid in dealing with the heart of man. He is making himself inhuman in order to understand humanity. An ignorance of the other world is boasted by many men of science; but in this matter their defect arises, not from ignorance of the other world, but from ignorance of this world. For the secrets about which anthropologists concern themselves can be best learnt, not from books or voyages, but from the ordinary commerce of man with man. The secret of why some savage tribe worships monkeys or the moon is not to be found even by travelling among those savages and taking down their answers in a notebook, although the cleverest man may pursue this course. The answer to the riddle is in England; it is in London; nay, it is in his own heart. When a man has discovered why men in Bond Street wear black hats he will at the same moment have discovered why men in Timbuctoo wear red feathers. The mystery in the heart of some savage war-dance should not be studied in books of scientific travel; it should be studied at a subscription ball. If a man desires to find out the origins of religions, let him not go to the Sandwich Islands; let him go to church. If a man wishes to know the origin of human society, to know what society, philosophically speaking, really is, let him not go into the British Museum; let him go into society.

This total misunderstanding of the real nature of ceremonial gives rise to the most awkward and dehumanized versions of the conduct of men in rude lands or ages. The man of science, not realizing that ceremonial is essentially a thing which is done without a reason, has to find a reason for every sort of ceremonial, and, as might be supposed, the reason is generally a very absurd one—absurd because it originates not in the simple mind of the barbarian, but in the sophisticated mind of the professor. The teamed man will say, for instance, "The natives of Mumbojumbo Land believe that the dead man can eat and will require food upon his journey to the other world. This is attested by the fact that they place food in the grave, and that any family not complying with this rite is the object of the anger of the priests and the tribe." To any one acquainted with humanity this way of talking is topsy-turvy. It is like saying, "The English in the twentieth century believed that a dead man could smell. This is attested by the fact that they always covered his grave with lilies, violets, or other flowers. Some priestly and tribal terrors were evidently attached to the neglect of this action, as we have records of several old ladies who were very much disturbed in mind because their wreaths had not arrived in time for the funeral." It may be of course that savages put food with a dead man because they think that a dead man can eat, or weapons with a dead man because they think that a dead man can fight. But personally I do not believe that they think anything of the kind. I believe they put food or weapons on the dead for the same reason that we put flowers, because it is an exceedingly natural and obvious thing to do. We do not understand, it is true, the emotion which makes us think it obvious and natural; but that is because, like all the important emotions of human existence it is essentially irrational. We do not understand the savage for the same reason that the savage does not understand himself. And the savage does not understand himself for the same reason that we do not understand ourselves either.

The obvious truth is that the moment any matter has passed through the human mind it is finally and for ever spoilt for all purposes of science. It has become a thing incurably mysterious and infinite; this mortal has put on immortality. Even what we call our material desires are spiritual, because they are human. Science can analyse a pork-chop, and say how much of it is phosphorus and how much is protein; but science cannot analyse any man's wish for a pork-chop, and say how much of it is hunger, how much custom, how much nervous fancy, how much a haunting love of the beautiful. The man's desire for the pork-chop remains literally as mystical and ethereal as his desire for heaven. All attempts, therefore, at a science of any human things, at a science of history, a science of folk-lore, a science of sociology, are by their nature not merely hopeless, but crazy. You can no more be certain in economic history that a man's desire for money was merely a desire for money than you can be certain in hagiology that a saint's desire for God was merely a desire for God. And this kind of vagueness in the primary phenomena of the study is an absolutely final blow to anything in the nature of a science. Men can construct a science with very few instruments, or with very plain instruments; but no one on earth could construct a science with unreliable instruments. A man might work out the whole of mathematics with a handful of pebbles, but not with a handful of clay which was always falling apart into new fragments, and falling together into new combinations. A man might measure heaven and earth with a reed, but not with a growing reed.

As one of the enormous follies of folk-lore, let us take the case of the transmigration of stories, and the alleged unity of their source. Story after story the scientific mythologists have cut out of its place in history, and pinned side by side with similar stories in their museum of fables. The process is industrious, it is fascinating, and the whole of it rests on one of the plainest fallacies in the world. That a story has been told all over the place at some time or other, not only does not prove that it never really happened; it does not even faintly indicate or make slightly more probable that it never happened. That a large number of fishermen have falsely asserted that they have caught a pike two feet long, does not in the least affect the question of whether any one ever really did so. That numberless journalists announce a Franco-German war merely for money is no evidence one way or the other upon the dark question of whether such a war ever occurred. Doubtless in a few hundred years the innumerable Franco-German wars that did not happen will have cleared the scientific mind of any belief in the legendary war of '70 which did. But that will be because if folk-lore students remain at all, their nature will be unchanged; and their services to folk-lore will be still as they are at present, greater than they know. For in truth these men do something far more god-like than studying legends; they create them.

There are two kinds of stories which the scientists say cannot be true, because everybody tells them. The first class consists of the stories which are told everywhere, because they are somewhat odd or clever; there is nothing in the world to prevent their having happened to somebody as an adventure any more than there is anything to prevent their having occurred, as they certainly did occur, to somebody as an idea. But they are not likely to have happened to many people. The second class of their "myths" consist of the stories that are told everywhere for the simple reason that they happen everywhere. Of the first class, for instance, we might take such an example as the story of William Tell, now generally ranked among legends upon the sole ground that it is found in the tales of other peoples. Now, it is obvious that this was told everywhere because whether true or fictitious it is what is called "a good story;" it is odd, exciting, and it has a climax. But to suggest that some such eccentric incident can never have happened in the whole history of archery, or that it did not happen to any particular person of whom it is told, is stark impudence. The idea of shooting at a mark attached to some valuable or beloved person is an idea doubtless that might easily have occurred to any inventive poet. But it is also an idea that might easily occur to any boastful archer. It might be one of the fantastic caprices of some story-teller. It might equally well be one of the fantastic caprices of some tyrant. It might occur first in real life and afterwards occur in legends. Or it might just as well occur first in legends and afterwards occur in real life. If no apple has ever been shot off a boy's head from the beginning of the world, it may be done to-morrow morning, and by somebody who has never heard of William Tell.

This type of tale, indeed, may be pretty fairly paralleled with the ordinary anecdote terminating in a repartee or an Irish bull. Such a retort as the famous *"je ne vois pas la necessite"* we have all seen attributed to Talleyrand, to Voltaire, to Henri Quatre, to an anonymous judge, and so on. But this variety does not in any way make it more likely that the thing was never said at all. It is highly likely that it was really said by somebody unknown. It is highly likely that it was really said by Talleyrand. In any case, it is not any more difficult to believe that the mot might have occurred to a man in conversation than to a man writing memoirs. It might have occurred to any of the men I have mentioned. But there is this point of distinction about it, that it is not likely to have occurred to all of them. And this is where the first class of so-called myth differs from the second to which I have previously referred. For there is a second class of incident found to be common to the stories of five or six heroes, say to Sigurd, to Hercules, to Rustem, to the Cid, and so on. And the peculiarity of this myth is that not only is it highly reasonable to imagine that it really happened to one hero, but it is highly reasonable to imagine that it really happened to all of them. Such a story, for instance, is that of a great man having his strength swayed or thwarted by the mysterious weakness of a woman. The anecdotal story, the story of William Tell, is as I have said, popular, because it is peculiar. But this kind of story, the story of Samson and Delilah of Arthur and Guinevere, is obviously popular because it is not peculiar. It is popular as good, quiet fiction is popular, because it tells the truth about people. If the ruin of Samson by a woman, and the ruin of Hercules by a woman, have a common legendary origin, it is gratifying to know that we can also explain, as a fable, the ruin of Nelson by a woman and the ruin of Parnell by a woman. And, indeed, I have no doubt whatever that, some centuries hence, the students of folk-lore will refuse altogether to believe that Elizabeth Barrett eloped with Robert Browning, and will prove their point up to the hilt by the unquestionable fact that the whole fiction of the period was full of such elopements from end to end.

Possibly the most pathetic of all the delusions of the modern students of primitive belief is the notion they have about the thing they call anthropomorphism. They believe that primitive men attributed phenomena to a god in human form in order to explain them, because his mind in its sullen limitation could not reach any further than his own clownish existence. The thunder was called the voice of a man, the lightning the eyes of a man, because by this explanation they were made more reasonable and comfortable. The final cure for all this kind of philosophy is to walk down a lane at night. Any one who does so will discover very quickly that men pictured something semi-human at the back of all things, not because such a thought was natural, but because it was supernatural; not because it made things more comprehensible, but because it made them a hundred times more incomprehensible and mysterious. For a man walking down a lane at night can see the conspicuous fact that as long as nature keeps to her own course, she has no power with us at all. As long as a tree is a tree, it is a top-heavy monster with a hundred arms, a thousand tongues, and only one leg. But so long as a tree is a tree, it does not frighten us at all. It begins to be something alien, to be something strange, only when it looks like ourselves. When a tree really looks like a man our knees knock under us. And when the whole universe looks like a man we fall on our faces.

Chapter 12
Paganism and Mr. Lowes Dickinson

f the New Paganism (or neo-Paganism), as it was preached flamboyantly by Mr. Swinburne or delicately by Walter Pater, there is no necessity to take any very grave account, except as a thing which left behind it incomparable exercises in the English language. The New Paganism is no longer new, and it never at any time bore the smallest resemblance to Paganism. The ideas about the ancient civilization which it has left loose in the public mind are certainly extraordinary enough. The term "pagan" is continually used in fiction and light literature as meaning a man without any religion, whereas a pagan was generally a man with about half a dozen. The pagans, according to this notion, were continually crowning themselves with flowers and dancing about in an irresponsible state, whereas, if there were two things that the best pagan civilization did honestly believe in, they were a rather too rigid dignity and a much too rigid responsibility. Pagans are depicted as above all things inebriate and lawless, whereas they were above all things reasonable and respectable. They are praised as disobedient when they had only one great virtue—civic obedience. They are envied and admired as shamelessly happy when they had only one great sin—despair.

Mr. Lowes Dickinson, the most pregnant and provocative of recent writers on this and similar subjects, is far too solid a man to have fallen into this old error of the mere anarchy of Paganism. In order to make hay of that Hellenic enthusiasm which has as its ideal mere appetite and egotism, it is not necessary to know much philosophy, but merely to know a little Greek. Mr. Lowes Dickinson knows a great deal of philosophy, and also a great deal of Greek, and his error, if error he has, is not that of the crude hedonist. But the contrast which he offers between Christianity and Paganism in the matter of moral ideals—a contrast which he states very ably in a paper called "How long halt ye?" which appeared in the Independent Review—does, I think, contain an error of a deeper kind. According to him, the ideal of Paganism was not, indeed, a mere frenzy of lust and liberty and caprice, but was an ideal of full and satisfied humanity. According to him, the ideal of Christianity was the ideal of asceticism. When I say that I think this idea wholly wrong as a matter of philosophy and history, I am not talking for the moment about any ideal Christianity of my own, or even of any primitive Christianity undefiled by after events. I am not, like so many modern Christian idealists, basing my case upon certain things which Christ said. Neither am I, like so many other Christian idealists, basing my case upon certain things that Christ forgot to say. I take historic Christianity with all its sins upon its head; I take it, as I would take Jacobinism, or Mormonism, or any other mixed or unpleasing human product, and I say that the meaning of its action was not to be found in asceticism. I say that its point of departure from Paganism was not asceticism. I say that its point of difference with the modern world was not asceticism. I say that St. Simeon Stylites had not his main inspiration in asceticism. I say that the main Christian impulse cannot be described as asceticism, even in the ascetics.

Let me set about making the matter clear. There is one broad fact about the relations of Christianity and Paganism which is so simple that many will smile at it, but which is so important that all moderns forget it. The primary fact about Christianity and Paganism is that one came after the other. Mr. Lowes Dickinson speaks of them as if they were parallel ideals—even speaks as if Paganism were the newer of the two, and the more fitted for a new age. He suggests that the Pagan ideal will be the ultimate good of man; but if that is so, we must at least ask with more curiosity than he allows for, why it was that man actually found his ultimate good on earth under the stars, and threw it away again. It is this extraordinary enigma to which I propose to attempt an answer.

There is only one thing in the modern world that has been face to face with Paganism; there is only one thing in the modern world which in that sense knows anything about Paganism: and that is Christianity. That fact is really the weak point in the whole of that hedonistic neo-Paganism of which I have spoken. All that genuinely remains of the ancient hymns or the ancient dances of Europe, all that has honestly come to us from the festivals of Phoebus or Pan, is to be found in the festivals of the Christian Church. If any one wants to hold the end of a chain which really goes back to the heathen mysteries, he had better take hold of a festoon of flowers at Easter or a string of sausages at Christmas. Everything else in the modern world is of Christian origin, even everything that seems most anti-Christian. The French Revolution is of Christian origin. The newspaper is of Christian origin. The anarchists are of Christian origin. Physical science is of Christian origin. The attack on Christianity is of Christian origin. There is one thing, and one thing only, in existence at the present day which can in any sense accurately be said to be of pagan origin, and that is Christianity.

The real difference between Paganism and Christianity is perfectly summed up in the difference between the pagan, or natural, virtues, and those three virtues of Christianity which the Church of Rome calls virtues of grace. The pagan, or rational, virtues are such things as justice and temperance, and Christianity has adopted them. The three mystical virtues which Christianity has not adopted, but invented, are faith, hope, and charity. Now much easy and foolish Christian rhetoric could easily be poured out upon those three words, but I desire to confine myself to the two facts which are evident about them. The first evident fact (in marked contrast to the delusion of the dancing pagan)—the first evident fact, I say, is that the pagan virtues, such as justice and temperance, are the sad virtues, and that the mystical virtues of faith, hope, and charity are the gay and exuberant virtues. And the second evident fact, which is even more evident, is the fact that the pagan virtues are the reasonable virtues, and that the Christian virtues of faith, hope, and charity are in their essence as unreasonable as they can be.

As the word "unreasonable" is open to misunderstanding, the matter may be more accurately put by saying that each one of these Christian or mystical virtues involves a paradox in its own nature, and that this is not true of any of the typically pagan or rationalist virtues. Justice consists in finding out a certain thing due to a certain man and giving it to him. Temperance consists in finding out the proper limit of a particular indulgence and adhering to that. But charity means pardoning what is unpardonable, or it is no virtue at all. Hope means hoping when things are hopeless, or it is no virtue at all. And faith means believing the incredible, or it is no virtue at all.

It is somewhat amusing, indeed, to notice the difference between the fate of these three paradoxes in the fashion of the modern mind. Charity is a fashionable virtue in our time; it is lit up by the gigantic firelight of Dickens. Hope is a fashionable virtue to-day; our attention has been arrested for it by the sudden and silver trumpet of Stevenson. But faith is unfashionable, and it is customary on every side to cast against it the fact that it is a paradox. Everybody mockingly repeats the famous childish definition that faith is "the power of believing that which we know to be untrue." Yet it is not one atom more paradoxical than hope or charity. Charity is the power of defending that which we know to be indefensible. Hope is the power of being cheerful in circumstances which we know to be desperate. It is true that there is a state of hope which belongs to bright prospects and the morning; but that is not the virtue of hope. The virtue of hope exists only in earthquake and, eclipse. It is true that there is a thing crudely called charity, which means charity to the deserving poor; but charity to the deserving is not charity at all, but justice. It is the undeserving who require it, and the ideal either does not exist at all, or exists wholly for them. For practical purposes it is at the hopeless moment that we require the hopeful man, and the virtue either does not exist at all, or begins to exist at that moment. Exactly at the instant when hope ceases to be reasonable it begins to be useful. Now the old pagan world went perfectly straightforward until it discovered that going straightforward is an enormous mistake. It was nobly and beautifully reasonable, and discovered in its death-pang this lasting and valuable truth, a heritage for the ages, that reasonableness will not do. The pagan age was truly an Eden or golden age, in this essential sense, that it is not to be recovered. And it is not to be recovered in this sense again that, while we are certainly jollier than the pagans, and much more right than the pagans, there is not one of us who can, by the utmost stretch of energy, be so sensible as the pagans. That naked innocence of the intellect cannot be recovered by any man after Christianity; and for this excellent reason, that every man after Christianity knows it to be misleading. Let me take an example, the first that occurs to the mind, of this impossible plainness in the pagan point of view. The greatest tribute to Christianity in the modern world is Tennyson's "Ulysses." The poet reads into the story of Ulysses the conception of an incurable desire to wander. But the real Ulysses does not desire to wander at all. He desires to get home. He displays his heroic and unconquerable qualities in resisting the misfortunes which baulk him; but that is all. There is no love of adventure for its own sake; that is a Christian product. There is no love of Penelope for her own sake; that is a Christian product. Everything in that old world would appear to have been clean and obvious. A good man was a good man; a bad man was a bad man. For this reason they had no charity; for charity is a reverent agnosticism towards the complexity of the soul. For this reason they had no such thing as the art of fiction, the novel; for the novel is a creation of the mystical idea of charity. For them a pleasant landscape was pleasant, and an unpleasant landscape unpleasant. Hence they had no idea of romance; for romance consists in thinking a thing more delightful because it is dangerous; it is a Christian idea. In a word, we cannot reconstruct or even imagine the beautiful and astonishing pagan world. It was a world in which common sense was really common.

My general meaning touching the three virtues of which I have spoken will now, I hope, be sufficiently clear. They are all three paradoxical, they are all three practical, and they are all three paradoxical because they are practical. it is the stress of ultimate need, and a terrible knowledge of things as they are, which led men to set up these riddles, and to die for them. Whatever may be the meaning of the contradiction, it is the fact that the only kind of hope that is of any use in a battle is a hope that denies arithmetic. Whatever may be the meaning of the contradiction, it is the fact that the only kind of charity which any weak spirit wants, or which any generous spirit feels, is the charity which forgives the sins that are like scarlet. Whatever may be the meaning of faith, it must always mean a certainty about something we cannot prove. Thus, for instance, we believe by faith in the existence of other people.

But there is another Christian virtue, a virtue far more obviously and histori-cally connected with Christianity, which will illustrate even better the connection between paradox and practical necessity. This virtue cannot be questioned in its capacity as a historical symbol; certainly Mr. Lowes Dickinson will not question it. It has been the boast of hundreds of the champions of Christianity. It has been the taunt of hundreds of the opponents of Christianity. It is, in essence, the basis of Mr. Lowes Dickinson's whole distinction between Christianity and Paganism. I mean, of course, the virtue of humility. I admit, of course, most readily, that a great deal of false Eastern humility (that is, of strictly ascetic humility) mixed itself with the main stream of European Christianity. We must not forget that when we speak of Christianity we are speaking of a whole continent for about a thousand years. But of this virtue even more than of the other three, I would maintain the general proposition adopted above. Civilization discovered Christian humility for the same urgent reason that it discovered faith and charity—that is, because Christian civilization had to discover it or die.

The great psychological discovery of Paganism, which turned it into Christian-

ity, can be expressed with some accuracy in one phrase. The pagan set out, with
admirable sense, to enjoy himself. By the end of his civilization he had discovered
that a man cannot enjoy himself and continue to enjoy anything else. Mr. Lowes
Dickinson has pointed out in words too excellent to need any further elucidation,
the absurd shallowness of those who imagine that the pagan enjoyed himself only
in a materialistic sense. Of course, he enjoyed himself, not only intellectually
even, he enjoyed himself morally, he enjoyed himself spiritually. But it was himself that he was enjoying; on the face of it, a very natural thing to do. Now, the
psychological discovery is merely this, that whereas it had been supposed that the
fullest possible enjoyment is to be found by extending our ego to infinity, the
truth is that the fullest possible enjoyment is to be found by reducing our ego to
zero.

   Humility is the thing which is for ever renewing the earth and the stars. It is
humility, and not duty, which preserves the stars from wrong, from the unpardonable wrong of casual resignation; it is through humility that the most ancient
heavens for us are fresh and strong. The curse that came before history has laid
on us all a tendency to be weary of wonders. If we saw the sun for the first time it
would be the most fearful and beautiful of meteors. Now that we see it for the
hundredth time we call it, in the hideous and blasphemous phrase of Wordsworth,
"the light of common day." We are inclined to increase our claims. We are inclined
to demand six suns, to demand a blue sun, to demand a green sun. Humility is
perpetually putting us back in the primal darkness. There all light is lightning,
startling and instantaneous. Until we understand that original dark, in which we
have neither sight nor expectation, we can give no hearty and childlike praise to
the splendid sensationalism of things. The terms "pessimism" and "optimism,"
like most modern terms, are unmeaning. But if they can be used in any vague
sense as meaning something, we may say that in this great fact pessimism is the
very basis of optimism. The man who destroys himself creates the universe. To the
humble man, and to the humble man alone, the sun is really a sun; to the humble
man, and to the humble man alone, the sea is really a sea. When he looks at all the
faces in the street, he does not only realize that men are alive, he realizes with a
dramatic pleasure that they are not dead.

   I have not spoken of another aspect of the discovery of humility as a psychological necessity, because it is more commonly insisted on, and is in itself
more obvious. But it is equally clear that humility is a permanent necessity as a
condition of effort and self-examination. It is one of the deadly fallacies of Jingo
politics that a nation is stronger for despising other nations. As a matter of fact,
the strongest nations are those, like Prussia or Japan, which began from very mean
beginnings, but have not been too proud to sit at the feet of the foreigner and
learn everything from him. Almost every obvious and direct victory has been the
victory of the plagiarist. This is, indeed, only a very paltry by-product of humility,
but it is a product of humility, and, therefore, it is successful. Prussia had no

Christian humility in its internal arrangements; hence its internal arrangements were miserable. But it had enough Christian humility slavishly to copy France (even down to Frederick the Great's poetry), and that which it had the humility to copy it had ultimately the honour to conquer. The case of the Japanese is even more obvious; their only Christian and their only beautiful quality is that they have humbled themselves to be exalted. All this aspect of humility, however, as connected with the matter of effort and striving for a standard set above us, I dismiss as having been sufficiently pointed out by almost all idealistic writers.

It may be worth while, however, to point out the interesting disparity in the matter of humility between the modern notion of the strong man and the actual records of strong men. Carlyle objected to the statement that no man could be a hero to his valet. Every sympathy can be extended towards him in the matter if he merely or mainly meant that the phrase was a disparagement of hero-worship. Hero-worship is certainly a generous and human impulse; the hero may be faulty, but the worship can hardly be. It may be that no man would be a hero to his valet. But any man would be a valet to his hero. But in truth both the proverb itself and Carlyle's stricture upon it ignore the most essential matter at issue. The ultimate psychological truth is not that no man is a hero to his valet. The ultimate psychological truth, the foundation of Christianity, is that no man is a hero to himself. Cromwell, according to Carlyle, was a strong man. According to Cromwell, he was a weak one.

The weak point in the whole of Carlyle's case for aristocracy lies, indeed, in his most celebrated phrase. Carlyle said that men were mostly fools. Christianity, with a surer and more reverent realism, says that they are all fools. This doctrine is sometimes called the doctrine of original sin. It may also be described as the doctrine of the equality of men. But the essential point of it is merely this, that whatever primary and far-reaching moral dangers affect any man, affect all men. All men can be criminals, if tempted; all men can be heroes, if inspired. And this doctrine does away altogether with Carlyle's pathetic belief (or any one else's pathetic belief) in "the wise few." There are no wise few. Every aristocracy that has ever existed has behaved, in all essential points, exactly like a small mob. Every oligarchy is merely a knot of men in the street—that is to say, it is very jolly, but not infallible. And no oligarchies in the world's history have ever come off so badly in practical affairs as the very proud oligarchies—the oligarchy of Poland, the oligarchy of Venice. And the armies that have most swiftly and suddenly broken their enemies in pieces have been the religious armies—the Moslem Armies, for instance, or the Puritan Armies. And a religious army may, by its nature, be defined as an army in which every man is taught not to exalt but to abase himself. Many modern Englishmen talk of themselves as the sturdy descendants of their sturdy Puritan fathers. As a fact, they would run away from a cow. If you asked one of their Puritan fathers, if you asked Bunyan, for instance, whether he was sturdy, he would have answered, with tears, that he was as weak as water. And because of this he would have borne tortures. And this virtue of humility, while being practical enough to win battles, will always be paradoxical enough to puzzle pedants. It is at one with the virtue of charity in this respect. Every generous person will admit that the one kind of sin which charity should cover is the sin which is inexcusable. And every generous person will equally agree that the one kind of pride which is wholly damnable is the pride of the man who has something to be proud of. The pride which, proportionally speaking, does not hurt the character, is the pride in things which reflect no credit on the person at all. Thus it does a man no harm to be proud of his country, and comparatively little harm to be proud of his remote ancestors. It does him more harm to be proud of having made money, because in that he has a little more reason for pride. It does him more harm still to be proud of what is nobler than money—intellect. And it does him most harm of all to value himself for the most valuable thing on earth—goodness. The man who is proud of what is really creditable to him is the Pharisee, the man whom Christ Himself could not forbear to strike.

My objection to Mr. Lowes Dickinson and the reassertors of the pagan ideal is, then, this. I accuse them of ignoring definite human discoveries in the moral world, discoveries as definite, though not as material, as the discovery of the circulation of the blood. We cannot go back to an ideal of reason and sanity. For mankind has discovered that reason does not lead to sanity. We cannot go back to an ideal of pride and enjoyment. For mankind has discovered that pride does not lead to enjoyment. I do not know by what extraordinary mental accident modern writers so constantly connect the idea of progress with the idea of independent thinking. Progress is obviously the antithesis of independent thinking. For under independent or individualistic thinking, every man starts at the beginning, and goes, in all probability, just as far as his father before him. But if there really be anything of the nature of progress, it must mean, above all things, the careful study and assumption of the whole of the past. I accuse Mr. Lowes Dickinson and his school of reaction in the only real sense. If he likes, let him ignore these great historic mysteries—the mystery of charity, the mystery of chivalry, the mystery of faith. If he likes, let him ignore the plough or the printing-press. But if we do revive and pursue the pagan ideal of a simple and rational self-completion we shall end—where Paganism ended. I do not mean that we shall end in destruction. I mean that we shall end in Christianity.

Chapter 13
Celts and Celtophiles

cience in the modern world has many uses; its chief use, however, is to provide long words to cover the errors of the rich. The word "kleptomania" is a vulgar example of what I mean. It is on a par with that strange theory, always advanced when a wealthy or prominent person is in the dock, that exposure is more of a punishment for the rich than for the poor. Of course, the very reverse is the truth. Exposure is more of a punishment for the poor than for the rich. The richer a man is the easier it is for him to be a tramp. The richer a man is the easier it is for him to be popular and generally respected in the Cannibal Islands. But the poorer a man is the more likely it is that he will have to use his past life whenever he wants to get a bed for the night. Honour is a luxury for aristocrats, but it is a necessity for hall-porters. This is a secondary matter, but it is an example of the general proposition I offer—the proposition that an enormous amount of modern ingenuity is expended on finding defences for the indefensible conduct of the powerful. As I have said above, these defences generally exhibit themselves most emphatically in the form of appeals to physical science. And of all the forms in which science, or pseudo-science, has come to the rescue of the rich and stupid, there is none so singular as the singular invention of the theory of races.

When a wealthy nation like the English discovers the perfectly patent fact that it is making a ludicrous mess of the government of a poorer nation like the Irish, it pauses for a moment in consternation, and then begins to talk about Celts and Teutons. As far as I can understand the theory, the Irish are Celts and the English are Teutons. Of course, the Irish are not Celts any more than the English are Teutons. I have not followed the ethnological discussion with much energy, but the last scientific conclusion which I read inclined on the whole to the summary that the English were mainly Celtic and the Irish mainly Teutonic. But no man alive, with even the glimmering of a real scientific sense, would ever dream of applying the terms "Celtic" or "Teutonic" to either of them in any positive or useful sense.

That sort of thing must be left to people who talk about the Anglo-Saxon race, and extend the expression to America. How much of the blood of the Angles and Saxons (whoever they were) there remains in our mixed British, Roman, German, Dane, Norman, and Picard stock is a matter only interesting to wild antiquaries. And how much of that diluted blood can possibly remain in that roaring whirlpool of America into which a cataract of Swedes, Jews, Germans, Irishmen, and Italians is perpetually pouring, is a matter only interesting to lunatics. It would have been wiser for the English governing class to have called upon some other god. All other gods, however weak and warring, at least boast of being constant. But science boasts of being in a flux for ever; boasts of being unstable as water.

And England and the English governing class never did call on this absurd deity of race until it seemed, for an instant, that they had no other god to call on. All the most genuine Englishmen in history would have yawned or laughed in your face if you had begun to talk about Anglo-Saxons. If you had attempted to substitute the ideal of race for the ideal of nationality, I really do not like to think what they would have said. I certainly should not like to have been the officer of Nelson who suddenly discovered his French blood on the eve of Trafalgar. I should not like to have been the Norfolk or Suffolk gentleman who had to expound to Admiral Blake by what demonstrable ties of genealogy he was irrevocably bound to the Dutch. The truth of the whole matter is very simple. Nationality exists, and has nothing in the world to do with race. Nationality is a thing like a church or a secret society; it is a product of the human soul and will; it is a spiritual product. And there are men in the modern world who would think anything and do anything rather than admit that anything could be a spiritual product.

A nation, however, as it confronts the modern world, is a purely spiritual product. Sometimes it has been born in independence, like Scotland. Sometimes it has been born in dependence, in subjugation, like Ireland. Sometimes it is a large thing cohering out of many smaller things, like Italy. Sometimes it is a small thing breaking away from larger things, like Poland. But in each and every case its quality is purely spiritual, or, if you will, purely psychological. It is a moment when five men become a sixth man. Every one knows it who has ever founded a club. It is a moment when five places become one place. Every one must know it who has ever had to repel an invasion. Mr. Timothy Healy, the most serious intellect in the present House of Commons, summed up nationality to perfection when he simply called it something for which people will die, As he excellently said in reply to Lord Hugh Cecil, "No one, not even the noble lord, would die for the meridian of Greenwich." And that is the great tribute to its purely psychological character. It is idle to ask why Greenwich should not cohere in this spiritual manner while Athens or Sparta did. It is like asking why a man falls in love with one woman and not with another.

Now, of this great spiritual coherence, independent of external circumstances, or of race, or of any obvious physical thing, Ireland is the most remarkable example. Rome conquered nations, but Ireland has conquered races. The Norman has gone there and become Irish, the Scotchman has gone there and become Irish, the Spaniard has gone there and become Irish, even the bitter soldier of Cromwell has gone there and become Irish. Ireland, which did not exist even politically, has been stronger than all the races that existed scientifically. The purest Germanic blood, the purest Norman blood, the purest blood of the passionate Scotch patriot, has not been so attractive as a nation without a flag. Ireland, unrecognized and oppressed, has easily absorbed races, as such trifles are easily absorbed. She has easily disposed of physical science, as such superstitions are easily disposed of. Nationality in its weakness has been stronger than ethnology in its strength. Five triumphant races have been absorbed, have been defeated by a defeated nationality.

This being the true and strange glory of Ireland, it is impossible to hear without impatience of the attempt so constantly made among her modern sympathizers to talk about Celts and Celticism. Who were the Celts? I defy anybody to say. Who are the Irish? I defy any one to be indifferent, or to pretend not to know. Mr. W. B. Yeats, the great Irish genius who has appeared in our time, shows his own admirable penetration in discarding altogether the argument from a Celtic race. But he does not wholly escape, and his followers hardly ever escape, the general objection to the Celtic argument. The tendency of that argument is to represent the Irish or the Celts as a strange and separate race, as a tribe of eccentrics in the modern world immersed in dim legends and fruitless dreams. Its tendency is to exhibit the Irish as odd, because they see the fairies. Its trend is to make the Irish seem weird and wild because they sing old songs and join in strange dances. But this is quite an error; indeed, it is the opposite of the truth. It is the English who are odd because they do not see the fairies. It is the inhabitants of Kensington who are weird and wild because they do not sing old songs and join in strange dances. In all this the Irish are not in the least strange and separate, are not in the least Celtic, as the word is commonly and popularly used. In all this the Irish are simply an ordinary sensible nation, living the life of any other ordinary and sensible nation which has not been either sodden with smoke or oppressed by money-lenders, or otherwise corrupted with wealth and science. There is nothing Celtic about having legends. It is merely human. The Germans, who are (I suppose) Teutonic, have hundreds of legends, wherever it happens that the Germans are human. There is nothing Celtic about loving poetry; the English loved poetry more, perhaps, than any other people before they came under the shadow of the chimney-pot and the shadow of the chimney-pot hat. It is not Ireland which is mad and mystic; it is Manchester which is mad and mystic, which is incredible, which is a wild exception among human things. Ireland has no need to play the silly game of the science of races; Ireland has no need to pretend to be a tribe of visionaries apart. In the matter of visions, Ireland is more than a nation, it is a model nation.

Chapter 14
On Certain Modern Writers and the
Institution of the Family

he family may fairly be considered, one would think, an ultimate human institution. Every one would admit that it has been the main cell and central unit of almost all societies hitherto, except, indeed, such societies as that of Lacedaemon, which went in for "efficiency," and has, therefore, perished, and left not a trace behind. Christianity, even enormous as was its revolution, did not alter this ancient and savage sanctity; it merely reversed it. It did not deny the trinity of father, mother, and child. It merely read it backwards, making it run child, mother, father. This it called, not the family, but the Holy Family, for many things are made holy by being turned upside down. But some sages of our own decadence have made a serious attack on the family. They have impugned it, as I think wrongly; and its defenders have defended it, and defended it wrongly. The common defence of the family is that, amid the stress and fickleness of life, it is peaceful, pleasant, and at one. But there is another defence of the family which is possible, and to me evident; this defence is that the family is not peaceful and not pleasant and not at one.

It is not fashionable to say much nowadays of the advantages of the small community. We are told that we must go in for large empires and large ideas. There is one advantage, however, in the small state, the city, or the village, which only the wilfully blind can overlook. The man who lives in a small community lives in a much larger world. He knows much more of the fierce varieties and uncompromising divergences of men. The reason is obvious. In a large community we can choose our companions. In a small community our companions are chosen for us. Thus in all extensive and highly civilized societies groups come into existence founded upon what is called sympathy, and shut out the real world more sharply than the gates of a monastery. There is nothing really narrow about the clan; the thing which is really narrow is the clique. The men of the clan live together because they all wear the same tartan or are all descended from the same sacred cow; but in their souls, by the divine luck of things, there will always be more colours than in any tartan. But the men of the clique live together because they have the same kind of soul, and their narrowness is a narrowness of spiritual coherence and contentment, like that which exists in hell. A big society exists in order to form cliques. A big society is a society for the promotion of narrowness. It is a machinery for the purpose of guarding the solitary and sensitive individual from all experience of the bitter and bracing human compromises. It is, in the most literal sense of the words, a society for the prevention of Christian knowledge.

We can see this change, for instance, in the modern transformation of the thing called a club. When London was smaller, and the parts of London more self-contained and parochial, the club was what it still is in villages, the opposite of what it is now in great cities. Then the club was valued as a place where a man could be sociable. Now the club is valued as a place where a man can be unsociable. The more the enlargement and elaboration of our civilization goes on the more the club ceases to be a place where a man can have a noisy argument, and becomes more and more a place where a man can have what is somewhat fantastically called a quiet chop. Its aim is to make a man comfortable, and to make a man comfortable is to make him the opposite of sociable. Sociability, like all good things, is full of discomforts, dangers, and renunciations. The club tends to produce the most degraded of all combinations—the luxurious anchorite, the man who combines the self-indulgence of Lucullus with the insane loneliness of St. Simeon Stylites.

If we were to-morrow morning snowed up in the street in which we live, we should step suddenly into a much larger and much wilder world than we have ever known. And it is the whole effort of the typically modern person to escape from the street in which he lives. First he invents modern hygiene and goes to Margate. Then he invents modern culture and goes to Florence. Then he invents modern imperialism and goes to Timbuctoo. He goes to the fantastic borders of the earth. He pretends to shoot tigers. He almost rides on a camel. And in all this he is still essentially fleeing from the street in which he was born; and of this flight he is always ready with his own explanation. He says he is fleeing from his street because it is dull; he is lying. He is really fleeing from his street because it is a great deal too exciting. It is exciting because it is exacting; it is exacting because it is alive. He can visit Venice because to him the Venetians are only Venetians; the people in his own street are men. He can stare at the Chinese because for him the Chinese are a passive thing to be stared at; if he stares at the old lady in the next garden, she becomes active. He is forced to flee, in short, from the too stimulating society of his equals—of free men, perverse, personal, deliberately different from himself. The street in Brixton is too glowing and overpowering. He has to soothe and quiet himself among tigers and vultures, camels and crocodiles. These creatures are indeed very different from himself. But they do not put their shape or colour or custom into a decisive intellectual competition with his own. They do not seek to destroy his principles and assert their own; the stranger monsters of the suburban street do seek to do this. The camel does not contort his features into a fine sneer because Mr. Robinson has not got a hump; the cultured gentleman at No. 5 does exhibit a sneer because Robinson has not got a dado. The vulture will not roar with laughter because a man does not fly; but the major at No. 9 will roar with laughter because a man does not smoke. The complaint we commonly have to make of our neighbours is that they will not, as we express it, mind their own business. We do not really mean that they will not mind their own business. If our neighbours did not mind their own business they would be asked abruptly for their rent, and would rapidly cease to be our neighbours. What we really mean when we say that they cannot mind their own business is something much deeper. We do not dislike them because they have so little force and fire that they cannot be interested in themselves. We dislike them because they have so much force and fire that they can be interested in us as well. What we dread about our neighbours, in short, is not the narrowness of their horizon, but their superb tendency to broaden it. And all aversions to ordinary humanity have this general character. They are not aversions to its feebleness (as is pretended), but to its energy. The misanthropes pretend that they despise humanity for its weakness. As a matter of fact, they hate it for its strength.

Of course, this shrinking from the brutal vivacity and brutal variety of common men is a perfectly reasonable and excusable thing as long as it does not pretend to any point of superiority. It is when it calls itself aristocracy or aestheticism or a superiority to the bourgeoisie that its inherent weakness has in justice to be pointed out. Fastidiousness is the most pardonable of vices; but it is the most unpardonable of virtues. Nietzsche, who represents most prominently this pretentious claim of the fastidious, has a description somewhere—a very powerful description in the purely literary sense—of the disgust and disdain which consume him at the sight of the common people with their common faces, their common voices, and their common minds. As I have said, this attitude is almost beautiful if we may regard it as pathetic. Nietzsche's aristocracy has about it all the sacredness that belongs to the weak. When he makes us feel that he cannot endure the innumerable faces, the incessant voices, the overpowering omnipresence which belongs to the mob, he will have the sympathy of anybody who has ever been sick on a steamer or tired in a crowded omnibus. Every man has hated mankind when he was less than a man. Every man has had humanity in his eyes like a blinding fog, humanity in his nostrils like a suffocating smell. But when Nietzsche has the incredible lack of humour and lack of imagination to ask us to believe that his aristocracy is an aristocracy of strong muscles or an aristocracy of strong wills, it is necessary to point out the truth. It is an aristocracy of weak nerves.

We make our friends; we make our enemies; but God makes our next-door neighbour. Hence he comes to us clad in all the careless terrors of nature; he is as strange as the stars, as reckless and indifferent as the rain. He is Man, the most terrible of the beasts. That is why the old religions and the old scriptural language showed so sharp a wisdom when they spoke, not of one's duty towards humanity, but one's duty towards one's neighbour. The duty towards humanity may often take the form of some choice which is personal or even pleasurable. That duty may be a hobby; it may even be a dissipation. We may work in the East End because we are peculiarly fitted to work in the East End, or because we think we are; we may fight for the cause of international peace because we are very fond of fighting. The most monstrous martyrdom, the most repulsive experience, may be the result of choice or a kind of taste. We may be so made as to be particularly fond of lunatics or specially interested in leprosy. We may love negroes because they are black or German Socialists because they are pedantic. But we have to love our neighbour because he is there—a much more alarming reason for a much more serious operation. He is the sample of humanity which is actually given us. Precisely because he may be anybody he is everybody. He is a symbol because he is an accident.

Doubtless men flee from small environments into lands that are very deadly. But this is natural enough; for they are not fleeing from death. They are fleeing from life. And this principle applies to ring within ring of the social system of humanity. It is perfectly reasonable that men should seek for some particular variety of the human type, so long as they are seeking for that variety of the human type, and not for mere human variety. It is quite proper that a British diplomatist should seek the society of Japanese generals, if what he wants is Japanese generals. But if what he wants is people different from himself, he had much better stop at home and discuss religion with the housemaid. It is quite reasonable that the village genius should come up to conquer London if what he wants is to conquer London. But if he wants to conquer something fundamentally and symbolically hostile and also very strong, he had much better remain where he is and have a row with the rector. The man in the suburban street is quite right if he goes to Ramsgate for the sake of Ramsgate—a difficult thing to imagine. But if, as he expresses it, he goes to Ramsgate "for a change," then he would have a much more romantic and even melodramatic change if he jumped over the wall into his neighbours garden. The consequences would be bracing in a sense far beyond the possibilities of Ramsgate hygiene.

Now, exactly as this principle applies to the empire, to the nation within the empire, to the city within the nation, to the street within the city, so it applies to the home within the street. The institution of the family is to be commended for precisely the same reasons that the institution of the nation, or the institution of the city, are in this matter to be commended. It is a good thing for a man to live in a family for the same reason that it is a good thing for a man to be besieged in a city. It is a good thing for a man to live in a family in the same sense that it is a beautiful and delightful thing for a man to be snowed up in a street. They all force him to realize that life is not a thing from outside, but a thing from inside. Above all, they all insist upon the fact that life, if it be a truly stimulating and fascinating life, is a thing which, of its nature, exists in spite of ourselves. The modern writers who have suggested, in a more or less open manner, that the family is a bad institution, have generally confined themselves to suggesting, with much sharpness, bitterness, or pathos, that perhaps the family is not always very congenial. Of course the family is a good institution because it is uncongenial. It is wholesome precisely because it contains so many divergencies and varieties. It is, as the sentimentalists say, like a little kingdom, and, like most other little kingdoms, is generally in a state of something resembling anarchy. It is exactly because our brother George is not interested in our religious difficulties, but is interested in the Trocadero Restaurant, that the family has some of the bracing qualities of the commonwealth. It is precisely because our uncle Henry does not approve of the theatrical ambitions of our sister Sarah that the family is like humanity. The men and women who, for good reasons and bad, revolt against the family, are, for good reasons and bad, simply revolting against mankind. Aunt Elizabeth is unreasonable, like mankind. Papa is excitable, like mankind Our youngest brother is mischievous, like mankind. Grandpapa is stupid, like the world; he is old, like the world.

Those who wish, rightly or wrongly, to step out of all this, do definitely wish to step into a narrower world. They are dismayed and terrified by the largeness and variety of the family. Sarah wishes to find a world wholly consisting of private theatricals; George wishes to think the Trocadero a cosmos. I do not say, for a moment, that the flight to this narrower life may not be the right thing for the individual, any more than I say the same thing about flight into a monastery. But I do say that anything is bad and artificial which tends to make these people succumb to the strange delusion that they are stepping into a world which is actually larger and more varied than their own. The best way that a man could test his readiness to encounter the common variety of mankind would be to climb down a chimney into any house at random, and get on as well as possible with the people inside. And that is essentially what each one of us did on the day that he was born.

This is, indeed, the sublime and special romance of the family. It is romantic because it is a toss-up. It is romantic because it is everything that its enemies call it. It is romantic because it is arbitrary. It is romantic because it is there. So long as you have groups of men chosen rationally, you have some special or sectarian atmosphere. It is when you have groups of men chosen irrationally that you have men. The element of adventure begins to exist; for an adventure is, by its nature, a thing that comes to us. It is a thing that chooses us, not a thing that we choose. Falling in love has been often regarded as the supreme adventure, the supreme romantic accident. In so much as there is in it something outside ourselves, something of a sort of merry fatalism, this is very true. Love does take us and transfigure and torture us. It does break our hearts with an unbearable beauty, like the unbearable beauty of music. But in so far as we have certainly something to do with the matter; in so far as we are in some sense prepared to fall in love and in some sense jump into it; in so far as we do to some extent choose and to some extent even judge—in all this falling in love is not truly romantic, is not truly adventurous at all. In this degree the supreme adventure is not falling in love. The supreme adventure is being born. There we do walk suddenly into a splendid and startling trap. There we do see something of which we have not dreamed before. Our father and mother do lie in wait for us and leap out on us, like brigands from a bush. Our uncle is a surprise. Our aunt is, in the beautiful common expression, a bolt from the blue. When we step into the family, by the act of being born, we do step into a world which is incalculable, into a world which has its own strange laws, into a world which could do without us, into a world that we have not made. In other words, when we step into the family we step into a fairy-tale.

This colour as of a fantastic narrative ought to cling to the family and to our relations with it throughout life. Romance is the deepest thing in life; romance is deeper even than reality. For even if reality could be proved to be misleading, it still could not be proved to be unimportant or unimpressive. Even if the facts are false, they are still very strange. And this strangeness of life, this unexpected and even perverse element of things as they fall out, remains incurably interesting. The circumstances we can regulate may become tame or pessimistic; but the "circumstances over which we have no control" remain god-like to those who, like Mr. Micawber, can call on them and renew their strength. People wonder why the novel is the most popular form of literature; people wonder why it is read more than books of science or books of metaphysics. The reason is very simple; it is merely that the novel is more true than they are. Life may sometimes legitimately appear as a book of science. Life may sometimes appear, and with a much greater legitimacy, as a book of metaphysics. But life is always a novel. Our existence may cease to be a song; it may cease even to be a beautiful lament. Our existence may not be an intelligible justice, or even a recognizable wrong. But our existence is still a story. In the fiery alphabet of every sunset is written, "to be continued in our next." If we have sufficient intellect, we can finish a philosophical and exact deduction, and be certain that we are finishing it right. With the adequate brain-power we could finish any scientific discovery, and be certain that we were finishing it right. But not with the most gigantic intellect could we finish the simplest or silliest story, and be certain that we were finishing it right. That is because a story has behind it, not merely intellect which is partly mechanical, but will, which is in its essence divine. The narrative writer can send his hero to the gallows if he likes in the last chapter but one. He can do it by the same divine caprice whereby he, the author, can go to the gallows himself, and to hell afterwards if he chooses. And the same civilization, the chivalric European civilization which asserted freewill in the thirteenth century, produced the thing called "fiction" in the eighteenth. When Thomas Aquinas asserted the spiritual liberty of man, he created all the bad novels in the circulating libraries.

But in order that life should be a story or romance to us, it is necessary that a great part of it, at any rate, should be settled for us without our permission. If we wish life to be a system, this may be a nuisance; but if we wish it to be a drama, it is an essential. It may often happen, no doubt, that a drama may be written by somebody else which we like very little. But we should like it still less if the author came before the curtain every hour or so, and forced on us the whole trouble of inventing the next act. A man has control over many things in his life; he has control over enough things to be the hero of a novel. But if he had control over everything, there would be so much hero that there would be no novel. And the reason why the lives of the rich are at bottom so tame and uneventful is simply that they can choose the events. They are dull because they are omnipotent. They fail to feel adventures because they can make the adventures. The thing which keeps life romantic and full of fiery possibilities is the existence of these great plain limitations which force all of us to meet the things we do not like or do not expect. It is vain for the supercilious moderns to talk of being in uncongenial surroundings. To be in a romance is to be in uncongenial surroundings. To be born into this earth is to be born into uncongenial surroundings, hence to be born into a romance. Of all these great limitations and frameworks which fashion and create the poetry and variety of life, the family is the most definite and important. Hence it is misunderstood by the moderns, who imagine that romance would exist most perfectly in a complete state of what they call liberty. They think that if a man makes a gesture it would be a startling and romantic matter that the sun should fall from the sky. But the startling and romantic thing about the sun is that it does not fall from the sky. They are seeking under every shape and form a world where there are no limitations—that is, a world where there are no outlines; that is, a world where there are no shapes. There is nothing baser than that infinity. They say they wish to be as strong as the universe, but they really wish the whole universe as weak as themselves.

Chapter 15
On Smart Novelists and the Smart Set

n one sense, at any rate, it is more valuable to read bad literature than good literature. Good literature may tell us the mind of one man; but bad literature may tell us the mind of many men. A good novel tells us the truth about its hero; but a bad novel tells us the truth about its author. It does much more than that, it tells us the truth about its readers; and, oddly enough, it tells us this all the more the more cynical and immoral be the motive of its manufacture. The more dishonest a book is as a book the more honest it is as a public document. A sincere novel exhibits the simplicity of one particular man; an insincere novel exhibits the simplicity of mankind. The pedantic decisions and definable readjustments of man may be found in scrolls and statute books and scriptures; but men's basic assumptions and everlasting energies are to be found in penny dreadfuls and halfpenny novelettes. Thus a man, like many men of real culture in our day, might learn from good literature nothing except the power to appreciate good literature. But from bad literature he might learn to govern empires and look over the map of mankind.

There is one rather interesting example of this state of things in which the weaker literature is really the stronger and the stronger the weaker. It is the case of what may be called, for the sake of an approximate description, the literature of aristocracy; or, if you prefer the description, the literature of snobbishness. Now if any one wishes to find a really effective and comprehensible and permanent case for aristocracy well and sincerely stated, let him read, not the modern philosophical conservatives, not even Nietzsche, let him read the Bow Bells Novelettes. Of the case of Nietzsche I am confessedly more doubtful. Nietzsche and the Bow Bells Novelettes have both obviously the same fundamental character; they both worship the tall man with curling moustaches and herculean bodily power, and they both worship him in a manner which is somewhat feminine and hysterical. Even here, however, the Novelette easily maintains its philosophical superiority, because it does attribute to the strong man those virtues which do commonly belong to him, such virtues as laziness and kindliness and a rather reckless benevolence, and a great dislike of hurting the weak. Nietzsche, on the other hand, attributes to the strong man that scorn against weakness which only exists among invalids. It is not, however, of the secondary merits of the great German philosopher, but of the primary merits of the Bow Bells Novelettes, that it is my present affair to speak. The picture of aristocracy in the popular sentimental novelette seems to me very satisfactory as a permanent political and philosophical guide. It may be inaccurate about details such as the title by which a baronet is addressed or the width of a mountain chasm which a baronet can conveniently leap, but it is not a bad description of the general idea and intention of aristocracy as they exist in human affairs. The essential dream of aristocracy is magnificence and valour; and if the Family Herald Supplement sometimes distorts or exaggerates these things, at least, it does not fall short in them. It never errs by making the mountain chasm too narrow or the title of the baronet insufficiently impressive. But above this sane reliable old literature of snobbishness there has arisen in our time another kind of literature of snobbishness which, with its much higher pretensions, seems to me worthy of very much less respect. Incidentally (if that matters), it is much better literature. But it is immeasurably worse philosophy, immeasurably worse ethics and politics, immeasurably worse vital rendering of aristocracy and humanity as they really are. From such books as those of which I wish now to speak we can discover what a clever man can do with the idea of aristocracy. But from the Family Herald Supplement literature we can learn what the idea of aristocracy can do with a man who is not clever. And when we know that we know English history.

This new aristocratic fiction must have caught the attention of everybody who has read the best fiction for the last fifteen years. It is that genuine or alleged literature of the Smart Set which represents that set as distinguished, not only by smart dresses, but by smart sayings. To the bad baronet, to the good baronet, to the romantic and misunderstood baronet who is supposed to be a bad baronet, but is a good baronet, this school has added a conception undreamed of in the former years—the conception of an amusing baronet. The aristocrat is not merely to be taller than mortal men and stronger and handsomer, he is also to be more witty. He is the long man with the short epigram. Many eminent, and deservedly eminent, modern novelists must accept some responsibility for having supported this worst form of snobbishness—an intellectual snobbishness. The talented author of "Dodo" is responsible for having in some sense created the fashion as a fashion. Mr. Hichens, in the "Green Carnation," reaffirmed the strange idea that young noblemen talk well; though his case had some vague biographical foundation, and in consequence an excuse. Mrs. Craigie is considerably guilty in the matter, although, or rather because, she has combined the aristocratic note with a note of some moral and even religious sincerity. When you are saving a man's soul, even in a novel, it is indecent to mention that he is a gentleman. Nor can blame in this matter be altogether removed from a man of much greater ability, and a man who has proved his possession of the highest of human instinct, the romantic instinct—I mean Mr. Anthony Hope. In a galloping, impossible melodrama like "The Prisoner of Zenda," the blood of kings fanned an excellent fantastic thread or theme. But the blood of kings is not a thing that can be taken seriously. And when, for example, Mr. Hope devotes so much serious and sympathetic study to the man called Tristram of Blent, a man who throughout burning boyhood thought of nothing but a silly old estate, we feel even in Mr. Hope the hint of this excessive concern about the oligarchic idea. It is hard for any ordinary person to feel so much interest in a young man whose whole aim is to own the house of Blent at the time when every other young man is owning the stars.

Mr. Hope, however, is a very mild case, and in him there is not only an element of romance, but also a fine element of irony which warns us against taking all this elegance too seriously. Above all, he shows his sense in not making his noblemen so incredibly equipped with impromptu repartee. This habit of insisting on the wit of the wealthier classes is the last and most servile of all the servilities. It is, as I have said, immeasurably more contemptible than the snobbishness of the novelette which describes the nobleman as smiling like an Apollo or riding a mad elephant. These may be exaggerations of beauty and courage, but beauty and courage are the unconscious ideals of aristocrats, even of stupid aristocrats.

The nobleman of the novelette may not be sketched with any very close or conscientious attention to the daily habits of noblemen. But he is something more important than a reality; he is a practical ideal. The gentleman of fiction may not copy the gentleman of real life; but the gentleman of real life is copying the gentleman of fiction. He may not be particularly good-looking, but he would rather be good-looking than anything else; he may not have ridden on a mad elephant, but he rides a pony as far as possible with an air as if he had. And, upon the whole, the upper class not only especially desire these qualities of beauty and courage, but in some degree, at any rate, especially possess them. Thus there is nothing really mean or sycophantic about the popular literature which makes all its marquises seven feet high. It is snobbish, but it is not servile. Its exaggeration is based on an exuberant and honest admiration; its honest admiration is based upon something which is in some degree, at any rate, really there. The English lower classes do not fear the English upper classes in the least; nobody could. They simply and freely and sentimentally worship them. The strength of the aristocracy is not in the aristocracy at all; it is in the slums. It is not in the House of Lords; it is not in the Civil Service; it is not in the Government offices; it is not even in the huge and disproportionate monopoly of the English land. It is in a certain spirit. It is in the fact that when a navvy wishes to praise a man, it comes readily to his tongue to say that he has behaved like a gentleman. From a democratic point of view he might as well say that he had behaved like a viscount. The oligarchic character of the modern English commonwealth does not rest, like many oligarchies, on the cruelty of the rich to the poor. It does not even rest on the kindness of the rich to the poor. It rests on the perennial and unfailing kindness of the poor to the rich.

The snobbishness of bad literature, then, is not servile; but the snobbishness of good literature is servile. The old-fashioned halfpenny romance where the duchesses sparkled with diamonds was not servile; but the new romance where they sparkle with epigrams is servile. For in thus attributing a special and startling degree of intellect and conversational or controversial power to the upper classes, we are attributing something which is not especially their virtue or even especially their aim. We are, in the words of Disraeli (who, being a genius and not a gentleman, has perhaps primarily to answer for the introduction of this method of flattering the gentry), we are performing the essential function of flattery which is flattering the people for the qualities they have not got. Praise may be gigantic and insane without having any quality of flattery so long as it is praise of something that is noticeably in existence. A man may say that a giraffe's head strikes the stars, or that a whale fills the German Ocean, and still be only in a rather excited state about a favourite animal. But when he begins to congratulate the giraffe on his feathers, and the whale on the elegance of his legs, we find ourselves confronted with that social element which we call flattery. The middle and lower orders of London can sincerely, though not perhaps safely, admire the health and grace of the English aristocracy. And this for the very simple reason that the aristocrats are, upon the whole, more healthy and graceful than the poor. But they cannot honestly admire the wit of the aristocrats. And this for the simple reason that the aristocrats are not more witty than the poor, but a very great deal less so. A man does not hear, as in the smart novels, these gems of verbal felicity dropped between diplomatists at dinner. Where he really does hear them is between two omnibus conductors in a block in Holborn. The witty peer whose impromptus fill the books of Mrs. Craigie or Miss Fowler, would, as a matter of fact, be torn to shreds in the art of conversation by the first boot-black he had the misfortune to fall foul of. The poor are merely sentimental, and very excusably sentimental, if they praise the gentleman for having a ready hand and ready money. But they are strictly slaves and sycophants if they praise him for having a ready tongue. For that they have far more themselves.

The element of oligarchical sentiment in these novels, however, has, I think, another and subtler aspect, an aspect more difficult to understand and more worth understanding. The modern gentleman, particularly the modern English gentle-man, has become so central and important in these books, and through them in the whole of our current literature and our current mode of thought, that certain qualities of his, whether original or recent, essential or accidental, have altered the quality of our English comedy. In particular, that stoical ideal, absurdly supposed to be the English ideal, has stiffened and chilled us. It is not the English ideal; but it is to some extent the aristocratic ideal; or it may be only the ideal of aristocracy in its autumn or decay. The gentleman is a Stoic because he is a sort of savage, because he is filled with a great elemental fear that some stranger will speak to him. That is why a third-class carriage is a community, while a first-class carriage is a place of wild hermits. But this matter, which is difficult, I may be permitted to approach in a more circuitous way.

The haunting element of ineffectualness which runs through so much of the witty and epigrammatic fiction fashionable during the last eight or ten years, which runs through such works of a real though varying ingenuity as "Dodo," or "Concerning Isabel Carnaby," or even "Some Emotions and a Moral," may be expressed in various ways, but to most of us I think it will ultimately amount to the same thing. This new frivolity is inadequate because there is in it no strong sense of an unuttered joy. The men and women who exchange the repartees may not only be hating each other, but hating even themselves. Any one of them might be bankrupt that day, or sentenced to be shot the next. They are joking, not because they are merry, but because they are not; out of the emptiness of the heart the mouth speaketh. Even when they talk pure nonsense it is a careful nonsense—a nonsense of which they are economical, or, to use the perfect expression of Mr. W. S. Gilbert in "Patience," it is such "precious nonsense." Even when they become light-headed they do not become light-hearted. All those who have read anything of the rationalism of the moderns know that their Reason is a sad thing. But even their unreason is sad.

The causes of this incapacity are also not very difficult to indicate. The chief of all, of course, is that miserable fear of being sentimental, which is the meanest of all the modern terrors—meaner even than the terror which produces hygiene. Everywhere the robust and uproarious humour has come from the men who were capable not merely of sentimentalism, but a very silly sentimentalism. There has been no humour so robust or uproarious as that of the sentimentalist Steele or the sentimentalist Sterne or the sentimentalist Dickens. These creatures who wept like women were the creatures who laughed like men. It is true that the humour of Micawber is good literature and that the pathos of little Nell is bad. But the kind of man who had the courage to write so badly in the one case is the kind of man who would have the courage to write so well in the other. The same unconsciousness, the same violent innocence, the same gigantesque scale of action which brought the Napoleon of Comedy his Jena brought him also his Moscow. And herein is especially shown the frigid and feeble limitations of our modern wits. They make violent efforts, they make heroic and almost pathetic efforts, but they cannot really write badly. There are moments when we almost think that they are achieving the effect, but our hope shrivels to nothing the moment we compare their little failures with the enormous imbecilities of Byron or Shakespeare.

For a hearty laugh it is necessary to have touched the heart. I do not know why touching the heart should always be connected only with the idea of touching it to compassion or a sense of distress. The heart can be touched to joy and triumph; the heart can be touched to amusement. But all our comedians are tragic comedians. These later fashionable writers are so pessimistic in bone and marrow that they never seem able to imagine the heart having any concern with mirth. When they speak of the heart, they always mean the pangs and disappointments of the emotional life. When they say that a man's heart is in the right place, they mean, apparently, that it is in his boots. Our ethical societies understand fellowship, but they do not understand good fellowship. Similarly, our wits understand talk, but not what Dr. Johnson called a good talk. In order to have, like Dr. Johnson, a good talk, it is emphatically necessary to be, like Dr. Johnson, a good man—to have friendship and honour and an abysmal tenderness. Above all, it is necessary to be openly and indecently humane, to confess with fulness all the primary pities and fears of Adam. Johnson was a clear-headed humorous man, and therefore he did not mind talking seriously about religion. Johnson was a brave man, one of the bravest that ever walked, and therefore he did not mind avowing to any one his consuming fear of death.

The idea that there is something English in the repression of one's feelings is one of those ideas which no Englishman ever heard of until England began to be governed exclusively by Scotchmen, Americans, and Jews. At the best, the idea is a generalization from the Duke of Wellington—who was an Irishman. At the worst, it is a part of that silly Teutonism which knows as little about England as it does about anthropology, but which is always talking about Vikings. As a matter of fact, the Vikings did not repress their feelings in the least. They cried like babies and kissed each other like girls; in short, they acted in that respect like Achilles and all strong heroes the children of the gods. And though the English nationality has probably not much more to do with the Vikings than the French nationality or the Irish nationality, the English have certainly been the children of the Vikings in the matter of tears and kisses. It is not merely true that all the most typically English men of letters, like Shakespeare and Dickens, Richardson and Thackeray, were sentimentalists. It is also true that all the most typically English men of action were sentimentalists, if possible, more sentimental. In the great Elizabethan age, when the English nation was finally hammered out, in the great eighteenth century when the British Empire was being built up everywhere, where in all these times, where was this symbolic stoical Englishman who dresses in drab and black and represses his feelings? Were all the Elizabethan palladins and pirates like that? Were any of them like that? Was Grenville concealing his emotions when he broke wine-glasses to pieces with his teeth and bit them till the blood poured down? Was Essex restraining his excitement when he threw his hat into the sea? Did Raleigh think it sensible to answer the Spanish guns only, as Stevenson says, with a flourish of insulting trumpets? Did Sydney ever miss an opportunity of making a theatrical remark in the whole course of his life and death? Were even the Puritans Stoics? The English Puritans repressed a good deal, but even they were too English to repress their feelings. It was by a great miracle of genius assuredly that Carlyle contrived to admire simultaneously two things so irreconcilably opposed as silence and Oliver Cromwell. Cromwell was the very reverse of a strong, silent man. Cromwell was always talking, when he was not crying. Nobody, I suppose, will accuse the author of "Grace Abounding" of being ashamed of his feelings. Milton, indeed, it might be possible to represent as a Stoic; in some sense he was a Stoic, just as he was a prig and a polygamist and several other unpleasant and heathen things. But when we have passed that great and desolate name, which may really be counted an exception, we find the tradition of English emotionalism immediately resumed and unbrokenly continuous. Whatever may have been the moral beauty of the passions of Etheridge and Dorset, Sedley and Buckingham, they cannot be accused of the fault of fastidiously concealing them. Charles the

Second was very popular with the English because, like all the jolly English kings, he displayed his passions. William the Dutchman was very unpopular with the English because, not being an Englishman, he did hide his emotions. He was, in fact, precisely the ideal Englishman of our modern theory; and precisely for that reason all the real Englishmen loathed him like leprosy. With the rise of the great England of the eighteenth century, we find this open and emotional tone still maintained in letters and politics, in arts and in arms. Perhaps the only quality which was possessed in common by the great Fielding, and the great Richardson was that neither of them hid their feelings. Swift, indeed, was hard and logical, because Swift was Irish. And when we pass to the soldiers and the rulers, the patriots and the empire-builders of the eighteenth century, we find, as I have said, that they were, If possible, more romantic than the romancers, more poetical than the poets. Chatham, who showed the world all his strength, showed the House of Commons all his weakness. Wolfe walked about the room with a drawn sword calling himself Caesar and Hannibal, and went to death with poetry in his mouth. Clive was a man of the same type as Cromwell or Bunyan, or, for the matter of that, Johnson—that is, he was a strong, sensible man with a kind of running spring of hysteria and melancholy in him. Like Johnson, he was all the more healthy because he was morbid. The tales of all the admirals and adventurers of that England are full of braggadocio, of sentimentality, of splendid affectation. But it is scarcely necessary to multiply examples of the essentially romantic Englishman when one example towers above them all. Mr. Rudyard Kipling has said complacently of the English, "We do not fall on the neck and kiss when we come together." It is true that this ancient and universal custom has vanished with the modern weakening of England. Sydney would have thought nothing of kissing Spenser. But I willingly concede that Mr. Broderick would not be likely to kiss Mr. Arnold-Foster, if that be any proof of the increased manliness and military greatness of England. But the Englishman who does not show his feelings has not altogether given up the power of seeing something English in the great sea-hero of the Napoleonic war. You cannot break the legend of Nelson. And across the sunset of that glory is written in flaming letters for ever the great English sentiment, "Kiss me, Hardy."

This ideal of self-repression, then, is, whatever else it is, not English. It is, perhaps, somewhat Oriental, it is slightly Prussian, but in the main it does not come, I think, from any racial or national source. It is, as I have said, in some sense aristocratic; it comes not from a people, but from a class. Even aristocracy, I think, was not quite so stoical in the days when it was really strong. But whether this unemotional ideal be the genuine tradition of the gentleman, or only one of the inventions of the modern gentleman (who may be called the decayed gentleman), it certainly has something to do with the unemotional quality in these society novels. From representing aristocrats as people who suppressed their feelings, it has been an easy step to representing aristocrats as people who had no feelings to suppress. Thus the modern oligarchist has made a virtue for the oligarchy of the hardness as well as the brightness of the diamond. Like a sonneteer addressing his lady in the seventeenth century, he seems to use the word "cold" almost as a eulogium, and the word "heartless" as a kind of compliment. Of course, in people so incurably kind-hearted and babyish as are the English gentry, it would be impossible to create anything that can be called positive cruelty; so in these books they exhibit a sort of negative cruelty. They cannot be cruel in acts, but they can be so in words. All this means one thing, and one thing only. It means that the living and invigorating ideal of England must be looked for in the masses; it must be looked for where Dickens found it—Dickens among whose glories it was to be a humorist, to be a sentimentalist, to be an optimist, to be a poor man, to be an Englishman, but the greatest of whose glories was that he saw all mankind in its amazing and tropical luxuriance, and did not even notice the aristocracy; Dickens, the greatest of whose glories was that he could not describe a gentleman.

Chapter 16
On Mr. McCabe and a Divine Frivolity

critic once remonstrated with me saying, with an air of indignant reasonableness, "If you must make jokes, at least you need not make them on such serious subjects." I replied with a natural simplicity and wonder, "About what other subjects can one make jokes except serious subjects?" It is quite useless to talk about profane jesting. All jesting is in its nature profane, in the sense that it must be the sudden realization that something which thinks itself solemn is not so very solemn after all. If a joke is not a joke about religion or morals, it is a joke about police-magistrates or scientific professors or undergraduates dressed up as Queen Victoria. And people joke about the police-magistrate more than they joke about the Pope, not because the police-magistrate is a more frivolous subject, but, on the contrary, because the police-magistrate is a more serious subject than the Pope. The Bishop of Rome has no jurisdiction in this realm of England; whereas the police-magistrate may bring his solemnity to bear quite suddenly upon us. Men make jokes about old scientific professors, even more than they make them about bishops—not because science is lighter than religion, but because science is always by its nature more solemn and austere than religion. It is not I; it is not even a particular class of journalists or jesters who make jokes about the matters which are of most awful import; it is the whole human race. If there is one thing more than another which any one will admit who has the smallest knowledge of the world, it is that men are always speaking gravely and earnestly and with the utmost possible care about the things that are not important, but always talking frivolously about the things that are. Men talk for hours with the faces of a college of cardinals about things like golf, or tobacco, or waistcoats, or party politics. But all the most grave and dreadful things in the world are the oldest jokes in the world—being married; being hanged.

One gentleman, however, Mr. McCabe, has in this matter made to me something that almost amounts to a personal appeal; and as he happens to be a man for whose sincerity and intellectual virtue I have a high respect, I do not feel inclined to let it pass without some attempt to satisfy my critic in the matter. Mr. McCabe devotes a considerable part of the last essay in the collection called "Christianity and Rationalism on Trial" to an objection, not to my thesis, but to my method, and a very friendly and dignified appeal to me to alter it. I am much inclined to defend myself in this matter out of mere respect for Mr. McCabe, and still more so out of mere respect for the truth which is, I think, in danger by his error, not only in this question, but in others. In order that there may be no injustice done in the matter, I will quote Mr. McCabe himself. "But before I follow Mr. Chesterton in some detail I would make a general observation on his method.

He is as serious as I am in his ultimate purpose, and I respect him for that. He knows, as I do, that humanity stands at a solemn parting of the ways. Towards some unknown goal it presses through the ages, impelled by an overmastering desire of happiness. To-day it hesitates, lightheartedly enough, but every serious thinker knows how momentous the decision may be. It is, apparently, deserting the path of religion and entering upon the path of secularism. Will it lose itself in quagmires of sensuality down this new path, and pant and toil through years of civic and industrial anarchy, only to learn it had lost the road, and must return to religion? Or will it find that at last it is leaving the mists and the quagmires behind it; that it is ascending the slope of the hill so long dimly discerned ahead, and making straight for the long-sought Utopia? This is the drama of our time, and every man and every woman should understand it.

"Mr. Chesterton understands it. Further, he gives us credit for understanding it. He has nothing of that paltry meanness or strange density of so many of his colleagues, who put us down as aimless iconoclasts or moral anarchists. He admits that we are waging a thankless war for what we take to be Truth and Progress. He is doing the same. But why, in the name of all that is reasonable, should we, when we are agreed on the momentousness of the issue either way, forthwith desert serious methods of conducting the controversy? Why, when the vital need of our time is to induce men and women to collect their thoughts occasionally, and be men and women—nay, to remember that they are really gods that hold the destinies of humanity on their knees—why should we think that this kaleidoscopic play of phrases is inopportune? The ballets of the Alhambra, and the fireworks of the Crystal Palace, and Mr. Chesterton's Daily News articles, have their place in life. But how a serious social student can think of curing the thoughtlessness of our generation by strained paradoxes; of giving people a sane grasp of social problems by literary sleight-of-hand; of settling important questions by a reckless shower of rocket-metaphors and inaccurate 'facts,' and the substitution of imagination for judgment, I cannot see."

I quote this passage with a particular pleasure, because Mr. McCabe certainly cannot put too strongly the degree to which I give him and his school credit for their complete sincerity and responsibility of philosophical attitude. I am quite certain that they mean every word they say. I also mean every word I say. But why is it that Mr. McCabe has some sort of mysterious hesitation about admitting that I mean every word I say; why is it that he is not quite as certain of my mental responsibility as I am of his mental responsibility? If we attempt to answer the question directly and well, we shall, I think, have come to the root of the matter by the shortest cut.

Mr. McCabe thinks that I am not serious but only funny, because Mr. McCabe thinks that funny is the opposite of serious. Funny is the opposite of not funny, and of nothing else. The question of whether a man expresses himself in a grotesque or laughable phraseology, or in a stately and restrained phraseology, is not a question of motive or of moral state, it is a question of instinctive language and self-expression. Whether a man chooses to tell the truth in long sentences or short jokes is a problem analogous to whether he chooses to tell the truth in French or German. Whether a man preaches his gospel grotesquely or gravely is merely like the question of whether he preaches it in prose or verse. The question of whether Swift was funny in his irony is quite another sort of question to the question of whether Swift was serious in his pessimism. Surely even Mr. McCabe would not maintain that the more funny "Gulliver" is in its method the less it can be sincere in its object. The truth is, as I have said, that in this sense the two qualities of fun and seriousness have nothing whatever to do with each other, they are no more comparable than black and triangular. Mr. Bernard Shaw is funny and sincere. Mr. George Robey is funny and not sincere. Mr. McCabe is sincere and not funny. The average Cabinet Minister is not sincere and not funny.

In short, Mr. McCabe is under the influence of a primary fallacy which I have found very common in men of the clerical type. Numbers of clergymen have from time to time reproached me for making jokes about religion; and they have almost always invoked the authority of that very sensible commandment which says, "Thou shalt not take the name of the Lord thy God in vain." Of course, I pointed out that I was not in any conceivable sense taking the name in vain. To take a thing and make a joke out of it is not to take it in vain. It is, on the contrary, to take it and use it for an uncommonly good object. To use a thing in vain means to use it without use. But a joke may be exceedingly useful; it may contain the whole earthly sense, not to mention the whole heavenly sense, of a situation. And those who find in the Bible the commandment can find in the Bible any number of the jokes. In the same book in which God's name is fenced from being taken in vain, God himself overwhelms Job with a torrent of terrible levities. The same book which says that God's name must not be taken vainly, talks easily and carelessly about God laughing and God winking. Evidently it is not here that we have to look for genuine examples of what is meant by a vain use of the name. And it is not very difficult to see where we have really to look for it. The people (as I tactfully pointed out to them) who really take the name of the Lord in vain are the clergymen themselves. The thing which is fundamentally and really frivolous is not a careless joke. The thing which is fundamentally and really frivolous is a careless solemnity. If Mr. McCabe really wishes to know what sort of guarantee of reality and solidity is afforded by the mere act of what is called talking seriously, let him spend a happy Sunday in going the round of the pulpits. Or, better still, let him drop in at the House of Commons or the House of Lords. Even Mr. McCabe would admit that these men are solemn—more solemn than I am. And even Mr. McCabe, I think, would admit that these men are frivolous—more frivolous than I am. Why should Mr. McCabe be so eloquent about the danger arising from fantastic and paradoxical writers? Why should he be so ardent in desiring grave and verbose writers? There are not so very many fantastic and paradoxical writers. But there are a gigantic number of grave and verbose writers; and it is by the efforts of the grave and verbose writers that everything that Mr. McCabe detests (and everything that I detest, for that matter) is kept in existence and energy. How can it have come about that a man as intelligent as Mr. McCabe can think that paradox and jesting stop the way? It is solemnity that is stopping the way in every department of modern effort. It is his own favourite "serious methods;" it is his own favourite "momentousness;" it is his own favourite "judgment" which stops the way everywhere. Every man who has ever headed a deputation to a minister knows this. Every man who has ever written a letter to the Times knows it. Every rich man who wishes to stop the mouths of the poor talks about "momentousness." Every Cabinet minister who has not got an answer suddenly develops a "judgment." Every sweater who uses vile methods recommends "serious methods." I said a moment ago that sincerity had nothing to do with solemnity, but I confess that I am not so certain that I was right. In the modern world, at any rate, I am not so sure that I was right. In the modern world solemnity is the direct enemy of sincerity. In the modern world sincerity is almost always on one side, and solemnity almost always on the other. The only answer possible to the fierce and glad attack of sincerity is the miserable answer of solemnity. Let Mr. McCabe, or any one else who is much concerned that we should be grave in order to be sincere, simply imagine the scene in some government office in which Mr. Bernard Shaw should head a Socialist deputation to Mr. Austen Chamberlain. On which side would be the solemnity? And on which the sincerity?

I am, indeed, delighted to discover that Mr. McCabe reckons Mr. Shaw along with me in his system of condemnation of frivolity. He said once, I believe, that he always wanted Mr. Shaw to label his paragraphs serious or comic. I do not know which paragraphs of Mr. Shaw are paragraphs to be labelled serious; but surely there can be no doubt that this paragraph of Mr. McCabe's is one to be labelled comic. He also says, in the article I am now discussing, that Mr. Shaw has the reputation of deliberately saying everything which his hearers do not expect him to say. I need not labour the inconclusiveness and weakness of this, because it has already been dealt with in my remarks on Mr. Bernard Shaw. Suffice it to say here that the only serious reason which I can imagine inducing any one person to listen to any other is, that the first person looks to the second person with an ardent faith and a fixed attention, expecting him to say what he does not expect him to say. It may be a paradox, but that is because paradoxes are true. It may not be rational, but that is because rationalism is wrong. But clearly it is quite true that whenever we go to hear a prophet or teacher we may or may not expect wit, we may or may not expect eloquence, but we do expect what we do not expect. We may not expect the true, we may not even expect the wise, but we do expect the unexpected. If we do not expect the unexpected, why do we go there at all? If we expect the expected, why do we not sit at home and expect it by ourselves? If Mr.

McCabe means merely this about Mr. Shaw, that he always has some unexpected application of his doctrine to give to those who listen to him, what he says is quite true, and to say it is only to say that Mr. Shaw is an original man. But if he means that Mr. Shaw has ever professed or preached any doctrine but one, and that his own, then what he says is not true. It is not my business to defend Mr. Shaw; as has been seen already, I disagree with him altogether. But I do not mind, on his behalf offering in this matter a flat defiance to all his ordinary opponents, such as Mr. McCabe. I defy Mr. McCabe, or anybody else, to mention one single instance in which Mr. Shaw has, for the sake of wit or novelty, taken up any position which was not directly deducible from the body of his doctrine as elsewhere expressed. I have been, I am happy to say, a tolerably close student of Mr. Shaw's utterances, and I request Mr. McCabe, if he will not believe that I mean anything else, to believe that I mean this challenge.

All this, however, is a parenthesis. The thing with which I am here immediately concerned is Mr. McCabe's appeal to me not to be so frivolous. Let me return to the actual text of that appeal. There are, of course, a great many things that I might say about it in detail. But I may start with saying that Mr. McCabe is in error in supposing that the danger which I anticipate from the disappearance of religion is the increase of sensuality. On the contrary, I should be inclined to anticipate a decrease in sensuality, because I anticipate a decrease in life. I do not think that under modern Western materialism we should have anarchy. I doubt whether we should have enough individual valour and spirit even to have liberty. It is quite an old-fashioned fallacy to suppose that our objection to scepticism is that it removes the discipline from life. Our objection to scepticism is that it removes the motive power. Materialism is not a thing which destroys mere restraint. Materialism itself is the great restraint. The McCabe school advocates a political liberty, but it denies spiritual liberty. That is, it abolishes the laws which could be broken, and substitutes laws that cannot. And that is the real slavery.

The truth is that the scientific civilization in which Mr. McCabe believes has one rather particular defect; it is perpetually tending to destroy that democracy or power of the ordinary man in which Mr. McCabe also believes. Science means specialism, and specialism means oligarchy. If you once establish the habit of trusting particular men to produce particular results in physics or astronomy, you leave the door open for the equally natural demand that you should trust particular men to do particular things in government and the coercing of men. If, you feel it to be reasonable that one beetle should be the only study of one man, and that one man the only student of that one beetle, it is surely a very harmless consequence to go on to say that politics should be the only study of one man, and that one man the only student of politics. As I have pointed out elsewhere in this book, the expert is more aristocratic than the aristocrat, because the aristocrat is only the man who lives well, while the expert is the man who knows better. But if we look at the progress of our scientific civilization we see a gradual increase everywhere of the specialist over the popular function. Once men sang together round a table in chorus; now one man sings alone, for the absurd reason that he can sing better. If scientific civilization goes on (which is most improbable) only one man will laugh, because he can laugh better than the rest.

I do not know that I can express this more shortly than by taking as a text the single sentence of Mr. McCabe, which runs as follows: "The ballets of the Alhambra and the fireworks of the Crystal Palace and Mr. Chesterton's Daily News articles have their places in life." I wish that my articles had as noble a place as either of the other two things mentioned. But let us ask ourselves (in a spirit of love, as Mr. Chadband would say), what are the ballets of the Alhambra? The ballets of the Alhambra are institutions in which a particular selected row of persons in pink go through an operation known as dancing. Now, in all commonwealths dominated by a religion—in the Christian commonwealths of the Middle Ages and in many rude societies—this habit of dancing was a common habit with everybody, and was not necessarily confined to a professional class. A person could dance without being a dancer; a person could dance without being a specialist; a person could dance without being pink. And, in proportion as Mr. McCabe's scientific civilization advances—that is, in proportion as religious civilization (or real civilization) decays—the more and more "well trained," the more and more pink, become the people who do dance, and the more and more numerous become the people who don't. Mr. McCabe may recognize an example of what I mean in the gradual discrediting in society of the ancient European waltz or dance with partners, and the substitution of that horrible and degrading oriental interlude which is known as skirt-dancing. That is the whole essence of decadence, the effacement of five people who do a thing for fun by one person who does it for money. Now it follows, therefore, that when Mr. McCabe says that the ballets of the Alhambra and my articles "have their place in life," it ought to be pointed out to him that he is doing his best to create a world in which dancing, properly speaking, will have no place in life at all. He is, indeed, trying to create a world in which there will be no life for dancing to have a place in. The very fact that Mr. McCabe thinks of dancing as a thing belonging to some hired women at the Alhambra is an illustration of the same principle by which he is able to think of religion as a thing belonging to some hired men in white neckties. Both these things are things which should not be done for us, but by us. If Mr. McCabe were really religious he would be happy. If he were really happy he would dance.

Briefly, we may put the matter in this way. The main point of modern life is not that the Alhambra ballet has its place in life. The main point, the main enormous tragedy of modern life, is that Mr. McCabe has not his place in the Alhambra ballet. The joy of changing and graceful posture, the joy of suiting the swing of music to the swing of limbs, the joy of whirling drapery, the joy of standing on one leg,—all these should belong by rights to Mr. McCabe and to me; in short, to the ordinary healthy citizen. Probably we should not consent to go through these evolutions. But that is because we are miserable moderns and rationalists. We do not merely love ourselves more than we love duty; we actually love ourselves more than we love joy.

When, therefore, Mr. McCabe says that he gives the Alhambra dances (and my articles) their place in life, I think we are justified in pointing out that by the very nature of the case of his philosophy and of his favourite civilization he gives them a very inadequate place. For (if I may pursue the too flattering parallel) Mr. McCabe thinks of the Alhambra and of my articles as two very odd and absurd things, which some special people do (probably for money) in order to amuse him. But if he had ever felt himself the ancient, sublime, elemental, human instinct to dance, he would have discovered that dancing is not a frivolous thing at all, but a very serious thing. He would have discovered that it is the one grave and chaste and decent method of expressing a certain class of emotions. And similarly, if he had ever had, as Mr. Shaw and I have had, the impulse to what he calls paradox, he would have discovered that paradox again is not a frivolous thing, but a very serious thing. He would have found that paradox simply means a certain defiant joy which belongs to belief. I should regard any civilization which was without a universal habit of uproarious dancing as being, from the full human point of view, a defective civilization. And I should regard any mind which had not got the habit in one form or another of uproarious thinking as being, from the full human point of view, a defective mind. It is vain for Mr. McCabe to say that a ballet is a part of him. He should be part of a ballet, or else he is only part of a man. It is in vain for him to say that he is "not quarrelling with the importation of humour into the controversy." He ought himself to be importing humour into every controversy; for unless a man is in part a humorist, he is only in part a man. To sum up the whole matter very simply, if Mr. McCabe asks me why I import frivolity into a discussion of the nature of man, I answer, because frivolity is a part of the nature of man. If he asks me why I introduce what he calls paradoxes into a philosophical problem, I answer, because all philosophical problems tend to become paradoxical. If he objects to my treating of life riotously, I reply that life is a riot. And I say that the Universe as I see it, at any rate, is very much more like the fireworks at the Crystal Palace than it is like his own philosophy. About the whole cosmos there is a tense and secret festivity—like preparations for Guy Fawkes' day. Eternity is the eve of something. I never look up at the stars without feeling that they are the fires of a schoolboy's rocket, fixed in their everlasting fall.

Chapter 17
On the Wit of Whistler

hat capable and ingenious writer, Mr. Arthur Symons, has included in a book of essays recently published, I believe, an apologia for "London Nights," in which he says that morality should be wholly subordinated to art in criticism, and he uses the somewhat singular argument that art or the worship of beauty is the same in all ages, while morality differs in every period and in every respect. He appears to defy his critics or his readers to mention any permanent feature or quality in ethics. This is surely a very curious example of that extravagant bias against morality which makes so many ultra-modern aesthetes as morbid and fanatical as any Eastern hermit. Unquestionably it is a very common phrase of modern intellectualism to say that the morality of one age can be entirely different to the morality of another. And like a great many other phrases of modern intellectualism, it means literally nothing at all. If the two moralities are entirely different, why do you call them both moralities? It is as if a man said, "Camels in various places are totally diverse; some have six legs, some have none, some have scales, some have feathers, some have horns, some have wings, some are green, some are triangular. There is no point which they have in common." The ordinary man of sense would reply, "Then what makes you call them all camels? What do you mean by a camel? How do you know a camel when you see one?" Of course, there is a permanent substance of morality, as much as there is a permanent substance of art; to say that is only to say that morality is morality, and that art is art. An ideal art-critic would, no doubt, see the enduring beauty under every school; equally an ideal moralist would see the enduring ethic under every code. But practically some of the best Englishmen that ever lived could see nothing but filth and idolatry in the starry piety of the Brahmin. And it is equally true that practically the greatest group of artists that the world has ever seen, the giants of the Renaissance, could see nothing but barbarism in the ethereal energy of Gothic.

This bias against morality among the modern aesthetes is nothing very much paraded. And yet it is not really a bias against morality; it is a bias against other people's morality. It is generally founded on a very definite moral preference for a certain sort of life, pagan, plausible, humane. The modern aesthete, wishing us to believe that he values beauty more than conduct, reads Mallarme, and drinks absinthe in a tavern. But this is not only his favourite kind of beauty; it is also his favourite kind of conduct. If he really wished us to believe that he cared for beauty only, he ought to go to nothing but Wesleyan school treats, and paint the sunlight in the hair of the Wesleyan babies. He ought to read nothing but very eloquent theological sermons by old-fashioned Presbyterian divines. Here the lack of all possible moral sympathy would prove that his interest was purely verbal or pictorial, as it is; in all the books he reads and writes he clings to the skirts of his own morality and his own immorality. The champion of l'art pour l'art is always denouncing Ruskin for his moralizing. If he were really a champion of l'art pour l'art, he would be always insisting on Ruskin for his style.

The doctrine of the distinction between art and morality owes a great part of its success to art and morality being hopelessly mixed up in the persons and performances of its greatest exponents. Of this lucky contradiction the very incarnation was Whistler. No man ever preached the impersonality of art so well; no man ever preached the impersonality of art so personally. For him pictures had nothing to do with the problems of character; but for all his fiercest admirers his character was, as a matter of fact far more interesting than his pictures. He gloried in standing as an artist apart from right and wrong. But he succeeded by talking from morning till night about his rights and about his wrongs. His talents were many, his virtues, it must be confessed, not many, beyond that kindness to tried friends, on which many of his biographers insist, but which surely is a quality of all sane men, of pirates and pickpockets; beyond this, his outstanding virtues limit themselves chiefly to two admirable ones—courage and an abstract love of good work. Yet I fancy he won at last more by those two virtues than by all his talents. A man must be something of a moralist if he is to preach, even if he is to preach unmorality. Professor Walter Raleigh, in his "In Memoriam: James McNeill Whistler," insists, truly enough, on the strong streak of an eccentric honesty in matters strictly pictorial, which ran through his complex and slightly confused character. "He would destroy any of his works rather than leave a careless or inexpressive touch within the limits of the frame. He would begin again a hundred times over rather than attempt by patching to make his work seem better than it was."

No one will blame Professor Raleigh, who had to read a sort of funeral oration over Whistler at the opening of the Memorial Exhibition, if, finding himself in that position, he confined himself mostly to the merits and the stronger qualities of his subject. We should naturally go to some other type of composition for a proper consideration of the weaknesses of Whistler. But these must never be omitted from our view of him. Indeed, the truth is that it was not so much a question of the weaknesses of Whistler as of the intrinsic and primary weakness of Whistler. He was one of those people who live up to their emotional incomes, who are always taut and tingling with vanity. Hence he had no strength to spare; hence he had no kindness, no geniality; for geniality is almost definable as strength to spare. He had no god-like carelessness; he never forgot himself; his whole life was, to use his own expression, an arrangement. He went in for "the art of living"—a miserable trick. In a word, he was a great artist; but emphatically not a great man. In this connection I must differ strongly with Professor Raleigh upon what is, from a superficial literary point of view, one of his most effective points. He compares Whistler's laughter to the laughter of another man who was a great man as well as a great artist. "His attitude to the public was exactly the attitude taken up by Robert Browning, who suffered as long a period of neglect and mistake, in those lines of 'The Ring and the Book'—

> " 'Well, British Public, ye who like me not,
> (God love you!) and will have your proper laugh
> At the dark question; laugh it! I'd laugh first.'

"Mr. Whistler," adds Professor Raleigh, "always laughed first." The truth is, I believe, that Whistler never laughed at all. There was no laughter in his nature; because there was no thoughtlessness and self-abandonment, no humility. I cannot understand anybody reading "The Gentle Art of Making Enemies" and thinking that there is any laughter in the wit. His wit is a torture to him. He twists himself into arabesques of verbal felicity; he is full of a fierce carefulness; he is inspired with the complete seriousness of sincere malice. He hurts himself to hurt his opponent. Browning did laugh, because Browning did not care; Browning did not care, because Browning was a great man. And when Browning said in brackets to the simple, sensible people who did not like his books, "God love you!" he was not sneering in the least. He was laughing—that is to say, he meant exactly what he said.

There are three distinct classes of great satirists who are also great men—that is to say, three classes of men who can laugh at something without losing their souls. The satirist of the first type is the man who, first of all enjoys himself, and then enjoys his enemies. In this sense he loves his enemy, and by a kind of exaggeration of Christianity he loves his enemy the more the more he becomes an enemy. He has a sort of overwhelming and aggressive happiness in his assertion of anger; his curse is as human as a benediction. Of this type of satire the great example is Rabelais. This is the first typical example of satire, the satire which is voluble, which is violent, which is indecent, but which is not malicious. The satire of Whistler was not this. He was never in any of his controversies simply happy; the proof of it is that he never talked absolute nonsense. There is a second type of mind which produces satire with the quality of greatness. That is embodied in the satirist whose passions are released and let go by some intolerable sense of wrong. He is maddened by the sense of men being maddened; his tongue becomes an unruly member, and testifies against all mankind. Such a man was Swift, in whom the *saeva indignatio* was a bitterness to others, because it was a bitterness to himself. Such a satirist Whistler was not. He did not laugh because he was happy, like Rabelais. But neither did he laugh because he was unhappy, like Swift.

The third type of great satire is that in which he satirist is enabled to rise superior to his victim in the only serious sense which superiority can bear, in that of pitying the sinner and respecting the man even while he satirises both. Such an achievement can be found in a thing like Pope's "Atticus" a poem in which the satirist feels that he is satirising the weaknesses which belong specially to literary genius. Consequently he takes a pleasure in pointing out his enemy's strength before he points out his weakness. That is, perhaps, the highest and most honourable form of satire. That is not the satire of Whistler. He is not full of a great sorrow for the wrong done to human nature; for him the wrong is altogether done to himself.

He was not a great personality, because he thought so much about himself. And the case is stronger even than that. He was sometimes not even a great artist, because he thought so much about art. Any man with a vital knowledge of the human psychology ought to have the most profound suspicion of anybody who claims to be an artist, and talks a great deal about art. Art is a right and human thing, like walking or saying one's prayers; but the moment it begins to be talked about very solemnly, a man may be fairly certain that the thing has come into a congestion and a kind of difficulty.

The artistic temperament is a disease that afflicts amateurs. It is a disease which arises from men not having sufficient power of expression to utter and get rid of the element of art in their being. It is healthful to every sane man to utter the art within him; it is essential to every sane man to get rid of the art within him at all costs. Artists of a large and wholesome vitality get rid of their art easily, as they breathe easily, or perspire easily. But in artists of less force, the thing becomes a pressure, and produces a definite pain, which is called the artistic temperament. Thus, very great artists are able to be ordinary men—men like Shakespeare or Browning. There are many real tragedies of the artistic temperament, tragedies of vanity or violence or fear. But the great tragedy of the artistic temperament is that it cannot produce any art.

Whistler could produce art; and in so far he was a great man. But he could not forget art; and in so far he was only a man with the artistic temperament. There can be no stronger manifestation of the man who is a really great artist than the fact that he can dismiss the subject of art; that he can, upon due occasion, wish art at the bottom of the sea. Similarly, we should always be much more inclined to trust a solicitor who did not talk about conveyancing over the nuts and wine. What we really desire of any man conducting any business is that the full force of an ordinary man should be put into that particular study. We do not desire that the full force of that study should be put into an ordinary man. We do not in the least wish that our particular law-suit should pour its energy into our barrister's games with his children, or rides on his bicycle, or meditations on the morning star. But we do, as a matter of fact, desire that his games with his children, and his rides on his bicycle, and his meditations on the morning star should pour something of their energy into our law-suit. We do desire that if he has gained any especial lung development from the bicycle, or any bright and pleasing metaphors from the morning star, that the should be placed at our disposal in that particular forensic controversy. In a word, we are very glad that he is an ordinary man, since that may help him to be an exceptional lawyer.

Whistler never ceased to be an artist. As Mr. Max Beerbohm pointed out in one of his extraordinarily sensible and sincere critiques, Whistler really regarded Whistler as his greatest work of art. The white lock, the single eyeglass, the remarkable hat—these were much dearer to him than any nocturnes or arrangements that he ever threw off. He could throw off the nocturnes; for some mysterious reason he could not throw off the hat. He never threw off from himself that disproportionate accumulation of aestheticism which is the burden of the amateur.

It need hardly be said that this is the real explanation of the thing which has puzzled so many dilettante critics, the problem of the extreme ordinariness of the behaviour of so many great geniuses in history. Their behaviour was so ordinary that it was not recorded; hence it was so ordinary that it seemed mysterious. Hence people say that Bacon wrote Shakespeare. The modern artistic temperament cannot understand how a man who could write such lyrics as Shakespeare wrote, could be as keen as Shakespeare was on business transactions in a little town in Warwickshire. The explanation is simple enough; it is that Shakespeare had a real lyrical impulse, wrote a real lyric, and so got rid of the impulse and went about his business. Being an artist did not prevent him from being an ordinary man, any more than being a sleeper at night or being a diner at dinner prevented him from being an ordinary man.

All very great teachers and leaders have had this habit of assuming their point of view to be one which was human and casual, one which would readily appeal to every passing man. If a man is genuinely superior to his fellows the first thing that he believes in is the equality of man. We can see this, for instance, in that strange and innocent rationality with which Christ addressed any motley crowd that happened to stand about Him. "What man of you having a hundred sheep, and losing one, would not leave the ninety and nine in the wilderness, and go after that which was lost?" Or, again, "What man of you if his son ask for bread will he give him a stone, or if he ask for a fish will he give him a serpent?" This plainness, this almost prosaic camaraderie, is the note of all very great minds.

To very great minds the things on which men agree are so immeasurably more important than the things on which they differ, that the latter, for all practical purposes, disappear. They have too much in them of an ancient laughter even to endure to discuss the difference between the hats of two men who were both born of a woman, or between the subtly varied cultures of two men who have both to die. The first-rate great man is equal with other men, like Shakespeare. The second-rate great man is on his knees to other men, like Whitman. The third-rate great man is superior to other men, like Whistler.

Chapter 18
The Fallacy of the Young Nation

o say that a man is an idealist is merely to say that he is a man; but, nevertheless, it might be possible to effect some valid distinction between one kind of idealist and another. One possible distinction, for instance, could be effected by saying that humanity is divided into conscious idealists and unconscious idealists. In a similar way, humanity is divided into conscious ritualists and unconscious ritualists. The curious thing is, in that example as in others, that it is the conscious ritualism which is comparatively simple, the unconscious ritual which is really heavy and complicated. The ritual which is comparatively rude and straightforward is the ritual which people call "ritualistic." It consists of plain things like bread and wine and fire, and men falling on their faces. But the ritual which is really complex, and many coloured, and elaborate, and needlessly formal, is the ritual which people enact without knowing it. It consists not of plain things like wine and fire, but of really peculiar, and local, and exceptional, and ingenious things—things like door-mats, and door-knockers, and electric bells, and silk hats, and white ties, and shiny cards, and confetti. The truth is that the modern man scarcely ever gets back to very old and simple things except when he is performing some religious mummery. The modern man can hardly get away from ritual except by entering a ritualistic church. In the case of these old and mystical formalities we can at least say that the ritual is not mere ritual; that the symbols employed are in most cases symbols which belong to a primary human poetry. The most ferocious opponent of the Christian ceremonials must admit that if Catholicism had not instituted the bread and wine, somebody else would most probably have done so. Any one with a poetical instinct will admit that to the ordinary human instinct bread symbolizes something which cannot very easily be symbolized otherwise; that wine, to the ordinary human instinct, symbolizes something which cannot very easily be symbolized otherwise. But white ties in the evening are ritual, and nothing else but ritual. No one would pretend that white ties in the evening are primary and poetical. Nobody would maintain that the ordinary human instinct would in any age or country tend to symbolize the idea of evening by a white necktie. Rather, the ordinary human instinct would, I imagine, tend to symbolize evening by cravats with some of the colours of the sunset, not white neckties, but tawny or crimson neckties—neckties of purple or olive, or some darkened gold. Mr. J. A. Kensit, for example, is under the impression that he is not a ritualist. But the daily life of Mr. J. A. Kensit, like that of any ordinary modern man, is, as a matter of fact, one continual and compressed catalogue of mystical mummery and flummery. To take one instance out of an inevitable hundred: I imagine that Mr. Kensit takes off his hat to a lady; and what can be more solemn and absurd, considered in the abstract, than, symbolizing the existence of the other sex by taking off a portion of your clothing and waving it in the air? This, I repeat, is not a natural and primitive symbol, like fire or food. A man might just as well have to take off his waistcoat to a lady; and if a man, by the social ritual of his civilization, had to take off his waistcoat to a lady, every chivalrous and sensible man would take off his waistcoat to a lady. In short, Mr. Kensit, and those who agree with him, may think, and quite sincerely think, that men give too much incense and ceremonial to their adoration of the other world. But nobody thinks that he can give too much incense and ceremonial to the adoration of this world. All men, then, are ritualists, but are either conscious or unconscious ritualists. The conscious ritualists are generally satisfied with a few very simple and elementary signs; the unconscious ritualists are not satisfied with anything short of the whole of human life, being almost insanely ritualistic. The first is called a ritualist because he invents and remembers one rite; the other is called an anti-ritualist because he obeys and forgets a thousand. And a somewhat similar distinction to this which I have drawn with some unavoidable length, between the conscious ritualist and the unconscious ritualist, exists between the conscious idealist and the unconscious idealist. It is idle to inveigh against cynics and materialists—there are no cynics, there are no materialists. Every man is idealistic; only it so often happens that he has the wrong ideal. Every man is incurably sentimental; but, unfortunately, it is so often a false sentiment. When we talk, for instance, of some unscrupulous commercial figure, and say that he would do anything for money, we use quite an inaccurate expression, and we slander him very much. He would not do anything for money. He would do some things for money; he would sell his soul for money, for instance; and, as Mirabeau humorously said, he would be quite wise "to take money for muck." He would oppress humanity for money; but then it happens that humanity and the soul are not things that he believes in; they are not his ideals. But he has his own dim and delicate ideals; and he would not violate these for money. He would not drink out of the soup-tureen, for money. He would not wear his coat-tails in front, for money. He would not spread a report that he had softening of the brain, for money. In the actual practice of life we find, in the matter of ideals, exactly what we have already found in the matter of ritual. We find that while there is a perfectly genuine danger of fanaticism from the men who have unworldly ideals, the permanent and urgent danger of fanaticism is from the men who have worldly ideals.

People who say that an ideal is a dangerous thing, that it deludes and intoxicates, are perfectly right. But the ideal which intoxicates most is the least idealistic kind of ideal. The ideal which intoxicates least is the very ideal ideal; that sobers us suddenly, as all heights and precipices and great distances do. Granted that it is a great evil to mistake a cloud for a cape; still, the cloud, which can be most easily mistaken for a cape, is the cloud that is nearest the earth. Similarly, we may grant that it may be dangerous to mistake an ideal for something practical. But we shall still point out that, in this respect, the most dangerous ideal of all is the ideal which looks a little practical. It is difficult to attain a high ideal; consequently, it is almost impossible to persuade ourselves that we have attained it. But it is easy to attain a low ideal; consequently, it is easier still to persuade ourselves that we have attained it when we have done nothing of the kind. To take a random example. It might be called a high ambition to wish to be an archangel; the man who entertained such an ideal would very possibly exhibit asceticism, or even frenzy, but not, I think, delusion. He would not think he was an archangel, and go about flapping his hands under the impression that they were wings. But suppose that a sane man had a low ideal; suppose he wished to be a gentleman. Any one who knows the world knows that in nine weeks he would have persuaded himself that he was a gentleman; and this being manifestly not the case, the result will be very real and practical dislocations and calamities in social life. It is not the wild ideals which wreck the practical world; it is the tame ideals.

The matter may, perhaps, be illustrated by a parallel from our modern politics. When men tell us that the old Liberal politicians of the type of Gladstone cared only for ideals, of course, they are talking nonsense—they cared for a great many other things, including votes. And when men tell us that modern politicians of the type of Mr. Chamberlain or, in another way, Lord Rosebery, care only for votes or for material interest, then again they are talking nonsense—these men care for ideals like all other men. But the real distinction which may be drawn is this, that to the older politician the ideal was an ideal, and nothing else. To the new politician his dream is not only a good dream, it is a reality. The old politician would have said, "It would be a good thing if there were a Republican Federation dominating the world." But the modern politician does not say, "It would be a good thing if there were a British Imperialism dominating the world." He says, "It is a good thing that there is a British Imperialism dominating the world;" whereas clearly there is nothing of the kind. The old Liberal would say "There ought to be a good Irish government in Ireland." But the ordinary modern Unionist does not say, "There ought to be a good English government in Ireland." He says, "There is a good English government in Ireland;" which is absurd. In short, the modern politicians seem to think that a man becomes practical merely by making assertions entirely about practical things. Apparently, a delusion does not matter as long as it is a materialistic delusion. Instinctively most of us feel that, as a practical matter, even the contrary is true. I certainly would much rather share my apartments with a gentleman who thought he was God than with a gentleman who thought he was a grasshopper. To be continually haunted by practical images and practical problems, to be constantly thinking of things as actual, as urgent, as in process of completion—these things do not prove a man to be practical; these things, indeed, are among the most ordinary signs of a lunatic. That our modern statesmen are materialistic is nothing against their being also morbid. Seeing angels in a vision may make a man a supernaturalist to excess. But merely seeing snakes in delirium tremens does not make him a naturalist.

And when we come actually to examine the main stock notions of our modern practical politicians, we find that those main stock notions are mainly delusions. A great many instances might be given of the fact. We might take, for example, the case of that strange class of notions which underlie the word "union," and all the eulogies heaped upon it. Of course, union is no more a good thing in itself than separation is a good thing in itself. To have a party in favour of union and a party in favour of separation is as absurd as to have a party in favour of going upstairs and a party in favour of going downstairs. The question is not whether we go up or down stairs, but where we are going to, and what we are going, for? Union is strength; union is also weakness. It is a good thing to harness two horses to a cart; but it is not a good thing to try and turn two hansom cabs into one four-wheeler. Turning ten nations into one empire may happen to be as feasible as turning ten shillings into one half-sovereign. Also it may happen to be as preposterous as turning ten terriers into one mastiff. The question in all cases is not a question of union or absence of union, but of identity or absence of identity. Owing to certain historical and moral causes, two nations may be so united as upon the whole to help each other. Thus England and Scotland pass their time in paying each other compliments; but their energies and atmospheres run distinct and parallel, and consequently do not clash. Scotland continues to be educated and Calvinistic; England continues to be uneducated and happy. But owing to certain other Moral and certain other political causes, two nations may be so united as only to hamper each other; their lines do clash and do not run parallel. Thus, for instance, England and Ireland are so united that the Irish can sometimes rule England, but can never rule Ireland. The educational systems, including the last Education Act, are here, as in the case of Scotland, a very good test of the matter. The overwhelming majority of Irishmen believe in a strict Catholicism; the overwhelming majority of Englishmen believe in a vague Protestantism. The Irish party in the Parliament of Union is just large enough to prevent the English education being indefinitely Protestant, and just small enough to prevent the Irish education being definitely Catholic. Here we have a state of things which no man in his senses would ever dream of wishing to continue if he had not been bewitched by the sentimentalism of the mere word "union."

This example of union, however, is not the example which I propose to take of the ingrained futility and deception underlying all the assumptions of the modern practical politician. I wish to speak especially of another and much more general delusion. It pervades the minds and speeches of all the practical men of all parties; and it is a childish blunder built upon a single false metaphor. I refer to the universal modern talk about young nations and new nations; about America being young, about New Zealand being new. The whole thing is a trick of words. America is not young, New Zealand is not new. It is a very discussable question whether they are not both much older than England or Ireland.

Of course we may use the metaphor of youth about America or the colonies, if we use it strictly as implying only a recent origin. But if we use it (as we do use it) as implying vigour, or vivacity, or crudity, or inexperience, or hope, or a long life before them or any of the romantic attributes of youth, then it is surely as clear as daylight that we are duped by a stale figure of speech. We can easily see the matter clearly by applying it to any other institution parallel to the institution of an independent nationality. If a club called "The Milk and Soda League" (let us say) was set up yesterday, as I have no doubt it was, then, of course, "The Milk and Soda League" is a young club in the sense that it was set up yesterday, but in no other sense. It may consist entirely of moribund old gentlemen. It may be moribund itself. We may call it a young club, in the light of the fact that it was founded yesterday. We may also call it a very old club in the light of the fact that it will most probably go bankrupt to-morrow. All this appears very obvious when we put it in this form. Any one who adopted the young-community delusion with regard to a bank or a butcher's shop would be sent to an asylum. But the whole modern political notion that America and the colonies must be very vigorous because they are very new, rests upon no better foundation. That America was founded long after England does not make it even in the faintest degree more probable that America will not perish a long time before England. That England existed before her colonies does not make it any the less likely that she will exist after her colonies. And when we look at the actual history of the world, we find that great European nations almost invariably have survived the vitality of their colonies. When we look at the actual history of the world, we find, that if there is a thing that is born old and dies young, it is a colony. The Greek colonies went to pieces long before the Greek civilization. The Spanish colonies have gone to pieces long before the nation of Spain—nor does there seem to be any reason to doubt the possibility or even the probability of the conclusion that the colonial civilization, which owes its origin to England, will be much briefer and much less vigorous than the civilization of England itself. The English nation will still be going the way of all European nations when the Anglo-Saxon race has gone the way of all fads. Now, of course, the interesting question is, have we, in the case of America and the colonies, any real evidence of a moral and intellectual youth as opposed to the indisputable triviality of a merely chronological youth? Consciously or unconsciously, we know that we have no such evidence, and consciously or unconsciously, therefore, we proceed to make it up. Of this pure and placid invention, a good example, for instance, can be found in a recent poem of Mr. Rudyard Kipling's. Speaking of the English people and the South African War Mr. Kipling says that "we fawned on the younger nations for the men that could shoot and ride." Some people considered this sentence insulting. All that I am concerned with at present is the evident fact that it is not true. The colonies provided very useful volunteer troops, but they did not provide the best troops, nor achieve the most successful exploits. The best work in the war on the English side was done, as might have been expected, by the best English regiments. The men who could shoot and ride were not the enthusiastic corn merchants from Melbourne, any more than they were the enthusiastic clerks from Cheapside. The men who could shoot and ride were the men who had been taught to shoot and ride in the discipline of the standing army of a great European power. Of course, the colonials are as brave and athletic as any other average white men. Of course, they acquitted themselves with reasonable credit. All I have here to indicate is that, for the purposes of this theory of the new nation, it is necessary to maintain that the colonial forces were more useful or more heroic than the gunners at Colenso or the Fighting Fifth. And of this contention there is not, and never has been, one stick or straw of evidence.

A similar attempt is made, and with even less success, to represent the literature of the colonies as something fresh and vigorous and important. The imperialist magazines are constantly springing upon us some genius from Queensland or Canada, through whom we are expected to smell the odours of the bush or the prairie. As a matter of fact, any one who is even slightly interested in literature as such (and I, for one, confess that I am only slightly interested in literature as such), will freely admit that the stories of these geniuses smell of nothing but printer's ink, and that not of first-rate quality. By a great effort of Imperial imagination the generous English people reads into these works a force and a novelty. But the force and the novelty are not in the new writers; the force and the novelty are in the ancient heart of the English. Anybody who studies them impartially will know that the first-rate writers of the colonies are not even particularly novel in their note and atmosphere, are not only not producing a new kind of good literature, but are not even in any particular sense producing a new kind of bad literature. The first-rate writers of the new countries are really almost exactly like the second-rate writers of the old countries. Of course they do feel the mystery of the wilderness, the mystery of the bush, for all simple and honest men feel this in Melbourne, or Margate, or South St. Pancras. But when they write most sincerely and most successfully, it is not with a background of the mystery of the bush, but with a background, expressed or assumed, of our own romantic cockney civilization. What really moves their souls with a kindly terror is not the mystery of the wilderness, but the Mystery of a Hansom Cab.

Of course there are some exceptions to this generalization. The one really arresting exception is Olive Schreiner, and she is quite as certainly an exception that proves the rule. Olive Schreiner is a fierce, brilliant, and realistic novelist; but she is all this precisely because she is not English at all. Her tribal kinship is with the country of Teniers and Maarten Maartens—that is, with a country of realists. Her literary kinship is with the pessimistic fiction of the continent; with the novelists whose very pity is cruel. Olive Schreiner is the one English colonial who is not conventional, for the simple reason that South Africa is the one English colony which is not English, and probably never will be. And, of course, there are individual exceptions in a minor way. I remember in particular some Australian tales by Mr. McIlwain which were really able and effective, and which, for that reason, I suppose, are not presented to the public with blasts of a trumpet. But my general contention if put before any one with a love of letters, will not be disputed if it is understood. It is not the truth that the colonial civilization as a whole is giving us, or shows any signs of giving us, a literature which will startle and renovate our own. It may be a very good thing for us to have an affectionate illusion in the matter; that is quite another affair. The colonies may have given England a new emotion; I only say that they have not given the world a new book.

Touching these English colonies, I do not wish to be misunderstood. I do not say of them or of America that they have not a future, or that they will not be great nations. I merely deny the whole established modern expression about them. I deny that they are "destined" to a future. I deny that they are "destined" to be great nations. I deny (of course) that any human thing is destined to be anything. All the absurd physical metaphors, such as youth and age, living and dying, are, when applied to nations, but pseudo-scientific attempts to conceal from men the awful liberty of their lonely souls.

In the case of America, indeed, a warning to this effect is instant and essential. America, of course, like every other human thing, can in spiritual sense live or die as much as it chooses. But at the present moment the matter which America has very seriously to consider is not how near it is to its birth and beginning, but how near it may be to its end. It is only a verbal question whether the American civilization is young; it may become a very practical and urgent question whether it is dying. When once we have cast aside, as we inevitably have after a moment's thought, the fanciful physical metaphor involved in the word "youth," what serious evidence have we that America is a fresh force and not a stale one? It has a great many people, like China; it has a great deal of money, like defeated Carthage or dying Venice. It is full of bustle and excitability, like Athens after its ruin, and all the Greek cities in their decline. It is fond of new things; but the old are always fond of new things. Young men read chronicles, but old men read newspapers. It admires strength and good looks; it admires a big and barbaric beauty in its women, for instance; but so did Rome when the Goth was at the gates. All these are things quite compatible with fundamental tedium and decay. There are three main shapes or symbols in which a nation can show itself essentially glad and great—by the heroic in government, by the heroic in arms, and by the heroic in art. Beyond government, which is, as it were, the very shape and body of a nation, the most significant thing about any citizen is his artistic attitude towards a holiday and his moral attitude towards a fight—that is, his way of accepting life and his way of accepting death.

Subjected to these eternal tests, America does not appear by any means as particularly fresh or untouched. She appears with all the weakness and weariness of modern England or of any other Western power. In her politics she has broken up exactly as England has broken up, into a bewildering opportunism and insincerity. In the matter of war and the national attitude towards war, her resemblance to England is even more manifest and melancholy. It may be said with rough accuracy that there are three stages in the life of a strong people. First, it is a small power, and fights small powers. Then it is a great power, and fights great powers. Then it is a great power, and fights small powers, but pretends that they are great powers, in order to rekindle the ashes of its ancient emotion and vanity. After that, the next step is to become a small power itself. England exhibited this symptom of decadence very badly in the war with the Transvaal; but America exhibited it worse in the war with Spain. There was exhibited more sharply and absurdly than anywhere else the ironic contrast between the very careless choice of a strong line and the very careful choice of a weak enemy. America added to all her other late Roman or Byzantine elements the element of the Caracallan triumph, the triumph over nobody.

But when we come to the last test of nationality, the test of art and letters, the case is almost terrible. The English colonies have produced no great artists; and that fact may prove that they are still full of silent possibilities and reserve force. But America has produced great artists. And that fact most certainly proves that she is full of a fine futility and the end of all things. Whatever the American men of genius are, they are not young gods making a young world. Is the art of Whistler a brave, barbaric art, happy and headlong? Does Mr. Henry James infect us with the spirit of a schoolboy? No; the colonies have not spoken, and they are safe. Their silence may be the silence of the unborn. But out of America has come a sweet and startling cry, as unmistakable as the cry of a dying man.

Chapter 19
Slum Novelists and the Slums

dd ideas are entertained in our time about the real nature of the doctrine of human fraternity. The real doctrine is something which we do not, with all our modern humanitarianism, very clearly understand, much less very closely practise. There is nothing, for instance, particularly undemocratic about kicking your butler downstairs. It may be wrong, but it is not unfraternal. In a certain sense, the blow or kick may be considered as a confession of equality: you are meeting your butler body to body; you are almost according him the privilege of the duel. There is nothing, undemocratic, though there may be something unreasonable, in expecting a great deal from the butler, and being filled with a kind of frenzy of surprise when he falls short of the divine stature. The thing which is really undemocratic and unfraternal is not to expect the butler to be more or less divine. The thing which is really undemocratic and unfraternal is to say, as so many modern humanitarians say, "Of course one must make allowances for those on a lower plane." All things considered indeed, it may be said, without undue exaggeration, that the really undemocratic and unfraternal thing is the common practice of not kicking the butler downstairs.

It is only because such a vast section of the modern world is out of sympathy with the serious democratic sentiment that this statement will seem to many to be lacking in seriousness. Democracy is not philanthropy; it is not even altruism or social reform. Democracy is not founded on pity for the common man; democracy is founded on reverence for the common man, or, if you will, even on fear of him. It does not champion man because man is so miserable, but because man is so sublime. It does not object so much to the ordinary man being a slave as to his not being a king, for its dream is always the dream of the first Roman republic, a nation of kings.

Next to a genuine republic, the most democratic thing in the world is a hereditary despotism. I mean a despotism in which there is absolutely no trace whatever of any nonsense about intellect or special fitness for the post. Rational despotism—that is, selective despotism—is always a curse to mankind, because with that you have the ordinary man misunderstood and misgoverned by some prig who has no brotherly respect for him at all. But irrational despotism is always democratic, because it is the ordinary man enthroned. The worst form of slavery is that which is called Caesarism, or the choice of some bold or brilliant man as despot because he is suitable. For that means that men choose a representative, not because he represents them, but because he does not. Men trust an ordinary man like George III or William IV. because they are themselves ordinary men and understand him. Men trust an ordinary man because they trust themselves. But men trust a great man because they do not trust themselves. And hence the worship of great men always appears in times of weakness and cowardice; we never hear of great men until the time when all other men are small.

Hereditary despotism is, then, in essence and sentiment democratic because it chooses from mankind at random. If it does not declare that every man may rule, it declares the next most democratic thing; it declares that any man may rule. Hereditary aristocracy is a far worse and more dangerous thing, because the numbers and multiplicity of an aristocracy make it sometimes possible for it to figure as an aristocracy of intellect. Some of its members will presumably have brains, and thus they, at any rate, will be an intellectual aristocracy within the social one. They will rule the aristocracy by virtue of their intellect, and they will rule the country by virtue of their aristocracy. Thus a double falsity will be set up, and millions of the images of God, who, fortunately for their wives and families, are neither gentlemen nor clever men, will be represented by a man like Mr. Balfour or Mr. Wyndham, because he is too gentlemanly to be called merely clever, and just too clever to be called merely a gentleman. But even an hereditary aristocracy may exhibit, by a sort of accident, from time to time some of the basically democratic quality which belongs to a hereditary despotism. It is amusing to think how much conservative ingenuity has been wasted in the defence of the House of Lords by men who were desperately endeavouring to prove that the House of Lords consisted of clever men. There is one really good defence of the House of Lords, though admirers of the peerage are strangely coy about using it; and that is, that the House of Lords, in its full and proper strength, consists of stupid men. It really would be a plausible defence of that otherwise indefensible body to point out that the clever men in the Commons, who owed their power to cleverness, ought in the last resort to be checked by the average man in the Lords, who owed their power to accident. Of course, there would be many answers to such a contention, as, for instance, that the House of Lords is largely no longer a House of Lords, but a House of tradesmen and financiers, or that the bulk of the commonplace nobility do not vote, and so leave the chamber to the prigs and the specialists and the mad old gentlemen with hobbies. But on some occasions the House of Lords, even under all these disadvantages, is in some sense representative. When all the peers flocked together to vote against Mr. Gladstone's second Home Rule Bill, for instance, those who said that the peers represented the English people, were perfectly right. All those dear old men who happened to be born peers were at that moment, and upon that question, the precise counterpart of all the dear old men who happened to be born paupers or middle-class gentlemen. That mob of peers did really represent the English people—that is to say, it was honest, ignorant, vaguely excited, almost unanimous, and obviously wrong. Of course, rational democracy is better as an expression of the public will than the haphazard hereditary method. While we are about having any kind of democracy, let it be rational democracy. But if we are to have any kind of oligarchy, let it be irrational oligarchy. Then at least we shall be ruled by men.

But the thing which is really required for the proper working of democracy is not merely the democratic system, or even the democratic philosophy, but the democratic emotion. The democratic emotion, like most elementary and indispensable things, is a thing difficult to describe at any time. But it is peculiarly difficult to describe it in our enlightened age, for the simple reason that it is peculiarly difficult to find it. It is a certain instinctive attitude which feels the things in which all men agree to be unspeakably important, and all the things in which they differ (such as mere brains) to be almost unspeakably unimportant. The nearest approach to it in our ordinary life would be the promptitude with which we should consider mere humanity in any circumstance of shock or death. We should say, after a somewhat disturbing discovery, "There is a dead man under the sofa." We should not be likely to say, "There is a dead man of considerable personal refinement under the sofa." We should say, "A woman has fallen into the water." We should not say, "A highly educated woman has fallen into the water." Nobody would say, "There are the remains of a clear thinker in your back garden." Nobody would say, "Unless you hurry up and stop him, a man with a very fine ear for music will have jumped off that cliff." But this emotion, which all of us have in connection with such things as birth and death, is to some people native and constant at all ordinary times and in all ordinary places. It was native to St. Francis of Assisi. It was native to Walt Whitman. In this strange and splendid degree it cannot be expected, perhaps, to pervade a whole commonwealth or a whole civilization; but one commonwealth may have it much more than another commonwealth, one civilization much more than another civilization. No community, perhaps, ever had it so much as the early Franciscans. No community, perhaps, ever had it so little as ours.

Everything in our age has, when carefully examined, this fundamentally un-democratic quality. In religion and morals we should admit, in the abstract, that the sins of the educated classes were as great as, or perhaps greater than, the sins of the poor and ignorant. But in practice the great difference between the mediaeval ethics and ours is that ours concentrate attention on the sins which are the sins of the ignorant, and practically deny that the sins which are the sins of the educated are sins at all. We are always talking about the sin of intemperate drinking, because it is quite obvious that the poor have it more than the rich. But we are always denying that there is any such thing as the sin of pride, because it would be quite obvious that the rich have it more than the poor. We are always ready to make a saint or prophet of the educated man who goes into cottages to give a little kindly advice to the uneducated. But the medieval idea of a saint or prophet was something quite different. The mediaeval saint or prophet was an uneducated man who walked into grand houses to give a little kindly advice to the educated. The old tyrants had enough insolence to despoil the poor, but they had not enough insolence to preach to them. It was the gentleman who oppressed the slums; but it was the slums that admonished the gentleman. And just as we are undemocratic in faith and morals, so we are, by the very nature of our attitude in such matters, undemocratic in the tone of our practical politics. It is a sufficient proof that we are not an essentially democratic state that we are always wondering what we shall do with the poor. If we were democrats, we should be wondering what the poor will do with us. With us the governing class is always saying to itself, "What laws shall we make?" In a purely democratic state it would be always saying, "What laws can we obey?" A purely democratic state perhaps there has never been. But even the feudal ages were in practice thus far democratic, that every feudal potentate knew that any laws which he made would in all probability return upon himself. His feathers might be cut off for breaking a sumptuary law. His head might be cut off for high treason. But the modern laws are almost always laws made to affect the governed class, but not the governing. We have public-house licensing laws, but not sumptuary laws. That is to say, we have laws against the festivity and hospitality of the poor, but no laws against the festivity and hospitality of the rich. We have laws against blasphemy—that is, against a kind of coarse and offensive speaking in which nobody but a rough and obscure man would be likely to indulge. But we have no laws against heresy—that is, against the intellectual poisoning of the whole people, in which only a prosperous and prominent man would be likely to be successful. The evil of aristocracy is not that it necessarily leads to the infliction of bad things or the suffering of sad ones; the evil of aristocracy is that it places everything in the hands of a class of people who can always inflict what they can never suffer. Whether what they inflict is, in their intention, good or bad, they become equally frivolous. The case against the governing class of modern England is not in the least that it is selfish; if you like, you may call the English oligarchs too fantastically unselfish. The case against them simply is that when they legislate for all men, they always omit themselves.

We are undemocratic, then, in our religion, as is proved by our efforts to "raise" the poor. We are undemocratic in our government, as is proved by our innocent attempt to govern them well. But above all we are undemocratic in our literature, as is proved by the torrent of novels about the poor and serious studies of the poor which pour from our publishers every month. And the more "modern" the book is the more certain it is to be devoid of democratic sentiment.

A poor man is a man who has not got much money. This may seem a simple and unnecessary description, but in the face of a great mass of modern fact and fiction, it seems very necessary indeed; most of our realists and sociologists talk about a poor man as if he were an octopus or an alligator. There is no more need to study the psychology of poverty than to study the psychology of bad temper, or the psychology of vanity, or the psychology of animal spirits. A man ought to know something of the emotions of an insulted man, not by being insulted, but simply by being a man. And he ought to know something of the emotions of a poor man, not by being poor, but simply by being a man. Therefore, in any writer who is describing poverty, my first objection to him will be that he has studied his subject. A democrat would have imagined it.

A great many hard things have been said about religious slumming and political or social slumming, but surely the most despicable of all is artistic slumming. The religious teacher is at least supposed to be interested in the costermonger because he is a man; the politician is in some dim and perverted sense interested in the costermonger because he is a citizen; it is only the wretched writer who is interested in the costermonger merely because he is a costermonger. Nevertheless, so long as he is merely seeking impressions, or in other words copy, his trade, though dull, is honest. But when he endeavours to represent that he is describing the spiritual core of a costermonger, his dim vices and his delicate virtues, then we must object that his claim is preposterous; we must remind him that he is a journalist and nothing else. He has far less psychological authority even than the foolish missionary. For he is in the literal and derivative sense a journalist, while the missionary is an eternalist. The missionary at least pretends to have a version of the man's lot for all time; the journalist only pretends to have a version of it from day to day. The missionary comes to tell the poor man that he is in the same condition with all men. The journalist comes to tell other people how different the poor man is from everybody else.

If the modern novels about the slums, such as novels of Mr. Arthur Morrison, or the exceedingly able novels of Mr. Somerset Maugham, are intended to be sensational, I can only say that that is a noble and reasonable object, and that they attain it. A sensation, a shock to the imagination, like the contact with cold water, is always a good and exhilarating thing; and, undoubtedly, men will always seek this sensation (among other forms) in the form of the study of the strange antics of remote or alien peoples. In the twelfth century men obtained this sensation by reading about dog-headed men in Africa. In the twentieth century they obtained it by reading about pig-headed Boers in Africa. The men of the twentieth century were certainly, it must be admitted, somewhat the more credulous of the two. For it is not recorded of the men in the twelfth century that they organized a sanguinary crusade solely for the purpose of altering the singular formation of the heads of the Africans. But it may be, and it may even legitimately be, that since all these monsters have faded from the popular mythology, it is necessary to have in our fiction the image of the horrible and hairy East-ender, merely to keep alive in us a fearful and childlike wonder at external peculiarities. But the Middle Ages (with a great deal more common sense than it would now be fashionable to admit) regarded natural history at bottom rather as a kind of joke; they regarded the soul as very important. Hence, while they had a natural history of dog-headed men, they did not profess to have a psychology of dog-headed men. They did not profess to mirror the mind of a dog-headed man, to share his tenderest secrets, or mount with his most celestial musings. They did not write novels about the semi-canine creature, attributing to him all the oldest morbidities and all the newest fads. It is permissible to present men as monsters if we wish to make the reader jump; and to make anybody jump is always a Christian act. But it is not permissible to present men as regarding themselves as monsters, or as making themselves jump. To summarize, our slum fiction is quite defensible as aesthetic fiction; it is not defensible as spiritual fact.

One enormous obstacle stands in the way of its actuality. The men who write it, and the men who read it, are men of the middle classes or the upper classes; at least, of those who are loosely termed the educated classes. Hence, the fact that it is the life as the refined man sees it proves that it cannot be the life as the unrefined man lives it. Rich men write stories about poor men, and describe them as speaking with a coarse, or heavy, or husky enunciation. But if poor men wrote novels about you or me they would describe us as speaking with some absurd shrill and affected voice, such as we only hear from a duchess in a three-act farce. The slum novelist gains his whole effect by the fact that some detail is strange to the reader; but that detail by the nature of the case cannot be strange in itself. It cannot be strange to the soul which he is professing to study. The slum novelist gains his effects by describing the same grey mist as draping the dingy factory and the dingy tavern. But to the man he is supposed to be studying there must be exactly the same difference between the factory and the tavern that there is to a middle-class man between a late night at the office and a supper at Pagani's. The slum novelist is content with pointing out that to the eye of his particular class a pickaxe looks dirty and a pewter pot looks dirty. But the man he is supposed to be studying sees the difference between them exactly as a clerk sees the difference between a ledger and an edition de luxe. The chiaroscuro of the life is inevitably lost; for to us the high lights and the shadows are a light grey. But the high lights and the shadows are not a light grey in that life any more than in any other. The kind of man who could really express the pleasures of the poor would be also the kind of man who could share them. In short, these books are not a record of the psychology of poverty. They are a record of the psychology of wealth and culture when brought in contact with poverty. They are not a description of the state of the slums. They are only a very dark and dreadful description of the state of the slummers. One might give innumerable examples of the essentially unsympathetic and unpopular quality of these realistic writers. But perhaps the simplest and most obvious example with which we could conclude is the mere fact that these writers are realistic. The poor have many other vices, but, at least, they are never realistic. The poor are melodramatic and romantic in grain; the poor all believe in high moral platitudes and copy-book maxims; probably this is the ultimate meaning of the great saying, "Blessed are the poor." Blessed are the poor, for they are always making life, or trying to make life like an Adelphi play. Some innocent educationalists and philanthropists (for even philanthropists can be innocent) have expressed a grave astonishment that the masses prefer shilling shockers to scientific treatises and melodramas to problem plays. The reason is very simple.

The realistic story is certainly more artistic than the melodramatic story. If what you desire is deft handling, delicate proportions, a unit of artistic atmosphere, the realistic story has a full advantage over the melodrama. In everything that is light and bright and ornamental the realistic story has a full advantage over the melodrama. But, at least, the melodrama has one indisputable advantage over the realistic story. The melodrama is much more like life. It is much more like man, and especially the poor man. It is very banal and very inartistic when a poor woman at the Adelphi says, "Do you think I will sell my own child?" But poor women in the Battersea High Road do say, "Do you think I will sell my own child?" They say it on every available occasion; you can hear a sort of murmur or babble of it all the way down the street. It is very stale and weak dramatic art (if that is all) when the workman confronts his master and says, "I'm a man." But a workman does say "I'm a man" two or three times every day. In fact, it is tedious, possibly, to hear poor men being melodramatic behind the footlights; but that is because one can always hear them being melodramatic in the street outside. In short, melodrama, if it is dull, is dull because it is too accurate. Somewhat the same problem exists in the case of stories about schoolboys. Mr. Kipling's "Stalky and Co." is much more amusing (if you are talking about amusement) than the late Dean Farrar's "Eric; or, Little by Little." But "Eric" is immeasurably more like real school-life. For real school-life, real boyhood, is full of the things of which Eric is full—priggishness, a crude piety, a silly sin, a weak but continual attempt at the heroic, in a word, melodrama. And if we wish to lay a firm basis for any efforts to help the poor, we must not become realistic and see them from the outside. We must become melodramatic, and see them from the inside. The novelist must not take out his notebook and say, "I am an expert." No; he must imitate the workman in the Adelphi play. He must slap himself on the chest and say, "I am a man."

Chapter 20
Concluding Remarks on the Importance of Orthodoxy

hether the human mind can advance or not, is a question too little discussed, for nothing can be more dangerous than to found our social philosophy on any theory which is debatable but has not been debated. But if we assume, for the sake of argument, that there has been in the past, or will be in the future, such a thing as a growth or improvement of the human mind itself, there still remains a very sharp objection to be raised against the modern version of that improvement. The vice of the modern notion of mental progress is that it is always something concerned with the breaking of bonds, the effacing of boundaries, the casting away of dogmas. But if there be such a thing as mental growth, it must mean the growth into more and more definite convictions, into more and more dogmas. The human brain is a machine for coming to conclusions; if it cannot come to conclusions it is rusty. When we hear of a man too clever to believe, we are hearing of something having almost the character of a contradiction in terms. It is like hearing of a nail that was too good to hold down a carpet; or a bolt that was too strong to keep a door shut. Man can hardly be defined, after the fashion of Carlyle, as an animal who makes tools; ants and beavers and many other animals make tools, in the sense that they make an apparatus. Man can be defined as an animal that makes dogmas. As he piles doctrine on doctrine and conclusion on conclusion in the formation of some tremendous scheme of philosophy and religion, he is, in the only legitimate sense of which the expression is capable, becoming more and more human. When he drops one doctrine after another in a refined scepticism, when he declines to tie himself to a system, when he says that he has outgrown definitions, when he says that he disbelieves in finality, when, in his own imagination, he sits as God, holding no form of creed but contemplating all, then he is by that very process sinking slowly backwards into the vagueness of the vagrant animals and the unconsciousness of the grass. Trees have no dogmas. Turnips are singularly broadminded.

If then, I repeat, there is to be mental advance, it must be mental advance in the construction of a definite philosophy of life. And that philosophy of life must be right and the other philosophies wrong. Now of all, or nearly all, the able modern writers whom I have briefly studied in this book, this is especially and pleasingly true, that they do each of them have a constructive and affirmative view, and that they do take it seriously and ask us to take it seriously. There is nothing merely sceptically progressive about Mr. Rudyard Kipling. There is nothing in the least broad minded about Mr. Bernard Shaw. The paganism of Mr. Lowes

Dickinson is more grave than any Christianity. Even the opportunism of Mr. H. G. Wells is more dogmatic than the idealism of anybody else. Somebody complained, I think, to Matthew Arnold that he was getting as dogmatic as Carlyle. He replied, "That may be true; but you overlook an obvious difference. I am dogmatic and right, and Carlyle is dogmatic and wrong." The strong humour of the remark ought not to disguise from us its everlasting seriousness and common sense; no man ought to write at all, or even to speak at all, unless he thinks that he is in truth and the other man in error. In similar style, I hold that I am dogmatic and right, while Mr. Shaw is dogmatic and wrong. But my main point, at present, is to notice that the chief among these writers I have discussed do most sanely and courageously offer themselves as dogmatists, as founders of a system. It may be true that the thing in Mr. Shaw most interesting to me, is the fact that Mr. Shaw is wrong. But it is equally true that the thing in Mr. Shaw most interesting to himself, is the fact that Mr. Shaw is right. Mr. Shaw may have none with him but himself; but it is not for himself he cares. It is for the vast and universal church, of which he is the only member.

The two typical men of genius whom I have mentioned here, and with whose names I have begun this book, are very symbolic, if only because they have shown that the fiercest dogmatists can make the best artists. In the fin de siecle atmosphere every one was crying out that literature should be free from all causes and all ethical creeds. Art was to produce only exquisite workmanship, and it was especially the note of those days to demand brilliant plays and brilliant short stories. And when they got them, they got them from a couple of moralists. The best short stories were written by a man trying to preach Imperialism. The best plays were written by a man trying to preach Socialism. All the art of all the artists looked tiny and tedious beside the art which was a by-product of propaganda.

The reason, indeed, is very simple. A man cannot be wise enough to be a great artist without being wise enough to wish to be a philosopher. A man cannot have the energy to produce good art without having the energy to wish to pass beyond it. A small artist is content with art; a great artist is content with nothing except everything. So we find that when real forces, good or bad, like Kipling and G. B. S., enter our arena, they bring with them not only startling and arresting art, but very startling and arresting dogmas. And they care even more, and desire us to care even more, about their startling and arresting dogmas than about their startling and arresting art. Mr. Shaw is a good dramatist, but what he desires more than anything else to be is a good politician. Mr. Rudyard Kipling is by divine caprice and natural genius an unconventional poet; but what he desires more than anything else to be is a conventional poet. He desires to be the poet of his people, bone of their bone, and flesh of their flesh, understanding their origins, celebrating their destiny. He desires to be Poet Laureate, a most sensible and honourable and public-spirited desire. Having been given by the gods originality— that is, disagreement with others—he desires divinely to agree with them. But the most striking instance of all, more striking, I think, even than either of these, is the instance of Mr. H. G. Wells. He began in a sort of insane infancy of pure art. He began by making a new heaven and a new earth, with the same irresponsible instinct by which men buy a new necktie or button-hole. He began by trifling with the stars and systems in order to make ephemeral anecdotes; he killed the universe for a joke. He has since become more and more serious, and has become, as men inevitably do when they become more and more serious, more and more parochial. He was frivolous about the twilight of the gods; but he is serious about the London omnibus. He was careless in "The Time Machine," for that dealt only with the destiny of all things; but he is careful, and even cautious, in "Mankind in the Making," for that deals with the day after to-morrow. He began with the end of the world, and that was easy. Now he has gone on to the beginning of the world, and that is difficult. But the main result of all this is the same as in the other cases. The men who have really been the bold artists, the realistic artists, the uncompromising artists, are the men who have turned out, after all, to be writing "with a purpose." Suppose that any cool and cynical art-critic, any art-critic fully impressed with the conviction that artists were greatest when they were most purely artistic, suppose that a man who professed ably a humane aestheticism, as did Mr. Max Beerbohm, or a cruel aestheticism, as did Mr. W. E. Henley, had cast his eye over the whole fictional literature which was recent in the year 1895, and had been asked to select the three most vigorous and promising and original artists and artistic works, he would, I think, most certainly have said that for a fine artistic audacity, for a real artistic delicacy, or for a whiff of true novelty in art, the things that stood first were "Soldiers Three," by a Mr. Rudyard Kipling; "Arms and the Man," by a Mr. Bernard Shaw; and "The Time Machine," by a man called Wells. And all these men have shown themselves ingrainedly didactic. You may express the matter if you will by saying that if we want doctrines we go to the great artists. But it is clear from the psychology of the matter that this is not the true statement; the true statement is that when we want any art tolerably brisk and bold we have to go to the doctrinaires.

In concluding this book, therefore, I would ask, first and foremost, that men such as these of whom I have spoken should not be insulted by being taken for artists. No man has any right whatever merely to enjoy the work of Mr. Bernard Shaw; he might as well enjoy the invasion of his country by the French. Mr. Shaw writes either to convince or to enrage us. No man has any business to be a Kiplingite without being a politician, and an Imperialist politician. If a man is first with us, it should be because of what is first with him. If a man convinces us at all, it should be by his convictions. If we hate a poem of Kipling's from political passion, we are hating it for the same reason that the poet loved it; if we dislike him because of his opinions, we are disliking him for the best of all possible reasons. If a man comes into Hyde Park to preach it is permissible to hoot him; but it is discourteous to applaud him as a performing bear. And an artist is only a performing bear compared with the meanest man who fancies he has anything to say.

There is, indeed, one class of modern writers and thinkers who cannot altogether be overlooked in this question, though there is no space here for a lengthy account of them, which, indeed, to confess the truth, would consist chiefly of abuse. I mean those who get over all these abysses and reconcile all these wars by talking about "aspects of truth," by saying that the art of Kipling represents one aspect of the truth, and the art of William Watson another; the art of Mr. Bernard Shaw one aspect of the truth, and the art of Mr. Cunningham Grahame another; the art of Mr. H. G. Wells one aspect, and the art of Mr. Coventry Patmore (say) another. I will only say here that this seems to me an evasion which has not even had the sense to disguise itself ingeniously in words. If we talk of a certain thing being an aspect of truth, it is evident that we claim to know what is truth; just as, if we talk of the hind leg of a dog, we claim to know what is a dog. Unfortunately, the philosopher who talks about aspects of truth generally also asks, "What is truth?" Frequently even he denies the existence of truth, or says it is inconceivable by the human intelligence. How, then, can he recognize its aspects? I should not like to be an artist who brought an architectural sketch to a builder, saying, "This is the south aspect of Sea-View Cottage. Sea-View Cottage, of course, does not exist." I should not even like very much to have to explain, under such circumstances, that Sea-View Cottage might exist, but was unthinkable by the human mind. Nor should I like any better to be the bungling and absurd metaphysician who professed to be able to see everywhere the aspects of a truth that is not there. Of course, it is perfectly obvious that there are truths in Kipling, that there are truths in Shaw or Wells. But the degree to which we can perceive them depends strictly upon how far we have a definite conception inside us of what is truth. It is ludicrous to suppose that the more sceptical we are the more we see good in everything. It is clear that the more we are certain what good is, the more we shall see good in everything.

I plead, then, that we should agree or disagree with these men. I plead that we should agree with them at least in having an abstract belief. But I know that there are current in the modern world many vague objections to having an abstract belief, and I feel that we shall not get any further until we have dealt with some of them. The first objection is easily stated.

A common hesitation in our day touching the use of extreme convictions is a sort of notion that extreme convictions specially upon cosmic matters, have been responsible in the past for the thing which is called bigotry. But a very small amount of direct experience will dissipate this view. In real life the people who are most bigoted are the people who have no convictions at all. The economists of the Manchester school who disagree with Socialism take Socialism seriously. It is the young man in Bond Street, who does not know what socialism means much less whether he agrees with it, who is quite certain that these socialist fellows are making a fuss about nothing. The man who understands the Calvinist philosophy enough to agree with it must understand the Catholic philosophy in order to disagree with it. It is the vague modern who is not at all certain what is right who is most certain that Dante was wrong. The serious opponent of the Latin Church in history, even in the act of showing that it produced great infamies, must know that it produced great saints. It is the hard-headed stockbroker, who knows no history and believes no religion, who is, nevertheless, perfectly convinced that all these priests are knaves. The Salvationist at the Marble Arch may be bigoted, but he is not too bigoted to yearn from a common human kinship after the dandy on church parade. But the dandy on church parade is so bigoted that he does not in the least yearn after the Salvationist at the Marble Arch. Bigotry may be roughly defined as the anger of men who have no opinions. It is the resistance offered to definite ideas by that vague bulk of people whose ideas are indefinite to excess. Bigotry may be called the appalling frenzy of the indifferent. This frenzy of the indifferent is in truth a terrible thing; it has made all monstrous and widely pervading persecutions. In this degree it was not the people who cared who ever persecuted; the people who cared were not sufficiently numerous. It was the people who did not care who filled the world with fire and oppression. It was the hands of the indifferent that lit the faggots; it was the hands of the indifferent that turned the rack. There have come some persecutions out of the pain of a passionate certainty; but these produced, not bigotry, but fanaticism—a very different and a somewhat admirable thing. Bigotry in the main has always been the pervading omnipotence of those who do not care crushing out those who care in darkness and blood.

There are people, however, who dig somewhat deeper than this into the possible evils of dogma. It is felt by many that strong philosophical conviction, while it does not (as they perceive) produce that sluggish and fundamentally frivolous condition which we call bigotry, does produce a certain concentration, exaggeration, and moral impatience, which we may agree to call fanaticism. They say, in brief, that ideas are dangerous things. In politics, for example, it is commonly urged against a man like Mr. Balfour, or against a man like Mr. John Morley, that a wealth of ideas is dangerous. The true doctrine on this point, again, is surely not very difficult to state. Ideas are dangerous, but the man to whom they are least dangerous is the man of ideas. He is acquainted with ideas, and moves among them like a lion-tamer. Ideas are dangerous, but the man to whom they are most dangerous is the man of no ideas. The man of no ideas will find the first idea fly to his head like wine to the head of a teetotaller. It is a common error, I think, among the Radical idealists of my own party and period to suggest that financiers and business men are a danger to the empire because they are so sordid or so materialistic. The truth is that financiers and business men are a danger to the empire because they can be sentimental about any sentiment, and idealistic about any ideal, any ideal that they find lying about. just as a boy who has not known much of women is apt too easily to take a woman for the woman, so these practical men, unaccustomed to causes, are always inclined to think that if a thing is proved to be an ideal it is proved to be the ideal. Many, for example, avowedly followed Cecil Rhodes because he had a vision. They might as well have followed him because he had a nose; a man without some kind of dream of perfection is quite as much of a monstrosity as a noseless man. People say of such a figure, in almost feverish whispers, "He knows his own mind," which is exactly like saying in equally feverish whispers, "He blows his own nose." Human nature simply cannot subsist without a hope and aim of some kind; as the sanity of the Old Testament truly said, where there is no vision the people perisheth. But it is precisely because an ideal is necessary to man that the man without ideals is in permanent danger of fanaticism. There is nothing which is so likely to leave a man open to the sudden and irresistible inroad of an unbalanced vision as the cultivation of business habits. All of us know angular business men who think that the earth is flat, or that Mr. Kruger was at the head of a great military despotism, or that men are graminivorous, or that Bacon wrote Shakespeare. Religious and philosophical beliefs are, indeed, as dangerous as fire, and nothing can take from them that beauty of danger. But there is only one way of really guarding ourselves against the excessive danger of them, and that is to be steeped in philosophy and soaked in religion.

Briefly, then, we dismiss the two opposite dangers of bigotry and fanaticism, bigotry which is a too great vagueness and fanaticism which is a too great concentration. We say that the cure for the bigot is belief; we say that the cure for the idealist is ideas. To know the best theories of existence and to choose the best from them (that is, to the best of our own strong conviction) appears to us the proper way to be neither bigot nor fanatic, but something more firm than a bigot and more terrible than a fanatic, a man with a definite opinion. But that definite opinion must in this view begin with the basic matters of human thought, and these must not be dismissed as irrelevant, as religion, for instance, is too often in our days dismissed as irrelevant. Even if we think religion insoluble, we cannot think it irrelevant. Even if we ourselves have no view of the ultimate verities, we must feel that wherever such a view exists in a man it must be more important than anything else in him. The instant that the thing ceases to be the unknowable, it becomes the indispensable. There can be no doubt, I think, that the idea does exist in our time that there is something narrow or irrelevant or even mean about attacking a man's religion, or arguing from it in matters of politics or ethics. There can be quite as little doubt that such an accusation of narrowness is itself almost grotesquely narrow. To take an example from comparatively current events: we all know that it was not uncommon for a man to be considered a scarecrow of bigotry and obscurantism because he distrusted the Japanese, or lamented the rise of the Japanese, on the ground that the Japanese were Pagans. Nobody would think that there was anything antiquated or fanatical about distrusting a people because of some difference between them and us in practice or political machinery. Nobody would think it bigoted to say of a people, "I distrust their influence because they are Protectionists." No one would think it narrow to say, "I lament their rise because they are Socialists, or Manchester Individualists, or strong believers in militarism and conscription." A difference of opinion about the nature of Parliaments matters very much; but a difference of opinion about the nature of sin does not matter at all. A difference of opinion about the object of taxation matters very much; but a difference of opinion about the object of human existence does not matter at all. We have a right to distrust a man who is in a different kind of municipality; but we have no right to mistrust a man who is in a different kind of cosmos. This sort of enlightenment is surely about the most unenlightened that it is possible to imagine. To recur to the phrase which I employed earlier, this is tantamount to saying that everything is important with the exception of everything. Religion is exactly the thing which cannot be left out—because it includes everything. The most absent-minded person cannot well pack his Gladstone-bag and leave out the bag. We have a general view of existence, whether we like it or not; it alters or, to speak more accurately, it creates and involves everything we say or do, whether we like it or not. If we regard the Cosmos as a dream, we regard the Fiscal Question as a dream. If we regard the Cosmos as a joke, we regard St. Paul's Cathedral as a joke. If everything is bad, then we must believe (if it be possible) that beer is bad; if everything be good, we are forced to the rather fantastic conclusion that scientific philanthropy is good. Every man in the street must hold a metaphysical system, and hold it firmly. The possibility is that he may have held it so firmly and so long as to have forgotten all about its existence.

This latter situation is certainly possible; in fact, it is the situation of the whole modern world. The modern world is filled with men who hold dogmas so strongly that they do not even know that they are dogmas. It may be said even that the modern world, as a corporate body, holds certain dogmas so strongly that it does not know that they are dogmas. It may be thought "dogmatic," for instance, in some circles accounted progressive, to assume the perfection or improvement of man in another world. But it is not thought "dogmatic" to assume the perfection or improvement of man in this world; though that idea of progress is quite as unproved as the idea of immortality, and from a rationalistic point of view quite as improbable. Progress happens to be one of our dogmas, and a dogma means a thing which is not thought dogmatic. Or, again, we see nothing "dogmatic" in the inspiring, but certainly most startling, theory of physical science, that we should collect facts for the sake of facts, even though they seem as useless as sticks and straws. This is a great and suggestive idea, and its utility may, if you will, be proving itself, but its utility is, in the abstract, quite as disputable as the utility of that calling on oracles or consulting shrines which is also said to prove itself. Thus, because we are not in a civilization which believes strongly in oracles or sacred places, we see the full frenzy of those who killed themselves to find the sepulchre of Christ. But being in a civilization which does believe in this dogma of fact for facts' sake, we do not see the full frenzy of those who kill themselves to find the North Pole. I am not speaking of a tenable ultimate utility which is true both of the Crusades and the polar explorations. I mean merely that we do see the superficial and aesthetic singularity, the startling quality, about the idea of men crossing a continent with armies to conquer the place where a man died. But we do not see the aesthetic singularity and startling quality of men dying in agonies to find a place where no man can live—a place only interesting because it is supposed to be the meeting-place of some lines that do not exist.

Let us, then, go upon a long journey and enter on a dreadful search. Let us, at least, dig and seek till we have discovered our own opinions. The dogmas we really hold are far more fantastic, and, perhaps, far more beautiful than we think. In the course of these essays I fear that I have spoken from time to time of rationalists and rationalism, and that in a disparaging sense. Being full of that kindliness which should come at the end of everything, even of a book, I apologize to the rationalists even for calling them rationalists. There are no rationalists. We all believe fairy-tales, and live in them. Some, with a sumptuous literary turn, believe in the existence of the lady clothed with the sun. Some, with a more rustic, elvish instinct, like Mr. McCabe, believe merely in the impossible sun itself. Some hold the undemonstrable dogma of the existence of God; some the equally undemonstrable dogma of the existence of the man next door.

Truths turn into dogmas the instant that they are disputed. Thus every man who utters a doubt defines a religion. And the scepticism of our time does not really destroy the beliefs, rather it creates them; gives them their limits and their plain and defiant shape. We who are Liberals once held Liberalism lightly as a truism. Now it has been disputed, and we hold it fiercely as a faith. We who believe in patriotism once thought patriotism to be reasonable, and thought little more about it. Now we know it to be unreasonable, and know it to be right. We who are Christians never knew the great philosophic common sense which inheres in that mystery until the anti-Christian writers pointed it out to us. The great march of mental destruction will go on. Everything will be denied. Everything will become a creed. It is a reasonable position to deny the stones in the street; it will be a religious dogma to assert them. It is a rational thesis that we are all in a dream; it will be a mystical sanity to say that we are all awake. Fires will be kindled to testify that two and two make four. Swords will be drawn to prove that leaves are green in summer. We shall be left defending, not only the incredible virtues and sanities of human life, but something more incredible still, this huge impossible universe which stares us in the face. We shall fight for visible prodigies as if they were invisible. We shall look on the impossible grass and the skies with a strange courage. We shall be of those who have seen and yet have believed.

All Things Considered

Chapter 1
The Case for the Ephemeral

cannot understand the people who take literature seriously; but I can love them, and I do. Out of my love I warn them to keep clear of this book. It is a collection of crude and shapeless papers upon current or rather flying subjects; and they must be published pretty much as they stand. They were written, as a rule, at the last moment; they were handed in the moment before it was too late, and I do not think that our commonwealth would have been shaken to its foundations if they had been handed in the moment after. They must go out now, with all their imperfections on their head, or rather on mine; for their vices are too vital to be improved with a blue pencil, or with anything I can think of, except dynamite.

Their chief vice is that so many of them are very serious; because I had no time to make them flippant. It is so easy to be solemn; it is so hard to be frivolous. Let any honest reader shut his eyes for a few moments, and approaching the secret tribunal of his soul, ask himself whether he would really rather be asked in the next two hours to write the front page of the *Times*, which is full of long leading articles, or the front page of *Tit-Bits*, which is full of short jokes. If the reader is the fine conscientious fellow I take him for, he will at once reply that he would rather on the spur of the moment write ten *Times* articles than one *Tit-Bits* joke. Responsibility, a heavy and cautious responsibility of speech, is the easiest thing in the world; anybody can do it. That is why so many tired, elderly, and wealthy men go in for politics. They are responsible, because they have not the strength of mind left to be irresponsible. It is more dignified to sit still than to dance the Barn Dance. It is also easier. So in these easy pages I keep myself on the whole on the level of the *Times*: it is only occasionally that I leap upwards almost to the level of *Tit-Bits*.

I resume the defence of this indefensible book. These articles have another disadvantage arising from the scurry in which they were written; they are too long-winded and elaborate. One of the great disadvantages of hurry is that it takes such a long time. If I have to start for High-gate this day week, I may perhaps go the shortest way. If I have to start this minute, I shall almost certainly go the longest. In these essays (as I read them over) I feel frightfully annoyed with myself for not getting to the point more quickly; but I had not enough leisure to be quick. There are several maddening cases in which I took two or three pages in attempting to describe an attitude of which the essence could be expressed in an epigram; only there was no time for epigrams. I do not repent of one shade of opinion here expressed; but I feel that they might have been expressed so much more briefly and precisely. For instance, these pages contain a sort of recurring protest against the boast of certain writers that they are merely recent. They brag that their philosophy of the universe is the last philosophy or the new philosophy, or the advanced and progressive philosophy. I have said much against a mere modernism. When I use the word "modernism," I am not alluding specially to the current quarrel in the Roman Catholic Church, though I am certainly astonished at any intellectual group accepting so weak and unphilosophical a name. It is incomprehensible to me that any thinker can calmly call himself a modernist; he might as well call himself a Thursdayite. But apart altogether from that particular disturbance, I am conscious of a general irritation expressed against the people who boast of their advancement and modernity in the discussion of religion. But I never succeeded in saying the quite clear and obvious thing that is really the matter with modernism. The real objection to modernism is simply that it is a form of snobbishness. It is an attempt to crush a rational opponent not by reason, but by some mystery of superiority, by hinting that one is specially up to date or particularly "in the know." To flaunt the fact that we have had all the last books from Germany is simply vulgar; like flaunting the fact that we have had all the last bonnets from Paris. To introduce into philosophical discussions a sneer at a creed's antiquity is like introducing a sneer at a lady's age. It is caddish because it is irrelevant. The pure modernist is merely a snob; he cannot bear to be a month behind the fashion.

Similarly I find that I have tried in these pages to express the real objection to philanthropists and have not succeeded. I have not seen the quite simple objection to the causes advocated by certain wealthy idealists; causes of which the cause called teetotalism is the strongest case. I have used many abusive terms about the thing, calling it Puritanism, or superciliousness, or aristocracy; but I have not seen and stated the quite simple objection to philanthropy; which is that it is religious persecution. Religious persecution does not consist in thumbscrews or fires of Smithfield; the essence of religious persecution is this: that the man who happens to have material power in the State, either by wealth or by official position, should govern his fellow-citizens not according to their religion or philosophy, but according to his own. If, for instance, there is such a thing as a vegetarian nation; if there is a great united mass of men who wish to live by the vegetarian morality, then I say in the emphatic words of the arrogant French marquis before the French Revolution, "Let them eat grass." Perhaps that French oligarch was a humanitarian; most oligarchs are. Perhaps when he told the peasants to eat grass he was recommending to them the hygienic simplicity of a vegetarian restaurant. But that is an irrelevant, though most fascinating, speculation. The point here is that if a nation is really vegetarian let its government force upon it the whole horrible weight of vegetarianism. Let its government give the national guests a State vegetarian banquet. Let its government, in the most literal and awful sense of the words, give them beans. That sort of tyranny is all very well; for it is the people tyrannising over all the persons. But "temperance reformers" are like a small group of vegetarians who should silently and systematically act on an ethical assumption entirely unfamiliar to the mass of the people. They would always be giving peerages to greengrocers. They would always be appointing Parliamentary Commissions to enquire into the private life of butchers. Whenever they found a man quite at their mercy, as a pauper or a convict or a lunatic, they would force him to add the final touch to his inhuman isolation by becoming a vegetarian. All the meals for school children will be vegetarian meals. All the State public houses will be vegetarian public houses. There is a very strong case for vegetarianism as compared with teetotalism. Drinking one glass of beer cannot by any philosophy be drunkenness; but killing one animal can, by this philosophy, be murder. The objection to both processes is not that the two creeds, teetotal and vegetarian, are not admissible; it is simply that they are not admitted. The thing is religious persecution because it is not based on the existing religion of the democracy. These people ask the poor to accept in practice what they know perfectly well that the poor would not accept in theory. That is the very definition of religious persecution. I was against the Tory attempt to force upon ordinary Englishmen a Catholic theology in which they do not believe. I am even more against the attempt to force upon them a Mohamedan morality which they actively deny.

Again, in the case of anonymous journalism I seem to have said a great deal without getting out the point very clearly. Anonymous journalism is dangerous, and is poisonous in our existing life simply because it is so rapidly becoming an anonymous life. That is the horrible thing about our contemporary atmosphere. Society is becoming a secret society. The modern tyrant is evil because of his elusiveness. He is more nameless than his slave. He is not more of a bully than the tyrants of the past; but he is more of a coward. The rich publisher may treat the poor poet better or worse than the old master workman treated the old apprentice. But the apprentice ran away and the master ran after him. Nowadays it is the poet who pursues and tries in vain to fix the fact of responsibility. It is the publisher who runs away. The clerk of Mr. Solomon gets the sack: the beautiful Greek slave of the Sultan Suliman also gets the sack; or the sack gets her. But though she is concealed under the black waves of the Bosphorus, at least her destroyer is not concealed. He goes behind golden trumpets riding on a white elephant. But in the case of the clerk it is almost as difficult to know where the dismissal comes from as to know where the clerk goes to. It may be Mr. Solomon or Mr. Solomon's manager, or Mr. Solomon's rich aunt in Cheltenham, or Mr. Soloman's rich creditor in Berlin. The elaborate machinery which was once used to make men responsible is now used solely in order to shift the responsibility. People talk about the pride of tyrants; but we in this age are not suffering from the pride of tyrants. We are suffering from the shyness of tyrants; from the shrinking modesty of tyrants. Therefore we must not encourage leader-writers to be shy; we must not inflame their already exaggerated modesty. Rather we must attempt to lure them to be vain and ostentatious; so that through ostentation they may at last find their way to honesty.

The last indictment against this book is the worst of all. It is simply this: that if all goes well this book will be unintelligible gibberish. For it is mostly concerned with attacking attitudes which are in their nature accidental and incapable of enduring. Brief as is the career of such a book as this, it may last just twenty minutes longer than most of the philosophies that it attacks. In the end it will not matter to us whether we wrote well or ill; whether we fought with flails or reeds. It will matter to us greatly on what side we fought.

Chapter 2
Cockneys and Their Jokes

 writer in the *Yorkshire Evening Post* is very angry indeed with my performances in this column. His precise terms of reproach are, "Mr. G. K. Chesterton is not a humourist: not even a Cockney humourist." I do not mind his saying that I am not a humourist— in which (to tell the truth) I think he is quite right. But I do resent his saying that I am not a Cockney. That envenomed arrow, I admit, went home. If a French writer said of me, "He is no metaphysician: not even an English metaphysician," I could swallow the insult to my metaphysics, but I should feel angry about the insult to my country. So I do not urge that I am a humourist; but I do insist that I am a Cockney. If I were a humourist, I should certainly be a Cockney humourist; if I were a saint, I should certainly be a Cockney saint. I need not recite the splendid catalogue of Cockney saints who have written their names on our noble old City churches. I need not trouble you with the long list of the Cockney humourists who have discharged their bills (or failed to discharge them) in our noble old City taverns. We can weep together over the pathos of the poor Yorkshireman, whose county has never produced some humour not intelligible to the rest of the world. And we can smile together when he says that somebody or other is "not even" a Cockney humourist like Samuel Johnson or Charles Lamb. It is surely sufficiently obvious that all the best humour that exists in our language is Cockney humour. Chaucer was a Cockney; he had his house close to the Abbey. Dickens was a Cockney; he said he could not think without the London streets. The London taverns heard always the quaintest conversation, whether it was Ben Johnson's at the Mermaid or Sam Johnson's at the Cock. Even in our own time it may be noted that the most vital and genuine humour is still written about London. Of this type is the mild and humane irony which marks Mr. Pett Ridge's studies of the small grey streets. Of this type is the simple but smashing laughter of the best tales of Mr. W. W. Jacobs, telling of the smoke and sparkle of the Thames. No; I concede that I am not a Cockney humourist. No; I am not worthy to be. Some time, after sad and strenuous after-lives; some time, after fierce and apocalyptic incarnations; in some strange world beyond the stars, I may become at last a Cockney humourist. In that potential paradise I may walk among the Cockney humourists, if not an equal, at least a companion. I may feel for a moment on my shoulder the hearty hand of Dryden and thread the labyrinths of the sweet insanity of Lamb. But that could only be if I were not only much cleverer, but much better than I am. Before I reach that sphere I shall have left behind, perhaps, the sphere that is inhabited by angels, and even passed that which is appropriated exclusively to the use of Yorkshiremen.

No; London is in this matter attacked upon its strongest ground. London is the largest of the bloated modern cities; London is the smokiest; London is the dirtiest; London is, if you will, the most sombre; London is, if you will, the most miserable. But London is certainly the most amusing and the most amused. You may prove that we have the most tragedy; the fact remains that we have the most comedy, that we have the most farce. We have at the very worst a splendid hypocrisy of humour. We conceal our sorrow behind a screaming derision. You speak of people who laugh through their tears; it is our boast that we only weep through our laughter. There remains always this great boast, perhaps the greatest boast that is possible to human nature. I mean the great boast that the most unhappy part of our population is also the most hilarious part. The poor can forget that social problem which we (the moderately rich) ought never to forget. Blessed are the poor; for they alone have not the poor always with them. The honest poor can sometimes forget poverty. The honest rich can never forget it.

I believe firmly in the value of all vulgar notions, especially of vulgar jokes. When once you have got hold of a vulgar joke, you may be certain that you have got hold of a subtle and spiritual idea. The men who made the joke saw something deep which they could not express except by something silly and emphatic. They saw something delicate which they could only express by something indelicate. I remember that Mr. Max Beerbohm (who has every merit except democracy) attempted to analyse the jokes at which the mob laughs. He divided them into three sections: jokes about bodily humiliation, jokes about things alien, such as foreigners, and jokes about bad cheese. Mr. Max Beerbohm thought he understood the first two forms; but I am not sure that he did. In order to understand vulgar humour it is not enough to be humorous. One must also be vulgar, as I am. And in the first case it is surely obvious that it is not merely at the fact of something being hurt that we laugh (as I trust we do) when a Prime Minister sits down on his hat. If that were so we should laugh whenever we saw a funeral. We do not laugh at the mere fact of something falling down; there is nothing humorous about leaves falling or the sun going down. When our house falls down we do not laugh. All the birds of the air might drop around us in a perpetual shower like a hailstorm without arousing a smile. If you really ask yourself why we laugh at a man sitting down suddenly in the street you will discover that the reason is not only recondite, but ultimately religious. All the jokes about men sitting down on their hats are really theological jokes; they are concerned with the Dual Nature of Man. They refer to the primary paradox that man is superior to all the things around him and yet is at their mercy.

Quite equally subtle and spiritual is the idea at the back of laughing at foreigners. It concerns the almost torturing truth of a thing being like oneself and yet not like oneself. Nobody laughs at what is entirely foreign; nobody laughs at a palm tree. But it is funny to see the familiar image of God disguised behind the black beard of a Frenchman or the black face of a Negro. There is nothing funny in the sounds that are wholly inhuman, the howling of wild beasts or of the wind.

But if a man begins to talk like oneself, but all the syllables come out different, then if one is a man one feels inclined to laugh, though if one is a gentleman one resists the inclination.

Mr. Max Beerbohm, I remember, professed to understand the first two forms of popular wit, but said that the third quite stumped him. He could not see why there should be anything funny about bad cheese. I can tell him at once. He has missed the idea because it is subtle and philosophical, and he was looking for something ignorant and foolish. Bad cheese is funny because it is (like the foreigner or the man fallen on the pavement) the type of the transition or transgression across a great mystical boundary. Bad cheese symbolises the change from the inorganic to the organic. Bad cheese symbolises the startling prodigy of matter taking on vitality. It symbolises the origin of life itself. And it is only about such solemn matters as the origin of life that the democracy condescends to joke. Thus, for instance, the democracy jokes about marriage, because marriage is a part of mankind. But the democracy would never deign to joke about Free Love, because Free Love is a piece of priggishness.

As a matter of fact, it will be generally found that the popular joke is not true to the letter, but is true to the spirit. The vulgar joke is generally in the oddest way the truth and yet not the fact. For instance, it is not in the least true that mothers-in-law are as a class oppressive and intolerable; most of them are both devoted and useful. All the mothers-in-law I have ever had were admirable. Yet the legend of the comic papers is profoundly true. It draws attention to the fact that it is much harder to be a nice mother-in-law than to be nice in any other conceivable relation of life. The caricatures have drawn the worst mother-in-law a monster, by way of expressing the fact that the best mother-in-law is a problem. The same is true of the perpetual jokes in comic papers about shrewish wives and henpecked husbands. It is all a frantic exaggeration, but it is an exaggeration of a truth; whereas all the modern mouthings about oppressed women are the exaggerations of a falsehood. If you read even the best of the intellectuals of to-day you will find them saying that in the mass of the democracy the woman is the chattel of her lord, like his bath or his bed. But if you read the comic literature of the democracy you will find that the lord hides under the bed to escape from the wrath of his chattel. This is not the fact, but it is much nearer the truth. Every man who is married knows quite well, not only that he does not regard his wife as a chattel, but that no man can conceivably ever have done so. The joke stands for an ultimate truth, and that is a subtle truth. It is one not very easy to state correctly. It can, perhaps, be most correctly stated by saying that, even if the man is the head of the house, he knows he is the figurehead.

But the vulgar comic papers are so subtle and true that they are even prophetic. If you really want to know what is going to happen to the future of our democracy, do not read the modern sociological prophecies, do not read even Mr. Wells's Utopias for this purpose, though you should certainly read them if you are fond of good honesty and good English. If you want to know what will happen, study the pages of *Snaps* or *Patchy Bits* as if they were the dark tablets graven with the oracles of the gods. For, mean and gross as they are, in all seriousness, they contain what is entirely absent from all Utopias and all the sociological conjectures of our time: they contain some hint of the actual habits and manifest desires of the English people. If we are really to find out what the democracy will ultimately do with itself, we shall surely find it, not in the literature which studies the people, but in the literature which the people studies.

I can give two chance cases in which the common or Cockney joke was a much better prophecy than the careful observations of the most cultured observer. When England was agitated, previous to the last General Election, about the existence of Chinese labour, there was a distinct difference between the tone of the politicians and the tone of the populace. The politicians who disapproved of Chinese labour were most careful to explain that they did not in any sense disapprove of Chinese. According to them, it was a pure question of legal propriety, of whether certain clauses in the contract of indenture were not inconsistent with our constitutional traditions: according to them, the case would have been the same if the people had been Kaffirs or Englishmen. It all sounded wonderfully enlightened and lucid; and in comparison the popular joke looked, of course, very poor. For the popular joke against the Chinese labourers was simply that they were Chinese; it was an objection to an alien type; the popular papers were full of gibes about pigtails and yellow faces. It seemed that the Liberal politicians were raising an intellectual objection to a doubtful document of State; while it seemed that the Radical populace were merely roaring with idiotic laughter at the sight of a Chinaman's clothes. But the popular instinct was justified, for the vices revealed were Chinese vices.

But there is another case more pleasant and more up to date. The popular papers always persisted in representing the New Woman or the Suffragette as an ugly woman, fat, in spectacles, with bulging clothes, and generally falling off a bicycle. As a matter of plain external fact, there was not a word of truth in this. The leaders of the movement of female emancipation are not at all ugly; most of them are extraordinarily good-looking. Nor are they at all indifferent to art or decorative costume; many of them are alarmingly attached to these things. Yet the popular instinct was right. For the popular instinct was that in this movement, rightly or wrongly, there was an element of indifference to female dignity, of a quite new willingness of women to be grotesque. These women did truly despise the pontifical quality of woman. And in our streets and around our Parliament we have seen the stately woman of art and culture turn into the comic woman of *Comic Bits*. And whether we think the exhibition justifiable or not, the prophecy of the comic papers is justified: the healthy and vulgar masses were conscious of a hidden enemy to their traditions who has now come out into the daylight, that the scriptures might be fulfilled. For the two things that a healthy person hates most between heaven and hell are a woman who is not dignified and a man who is.

Chapter 3
The Fallacy of Success

here has appeared in our time a particular class of books and articles which I sincerely and solemnly think may be called the silliest ever known among men. They are much more wild than the wildest romances of chivalry and much more dull than the dullest religious tract. Moreover, the romances of chivalry were at least about chivalry; the religious tracts are about religion. But these things are about nothing; they are about what is called Success. On every bookstall, in every magazine, you may find works telling people how to succeed. They are books showing men how to succeed in everything; they are written by men who cannot even succeed in writing books. To begin with, of course, there is no such thing as Success. Or, if you like to put it so, there is nothing that is not successful. That a thing is successful merely means that it is; a millionaire is successful in being a millionaire and a donkey in being a donkey. Any live man has succeeded in living; any dead man may have succeeded in committing suicide. But, passing over the bad logic and bad philosophy in the phrase, we may take it, as these writers do, in the ordinary sense of success in obtaining money or worldly position. These writers profess to tell the ordinary man how he may succeed in his trade or speculation—how, if he is a builder, he may succeed as a builder; how, if he is a stockbroker, he may succeed as a stockbroker. They profess to show him how, if he is a grocer, he may become a sporting yachtsman; how, if he is a tenth-rate journalist, he may become a peer; and how, if he is a German Jew, he may become an Anglo-Saxon. This is a definite and business-like proposal, and I really think that the people who buy these books (if any people do buy them) have a moral, if not a legal, right to ask for their money back. Nobody would dare to publish a book about electricity which literally told one nothing about electricity; no one would dare to publish an article on botany which showed that the writer did not know which end of a plant grew in the earth. Yet our modern world is full of books about Success and successful people which literally contain no kind of idea, and scarcely any kind of verbal sense.

It is perfectly obvious that in any decent occupation (such as bricklaying or writing books) there are only two ways (in any special sense) of succeeding. One is by doing very good work, the other is by cheating. Both are much too simple to require any literary explanation. If you are in for the high jump, either jump higher than any one else, or manage somehow to pretend that you have done so. If you want to succeed at whist, either be a good whist-player, or play with marked cards. You may want a book about jumping; you may want a book about whist; you may want a book about cheating at whist. But you cannot want a book about Success. Especially you cannot want a book about Success such as those which you can now find scattered by the hundred about the book-market. You may want to jump or to play cards; but you do not want to read wandering statements to the effect that jumping is jumping, or that games are won by winners. If these writers, for instance, said anything about success in jumping it would be something like this: "The jumper must have a clear aim before him. He must desire definitely to jump higher than the other men who are in for the same competition. He must let no feeble feelings of mercy (sneaked from the sickening Little Englanders and Pro-Boers) prevent him from trying to *do his best*. He must remember that a competition in jumping is distinctly competitive, and that, as Darwin has gloriously demonstrated, THE WEAKEST GO TO THE WALL." That is the kind of thing the book would say, and very useful it would be, no doubt, if read out in a low and tense voice to a young man just about to take the high jump. Or suppose that in the course of his intellectual rambles the philosopher of Success dropped upon our other case, that of playing cards, his bracing advice would run—"In playing cards it is very necessary to avoid the mistake (commonly made by maudlin humanitarians and Free Traders) of permitting your opponent to win the game. You must have grit and snap and go *in to win*. The days of idealism and superstition are over. We live in a time of science and hard common sense, and it has now been definitely proved that in any game where two are playing IF ONE DOES NOT WIN THE OTHER WILL." It is all very stirring, of course; but I confess that if I were playing cards I would rather have some decent little book which told me the rules of the game. Beyond the rules of the game it is all a question either of talent or dishonesty; and I will undertake to provide either one or the other—which, it is not for me to say.

Turning over a popular magazine, I find a queer and amusing example. There is an article called "The Instinct that Makes People Rich." It is decorated in front with a formidable portrait of Lord Rothschild. There are many definite methods, honest and dishonest, which make people rich; the only "instinct" I know of which does it is that instinct which theological Christianity crudely describes as "the sin of avarice." That, however, is beside the present point. I wish to quote the following exquisite paragraphs as a piece of typical advice as to how to succeed. It is so practical; it leaves so little doubt about what should be our next step—

"The name of Vanderbilt is synonymous with wealth gained by modern enterprise. 'Cornelius,' the founder of the family, was the first of the great American magnates of commerce. He started as the son of a poor farmer; he ended as a millionaire twenty times over.

"He had the money-making instinct. He seized his opportunities, the opportunities that were given by the application of the steam-engine to ocean traffic, and by the birth of railway locomotion in the wealthy but undeveloped United States of America, and consequently he amassed an immense fortune.

"Now it is, of course, obvious that we cannot all follow exactly in the footsteps of this great railway monarch. The precise opportunities that fell to him do not occur to us. Circumstances have changed. But, although this is so, still, in our own sphere and in our own circumstances, we *can* follow his general methods; we can seize those opportunities that are given us, and give ourselves a very fair chance of attaining riches."

In such strange utterances we see quite clearly what is really at the bottom of all these articles and books. It is not mere business; it is not even mere cynicism. It is mysticism; the horrible mysticism of money. The writer of that passage did not really have the remotest notion of how Vanderbilt made his money, or of how anybody else is to make his. He does, indeed, conclude his remarks by advocating some scheme; but it has nothing in the world to do with Vanderbilt. He merely wished to prostrate himself before the mystery of a millionaire. For when we really worship anything, we love not only its clearness but its obscurity. We exult in its very invisibility. Thus, for instance, when a man is in love with a woman he takes special pleasure in the fact that a woman is unreasonable. Thus, again, the very pious poet, celebrating his Creator, takes pleasure in saying that God moves in a mysterious way. Now, the writer of the paragraph which I have quoted does not seem to have had anything to do with a god, and I should not think (judging by his extreme unpracticality) that he had ever been really in love with a woman. But the thing he does worship—Vanderbilt—he treats in exactly this mystical manner. He really revels in the fact his deity Vanderbilt is keeping a secret from him. And it fills his soul with a sort of transport of cunning, an ecstasy of priestcraft, that he should pretend to be telling to the multitude that terrible secret which he does not know.

Speaking about the instinct that makes people rich, the same writer remarks—

"In olden days its existence was fully understood. The Greeks enshrined it in the story of Midas, of the 'Golden Touch.' Here was a man who turned everything he laid his hands upon into gold. His life was a progress amidst riches. Out of everything that came in his way he created the precious metal. 'A foolish legend,' said the wiseacres of the Victorian age. 'A truth,' say we of to-day. We all know of such men. We are ever meeting or reading about such persons who turn everything they touch into gold. Success dogs their very footsteps. Their life's pathway leads unerringly upwards. They cannot fail."

Unfortunately, however, Midas could fail; he did. His path did not lead unerringly upward. He starved because whenever he touched a biscuit or a ham sandwich it turned to gold. That was the whole point of the story, though the writer has to suppress it delicately, writing so near to a portrait of Lord Rothschild. The old fables of mankind are, indeed, unfathomably wise; but we must not have them expurgated in the interests of Mr. Vanderbilt. We must not have King Midas represented as an example of success; he was a failure of an unusually painful kind. Also, he had the ears of an ass. Also (like most other prominent and wealthy persons) he endeavoured to conceal the fact. It was his barber (if I remember right) who had to be treated on a confidential footing with regard to this peculiarity; and his barber, instead of behaving like a go-ahead person of the Succeed-at-all-costs school and trying to blackmail King Midas, went away and whispered this splendid piece of society scandal to the reeds, who enjoyed it enormously. It is said that they also whispered it as the winds swayed them to and fro. I look reverently at the portrait of Lord Rothschild; I read reverently about the exploits of Mr. Vanderbilt. I know that I cannot turn everything I touch to gold; but then I also know that I have never tried, having a preference for other substances, such as grass, and good wine. I know that these people have certainly succeeded in something; that they have certainly overcome somebody; I know that they are kings in a sense that no men were ever kings before; that they create markets and bestride continents. Yet it always seems to me that there is some small domestic fact that they are hiding, and I have sometimes thought I heard upon the wind the laughter and whisper of the reeds.

At least, let us hope that we shall all live to see these absurd books about Success covered with a proper derision and neglect. They do not teach people to be successful, but they do teach people to be snobbish; they do spread a sort of evil poetry of worldliness. The Puritans are always denouncing books that inflame lust; what shall we say of books that inflame the viler passions of avarice and pride? A hundred years ago we had the ideal of the Industrious Apprentice; boys were told that by thrift and work they would all become Lord Mayors. This was fallacious, but it was manly, and had a minimum of moral truth. In our society, temperance will not help a poor man to enrich himself, but it may help him to respect himself. Good work will not make him a rich man, but good work may make him a good workman. The Industrious Apprentice rose by virtues few and narrow indeed, but still virtues. But what shall we say of the gospel preached to the new Industrious Apprentice; the Apprentice who rises not by his virtues, but avowedly by his vices?

Chapter 4
On Running After One's Hat

feel an almost savage envy on hearing that London has been flooded in my absence, while I am in the mere country. My own Battersea has been, I understand, particularly favoured as a meeting of the waters. Battersea was already, as I need hardly say, the most beautiful of human localities. Now that it has the additional splendour of great sheets of water, there must be something quite incomparable in the landscape (or waterscape) of my own romantic town. Battersea must be a vision of Venice. The boat that brought the meat from the butcher's must have shot along those lanes of rippling silver with the strange smoothness of the gondola. The greengrocer who brought cabbages to the corner of the Latchmere Road must have leant upon the oar with the unearthly grace of the gondolier. There is nothing so perfectly poetical as an island; and when a district is flooded it becomes an archipelago.

Some consider such romantic views of flood or fire slightly lacking in reality. But really this romantic view of such inconveniences is quite as practical as the other. The true optimist who sees in such things an opportunity for enjoyment is quite as logical and much more sensible than the ordinary "Indignant Ratepayer" who sees in them an opportunity for grumbling. Real pain, as in the case of being burnt at Smithfield or having a toothache, is a positive thing; it can be supported, but scarcely enjoyed. But, after all, our toothaches are the exception, and as for being burnt at Smithfield, it only happens to us at the very longest intervals. And most of the inconveniences that make men swear or women cry are really sentimental or imaginative inconveniences—things altogether of the mind. For instance, we often hear grown-up people complaining of having to hang about a railway station and wait for a train. Did you ever hear a small boy complain of having to hang about a railway station and wait for a train? No; for to him to be inside a railway station is to be inside a cavern of wonder and a palace of poetical pleasures. Because to him the red light and the green light on the signal are like a new sun and a new moon. Because to him when the wooden arm of the signal falls down suddenly, it is as if a great king had thrown down his staff as a signal and started a shrieking tournament of trains. I myself am of little boys' habit in this matter. They also serve who only stand and wait for the two fifteen. Their meditations may be full of rich and fruitful things. Many of the most purple hours of my life have been passed at Clapham Junction, which is now, I suppose, under water. I have been there in many moods so fixed and mystical that the water might well have come up to my waist before I noticed it particularly. But in the case of all such annoyances, as I have said, everything depends upon the emotional point of view. You can safely apply the test to almost every one of the things that are currently talked of as the typical nuisance of daily life.

For instance, there is a current impression that it is unpleasant to have to run after one's hat. Why should it be unpleasant to the well-ordered and pious mind? Not merely because it is running, and running exhausts one. The same people run much faster in games and sports. The same people run much more eagerly after an uninteresting little leather ball than they will after a nice silk hat. There is an idea that it is humiliating to run after one's hat; and when people say it is humiliating they mean that it is comic. It certainly is comic; but man is a very comic creature, and most of the things he does are comic—eating, for instance. And the most comic things of all are exactly the things that are most worth doing—such as making love. A man running after a hat is not half so ridiculous as a man running after a wife.

Now a man could, if he felt rightly in the matter, run after his hat with the manliest ardour and the most sacred joy. He might regard himself as a jolly huntsman pursuing a wild animal, for certainly no animal could be wilder. In fact, I am inclined to believe that hat-hunting on windy days will be the sport of the upper classes in the future. There will be a meet of ladies and gentlemen on some high ground on a gusty morning. They will be told that the professional attendants have started a hat in such-and-such a thicket, or whatever be the technical term. Notice that this employment will in the fullest degree combine sport with humanitarianism. The hunters would feel that they were not inflicting pain. Nay, they would feel that they were inflicting pleasure, rich, almost riotous pleasure, upon the people who were looking on. When last I saw an old gentleman running after his hat in Hyde Park, I told him that a heart so benevolent as his ought to be filled with peace and thanks at the thought of how much unaffected pleasure his every gesture and bodily attitude were at that moment giving to the crowd.

The same principle can be applied to every other typical domestic worry. A gentleman trying to get a fly out of the milk or a piece of cork out of his glass of wine often imagines himself to be irritated. Let him think for a moment of the patience of anglers sitting by dark pools, and let his soul be immediately irradiated with gratification and repose. Again, I have known some people of very modern views driven by their distress to the use of theological terms to which they attached no doctrinal significance, merely because a drawer was jammed tight and they could not pull it out. A friend of mine was particularly afflicted in this way. Every day his drawer was jammed, and every day in consequence it was something else that rhymes to it. But I pointed out to him that this sense of wrong was really subjective and relative; it rested entirely upon the assumption that the drawer could, should, and would come out easily. "But if," I said, "you picture to yourself that you are pulling against some powerful and oppressive enemy, the struggle will become merely exciting and not exasperating. Imagine that you are tugging up a lifeboat out of the sea. Imagine that you are roping up a fellow-creature out of an Alpine crevass. Imagine even that you are a boy again and engaged in a tug-of-war between French and English." Shortly after saying this I left him; but I have no doubt at all that my words bore the best possible fruit. I have no doubt that every day of his life he hangs on to the handle of that drawer with a flushed face and eyes bright with battle, uttering encouraging shouts to himself, and seeming to hear all round him the roar of an applauding ring.

So I do not think that it is altogether fanciful or incredible to suppose that even the floods in London may be accepted and enjoyed poetically. Nothing beyond inconvenience seems really to have been caused by them; and inconvenience, as I have said, is only one aspect, and that the most unimaginative and accidental aspect of a really romantic situation. An adventure is only an inconvenience rightly considered. An inconvenience is only an adventure wrongly considered. The water that girdled the houses and shops of London must, if anything, have only increased their previous witchery and wonder. For as the Roman Catholic priest in the story said: "Wine is good with everything except water," and on a similar principle, water is good with everything except wine.

Chapter 5
The Vote and the House

ost of us will be canvassed soon, I suppose; some of us may even canvass. Upon which side, of course, nothing will induce me to state, beyond saying that by a remarkable coincidence it will in every case be the only side in which a high-minded, public-spirited, and patriotic citizen can take even a momentary interest. But the general question of canvassing itself, being a non-party question, is one which we may be permitted to approach. The rules for canvassers are fairly familiar to any one who has ever canvassed. They are printed on the little card which you carry about with you and lose. There is a statement, I think, that you must not offer a voter food or drink. However hospitable you may feel towards him in his own house, you must not carry his lunch about with you. You must not produce a veal cutlet from your tail-coat pocket. You must not conceal poached eggs about your person. You must not, like a kind of conjurer, produce baked potatoes from your hat. In short, the canvasser must not feed the voter in any way. Whether the voter is allowed to feed the canvasser, whether the voter may give the canvasser veal cutlets and baked potatoes, is a point of law on which I have never been able to inform myself. When I found myself canvassing a gentleman, I have sometimes felt tempted to ask him if there was any rule against his giving me food and drink; but the matter seemed a delicate one to approach. His attitude to me also sometimes suggested a doubt as to whether he would, even if he could. But there are voters who might find it worth while to discover if there is any law against bribing a canvasser. They might bribe him to go away.

The second veto for canvassers which was printed on the little card said that you must not persuade any one to personate a voter. I have no idea what it means. To dress up as an average voter seems a little vague. There is no well-recognised uniform, as far as I know, with civic waistcoat and patriotic whiskers. The enterprise resolves itself into one somewhat similar to the enterprise of a rich friend of mine who went to a fancy-dress ball dressed up as a gentleman. Perhaps it means that there is a practice of personating some individual voter. The canvasser creeps to the house of his fellow-conspirator carrying a make-up in a bag. He produces from it a pair of white moustaches and a single eyeglass, which are sufficient to give the most commonplace person a startling resemblance to the Colonel at No. 80. Or he hurriedly affixes to his friend that large nose and that bald head which are all that is essential to an illusion of the presence of Professor Budger. I do not undertake to unravel these knots. I can only say that when I was a canvasser I was told by the little card, with every circumstance of seriousness and authority, that I was not to persuade anybody to personate a voter: and I can lay my hand upon my heart and affirm that I never did.

The third injunction on the card was one which seemed to me, if interpreted exactly and according to its words, to undermine the very foundations of our politics. It told me that I must not "threaten a voter with any consequence whatever." No doubt this was intended to apply to threats of a personal and illegitimate character; as, for instance, if a wealthy candidate were to threaten to raise all the rents, or to put up a statue of himself. But as verbally and grammatically expressed, it certainly would cover those general threats of disaster to the whole community which are the main matter of political discussion. When a canvasser says that if the opposition candidate gets in the country will be ruined, he is threatening the voters with certain consequences. When the Free Trader says that if Tariffs are adopted the people in Brompton or Bayswater will crawl about eating grass, he is threatening them with consequences. When the Tariff Reformer says that if Free Trade exists for another year St. Paul's Cathedral will be a ruin and Ludgate Hill as deserted as Stonehenge, he is also threatening. And what is the good of being a Tariff Reformer if you can't say that? What is the use of being a politician or a Parliamentary candidate at all if one cannot tell the people that if the other man gets in, England will be instantly invaded and enslaved, blood be pouring down the Strand, and all the English ladies carried off into harems. But these things are, after all, consequences, so to speak.

The majority of refined persons in our day may generally be heard abusing the practice of canvassing. In the same way the majority of refined persons (commonly the same refined persons) may be heard abusing the practice of interviewing celebrities. It seems a very singular thing to me that this refined world reserves all its indignation for the comparatively open and innocent element in both walks of life. There is really a vast amount of corruption and hypocrisy in our election politics; about the most honest thing in the whole mess is the canvassing. A man has not got a right to "nurse" a constituency with aggressive charities, to buy it with great presents of parks and libraries, to open vague vistas of future benevolence; all this, which goes on unrebuked, is bribery and nothing else. But a man has got the right to go to another free man and ask him with civility whether he will vote for him. The information can be asked, granted, or refused without any loss of dignity on either side, which is more than can be said of a park. It is the same with the place of interviewing in journalism. In a trade where there are labyrinths of insincerity, interviewing is about the most simple and the most sincere thing there is. The canvasser, when he wants to know a man's opinions, goes and asks him. It may be a bore; but it is about as plain and straight a thing as he could do. So the interviewer, when he wants to know a man's opinions, goes and asks him. Again, it may be a bore; but again, it is about as plain and straight as anything could be. But all the other real and systematic cynicisms of our journalism pass without being vituperated and even without being known—the financial motives of policy, the misleading posters, the suppression of just letters of complaint. A statement about a man may be infamously untrue, but it is read calmly. But a statement by a man to an interviewer is felt as indefensibly vulgar. That the paper should misrepresent him is nothing; that he should represent himself is bad taste. The whole error in both cases lies in the fact that the refined persons are attacking politics and journalism on the ground of vulgarity. Of course, politics and journalism are, as it happens, very vulgar. But their vulgarity is not the worst thing about them. Things are so bad with both that by this time their vulgarity is the best thing about them. Their vulgarity is at least a noisy thing; and their great danger is that silence that always comes before decay. The conversational persuasion at elections is perfectly human and rational; it is the silent persuasions that are utterly damnable.

If it is true that the Commons' House will not hold all the Commons, it is a very good example of what we call the anomalies of the English Constitution. It is also, I think, a very good example of how highly undesirable those anomalies really are. Most Englishmen say that these anomalies do not matter; they are not ashamed of being illogical; they are proud of being illogical. Lord Macaulay (a very typical Englishman, romantic, prejudiced, poetical), Lord Macaulay said that he would not lift his hand to get rid of an anomaly that was not also a grievance. Many other sturdy romantic Englishmen say the same. They boast of our anomalies; they boast of our illogicality; they say it shows what a practical people we are. They are utterly wrong. Lord Macaulay was in this matter, as in a few others, utterly wrong. Anomalies do matter very much, and do a great deal of harm; abstract illogicalities do matter a great deal, and do a great deal of harm. And this for a reason that any one at all acquainted with human nature can see for himself. All injustice begins in the mind. And anomalies accustom the mind to the idea of unreason and untruth. Suppose I had by some prehistoric law the power of forcing every man in Battersea to nod his head three times before he got out of bed. The practical politicians might say that this power was a harmless anomaly; that it was not a grievance. It could do my subjects no harm; it could do me no good. The people of Battersea, they would say, might safely submit to it. But the people of Battersea could not safely submit to it, for all that. If I had nodded their heads for them for fifty years I could cut off their heads for them at the end of it with immeasurably greater ease. For there would have permanently sunk into every man's mind the notion that it was a natural thing for me to have a fantastic and irrational power. They would have grown accustomed to insanity.

For, in order that men should resist injustice, something more is necessary than that they should think injustice unpleasant. They must think injustice *absurd*; above all, they must think it startling. They must retain the violence of a virgin astonishment. That is the explanation of the singular fact which must have struck many people in the relations of philosophy and reform. It is the fact (I mean) that optimists are more practical reformers than pessimists. Superficially, one would imagine that the railer would be the reformer; that the man who thought that everything was wrong would be the man to put everything right. In historical practice the thing is quite the other way; curiously enough, it is the man who likes things as they are who really makes them better. The optimist Dickens has achieved more reforms than the pessimist Gissing. A man like Rousseau has far too rosy a theory of human nature; but he produces a revolution. A man like David Hume thinks that almost all things are depressing; but he is a Conservative, and wishes to keep them as they are. A man like Godwin believes existence to be kindly; but he is a rebel. A man like Carlyle believes existence to be cruel; but he is a Tory. Everywhere the man who alters things begins by liking things. And the real explanation of this success of the optimistic reformer, of this failure of the pessimistic reformer, is, after all, an explanation of sufficient simplicity. It is because the optimist can look at wrong not only with indignation, but with a startled indignation. When the pessimist looks at any infamy, it is to him, after all, only a repetition of the infamy of existence. The Court of Chancery is indefensible—like mankind. The Inquisition is abominable—like the universe. But the optimist sees injustice as something discordant and unexpected, and it stings him into action. The pessimist can be enraged at wrong; but only the optimist can be surprised at it.

And it is the same with the relations of an anomaly to the logical mind. The pessimist resents evil (like Lord Macaulay) solely because it is a grievance. The optimist resents it also, because it is an anomaly; a contradiction to his conception of the course of things. And it is not at all unimportant, but on the contrary most important, that this course of things in politics and elsewhere should be lucid, explicable and defensible. When people have got used to unreason they can no longer be startled at injustice. When people have grown familiar with an anomaly, they are prepared to that extent for a grievance; they may think the grievance grievous, but they can no longer think it strange. Take, if only as an excellent example, the very matter alluded to before; I mean the seats, or rather the lack of seats, in the House of Commons. Perhaps it is true that under the best conditions it would never happen that every member turned up. Perhaps a complete attendance would never actually be. But who can tell how much influence in keeping members away may have been exerted by this calm assumption that they would stop away? How can any man be expected to help to make a full attendance when he knows that a full attendance is actually forbidden? How can the men who make up the Chamber do their duty reasonably when the very men who built the House have not done theirs reasonably? If the trumpet give an uncertain sound, who shall prepare himself for the battle? And what if the remarks of the trumpet take this form, "I charge you as you love your King and country to come to this Council. And I know you won't."

Chapter 6
Conceit and Caricature

f a man must needs be conceited, it is certainly better that he should be conceited about some merits or talents that he does not really possess. For then his vanity remains more or less superficial; it remains a mere mistake of fact, like that of a man who thinks he inherits the royal blood or thinks he has an infallible system for Monte Carlo. Because the merit is an unreal merit, it does not corrupt or sophisticate his real merits. He is vain about the virtue he has not got; but he may be humble about the virtues that he has got. His truly honourable qualities remain in their primordial innocence; he cannot see them and he cannot spoil them. If a man's mind is erroneously possessed with the idea that he is a great violinist, that need not prevent his being a gentleman and an honest man. But if once his mind is possessed in any strong degree with the knowledge that he is a gentleman, he will soon cease to be one.

But there is a third kind of satisfaction of which I have noticed one or two examples lately—another kind of satisfaction which is neither a pleasure in the virtues that we do possess nor a pleasure in the virtues we do not possess. It is the pleasure which a man takes in the presence or absence of certain things in himself without ever adequately asking himself whether in his case they constitute virtues at all. A man will plume himself because he is not bad in some particular way, when the truth is that he is not good enough to be bad in that particular way. Some priggish little clerk will say, "I have reason to congratulate myself that I am a civilised person, and not so bloodthirsty as the Mad Mullah." Somebody ought to say to him, "A really good man would be less bloodthirsty than the Mullah. But you are less bloodthirsty, not because you are more of a good man, but because you are a great deal less of a man. You are not bloodthirsty, not because you would spare your enemy, but because you would run away from him." Or again, some Puritan with a sullen type of piety would say, "I have reason to congratulate myself that I do not worship graven images like the old heathen Greeks." And again somebody ought to say to him, "The best religion may not worship graven images, because it may see beyond them. But if you do not worship graven images, it is only because you are mentally and morally quite incapable of graving them. True religion, perhaps, is above idolatry. But you are below idolatry. You are not holy enough yet to worship a lump of stone."

Mr. F. C. Gould, the brilliant and felicitous caricaturist, recently delivered a most interesting speech upon the nature and atmosphere of our modern English caricature. I think there is really very little to congratulate oneself about in the condition of English caricature. There are few causes for pride; probably the greatest cause for pride is Mr. F. C. Gould. But Mr. F. C. Gould, forbidden by modesty to adduce this excellent ground for optimism, fell back upon saying a thing which is said by numbers of other people, but has not perhaps been said lately with the full authority of an eminent cartoonist. He said that he thought "that they might congratulate themselves that the style of caricature which found acceptation nowadays was very different from the lampoon of the old days." Continuing, he said, according to the newspaper report, "On looking back to the political lampoons of Rowlandson's and Gilray's time they would find them coarse and brutal. In some countries abroad still, 'even in America,' the method of political caricature was of the bludgeon kind. The fact was we had passed the bludgeon stage. If they were brutal in attacking a man, even for political reasons, they roused sympathy for the man who was attacked. What they had to do was to rub in the point they wanted to emphasise as gently as they could." (Laughter and applause.)

Anybody reading these words, and anybody who heard them, will certainly feel that there is in them a great deal of truth, as well as a great deal of geniality. But along with that truth and with that geniality there is a streak of that erroneous type of optimism which is founded on the fallacy of which I have spoken above. Before we congratulate ourselves upon the absence of certain faults from our nation or society, we ought to ask ourselves why it is that these faults are absent. Are we without the fault because we have the opposite virtue? Or are we without the fault because we have the opposite fault? It is a good thing assuredly, to be innocent of any excess; but let us be sure that we are not innocent of excess merely by being guilty of defect. Is it really true that our English political satire is so moderate because it is so magnanimous, so forgiving, so saintly? Is it penetrated through and through with a mystical charity, with a psychological tenderness? Do we spare the feelings of the Cabinet Minister because we pierce through all his apparent crimes and follies down to the dark virtues of which his own soul is unaware? Do we temper the wind to the Leader of the Opposition because in our all-embracing heart we pity and cherish the struggling spirit of the Leader of the Opposition? Briefly, have we left off being brutal because we are too grand and generous to be brutal? Is it really true that we are *better* than brutality? Is it really true that we have *passed* the bludgeon stage?

I fear that there is, to say the least of it, another side to the matter. Is it not only too probable that the mildness of our political satire, when compared with the political satire of our fathers, arises simply from the profound unreality of our current politics? Rowlandson and Gilray did not fight merely because they were naturally pothouse pugilists; they fought because they had something to fight about. It is easy enough to be refined about things that do not matter; but men kicked and plunged a little in that portentous wrestle in which swung to and fro, alike dizzy with danger, the independence of England, the independence of Ireland, the independence of France. If we wish for a proof of this fact that the lack of refinement did not come from mere brutality, the proof is easy. The proof is that in that struggle no personalities were more brutal than the really refined personalities. None were more violent and intolerant than those who were by nature polished and sensitive. Nelson, for instance, had the nerves and good manners of a woman: nobody in his senses, I suppose, would call Nelson "brutal." But when he was touched upon the national matter, there sprang out of him a spout of oaths, and he could only tell men to "Kill! kill! kill the d—— d Frenchmen." It would be as easy to take examples on the other side. Camille Desmoulins was a man of much the same type, not only elegant and sweet in temper, but almost tremulously tender and humanitarian. But he was ready, he said, "to embrace Liberty upon a pile of corpses." In Ireland there were even more instances. Robert Emmet was only one famous example of a whole family of men at once sensitive and savage. I think that Mr. F.C. Gould is altogether wrong in talking of this political ferocity as if it were some sort of survival from ruder conditions, like a flint axe or a hairy man. Cruelty is, perhaps, the worst kind of sin. Intellectual cruelty is certainly the worst kind of cruelty. But there is nothing in the least barbaric or ignorant about intellectual cruelty. The great Renaissance artists who mixed colours exquisitely mixed poisons equally exquisitely; the great Renaissance princes who designed instruments of music also designed instruments of torture. Barbarity, malignity, the desire to hurt men, are the evil things generated in atmospheres of intense reality when great nations or great causes are at war. We may, perhaps, be glad that we have not got them: but it is somewhat dangerous to be proud that we have not got them. Perhaps we are hardly great enough to have them. Perhaps some great virtues have to be generated, as in men like Nelson or Emmet, before we can have these vices at all, even as temptations. I, for one, believe that if our caricaturists do not hate their enemies, it is not because they are too big to hate them, but because their enemies are not big enough to hate. I do not think we have passed the bludgeon stage. I believe we have not come to the bludgeon stage. We must be better, braver, and purer men than we are before we come to the bludgeon stage.

Let us then, by all means, be proud of the virtues that we have not got; but let us not be too arrogant about the virtues that we cannot help having. It may be that a man living on a desert island has a right to congratulate himself upon the fact that he can meditate at his ease. But he must not congratulate himself on the fact that he is on a desert island, and at the same time congratulate himself on the self-restraint he shows in not going to a ball every night. Similarly our England may have a right to congratulate itself upon the fact that her politics are very quiet, amicable, and humdrum. But she must not congratulate herself upon that fact and also congratulate herself upon the self-restraint she shows in not tearing herself and her citizens into rags. Between two English Privy Councillors polite language is a mark of civilisation, but really not a mark of magnanimity.

Allied to this question is the kindred question on which we so often hear an innocent British boast—the fact that our statesmen are privately on very friendly relations, although in Parliament they sit on opposite sides of the House. Here, again, it is as well to have no illusions. Our statesmen are not monsters of mystical generosity or insane logic, who are really able to hate a man from three to twelve and to love him from twelve to three. If our social relations are more peaceful than those of France or America or the England of a hundred years ago, it is simply because our politics are more peaceful; not improbably because our politics are more fictitious. If our statesmen agree more in private, it is for the very simple reason that they agree more in public. And the reason they agree so much in both cases is really that they belong to one social class; and therefore the dining life is the real life. Tory and Liberal statesmen like each other, but it is not because they are both expansive; it is because they are both exclusive.

Chapter 7
Patriotism and Sport

notice that some papers, especially papers that call themselves patriotic, have fallen into quite a panic over the fact that we have been twice beaten in the world of sport, that a Frenchman has beaten us at golf, and that Belgians have beaten us at rowing. I suppose that the incidents are important to any people who ever believed in the self-satisfied English legend on this subject. I suppose that there are men who vaguely believe that we could never be beaten by a Frenchman, despite the fact that we have often been beaten by Frenchmen, and once by a Frenchwoman. In the old pictures in *Punch* you will find a recurring piece of satire. The English caricaturists always assumed that a Frenchman could not ride to hounds or enjoy English hunting. It did not seem to occur to them that all the people who founded English hunting were Frenchmen. All the Kings and nobles who originally rode to hounds spoke French. Large numbers of those Englishmen who still ride to hounds have French names. I suppose that the thing is important to any one who is ignorant of such evident matters as these. I suppose that if a man has ever believed that we English have some sacred and separate right to be athletic, such reverses do appear quite enormous and shocking. They feel as if, while the proper sun was rising in the east, some other and unexpected sun had begun to rise in the north-north-west by north. For the benefit, the moral and intellectual benefit of such people, it may be worth while to point out that the Anglo-Saxon has in these cases been defeated precisely by those competitors whom he has always regarded as being out of the running; by Latins, and by Latins of the most easy and unstrenuous type; not only by Frenchman, but by Belgians. All this, I say, is worth telling to any intelligent person who believes in the haughty theory of Anglo-Saxon superiority. But, then, no intelligent person does believe in the haughty theory of Anglo-Saxon superiority. No quite genuine Englishman ever did believe in it. And the genuine Englishman these defeats will in no respect dismay.

The genuine English patriot will know that the strength of England has never depended upon any of these things; that the glory of England has never had anything to do with them, except in the opinion of a large section of the rich and a loose section of the poor which copies the idleness of the rich. These people will, of course, think too much of our failure, just as they thought too much of our success. The typical Jingoes who have admired their countrymen too much for being conquerors will, doubtless, despise their countrymen too much for being conquered. But the Englishman with any feeling for England will know that athletic failures do not prove that England is weak, any more than athletic successes proved that England was strong. The truth is that athletics, like all other things, especially modern, are insanely individualistic. The Englishmen who win sporting prizes are exceptional among Englishmen, for the simple reason that they are exceptional even among men. English athletes represent England just about as much as Mr. Barnum's freaks represent America. There are so few of such people in the whole world that it is almost a toss-up whether they are found in this or that country.

If any one wants a simple proof of this, it is easy to find. When the great English athletes are not exceptional Englishmen they are generally not Englishmen at all. Nay, they are often representatives of races of which the average tone is specially incompatible with athletics. For instance, the English are supposed to rule the natives of India in virtue of their superior hardiness, superior activity, superior health of body and mind. The Hindus are supposed to be our subjects because they are less fond of action, less fond of openness and the open air. In a word, less fond of cricket. And, substantially, this is probably true, that the Indians are less fond of cricket. All the same, if you ask among Englishmen for the very best cricket-player, you will find that he is an Indian. Or, to take another case: it is, broadly speaking, true that the Jews are, as a race, pacific, intellectual, indifferent to war, like the Indians, or, perhaps, contemptuous of war, like the Chinese: nevertheless, of the very good prize-fighters, one or two have been Jews.

This is one of the strongest instances of the particular kind of evil that arises from our English form of the worship of athletics. It concentrates too much upon the success of individuals. It began, quite naturally and rightly, with wanting England to win. The second stage was that it wanted some Englishmen to win. The third stage was (in the ecstasy and agony of some special competition) that it wanted one particular Englishman to win. And the fourth stage was that when he had won, it discovered that he was not even an Englishman.

This is one of the points, I think, on which something might really be said for Lord Roberts and his rather vague ideas which vary between rifle clubs and conscription. Whatever may be the advantages or disadvantages otherwise of the idea, it is at least an idea of procuring equality and a sort of average in the athletic capacity of the people; it might conceivably act as a corrective to our mere tendency to see ourselves in certain exceptional athletes. As it is, there are millions of Englishmen who really think that they are a muscular race because C.B. Fry is an Englishman. And there are many of them who think vaguely that athletics must belong to England because Ranjitsinhji is an Indian.

But the real historic strength of England, physical and moral, has never had anything to do with this athletic specialism; it has been rather hindered by it. Somebody said that the Battle of Waterloo was won on Eton playing-fields. It was a particularly unfortunate remark, for the English contribution to the victory of Waterloo depended very much more than is common in victories upon the steadiness of the rank and file in an almost desperate situation. The Battle of Waterloo was won by the stubbornness of the common soldier—that is to say, it was won by the man who had never been to Eton. It was absurd to say that Waterloo was won on Eton cricket-fields. But it might have been fairly said that Waterloo was won on the village green, where clumsy boys played a very clumsy cricket. In a word, it was the average of the nation that was strong, and athletic glories do not indicate much about the average of a nation. Waterloo was not won by good cricket-players. But Waterloo was won by bad cricket-players, by a mass of men who had some minimum of athletic instincts and habits.

It is a good sign in a nation when such things are done badly. It shows that all the people are doing them. And it is a bad sign in a nation when such things are done very well, for it shows that only a few experts and eccentrics are doing them, and that the nation is merely looking on. Suppose that whenever we heard of walking in England it always meant walking forty-five miles a day without fatigue. We should be perfectly certain that only a few men were walking at all, and that all the other British subjects were being wheeled about in Bath-chairs. But if when we hear of walking it means slow walking, painful walking, and frequent fatigue, then we know that the mass of the nation still is walking. We know that England is still literally on its feet.

The difficulty is therefore that the actual raising of the standard of athletics has probably been bad for national athleticism. Instead of the tournament being a healthy *mêlée* into which any ordinary man would rush and take his chance, it has become a fenced and guarded tilting-yard for the collision of particular champions against whom no ordinary man would pit himself or even be permitted to pit himself. If Waterloo was won on Eton cricket-fields it was because Eton cricket was probably much more careless then than it is now. As long as the game was a game, everybody wanted to join in it. When it becomes an art, every one wants to look at it. When it was frivolous it may have won Waterloo: when it was serious and efficient it lost Magersfontein.

In the Waterloo period there was a general rough-and-tumble athleticism among average Englishmen. It cannot be re-created by cricket, or by conscription, or by any artificial means. It was a thing of the soul. It came out of laughter, religion, and the spirit of the place. But it was like the modern French duel in this—that it might happen to anybody. If I were a French journalist it might really happen that Monsieur Clemenceau might challenge me to meet him with pistols. But I do not think that it is at all likely that Mr. C. B. Fry will ever challenge me to meet him with cricket-bats.

Chapter 8
An Essay on Two Cities

little while ago I fell out of England into the town of Paris. If a man fell out of the moon into the town of Paris he would know that it was the capital of a great nation. If, however, he fell (perhaps off some other side of the moon) so as to hit the city of London, he would not know so well that it was the capital of a great nation; at any rate, he would not know that the nation was so great as it is. This would be so even on the assumption that the man from the moon could not read our alphabet, as presumably he could not, unless elementary education in that planet has gone to rather unsuspected lengths. But it is true that a great part of the distinctive quality which separates Paris from London may be even seen in the names. Real democrats always insist that England is an aristocratic country. Real aristocrats always insist (for some mysterious reason) that it is a democratic country. But if any one has any real doubt about the matter let him consider simply the names of the streets. Nearly all the streets out of the Strand, for instance, are named after the first name, second name, third name, fourth, fifth, and sixth names of some particular noble family; after their relations, connections, or places of residence—Arundel Street, Norfolk Street, Villiers Street, Bedford Street, Southampton Street, and any number of others. The names are varied, so as to introduce the same family under all sorts of different surnames. Thus we have Arundel Street and also Norfolk Street; thus we have Buckingham Street and also Villiers Street. To say that this is not aristocracy is simply intellectual impudence. I am an ordinary citizen, and my name is Gilbert Keith Chesterton; and I confess that if I found three streets in a row in the Strand, the first called Gilbert Street, the second Keith Street, and the third Chesterton Street, I should consider that I had become a somewhat more important person in the commonwealth than was altogether good for its health. If Frenchmen ran London (which God forbid!), they would think it quite as ludicrous that those streets should be named after the Duke of Buckingham as that they should be named after me. They are streets out of one of the main thoroughfares of London. If French methods were adopted, one of them would be called Shakspere Street, another Cromwell Street, another Wordsworth Street; there would be statues of each of these persons at the end of each of these streets, and any streets left over would be named after the date on which the Reform Bill was passed or the Penny Postage established.

Suppose a man tried to find people in London by the names of the places. It would make a fine farce, illustrating our illogicality. Our hero having once realised that Buckingham Street was named after the Buckingham family, would naturally walk into Buckingham Palace in search of the Duke of Buckingham. To his astonishment he would meet somebody quite different. His simple lunar logic would lead him to suppose that if he wanted the Duke of Marlborough (which seems unlikely) he would find him at Marlborough House. He would find the Prince of Wales. When at last he understood that the Marlboroughs live at Blenheim, named after the great Marlborough's victory, he would, no doubt, go there. But he would again find himself in error if, acting upon this principle, he tried to find the Duke of Wellington, and told the cabman to drive to Waterloo. I wonder that no one has written a wild romance about the adventures of such an alien, seeking the great English aristocrats, and only guided by the names; looking for the Duke of Bedford in the town of that name, seeking for some trace of the Duke of Norfolk in Norfolk. He might sail for Wellington in New Zealand to find the ancient seat of the Wellingtons. The last scene might show him trying to learn Welsh in order to converse with the Prince of Wales.

But even if the imaginary traveller knew no alphabet of this earth at all, I think it would still be possible to suppose him seeing a difference between London and Paris, and, upon the whole, the real difference. He would not be able to read the words "Quai Voltaire;" but he would see the sneering statue and the hard, straight roads; without having heard of Voltaire he would understand that the city was Voltairean. He would not know that Fleet Street was named after the Fleet Prison. But the same national spirit which kept the Fleet Prison closed and narrow still keeps Fleet Street closed and narrow. Or, if you will, you may call Fleet Street cosy, and the Fleet Prison cosy. I think I could be more comfortable in the Fleet Prison, in an English way of comfort, than just under the statue of Voltaire. I think that the man from the moon would know France without knowing French; I think that he would know England without having heard the word. For in the last resort all men talk by signs. To talk by statues is to talk by signs; to talk by cities is to talk by signs. Pillars, palaces, cathedrals, temples, pyramids, are an enormous dumb alphabet: as if some giant held up his fingers of stone. The most important things at the last are always said by signs, even if, like the Cross on St. Paul's, they are signs in heaven. If men do not understand signs, they will never understand words.

For my part, I should be inclined to suggest that the chief object of education should be to restore simplicity. If you like to put it so, the chief object of education is not to learn things; nay, the chief object of education is to unlearn things. The chief object of education is to unlearn all the weariness and wickedness of the world and to get back into that state of exhilaration we all instinctively celebrate when we write by preference of children and of boys. If I were an examiner appointed to examine all examiners (which does not at present appear probable), I would not only ask the teachers how much knowledge they had imparted; I would ask them how much splendid and scornful ignorance they had erected, like some royal tower in arms. But, in any case, I would insist that people should have so much simplicity as would enable them to see things suddenly and to see things as they are. I do not care so much whether they can read the names over the shops. I do care very much whether they can read the shops. I do not feel deeply troubled as to whether they can tell where London is on the map so long as they can tell where Brixton is on the way home. I do not even mind whether they can put two and two together in the mathematical sense; I am content if they can put two and two together in the metaphorical sense. But all this longer statement of an obvious view comes back to the metaphor I have employed. I do not care a dump whether they know the alphabet, so long as they know the dumb alphabet.

Unfortunately, I have noticed in many aspects of our popular education that this is not done at all. One teaches our London children to see London with abrupt and simple eyes. And London is far more difficult to see properly than any other place. London is a riddle. Paris is an explanation. The education of the Parisian child is something corresponding to the clear avenues and the exact squares of Paris. When the Parisian boy has done learning about the French reason and the Roman order he can go out and see the thing repeated in the shapes of many shining public places, in the angles of many streets. But when the English boy goes out, after learning about a vague progress and idealism, he cannot see it anywhere. He cannot see anything anywhere, except Sapolio and the *Daily Mail*. We must either alter London to suit the ideals of our education, or else alter our education to suit the great beauty of London.

Chapter 9
French and English

It is obvious that there is a great deal of difference between being international and being cosmopolitan. All good men are international. Nearly all bad men are cosmopolitan. If we are to be international we must be national. And it is largely because those who call themselves the friends of peace have not dwelt sufficiently on this distinction that they do not impress the bulk of any of the nations to which they belong. International peace means a peace between nations, not a peace after the destruction of nations, like the Buddhist peace after the destruction of personality. The golden age of the good European is like the heaven of the Christian: it is a place where people will love each other; not like the heaven of the Hindu, a place where they will be each other. And in the case of national character this can be seen in a curious way. It will generally be found, I think, that the more a man really appreciates and admires the soul of another people the less he will attempt to imitate it; he will be conscious that there is something in it too deep and too unmanageable to imitate. The Englishman who has a fancy for France will try to be French; the Englishman who admires France will remain obstinately English. This is to be particularly noticed in the case of our relations with the French, because it is one of the outstanding peculiarities of the French that their vices are all on the surface, and their extraordinary virtues concealed. One might almost say that their vices are the flower of their virtues.

Thus their obscenity is the expression of their passionate love of dragging all things into the light. The avarice of their peasants means the independence of their peasants. What the English call their rudeness in the streets is a phase of their social equality. The worried look of their women is connected with the responsibility of their women; and a certain unconscious brutality of hurry and gesture in the men is related to their inexhaustible and extraordinary military courage. Of all countries, therefore, France is the worst country for a superficial fool to admire. Let a fool hate France: if the fool loves it he will soon be a knave. He will certainly admire it, not only for the things that are not creditable, but actually for the things that are not there. He will admire the grace and indolence of the most industrious people in the world. He will admire the romance and fantasy of the most determinedly respectable and commonplace people in the world. This mistake the Englishman will make if he admires France too hastily; but the mistake that he makes about France will be slight compared with the mistake that he makes about himself. An Englishman who professes really to like French realistic novels, really to be at home in a French modern theatre, really to experience no shock on first seeing the savage French caricatures, is making a mistake very dangerous for his own sincerity. He is admiring something he does not understand. He is reaping where he has not sown, and taking up where he has not laid down; he is trying to taste the fruit when he has never toiled over the tree. He is trying to pluck the exquisite fruit of French cynicism, when he has never tilled the rude but rich soil of French virtue.

The thing can only be made clear to Englishmen by turning it round. Suppose a Frenchman came out of democratic France to live in England, where the shadow of the great houses still falls everywhere, and where even freedom was, in its origin, aristocratic. If the Frenchman saw our aristocracy and liked it, if he saw our snobbishness and liked it, if he set himself to imitate it, we all know what we should feel. We all know that we should feel that that particular Frenchman was a repulsive little gnat. He would be imitating English aristocracy; he would be imitating the English vice. But he would not even understand the vice he plagiarised: especially he would not understand that the vice is partly a virtue. He would not understand those elements in the English which balance snobbishness and make it human: the great kindness of the English, their hospitality, their unconscious poetry, their sentimental conservatism, which really admires the gentry. The French Royalist sees that the English like their King. But he does not grasp that while it is base to worship a King, it is almost noble to worship a powerless King. The impotence of the Hanoverian Sovereigns has raised the English loyal subject almost to the chivalry and dignity of a Jacobite. The Frenchman sees that the English servant is respectful: he does not realise that he is also disrespectful; that there is an English legend of the humorous and faithful servant, who is as much a personality as his master; the Caleb Balderstone, the Sam Weller. He sees that the English do admire a nobleman; he does not allow for the fact that they admire a nobleman most when he does not behave like one. They like a noble to be unconscious and amiable: the slave may be humble, but the master must not be proud. The master is Life, as they would like to enjoy it; and among the joys they desire in him there is none which they desire more sincerely than that of generosity, of throwing money about among mankind, or, to use the noble mediæval word, largesse—the joy of largeness. That is why a cabman tells you are no gentleman if you give him his correct fare. Not only his pocket, but his soul is hurt. You have wounded his ideal. You have defaced his vision of the perfect aristocrat. All this is really very subtle and elusive; it is very difficult to separate what is mere slavishness from what is a sort of vicarious nobility in the English love of a lord. And no Frenchman could easily grasp it at all. He would think it was mere slavishness; and if he liked it, he would be a slave. So every Englishman must (at first) feel French candour to be mere brutality. And if he likes it, he is a brute. These national merits must not be understood so easily. It requires long years of plenitude and quiet, the slow growth of great parks, the seasoning of oaken beams, the dark enrichment of red wine in cellars and in inns, all the leisure and the life of England through many centuries, to produce at last the generous and genial fruit of English snobbishness. And it requires battery and barricade, songs in the streets, and ragged men dead for an idea, to produce and justify the terrible flower of French indecency.

When I was in Paris a short time ago, I went with an English friend of mine to an extremely brilliant and rapid succession of French plays, each occupying about twenty minutes. They were all astonishingly effective; but there was one of them which was so effective that my friend and I fought about it outside, and had almost to be separated by the police. It was intended to indicate how men really behaved in a wreck or naval disaster, how they break down, how they scream, how they fight each other without object and in a mere hatred of everything. And then there was added, with all that horrible irony which Voltaire began, a scene in which a great statesman made a speech over their bodies, saying that they were all heroes and had died in a fraternal embrace. My friend and I came out of this theatre, and as he had lived long in Paris, he said, like a Frenchman: "What admirable artistic arrangement! Is it not exquisite?" "No," I replied, assuming as far as possible the traditional attitude of John Bull in the pictures in *Punch*—"No, it is not exquisite. Perhaps it is unmeaning; if it is unmeaning I do not mind. But if it has a meaning I know what the meaning is; it is that under all their pageant of chivalry men are not only beasts, but even hunted beasts. I do not know much of humanity, especially when humanity talks in French. But I know when a thing is meant to uplift the human soul, and when it is meant to depress it. I know that 'Cyrano de Bergerac' (where the actors talked even quicker) was meant to encourage man. And I know that this was meant to discourage him." "These sentimental and moral views of art," began my friend, but I broke into his words as a light broke into my mind. "Let me say to you," I said, "what Jaurès said to Liebknecht at the Socialist Conference: 'You have not died on the barricades'. You are an Englishman, as I am, and you ought to be as amiable as I am. These people have some right to be terrible in art, for they have been terrible in politics. They may endure mock tortures on the stage; they have seen real tortures in the streets. They have been hurt for the idea of Democracy. They have been hurt for the idea of Catholicism. It is not so utterly unnatural to them that they should be hurt for the idea of literature. But, by blazes, it is altogether unnatural to me! And the worst thing of all is that I, who am an Englishman, loving comfort, should find comfort in such things as this. The French do not seek comfort here, but rather unrest. This restless people seeks to keep itself in a perpetual agony of the revolutionary mood. Frenchmen, seeking revolution, may find the humiliation of humanity inspiring. But God forbid that two pleasure-seeking Englishmen should ever find it pleasant!"

Chapter 10
The Zola Controversy

he difference between two great nations can be illustrated by the coincidence that at this moment both France and England are engaged in discussing the memorial of a literary man. France is considering the celebration of the late Zola, England is considering that of the recently deceased Shakspere. There is some national significance, it may be, in the time that has elapsed. Some will find impatience and indelicacy in this early attack on Zola or deification of him; but the nation which has sat still for three hundred years after Shakspere's funeral may be considered, perhaps, to have carried delicacy too far. But much deeper things are involved than the mere matter of time. The point of the contrast is that the French are discussing whether there shall be any monument, while the English are discussing only what the monument shall be. In other words, the French are discussing a living question, while we are discussing a dead one. Or rather, not a dead one, but a settled one, which is quite a different thing.

When a thing of the intellect is settled it is not dead: rather it is immortal. The multiplication table is immortal, and so is the fame of Shakspere. But the fame of Zola is not dead or not immortal; it is at its crisis, it is in the balance; and may be found wanting. The French, therefore, are quite right in considering it a living question. It is still living as a question, because it is not yet solved. But Shakspere is not a living question: he is a living answer.

For my part, therefore, I think the French Zola controversy much more practical and exciting than the English Shakspere one. The admission of Zola to the Panthéon may be regarded as defining Zola's position. But nobody could say that a statue of Shakspere, even fifty feet high, on the top of St. Paul's Cathedral, could define Shakspere's position. It only defines our position towards Shakspere. It is he who is fixed; it is we who are unstable. The nearest approach to an English parallel to the Zola case would be furnished if it were proposed to put some savagely controversial and largely repulsive author among the ashes of the greatest English poets. Suppose, for instance, it were proposed to bury Mr. Rudyard Kipling in Westminster Abbey; first, because he is still alive (and here I think even he himself might admit the justice of my protest); and second, because I should like to reserve that rapidly narrowing space for the great permanent examples, not for the interesting foreign interruptions, of English literature. I would not have either Mr. Kipling or Mr. George Moore in Westminster Abbey, though Mr. Kipling has certainly caught even more cleverly than Mr. Moore the lucid and cool cruelty of the French short story. I am very sure that Geoffrey Chaucer and Joseph Addison get on very well together in the Poets' Corner, despite the centuries that sunder them. But I feel that Mr. George Moore would be much happier in Pere-la-Chaise, with a riotous statue by Rodin on the top of him; and Mr. Kipling much happier under some huge Asiatic monument, carved with all the cruelties of the gods.

As to the affair of the English monument to Shakspere, every people has its own mode of commemoration, and I think there is a great deal to be said for ours. There is the French monumental style, which consists in erecting very pompous statues, very well done. There is the German monumental style, which consists in erecting very pompous statues, badly done. And there is the English monumental method, the great English way with statues, which consists in not erecting them at all. A statue may be dignified; but the absence of a statue is always dignified. For my part, I feel there is something national, something wholesomely symbolic, in the fact that there is no statue of Shakspere. There is, of course, one in Leicester Square; but the very place where it stands shows that it was put up by a foreigner for foreigners. There is surely something modest and manly about not attempting to express our greatest poet in the plastic arts in which we do not excel. We honour Shakspere as the Jews honour God—by not daring to make of him a graven image. Our sculpture, our statues, are good enough for bankers and philanthropists, who are our curse: not good enough for him, who is our benediction. Why should we celebrate the very art in which we triumph by the very art in which we fail?

England is most easily understood as the country of amateurs. It is especially the country of amateur soldiers (that is, of Volunteers), of amateur statesmen (that is, of aristocrats), and it is not unreasonable or out of keeping that it should be rather specially the country of a careless and lounging view of literature. Shakspere has no academic monument for the same reason that he had no academic education. He had small Latin and less Greek, and (in the same spirit) he has never been commemorated in Latin epitaphs or Greek marble. If there is nothing clear and fixed about the emblems of his fame, it is because there was nothing clear and fixed about the origins of it. Those great schools and Universities which watch a man in his youth may record him in his death; but Shakspere had no such unifying traditions. We can only say of him what we can say of Dickens. We can only say that he came from nowhere and that he went everywhere. For him a monument in any place is out of place. A cold statue in a certain square is unsuitable to him as it would be unsuitable to Dickens. If we put up a statue of Dickens in Portland Place to-morrow we should feel the stiffness as unnatural. We should fear that the statue might stroll about the street at night.

But in France the question of whether Zola shall go to the Panthéon when he is dead is quite as practicable as the question whether he should go to prison when he was alive. It is the problem of whether the nation shall take one turn of thought or another. In raising a monument to Zola they do not raise merely a trophy, but a finger-post. The question is one which will have to be settled in most European countries; but like all such questions, it has come first to a head in France; because

France is the battlefield of Christendom. That question is, of course, roughly this: whether in that ill-defined area of verbal licence on certain dangerous topics it is an extenuation of indelicacy or an aggravation of it that the indelicacy was deliberate and solemn. Is indecency more indecent if it is grave, or more indecent if it is gay? For my part, I belong to an old school in this matter. When a book or a play strikes me as a crime, I am not disarmed by being told that it is a serious crime. If a man has written something vile, I am not comforted by the explanation that he quite meant to do it. I know all the evils of flippancy; I do not like the man who laughs at the sight of virtue. But I prefer him to the man who weeps at the sight of virtue and complains bitterly of there being any such thing. I am not reassured, when ethics are as wild as cannibalism, by the fact that they are also as grave and sincere as suicide. And I think there is an obvious fallacy in the bitter contrasts drawn by some moderns between the aversion to Ibsen's "Ghosts" and the popularity of some such joke as "Dear Old Charlie." Surely there is nothing mysterious or unphilosophic in the popular preference. The joke of "Dear Old Charlie" is passed—because it is a joke. "Ghosts" are exorcised—because they are ghosts.

This is, of course, the whole question of Zola. I am grown up, and I do not worry myself much about Zola's immorality. The thing I cannot stand is his morality. If ever a man on this earth lived to embody the tremendous text, "But if the light in your body be darkness, how great is the darkness," it was certainly he. Great men like Ariosto, Rabelais, and Shakspere fall in foul places, flounder in violent but venial sin, sprawl for pages, exposing their gigantic weakness, are dirty, are indefensible; and then they struggle up again and can still speak with a convincing kindness and an unbroken honour of the best things in the world: Rabelais, of the instruction of ardent and austere youth; Ariosto, of holy chivalry; Shakspere, of the splendid stillness of mercy. But in Zola even the ideals are undesirable; Zola's mercy is colder than justice—nay, Zola's mercy is more bitter in the mouth than injustice. When Zola shows us an ideal training he does not take us, like Rabelais, into the happy fields of humanist learning. He takes us into the schools of inhumanist learning, where there are neither books nor flowers, nor wine nor wisdom, but only deformities in glass bottles, and where the rule is taught from the exceptions. Zola's truth answers the exact description of the skeleton in the cupboard; that is, it is something of which a domestic custom forbids the discovery, but which is quite dead, even when it is discovered. Macaulay said that the Puritans hated bear-baiting, not because it gave pain to the bear, but because it gave pleasure to the spectators. Of such substance also was this Puritan who had lost his God. A Puritan of this type is worse than the Puritan who hates pleasure because there is evil in it. This man actually hates evil because there is pleasure in it. Zola was worse than a pornographer, he was a pessimist. He did worse than encourage sin: he encouraged discouragement. He made lust loathsome because to him lust meant life.

Chapter 11
Oxford from Without

ome time ago I ventured to defend that race of hunted and persecuted outlaws, the Bishops; but until this week I had no idea of how much persecuted they were. For instance, the Bishop of Birmingham made some extremely sensible remarks in the House of Lords, to the effect that Oxford and Cambridge were (as everybody knows they are) far too much merely plutocratic playgrounds. One would have thought that an Anglican Bishop might be allowed to know something about the English University system, and even to have, if anything, some bias in its favour. But (as I pointed out) the rollicking Radicalism of Bishops has to be restrained. The man who writes the notes in the weekly paper called the *Outlook* feels that it is his business to restrain it. The passage has such simple sublimity that I must quote it—

"Dr. Gore talked unworthily of his reputation when he spoke of the older Universities as playgrounds for the rich and idle. In the first place, the rich men there are not idle. Some of the rich men are, and so are some of the poor men. On the whole, the sons of noble and wealthy families keep up the best traditions of academic life."

So far this seems all very nice. It is a part of the universal principle on which Englishmen have acted in recent years. As you will not try to make the best people the most powerful people, persuade yourselves that the most powerful people are the best people. Mad Frenchmen and Irishmen try to realise the ideal. To you belongs the nobler (and much easier) task of idealising the real. First give your Universities entirely into the power of the rich; then let the rich start traditions; and then congratulate yourselves on the fact that the sons of the rich keep up these traditions. All that is quite simple and jolly. But then this critic, who crushes Dr. Gore from the high throne of the *Outlook*, goes on in a way that is really perplexing. "It is distinctly advantageous," he says, "that rich and poor—*i. e.*, young men with a smooth path in life before them, and those who have to hew out a road for themselves—should be brought into association. Each class learns a great deal from the other. On the one side, social conceit and exclusiveness give way to the free spirit of competition amongst all classes; on the other side, angularities and prejudices are rubbed away." Even this I might have swallowed. But the paragraph concludes with this extraordinary sentence: "We get the net result in such careers as those of Lord Milner, Lord Curzon, and Mr. Asquith."

Those three names lay my intellect prostrate. The rest of the argument I understand quite well. The social exclusiveness of aristocrats at Oxford and Cambridge gives way before the free spirit of competition amongst all classes. That is to say, there is at Oxford so hot and keen a struggle, consisting of coal-heavers,

London clerks, gypsies, navvies, drapers' assistants, grocers' assistants—in short, all the classes that make up the bulk of England—there is such a fierce competition at Oxford among all these people that in its presence aristocratic exclusiveness gives way. That is all quite clear. I am not quite sure about the facts, but I quite understand the argument. But then, having been called upon to contemplate this bracing picture of a boisterous turmoil of all the classes of England, I am suddenly asked to accept as example of it, Lord Milner, Lord Curzon, and the present Chancellor of the Exchequer. What part do these gentlemen play in the mental process? Is Lord Curzon one of the rugged and ragged poor men whose angularities have been rubbed away? Or is he one of those whom Oxford immediately deprived of all kind of social exclusiveness? His Oxford reputation does not seem to bear out either account of him. To regard Lord Milner as a typical product of Oxford would surely be unfair. It would be to deprive the educational tradition of Germany of one of its most typical products. English aristocrats have their faults, but they are not at all like Lord Milner. What Mr. Asquith was meant to prove, whether he was a rich man who lost his exclusiveness, or a poor man who lost his angles, I am utterly unable to conceive.

There is, however, one mild but very evident truth that might perhaps be mentioned. And it is this: that none of those three excellent persons is, or ever has been, a poor man in the sense that that word is understood by the overwhelming majority of the English nation. There are no poor men at Oxford in the sense that the majority of men in the street are poor. The very fact that the writer in the *Outlook* can talk about such people as poor shows that he does not understand what the modern problem is. His kind of poor man rather reminds me of the Earl in the ballad by that great English satirist, Sir W.S. Gilbert, whose angles (very acute angles) had, I fear, never been rubbed down by an old English University. The reader will remember that when the Periwinkle-girl was adored by two Dukes, the poet added—

> "A third adorer had the girl,
> A man of lowly station;
> A miserable grovelling Earl
> Besought her approbation."

Perhaps, indeed, some allusion to our University system, and to the universal clash in it of all the classes of the community, may be found in the verse a little farther on, which says—

> "He'd had, it happily befell,
> A decent education;
> His views would have befitted well
> A far superior station."

Possibly there was as simple a chasm between Lord Curzon and Lord Milner. But I am afraid that the chasm will become almost imperceptible, a microscopic crack, if we compare it with the chasm that separates either or both of them from the people of this country.

Of course the truth is exactly as the Bishop of Birmingham put it. I am sure that he did not put it in any unkindly or contemptuous spirit towards those old English seats of learning, which whether they are or are not seats of learning, are, at any rate, old and English, and those are two very good things to be. The Old English University is a playground for the governing class. That does not prove that it is a bad thing; it might prove that it was a very good thing. Certainly if there is a governing class, let there be a playground for the governing class. I would much rather be ruled by men who know how to play than by men who do not know how to play. Granted that we are to be governed by a rich section of the community, it is certainly very important that that section should be kept tolerably genial and jolly. If the sensitive man on the *Outlook* does not like the phrase, "Playground of the rich," I can suggest a phrase that describes such a place as Oxford perhaps with more precision. It is a place for humanising those who might otherwise be tyrants, or even experts.

To pretend that the aristocrat meets all classes at Oxford is too ludicrous to be worth discussion. But it may be true that he meets more different kinds of men than he would meet under a strictly aristocratic *regime* of private tutors and small schools. It all comes back to the fact that the English, if they were resolved to have an aristocracy, were at least resolved to have a good-natured aristocracy. And it is due to them to say that almost alone among the peoples of the world, they have succeeded in getting one. One could almost tolerate the thing, if it were not for the praise of it. One might endure Oxford, but not the *Outlook*.

When the poor man at Oxford loses his angles (which means, I suppose, his independence), he may perhaps, even if his poverty is of that highly relative type possible at Oxford, gain a certain amount of worldly advantage from the surrender of those angles. I must confess, however, that I can imagine nothing nastier than to lose one's angles. It seems to me that a desire to retain some angles about one's person is a desire common to all those human beings who do not set their ultimate hopes upon looking like Humpty-Dumpty. Our angles are simply our shapes. I cannot imagine any phrase more full of the subtle and exquisite vileness which is poisoning and weakening our country than such a phrase as this, about the desirability of rubbing down the angularities of poor men. Reduced to permanent and practical human speech, it means nothing whatever except the corrupting of that first human sense of justice which is the critic of all human institutions.

It is not in any such spirit of facile and reckless reassurance that we should approach the really difficult problem of the delicate virtues and the deep dangers of our two historic seats of learning. A good son does not easily admit that his sick mother is dying; but neither does a good son cheerily assert that she is "all right." There are many good arguments for leaving the two historic Universities exactly as they are. There are many good arguments for smashing them or altering them entirely. But in either case the plain truth told by the Bishop of Birmingham remains. If these Universities were destroyed, they would not be destroyed as Universities. If they are preserved, they will not be preserved as Universities. They will be preserved strictly and literally as playgrounds; places valued for their hours of leisure more than for their hours of work. I do not say that this is unreasonable; as a matter of private temperament I find it attractive. It is not only possible to say a great deal in praise of play; it is really possible to say the highest things in praise of it. It might reasonably be maintained that the true object of all human life is play. Earth is a task garden; heaven is a playground. To be at last in such secure innocence that one can juggle with the universe and the stars, to be so good that one can treat everything as a joke—that may be, perhaps, the real end and final holiday of human souls. When we are really holy we may regard the Universe as a lark; so perhaps it is not essentially wrong to regard the University as a lark. But the plain and present fact is that our upper classes do regard the University as a lark, and do not regard it as a University. It also happens very often that through some oversight they neglect to provide themselves with that extreme degree of holiness which I have postulated as a necessary preliminary to such indulgence in the higher frivolity.

Humanity, always dreaming of a happy race, free, fantastic, and at ease, has sometimes pictured them in some mystical island, sometimes in some celestial city, sometimes as fairies, gods, or citizens of Atlantis. But one method in which it has often indulged is to picture them as aristocrats, as a special human class that could actually be seen hunting in the woods or driving about the streets. And this never was (as some silly Germans say) a worship of pride and scorn; mankind never really admired pride; mankind never had any thing but a scorn for scorn. It was a worship of the spectacle of happiness; especially of the spectacle of youth. This is what the old Universities in their noblest aspect really are; and this is why there is always something to be said for keeping them as they are. Aristocracy is not a tyranny; it is not even merely a spell. It is a vision. It is a deliberate indulgence in a certain picture of pleasure painted for the purpose; every Duchess is (in an innocent sense) painted, like Gainsborough's "Duchess of Devonshire." She is only beautiful because, at the back of all, the English people wanted her to be beautiful. In the same way, the lads at Oxford and Cambridge are only larking because England, in the depths of its solemn soul, really wishes them to lark. All this is very human and pardonable, and would be even harmless if there were no such things in the world as danger and honour and intellectual responsibility. But if aristocracy is a vision, it is perhaps the most unpractical of all visions. It is not a working way of doing things to put all your happiest people on a lighted platform and stare only at them. It is not a working way of managing education to be entirely content with the mere fact that you have (to a degree unexampled in the world) given the luckiest boys the jolliest time. It would be easy enough, like the writer in the *Outlook*, to enjoy the pleasures and deny the perils. Oh what a happy place England would be to live in if only one did not love it!

Chapter 12
Woman

correspondent has written me an able and interesting letter in the matter of some allusions of mine to the subject of communal kitchens. He defends communal kitchens very lucidly from the standpoint of the calculating collectivist; but, like many of his school, he cannot apparently grasp that there is another test of the whole matter, with which such calculation has nothing at all to do. He knows it would be cheaper if a number of us ate at the same time, so as to use the same table. So it would. It would also be cheaper if a number of us slept at different times, so as to use the same pair of trousers. But the question is not how cheap are we buying a thing, but what are we buying? It is cheap to own a slave. And it is cheaper still to be a slave.

My correspondent also says that the habit of dining out in restaurants, etc., is growing. So, I believe, is the habit of committing suicide. I do not desire to connect the two facts together. It seems fairly clear that a man could not dine at a restaurant because he had just committed suicide; and it would be extreme, perhaps, to suggest that he commits suicide because he has just dined at a restaurant. But the two cases, when put side by side, are enough to indicate the falsity and poltroonery of this eternal modern argument from what is in fashion. The question for brave men is not whether a certain thing is increasing; the question is whether we are increasing it. I dine very often in restaurants because the nature of my trade makes it convenient: but if I thought that by dining in restaurants I was working for the creation of communal meals, I would never enter a restaurant again; I would carry bread and cheese in my pocket or eat chocolate out of automatic machines. For the personal element in some things is sacred. I heard Mr. Will Crooks put it perfectly the other day: "The most sacred thing is to be able to shut your own door."

My correspondent says, "Would not our women be spared the drudgery of cooking and all its attendant worries, leaving them free for higher culture?" The first thing that occurs to me to say about this is very simple, and is, I imagine, a part of all our experience. If my correspondent can find any way of preventing women from worrying, he will indeed be a remarkable man. I think the matter is a much deeper one. First of all, my correspondent overlooks a distinction which is elementary in our human nature. Theoretically, I suppose, every one would like to be freed from worries. But nobody in the world would always like to be freed from worrying occupations. I should very much like (as far as my feelings at the moment go) to be free from the consuming nuisance of writing this article. But it does not follow that I should like to be free from the consuming nuisance of being a journalist. Because we are worried about a thing, it does not follow that we are not interested in it. The truth is the other way. If we are not interested, why on earth should we be worried? Women are worried about housekeeping, but those that are most interested are the most worried. Women are still more worried about their husbands and their children. And I suppose if we strangled the children and poleaxed the husbands it would leave women free for higher culture. That is, it would leave them free to begin to worry about that. For women would worry about higher culture as much as they worry about everything else.

I believe this way of talking about women and their higher culture is almost entirely a growth of the classes which (unlike the journalistic class to which I belong) have always a reasonable amount of money. One odd thing I specially notice. Those who write like this seem entirely to forget the existence of the working and wage-earning classes. They say eternally, like my correspondent, that the ordinary woman is always a drudge. And what, in the name of the Nine Gods, is the ordinary man? These people seem to think that the ordinary man is a Cabinet Minister. They are always talking about man going forth to wield power, to carve his own way, to stamp his individuality on the world, to command and to be obeyed. This may be true of a certain class. Dukes, perhaps, are not drudges; but, then, neither are Duchesses. The Ladies and Gentlemen of the Smart Set are quite free for the higher culture, which consists chiefly of motoring and Bridge. But the ordinary man who typifies and constitutes the millions that make up our civilisation is no more free for the higher culture than his wife is.

Indeed, he is not so free. Of the two sexes the woman is in the more powerful position. For the average woman is at the head of something with which she can do as she likes; the average man has to obey orders and do nothing else. He has to put one dull brick on another dull brick, and do nothing else; he has to add one dull figure to another dull figure, and do nothing else. The woman's world is a small one, perhaps, but she can alter it. The woman can tell the tradesman with whom she deals some realistic things about himself. The clerk who does this to the manager generally gets the sack, or shall we say (to avoid the vulgarism), finds himself free for higher culture. Above all, as I said in my previous article, the woman does work which is in some small degree creative and individual. She can put the flowers or the furniture in fancy arrangements of her own. I fear the bricklayer cannot put the bricks in fancy arrangements of his own, without disaster to himself and others. If the woman is only putting a patch into a carpet, she can choose the thing with regard to colour. I fear it would not do for the office boy dispatching a parcel to choose his stamps with a view to colour; to prefer the tender mauve of the sixpenny to the crude scarlet of the penny stamp. A woman cooking may not always cook artistically; still she can cook artistically. She can introduce a personal and imperceptible alteration into the composition of a soup. The clerk is not encouraged to introduce a personal and imperceptible alteration into the figures in a ledger.

The trouble is that the real question I raised is not discussed. It is argued as a problem in pennies, not as a problem in people. It is not the proposals of these reformers that I feel to be false so much as their temper and their arguments. I am not nearly so certain that communal kitchens are wrong as I am that the defenders of communal kitchens are wrong. Of course, for one thing, there is a vast difference between the communal kitchens of which I spoke and the communal meal (*monstrum horrendum, informe*) which the darker and wilder mind of my correspondent diabolically calls up. But in both the trouble is that their defenders will not defend them humanly as human institutions. They will not interest themselves in the staring psychological fact that there are some things that a man or a woman, as the case may be, wishes to do for himself or herself. He or she must do it inventively, creatively, artistically, individually—in a word, badly. Choosing your wife (say) is one of these things. Is choosing your husband's dinner one of these things? That is the whole question: it is never asked.

And then the higher culture. I know that culture. I would not set any man free for it if I could help it. The effect of it on the rich men who are free for it is so horrible that it is worse than any of the other amusements of the millionaire—worse than gambling, worse even than philanthropy. It means thinking the smallest poet in Belgium greater than the greatest poet of England. It means losing every democratic sympathy. It means being unable to talk to a navvy about sport, or about beer, or about the Bible, or about the Derby, or about patriotism, or about anything whatever that he, the navvy, wants to talk about. It means taking literature seriously, a very amateurish thing to do. It means pardoning indecency only when it is gloomy indecency. Its disciples will call a spade a spade; but only when it is a grave-digger's spade. The higher culture is sad, cheap, impudent, unkind, without honesty and without ease. In short, it is "high." That abominable word (also applied to game) admirably describes it.

No; if you were setting women free for something else, I might be more melted. If you can assure me, privately and gravely, that you are setting women free to dance on the mountains like mænads, or to worship some monstrous goddess, I will make a note of your request. If you are quite sure that the ladies in Brixton, the moment they give up cooking, will beat great gongs and blow horns to Mumbo-Jumbo, then I will agree that the occupation is at least human and is more or less entertaining. Women have been set free to be Bacchantes; they have been set free to be Virgin Martyrs; they have been set free to be Witches. Do not ask them now to sink so low as the higher culture.

I have my own little notions of the possible emancipation of women; but I suppose I should not be taken very seriously if I propounded them. I should favour anything that would increase the present enormous authority of women and their creative action in their own homes. The average woman, as I have said, is a despot; the average man is a serf. I am for any scheme that any one can suggest that will make the average woman more of a despot. So far from wishing her to get her cooked meals from outside, I should like her to cook more wildly and at her own will than she does. So far from getting always the same meals from the same place, let her invent, if she likes, a new dish every day of her life. Let woman be more of a maker, not less. We are right to talk about "Woman;" only blackguards talk about women. Yet all men talk about men, and that is the whole difference. Men represent the deliberative and democratic element in life. Woman represents the despotic.

Chapter 13
The Modern Martyr

he incident of the Suffragettes who chained themselves with iron chains to the railings of Downing Street is a good ironical allegory of most modern martyrdom. It generally consists of a man chaining himself up and then complaining that he is not free. Some say that such larks retard the cause of female suffrage, others say that such larks alone can advance it; as a matter of fact, I do not believe that they have the smallest effect one way or the other.

The modern notion of impressing the public by a mere demonstration of unpopularity, by being thrown out of meetings or thrown into jail is largely a mistake. It rests on a fallacy touching the true popular value of martyrdom. People look at human history and see that it has often happened that persecutions have not only advertised but even advanced a persecuted creed, and given to its validity the public and dreadful witness of dying men. The paradox was pictorially expressed in Christian art, in which saints were shown brandishing as weapons the very tools that had slain them. And because his martyrdom is thus a power to the martyr, modern people think that any one who makes himself slightly uncomfortable in public will immediately be uproariously popular. This element of inadequate martyrdom is not true only of the Suffragettes; it is true of many movements I respect and some that I agree with. It was true, for instance, of the Passive Resisters, who had pieces of their furniture sold up. The assumption is that if you show your ordinary sincerity (or even your political ambition) by being a nuisance to yourself as well as to other people, you will have the strength of the great saints who passed through the fire. Any one who can be hustled in a hall for five minutes, or put in a cell for five days, has achieved what was meant by martyrdom, and has a halo in the Christian art of the future. Miss Pankhurst will be represented holding a policeman in each hand—the instruments of her martyrdom. The Passive Resister will be shown symbolically carrying the teapot that was torn from him by tyrannical auctioneers.

But there is a fallacy in this analogy of martyrdom. The truth is that the special impressiveness which does come from being persecuted only happens in the case of extreme persecution. For the fact that the modern enthusiast will undergo some inconvenience for the creed he holds only proves that he does hold it, which no one ever doubted. No one doubts that the Nonconformist minister cares more for Nonconformity than he does for his teapot. No one doubts that Miss Pankhurst wants a vote more than she wants a quiet afternoon and an armchair. All our ordinary intellectual opinions are worth a bit of a row: I remember during the Boer War fighting an Imperialist clerk outside the Queen's Hall, and giving and receiving a bloody nose; but I did not think it one of the incidents that produce the psychological effect of the Roman amphitheatre or the stake at Smithfield. For in that impression there is something more than the mere fact that a man is sincere enough to give his time or his comfort. Pagans were not impressed by the torture of Christians merely because it showed that they honestly held their opinion; they knew that millions of people honestly held all sorts of opinions. The point of such extreme martyrdom is much more subtle. It is that it gives an appearance of a man having something quite specially strong to back him up, of his drawing upon some power. And this can only be proved when all his physical contentment is destroyed; when all the current of his bodily being is reversed and turned to pain. If a man is seen to be roaring with laughter all the time that he is skinned alive, it would not be unreasonable to deduce that somewhere in the recesses of his mind he had thought of a rather good joke. Similarly, if men smiled and sang (as they did) while they were being boiled or torn in pieces, the spectators felt the presence of something more than mere mental honesty: they felt the presence of some new and unintelligible kind of pleasure, which, presumably, came from somewhere. It might be a strength of madness, or a lying spirit from Hell; but it was something quite positive and extraordinary; as positive as brandy and as extraordinary as conjuring. The Pagan said to himself: "If Christianity makes a man happy while his legs are being eaten by a lion, might it not make me happy while my legs are still attached to me and walking down the street?" The Secularists laboriously explain that martyrdoms do not prove a faith to be true, as if anybody was ever such a fool as to suppose that they did. What they did prove, or, rather, strongly suggest, was that something had entered human psychology which was stronger than strong pain. If a young girl, scourged and bleeding to death, saw nothing but a crown descending on her from God, the first mental step was not that her philosophy was correct, but that she was certainly feeding on something. But this particular point of psychology does not arise at all in the modern cases of mere public discomfort or inconvenience. The causes of Miss Pankhurst's cheerfulness require no mystical explanations. If she were being burned alive as a witch, if she then looked up in unmixed rapture and saw a ballot-box descending out of heaven, then I should say that the incident, though not conclusive, was frightfully impressive. It would not prove logically that she ought to have the vote, or that anybody ought to have the vote. But it would prove this: that there was, for some reason, a sacramental reality in the vote, that the soul could take the vote and feed on it; that it was in itself a positive and overpowering pleasure, capable of being pitted against positive and overpowering pain.

I should advise modern agitators, therefore, to give up this particular method: the method of making very big efforts to get a very small punishment. It does not really go down at all; the punishment is too small, and the efforts are too obvious. It has not any of the effectiveness of the old savage martyrdom, because it does not leave the victim absolutely alone with his cause, so that his cause alone can support him. At the same time it has about it that element of the pantomimic and

the absurd, which was the cruellest part of the slaying and the mocking of the
real prophets. St. Peter was crucified upside down as a huge inhuman joke; but
his human seriousness survived the inhuman joke, because, in whatever posture,
he had died for his faith. The modern martyr of the Pankhurst type courts the
absurdity without making the suffering strong enough to eclipse the absurdity.
She is like a St. Peter who should deliberately stand on his head for ten seconds
and then expect to be canonised for it.

Or, again, the matter might be put in this way. Modern martyrdoms fail even
as demonstrations, because they do not prove even that the martyrs are completely
serious. I think, as a fact, that the modern martyrs generally are serious, perhaps
a trifle too serious. But their martyrdom does not prove it; and the public does
not always believe it. Undoubtedly, as a fact, Dr. Clifford is quite honourably
indignant with what he considers to be clericalism, but he does not prove it by
having his teapot sold; for a man might easily have his teapot sold as an actress
has her diamonds stolen—as a personal advertisement. As a matter of fact, Miss
Pankhurst is quite in earnest about votes for women. But she does not prove it by
being chucked out of meetings. A person might be chucked out of meetings just
as young men are chucked out of music-halls—for fun. But no man has himself
eaten by a lion as a personal advertisement. No woman is broiled on a gridiron
for fun. That is where the testimony of St. Perpetua and St. Faith comes in.
Doubtless it is no fault of these enthusiasts that they are not subjected to the old
and searching penalties; very likely they would pass through them as triumphantly
as St. Agatha. I am simply advising them upon a point of policy, things being
as they are. And I say that the average man is not impressed with their sacrifices
simply because they are not and cannot be more decisive than the sacrifices which
the average man himself would make for mere fun if he were drunk. Drunkards
would interrupt meetings and take the consequences. And as for selling a teapot,
it is an act, I imagine, in which any properly constituted drunkard would take a
positive pleasure. The advertisement is not good enough; it does not tell. If I
were really martyred for an opinion (which is more improbable than words can say),
it would certainly only be for one or two of my most central and sacred opinions.
I might, perhaps, be shot for England, but certainly not for the British Empire. I
might conceivably die for political freedom, but I certainly wouldn't die for Free
Trade. But as for kicking up the particular kind of shindy that the Suffragettes
are kicking up, I would as soon do it for my shallowest opinion as for my deepest
one. It never could be anything worse than an inconvenience; it never could be
anything better than a spree. Hence the British public, and especially the working
classes, regard the whole demonstration with fundamental indifference; for, while
it is a demonstration that probably is adopted from the most fanatical motives, it
is a demonstration which might be adopted from the most frivolous.

Chapter 14
On Political Secrecy

enerally, instinctively, in the absence of any special reason, human-ity hates the idea of anything being hidden—that is, it hates the idea of anything being successfully hidden. Hide-and-seek is a popular pastime; but it assumes the truth of the text, "Seek and ye shall find." Ordinary mankind (gigantic and unconquerable in its power of joy) can get a great deal of pleasure out of a game called "hide the thimble," but that is only because it is really a game of "see the thimble." Suppose that at the end of such a game the thimble had not been found at all; suppose its place was unknown for ever: the result on the players would not be playful, it would be tragic. That thimble would hag-ride all their dreams. They would all die in asylums. The pleasure is all in the poignant moment of passing from not knowing to knowing. Mystery stories are very popular, especially when sold at sixpence; but that is because the author of a mystery story reveals. He is enjoyed not because he creates mystery, but because he destroys mystery. Nobody would have the courage to publish a detective-story which left the problem exactly where it found it. That would rouse even the London public to revolution. No one dare publish a detective-story that did not detect.

There are three broad classes of the special things in which human wisdom does permit privacy. The first is the case I have mentioned—that of hide-and-seek, or the police novel, in which it permits privacy only in order to explode and smash privacy. The author makes first a fastidious secret of how the Bishop was murdered, only in order that he may at last declare, as from a high tower, to the whole democracy the great glad news that he was murdered by the governess. In that case, ignorance is only valued because being ignorant is the best and purest preparation for receiving the horrible revelations of high life. Somewhat in the same way being an agnostic is the best and purest preparation for receiving the happy revelations of St. John.

This first sort of secrecy we may dismiss, for its whole ultimate object is not to keep the secret, but to tell it. Then there is a second and far more important class of things which humanity does agree to hide. They are so important that they cannot possibly be discussed here. But every one will know the kind of things I mean. In connection with these, I wish to remark that though they are, in one sense, a secret, they are also always a "sécret de Polichinelle." Upon sex and such matters we are in a human freemasonry; the freemasonry is disciplined, but the freemasonry is free. We are asked to be silent about these things, but we are not asked to be ignorant about them. On the contrary, the fundamental human argument is entirely the other way. It is the thing most common to humanity that is most veiled by humanity. It is exactly because we all know that it is there that we need not say that it is there.

Then there is a third class of things on which the best civilisation does permit privacy, does resent all inquiry or explanation. This is in the case of things
which need not be explained, because they cannot be explained, things too airy,
instinctive, or intangible—caprices, sudden impulses, and the more innocent kind
of prejudice. A man must not be asked why he is talkative or silent, for the simple
reason that he does not know. A man is not asked (even in Germany) why he walks
slow or quick, simply because he could not answer. A man must take his own road
through a wood, and make his own use of a holiday. And the reason is this: not
because he has a strong reason, but actually because he has a weak reason; because
he has a slight and fleeting feeling about the matter which he could not explain to
a policeman, which perhaps the very appearance of a policeman out of the bushes
might destroy. He must act on the impulse, because the impulse is unimportant,
and he may never have the same impulse again. If you like to put it so he must
act on the impulse because the impulse is not worth a moment's thought. All
these fancies men feel should be private; and even Fabians have never proposed
to interfere with them.

Now, for the last fortnight the newspapers have been full of very varied com-
ments upon the problem of the secrecy of certain parts of our political finance,
and especially of the problem of the party funds. Some papers have failed entirely
to understand what the quarrel is about. They have urged that Irish members
and Labour members are also under the shadow, or, as some have said, even more
under it. The ground of this frantic statement seems, when patiently considered,
to be simply this: that Irish and Labour members receive money for what they do.
All persons, as far as I know, on this earth receive money for what they do; the
only difference is that some people, like the Irish members, do it.

I cannot imagine that any human being could think any other human being
capable of maintaining the proposition that men ought not to receive money.
The simple point is that, as we know that some money is given rightly and some
wrongly, an elementary common-sense leads us to look with indifference at the
money that is given in the middle of Ludgate Circus, and to look with particular
suspicion at the money which a man will not give unless he is shut up in a box or a
bathing-machine. In short, it is too silly to suppose that anybody could ever have
discussed the desirability of funds. The only thing that even idiots could ever
have discussed is the concealment of funds. Therefore, the whole question that we
have to consider is whether the concealment of political money-transactions, the
purchase of peerages, the payment of election expenses, is a kind of concealment
that falls under any of the three classes I have mentioned as those in which human
custom and instinct does permit us to conceal. I have suggested three kinds of
secrecy which are human and defensible. Can this institution be defended by
means of any of them?

Now the question is whether this political secrecy is of any of the kinds that can be called legitimate. We have roughly divided legitimate secrets into three classes. First comes the secret that is only kept in order to be revealed, as in the detective stories; secondly, the secret which is kept because everybody knows it, as in sex; and third, the secret which is kept because it is too delicate and vague to be explained at all, as in the choice of a country walk. Do any of these broad human divisions cover such a case as that of secrecy of the political and party finances? It would be absurd, and even delightfully absurd, to pretend that any of them did. It would be a wild and charming fancy to suggest that our politicians keep political secrets only that they may make political revelations. A modern peer only pretends that he has earned his peerage in order that he may more dramatically declare, with a scream of scorn and joy, that he really bought it. The Baronet pretends that he deserved his title only in order to make more exquisite and startling the grand historical fact that he did not deserve it. Surely this sounds improbable. Surely all our statesmen cannot be saving themselves up for the excitement of a death-bed repentance. The writer of detective tales makes a man a duke solely in order to blast him with a charge of burglary. But surely the Prime Minister does not make a man a duke solely in order to blast him with a charge of bribery. No; the detective-tale theory of the secrecy of political funds must (with a sigh) be given up.

Neither can we say that the thing is explained by that second case of human secrecy which is so secret that it is hard to discuss it in public. A decency is preserved about certain primary human matters precisely because every one knows all about them. But the decency touching contributions, purchases, and peerages is not kept up because most ordinary men know what is happening; it is kept up precisely because most ordinary men do not know what is happening. The ordinary curtain of decorum covers normal proceedings. But no one will say that being bribed is a normal proceeding.

And if we apply the third test to this problem of political secrecy, the case is even clearer and even more funny. Surely no one will say that the purchase of peerages and such things are kept secret because they are so light and impulsive and unimportant that they must be matters of individual fancy. A child sees a flower and for the first time feels inclined to pick it. But surely no one will say that a brewer sees a coronet and for the first time suddenly thinks that he would like to be a peer. The child's impulse need not be explained to the police, for the simple reason that it could not be explained to anybody. But does any one believe that the laborious political ambitions of modern commercial men ever have this airy and incommunicable character? A man lying on the beach may throw stones into the sea without any particular reason. But does any one believe that the brewer throws bags of gold into the party funds without any particular reason? This theory of the secrecy of political money must also be regretfully abandoned; and with it the two other possible excuses as well. This secrecy is one which cannot be justified as a sensational joke nor as a common human freemasonry, nor as an indescribable personal whim. Strangely enough, indeed, it violates all three conditions and classes at once. It is not hidden in order to be revealed: it is hidden in order to be hidden. It is not kept secret because it is a common secret of mankind, but because mankind must not get hold of it. And it is not kept secret because it is too unimportant to be told, but because it is much too important to bear telling. In short, the thing we have is the real and perhaps rare political phenomenon of an occult government. We have an exoteric and an esoteric doctrine. England is really ruled by priestcraft, but not by priests. We have in this country all that has ever been alleged against the evil side of religion; the peculiar class with privileges, the sacred words that are unpronounceable; the important things known only to the few. In fact we lack nothing except the religion.

Chapter 15
Edward VII and Scotland

have received a serious, and to me, at any rate, an impressive remonstrance from the Scottish Patriotic Association. It appears that I recently referred to Edward VII. of Great Britain and Ireland, King, Defender of the Faith, under the horrible description of the King of England. The Scottish Patriotic Association draws my attention to the fact that by the provisions of the Act of Union, and the tradition of nationality, the monarch should be referred to as the King of Britain. The blow thus struck at me is particularly wounding because it is particularly unjust. I believe in the reality of the independent nationalities under the British Crown much more passionately and positively than any other educated Englishman of my acquaintance believes in it. I am quite certain that Scotland is a nation; I am quite certain that nationality is the key of Scotland; I am quite certain that all our success with Scotland has been due to the fact that we have in spirit treated it as a nation. I am quite certain that Ireland is a nation; I am quite certain that nationality is the key to Ireland; I am quite certain that all our failure in Ireland arose from the fact that we would not in spirit treat it as a nation. It would be difficult to find, even among the innumerable examples that exist, a stronger example of the immensely superior importance of sentiment to what is called practicality than this case of the two sister nations. It is not that we have encouraged a Scotchman to be rich; it is not that we have encouraged a Scotchman to be active; it is not that we have encouraged a Scotchman to be free. It is that we have quite definitely encouraged a Scotchman to be Scotch.

A vague, but vivid impression was received from all our writers of history, philosophy, and rhetoric that the Scottish element was something really valuable in itself, was something which even Englishmen were forced to recognise and respect. If we ever admitted the beauty of Ireland, it was as something which might be loved by an Englishman but which could hardly be respected even by an Irishman. A Scotchman might be proud of Scotland; it was enough for an Irishman that he could be fond of Ireland. Our success with the two nations has been exactly proportioned to our encouragement of their independent national emotion; the one that we would not treat nationally has alone produced Nationalists. The one nation that we would not recognise as a nation in theory is the one that we have been forced to recognise as a nation in arms. The Scottish Patriotic Association has no need to draw my attention to the importance of the separate national sentiment or the need of keeping the Border as a sacred line. The case is quite sufficiently proved by the positive history of Scotland. The place of Scottish loyalty to England has been taken by English admiration of Scotland. They do not need to envy us our titular leadership, when we seem to envy them their separation.

I wish to make very clear my entire sympathy with the national sentiment of the Scottish Patriotic Association. But I wish also to make clear this very enlightening comparison between the fate of Scotch and of Irish patriotism. In life it is always the little facts that express the large emotions, and if the English once respected Ireland as they respect Scotland, it would come out in a hundred small ways. For instance, there are crack regiments in the British Army which wear the kilt—the kilt which, as Macaulay says with perfect truth, was regarded by nine Scotchmen out of ten as the dress of a thief. The Highland officers carry a silver-hilted version of the old barbarous Gaelic broadsword with a basket-hilt, which split the skulls of so many English soldiers at Killiecrankie and Prestonpans. When you have a regiment of men in the British Army carrying ornamental silver shillelaghs you will have done the same thing for Ireland, and not before—or when you mention Brian Boru with the same intonation as Bruce.

Let me be considered therefore to have made quite clear that I believe with a quite special intensity in the independent consideration of Scotland and Ireland as apart from England. I believe that, in the proper sense of the words, Scotland is an independent nation, even if Edward VII. is the King of Scotland. I believe that, in the proper sense of words, Ireland is an independent nation, even if Edward VII. is King of Ireland. But the fact is that I have an even bolder and wilder belief than either of these. I believe that England is an independent nation. I believe that England also has its independent colour and history, and meaning. I believe that England could produce costumes quite as queer as the kilt; I believe that England has heroes fully as untranslateable as Brian Boru, and consequently I believe that Edward VII. is, among his innumerable other functions, really King of England. If my Scotch friends insist, let us call it one of his quite obscure, unpopular, and minor titles; one of his relaxations. A little while ago he was Duke of Cornwall; but for a family accident he might still have been King of Hanover. Nor do I think that we should blame the simple Cornishmen if they spoke of him in a rhetorical moment by his Cornish title, nor the well-meaning Hanoverians if they classed him with Hanoverian Princes.

Now it so happens that in the passage complained of I said the King of England merely because I meant the King of England. I was speaking strictly and especially of English Kings, of Kings in the tradition of the old Kings of England. I wrote as an English nationalist keenly conscious of the sacred boundary of the Tweed that keeps (or used to keep) our ancient enemies at bay. I wrote as an English nationalist resolved for one wild moment to throw off the tyranny of the Scotch and Irish who govern and oppress my country. I felt that England was at least spiritually guarded against these surrounding nationalities. I dreamed that the Tweed was guarded by the ghosts of Scropes and Percys; I dreamed that St. George's Channel was guarded by St. George. And in this insular security I spoke deliberately and specifically of the King of England, of the representative of the Tudors and

Plantagenets. It is true that the two Kings of England, of whom I especially spoke, Charles II. and George III., had both an alien origin, not very recent and not very remote. Charles II. came of a family originally Scotch. George III. came of a family originally German. But the same, so far as that goes, could be said of the English royal houses when England stood quite alone. The Plantagenets were originally a French family. The Tudors were originally a Welsh family. But I was not talking of the amount of English sentiment in the English Kings. I was talking of the amount of English sentiment in the English treatment and popularity of the English Kings. With that Ireland and Scotland have nothing whatever to do.

Charles II. may, for all I know, have not only been King of Scotland; he may, by virtue of his temper and ancestry, have been a Scotch King of Scotland. There was something Scotch about his combination of clear-headedness with sensuality. There was something Scotch about his combination of doing what he liked with knowing what he was doing. But I was not talking of the personality of Charles, which may have been Scotch. I was talking of the popularity of Charles, which was certainly English. One thing is quite certain: whether or no he ever ceased to be a Scotch man, he ceased as soon as he conveniently could to be a Scotch King. He had actually tried the experiment of being a national ruler north of the Tweed, and his people liked him as little as he liked them. Of Presbyterianism, of the Scottish religion, he left on record the exquisitely English judgment that it was "no religion for a gentleman." His popularity then was purely English; his royalty was purely English; and I was using the words with the utmost narrowness and deliberation when I spoke of this particular popularity and royalty as the popularity and royalty of a King of England. I said of the English people specially that they like to pick up the King's crown when he has dropped it. I do not feel at all sure that this does apply to the Scotch or the Irish. I think that the Irish would knock his crown off for him. I think that the Scotch would keep it for him after they had picked it up.

For my part, I should be inclined to adopt quite the opposite method of asserting nationality. Why should good Scotch nationalists call Edward VII. the King of Britain? They ought to call him King Edward I. of Scotland. What is Britain? Where is Britain? There is no such place. There never was a nation of Britain; there never was a King of Britain; unless perhaps Vortigern or Uther Pendragon had a taste for the title. If we are to develop our Monarchy, I should be altogether in favour of developing it along the line of local patriotism and of local proprietorship in the King. I think that the Londoners ought to call him the King of London, and the Liverpudlians ought to call him the King of Liverpool. I do not go so far as to say that the people of Birmingham ought to call Edward VII. the King of Birmingham; for that would be high treason to a holier and more established power. But I think we might read in the papers: "The King of Brighton left Brighton at half-past two this afternoon," and then immediately afterwards, "The King of Worthing entered Worthing at ten minutes past three." Or, "The people of Margate bade a reluctant farewell to the popular King of Margate this morning," and then, "His Majesty the King of Ramsgate returned to his country and capital this afternoon after his long sojourn in strange lands." It might be pointed out that by a curious coincidence the departure of the King of Oxford occurred a very short time before the triumphal arrival of the King of Reading. I cannot imagine any method which would more increase the kindly and normal relations between the Sovereign and his people. Nor do I think that such a method would be in any sense a depreciation of the royal dignity; for, as a matter of fact, it would put the King upon the same platform with the gods. The saints, the most exalted of human figures, were also the most local. It was exactly the men whom we most easily connected with heaven whom we also most easily connected with earth.

Chapter 16
Thoughts Around Koepenick

famous and epigrammatic author said that life copied literature; it seems clear that life really caricatures it. I suggested recently that the Germans submitted to, and even admired, a solemn and theatrical assertion of authority. A few hours after I had sent up my "copy," I saw the first announcement of the affair of the comic Captain at Koepenick. The most absurd part of this absurd fraud (at least, to English eyes) is one which, oddly enough, has received comparatively little comment. I mean the point at which the Mayor asked for a warrant, and the Captain pointed to the bayonets of his soldiery and said. "These are my authority." One would have thought any one would have known that no soldier would talk like that. The dupes were blamed for not knowing that the man wore the wrong cap or the wrong sash, or had his sword buckled on the wrong way; but these are technicalities which they might surely be excused for not knowing. I certainly should not know if a soldier's sash were on inside out or his cap on behind before. But I should know uncommonly well that genuine professional soldiers do not talk like Adelphi villains and utter theatrical epigrams in praise of abstract violence.

We can see this more clearly, perhaps, if we suppose it to be the case of any other dignified and clearly distinguishable profession. Suppose a Bishop called upon me. My great modesty and my rather distant reverence for the higher clergy might lead me certainly to a strong suspicion that any Bishop who called on me was a bogus Bishop. But if I wished to test his genuineness I should not dream of attempting to do so by examining the shape of his apron or the way his gaiters were done up. I have not the remotest idea of the way his gaiters ought to be done up. A very vague approximation to an apron would probably take me in; and if he behaved like an approximately Christian gentleman he would be safe enough from my detection. But suppose the Bishop, the moment he entered the room, fell on his knees on the mat, clasped his hands, and poured out a flood of passionate and somewhat hysterical extempore prayer, I should say at once and without the smallest hesitation, "Whatever else this man is, he is not an elderly and wealthy cleric of the Church of England. They don't do such things." Or suppose a man came to me pretending to be a qualified doctor, and flourished a stethoscope, or what he said was a stethoscope. I am glad to say that I have not even the remotest notion of what a stethoscope looks like; so that if he flourished a musical-box or a coffee-mill it would be all one to me. But I do think that I am not exaggerating my own sagacity if I say that I should begin to suspect the doctor if on entering my room he flung his legs and arms about, crying wildly, "Health! Health! priceless gift of Nature! I possess it! I overflow with it! I yearn to impart it! Oh, the sacred rapture of imparting health!" In that case I should suspect him of being rather in a position to receive than to offer medical superintendence.

Now, it is no exaggeration at all to say that any one who has ever known any soldiers (I can only answer for English and Irish and Scotch soldiers) would find it just as easy to believe that a real Bishop would grovel on the carpet in a religious ecstasy, or that a real doctor would dance about the drawing-room to show the invigorating effects of his own medicine, as to believe that a soldier, when asked for his authority, would point to a lot of shining weapons and declare symbolically that might was right. Of course, a real soldier would go rather red in the face and huskily repeat the proper formula, whatever it was, as that he came in the King's name.

Soldiers have many faults, but they have one redeeming merit; they are never worshippers of force. Soldiers more than any other men are taught severely and systematically that might is not right. The fact is obvious. The might is in the hundred men who obey. The right (or what is held to be right) is in the one man who commands them. They learn to obey symbols, arbitrary things, stripes on an arm, buttons on a coat, a title, a flag. These may be artificial things; they may be unreasonable things; they may, if you will, be wicked things; but they are weak things. They are not Force, and they do not look like Force. They are parts of an idea: of the idea of discipline; if you will, of the idea of tyranny; but still an idea. No soldier could possibly say that his own bayonets were his authority. No soldier could possibly say that he came in the name of his own bayonets. It would be as absurd as if a postman said that he came inside his bag. I do not, as I have said, underrate the evils that really do arise from militarism and the military ethic. It tends to give people wooden faces and sometimes wooden heads. It tends moreover (both through its specialisation and through its constant obedience) to a certain loss of real independence and strength of character. This has almost always been found when people made the mistake of turning the soldier into a statesman, under the mistaken impression that he was a strong man. The Duke of Wellington, for instance, was a strong soldier and therefore a weak statesman. But the soldier is always, by the nature of things, loyal to something. And as long as one is loyal to something one can never be a worshipper of mere force. For mere force, violence in the abstract, is the enemy of anything we love. To love anything is to see it at once under lowering skies of danger. Loyalty implies loyalty in misfortune; and when a soldier has accepted any nation's uniform he has already accepted its defeat.

Nevertheless, it does appear to be possible in Germany for a man to point to fixed bayonets and say, "These are my authority," and yet to convince ordinarily sane men that he is a soldier. If this is so, it does really seem to point to some habit of high-falutin' in the German nation, such as that of which I spoke previously. It almost looks as if the advisers, and even the officials, of the German Army had become infected in some degree with the false and feeble doctrine that might is right. As this doctrine is invariably preached by physical weaklings like Nietzsche it is a very serious thing even to entertain the supposition that it is affecting men who have really to do military work. It would be the end of German soldiers to be affected by German philosophy. Energetic people use energy as a means, but only very tired people ever use energy as a reason. Athletes go in for games, because athletes desire glory. Invalids go in for calisthenics; for invalids (alone of all human beings) desire strength. So long as the German Army points to its heraldic eagle and says, "I come in the name of this fierce but fabulous animal," the German Army will be all right. If ever it says, "I come in the name of bayonets," the bayonets will break like glass, for only the weak exhibit strength without an aim.

At the same time, as I said before, do not let us forget our own faults. Do not let us forget them any the more easily because they are the opposite to the German faults. Modern England is too prone to present the spectacle of a person who is enormously delighted because he has not got the contrary disadvantages to his own. The Englishman is always saying "My house is not damp" at the moment when his house is on fire. The Englishman is always saying, "I have thrown off all traces of anæmia" in the middle of a fit of apoplexy. Let us always remember that if an Englishman wants to swindle English people, he does not dress up in the uniform of a soldier. If an Englishman wants to swindle English people he would as soon think of dressing up in the uniform of a messenger boy. Everything in England is done unofficially, casually, by conversations and cliques. The one Parliament that really does rule England is a secret Parliament; the debates of which must not be published—the Cabinet. The debates of the Commons are sometimes important; but only the debates in the Lobby, never the debates in the House. Journalists do control public opinion; but it is not controlled by the arguments they publish—it is controlled by the arguments between the editor and sub-editor, which they do not publish. This casualness is our English vice. It is at once casual and secret. Our public life is conducted privately. Hence it follows that if an English swindler wished to impress us, the last thing he would think of doing would be to put on a uniform. He would put on a polite slouching air and a careless, expensive suit of clothes; he would stroll up to the Mayor, be so awfully sorry to disturb him, find he had forgotten his card-case, mention, as if he were ashamed of it, that he was the Duke of Mercia, and carry the whole thing through with the air of a man who could get two hundred witnesses and two thousand retainers, but who was too tired to call any of them. And if he did it very well I strongly suspect that he would be as successful as the indefensible Captain at Koepenick.

Our tendency for many centuries past has been, not so much towards creating an aristocracy (which may or may not be a good thing in itself), as towards substituting an aristocracy for everything else. In England we have an aristocracy instead of a religion. The nobility are to the English poor what the saints and the fairies are to the Irish poor, what the large devil with a black face was to the Scotch poor—the poetry of life. In the same way in England we have an aristocracy instead of a Government. We rely on a certain good humour and education in the upper class to interpret to us our contradictory Constitution. No educated man born of woman will be quite so absurd as the system that he has to administer. In short, we do not get good laws to restrain bad people. We get good people to restrain bad laws. And last of all we in England have an aristocracy instead of an Army. We have an Army of which the officers are proud of their families and ashamed of their uniforms. If I were a king of any country whatever, and one of my officers were ashamed of my uniform, I should be ashamed of my officer. Beware, then, of the really well-bred and apologetic gentleman whose clothes are at once quiet and fashionable, whose manner is at once diffident and frank. Beware how you admit him into your domestic secrets, for he may be a bogus Earl. Or, worse still, a real one.

Chapter 17
The Boy

 have no sympathy with international aggression when it is taken seriously, but I have a certain dark and wild sympathy with it when it is quite absurd. Raids are all wrong as practical politics, but they are human and imaginable as practical jokes. In fact, almost any act of ragging or violence can be forgiven on this strict condition—that it is of no use at all to anybody. If the aggressor gets anything out of it, then it is quite unpardonable. It is damned by the least hint of utility or profit. A man of spirit and breeding may brawl, but he does not steal. A gentleman knocks off his friend's hat; but he does not annex his friend's hat. For this reason (as Mr. Belloc has pointed out somewhere), the very militant French people have always returned after their immense raids—the raids of Godfrey the Crusader, the raids of Napoleon; "they are sucked back, having accomplished nothing but an epic."

Sometimes I see small fragments of information in the newspapers which make my heart leap with an irrational patriotic sympathy. I have had the misfortune to be left comparatively cold by many of the enterprises and proclamations of my country in recent times. But the other day I found in the *Tribune* the following paragraph, which I may be permitted to set down as an example of the kind of international outrage with which I have by far the most instinctive sympathy. There is something attractive, too, in the austere simplicity with which the affair is set forth—

"Geneva, Oct. 31.

"The English schoolboy Allen, who was arrested at Lausanne railway station on Saturday, for having painted red the statue of General Jomini of Payerne, was liberated yesterday, after paying a fine of £24. Allen has proceeded to Germany, where he will continue his studies. The people of Payerne are indignant, and clamoured for his detention in prison."

Now I have no doubt that ethics and social necessity require a contrary attitude, but I will freely confess that my first emotions on reading of this exploit were those of profound and elemental pleasure. There is something so large and simple about the operation of painting a whole stone General a bright red. Of course I can understand that the people of Payerne were indignant. They had passed to their homes at twilight through the streets of that beautiful city (or is it a province?), and they had seen against the silver ending of the sunset the grand grey figure of the hero of that land remaining to guard the town under the stars. It certainly must have been a shock to come out in the broad white morning and find a large vermilion General staring under the staring sun. I do not blame them at all for clamouring for the schoolboy's detention in prison; I dare say a little detention in prison would do him no harm. Still, I think the immense act has something about it human and excusable; and when I endeavour to analyse the reason of this feeling I find it to lie, not in the fact that the thing was big or bold or successful, but in the fact that the thing was perfectly useless to everybody, including the person who did it. The raid ends in itself; and so Master Allen is sucked back again, having accomplished nothing but an epic.

There is one thing which, in the presence of average modern journalism, is perhaps worth saying in connection with such an idle matter as this. The morals of a matter like this are exactly like the morals of anything else; they are concerned with mutual contract, or with the rights of independent human lives. But the whole modern world, or at any rate the whole modern Press, has a perpetual and consuming terror of plain morals. Men always attempt to avoid condemning a thing upon merely moral grounds. If I beat my grandmother to death to-morrow in the middle of Battersea Park, you may be perfectly certain that people will say everything about it except the simple and fairly obvious fact that it is wrong. Some will call it insane; that is, will accuse it of a deficiency of intelligence. This is not necessarily true at all. You could not tell whether the act was unintelligent or not unless you knew my grandmother. Some will call it vulgar, disgusting, and the rest of it; that is, they will accuse it of a lack of manners. Perhaps it does show a lack of manners; but this is scarcely its most serious disadvantage. Others will talk about the loathsome spectacle and the revolting scene; that is, they will accuse it of a deficiency of art, or æsthetic beauty. This again depends on the circumstances: in order to be quite certain that the appearance of the old lady has definitely deteriorated under the process of being beaten to death, it is necessary for the philosophical critic to be quite certain how ugly she was before. Another school of thinkers will say that the action is lacking in efficiency: that it is an uneconomic waste of a good grandmother. But that could only depend on the value, which is again an individual matter. The only real point that is worth mentioning is that the action is wicked, because your grandmother has a right not to be beaten to death. But of this simple moral explanation modern journalism has, as I say, a standing fear. It will call the action anything else—mad, bestial, vulgar, idiotic, rather than call it sinful.

One example can be found in such cases as that of the prank of the boy and the statue. When some trick of this sort is played, the newspapers opposed to it always describe it as "a senseless joke." What is the good of saying that? Every joke is a senseless joke. A joke is by its nature a protest against sense. It is no good attacking nonsense for being successfully nonsensical. Of course it is nonsensical to paint a celebrated Italian General a bright red; it is as nonsensical as "Alice in Wonderland." It is also, in my opinion, very nearly as funny. But the real answer to the affair is not to say that it is nonsensical or even to say that it is not funny, but to point out that it is wrong to spoil statues which belong to other people. If the modern world will not insist on having some sharp and definite moral law, capable of resisting the counter-attractions of art and humour, the modern world will simply be given over as a spoil to anybody who can manage to do a nasty thing in a nice way. Every murderer who can murder entertainingly will be allowed to murder. Every burglar who burgles in really humorous attitudes will burgle as much as he likes.

There is another case of the thing that I mean. Why on earth do the newspapers, in describing a dynamite outrage or any other political assassination, call it a "dastardly outrage" or a cowardly outrage? It is perfectly evident that it is not dastardly in the least. It is perfectly evident that it is about as cowardly as the Christians going to the lions. The man who does it exposes himself to the chance of being torn in pieces by two thousand people. What the thing is, is not cowardly, but profoundly and detestably wicked. The man who does it is very infamous and very brave. But, again, the explanation is that our modern Press would rather appeal to physical arrogance, or to anything, rather than appeal to right and wrong.

In most of the matters of modern England, the real difficulty is that there is a negative revolution without a positive revolution. Positive aristocracy is breaking up without any particular appearance of positive democracy taking its place. The polished class is becoming less polished without becoming less of a class; the nobleman who becomes a guinea-pig keeps all his privileges but loses some of his tradition; he becomes less of a gentleman without becoming less of a nobleman. In the same way (until some recent and happy revivals) it seemed highly probable that the Church of England would cease to be a religion long before it had ceased to be a Church. And in the same way, the vulgarisation of the old, simple middle class does not even have the advantage of doing away with class distinctions; the vulgar man is always the most distinguished, for the very desire to be distinguished is vulgar.

At the same time, it must be remembered that when a class has a morality it does not follow that it is an adequate morality. The middle-class ethic was inadequate for some purposes; so is the public-school ethic, the ethic of the upper classes. On this last matter of the public schools Dr. Spenser, the Head Master of University College School, has lately made some valuable observations. But even he, I think, overstates the claim of the public schools. "The strong point of the English public schools," he says, "has always lain in their efficiency as agencies for the formation of character and for the inculcation of the great notion of obligation which distinguishes a gentleman. On the physical and moral sides the public-school men of England are, I believe, unequalled." And he goes on to say that it is on the mental side that they are defective. But, as a matter of fact, the public-school training is in the strict sense defective upon the moral side also; it leaves out about half of morality. Its just claim is that, like the old middle class (and the Zulus), it trains some virtues and therefore suits some people for some situations. Put an old English merchant to serve in an army and he would have been irritated and clumsy. Put the men from English public schools to rule

Ireland, and they make the greatest hash in human history.

Touching the morality of the public schools, I will take one point only, which is enough to prove the case. People have got into their heads an extraordinary idea that English public-school boys and English youth generally are taught to tell the truth. They are taught absolutely nothing of the kind. At no English public school is it even suggested, except by accident, that it is a man's duty to tell the truth. What is suggested is something entirely different: that it is a man's duty not to tell lies. So completely does this mistake soak through all civilisation that we hardly ever think even of the difference between the two things. When we say to a child, "You must tell the truth," we do merely mean that he must refrain from verbal inaccuracies. But the thing we never teach at all is the general duty of telling the truth, of giving a complete and fair picture of anything we are talking about, of not misrepresenting, not evading, not suppressing, not using plausible arguments that we know to be unfair, not selecting unscrupulously to prove an *ex parte* case, not telling all the nice stories about the Scotch, and all the nasty stories about the Irish, not pretending to be disinterested when you are really angry, not pretending to be angry when you are really only avaricious. The one thing that is never taught by any chance in the atmosphere of public schools is exactly that—that there is a whole truth of things, and that in knowing it and speaking it we are happy.

If any one has the smallest doubt of this neglect of truth in public schools he can kill his doubt with one plain question. Can any one on earth believe that if the seeing and telling of the whole truth were really one of the ideals of the English governing class, there could conceivably exist such a thing as the English party system? Why, the English party system is founded upon the principle that telling the whole truth does not matter. It is founded upon the principle that half a truth is better than no politics. Our system deliberately turns a crowd of men who might be impartial into irrational partisans. It teaches some of them to tell lies and all of them to believe lies. It gives every man an arbitrary brief that he has to work up as best he may and defend as best he can. It turns a room full of citizens into a room full of barristers. I know that it has many charms and virtues, fighting and good-fellowship; it has all the charms and virtues of a game. I only say that it would be a stark impossibility in a nation which believed in telling the truth.

Chapter 18
Limericks and Counsels of Perfection

t is customary to remark that modern problems cannot easily be attacked because they are so complex. In many cases I believe it is really because they are so simple. Nobody would believe in such simplicity of scoundrelism even if it were pointed out. People would say that the truth was a charge of mere melodramatic villainy; forgetting that nearly all villains really are melodramatic. Thus, for instance, we say that some good measures are frustrated or some bad officials kept in power by the press and confusion of public business; whereas very often the reason is simple healthy human bribery. And thus especially we say that the Yellow Press is exaggerative, over-emotional, illiterate, and anarchical, and a hundred other long words; whereas the only objection to it is that it tells lies. We waste our fine intellects in finding exquisite phraseology to fit a man, when in a well-ordered society we ought to be finding handcuffs to fit him.

This criticism of the modern type of righteous indignation must have come into many people's minds, I think, in reading Dr. Horton's eloquent expressions of disgust at the "corrupt Press," especially in connection with the Limerick craze. Upon the Limerick craze itself, I fear Dr. Horton will not have much effect; such fads perish before one has had time to kill them. But Dr. Horton's protest may really do good if it enables us to come to some clear understanding about what is really wrong with the popular Press, and which means it might be useful and which permissible to use for its reform. We do not want a censorship of the Press; but we are long past talking about that. At present it is not we that silence the Press; it is the Press that silences us. It is not a case of the Commonwealth settling how much the editors shall say; it is a case of the editors settling how much the Commonwealth shall know. If we attack the Press we shall be rebelling, not repressing. But shall we attack it?

Now it is just here that the chief difficulty occurs. It arises from the very rarity and rectitude of those minds which commonly inaugurate such crusades. I have the warmest respect for Dr. Horton's thirst after righteousness; but it has always seemed to me that his righteousness would be more effective without his refinement. The curse of the Nonconformists is their universal refinement. They dimly connect being good with being delicate, and even dapper; with not being grotesque or loud or violent; with not sitting down on one's hat. Now it is always a pleasure to be loud and violent, and sometimes it is a duty. Certainly it has nothing to do with sin; a man can be loudly and violently virtuous—nay, he can be loudly and violently saintly, though that is not the type of saintliness that we recognise in Dr. Horton. And as for sitting on one's hat, if it is done for any sublime object (as, for instance, to amuse the children), it is obviously an act of very beautiful self-sacrifice, the destruction and surrender of the symbol of personal dignity upon the shrine of public festivity. Now it will not do to attack the modern editor merely for being unrefined, like the great mass of mankind. We must be able to say that he is immoral, not that he is undignified or ridiculous. I do not mind the Yellow Press editor sitting on his hat. My only objection to him begins to dawn when he attempts to sit on my hat; or, indeed (as is at present the case), when he proceeds to sit on my head.

But in reading between the lines of Dr. Horton's invective one continually feels that he is not only angry with the popular Press for being unscrupulous: he is partly angry with the popular Press for being popular. He is not only irritated with Limericks for causing a mean money-scramble; he is also partly irritated with Limericks for being Limericks. The enormous size of the levity gets on his nerves, like the glare and blare of Bank Holiday. Now this is a motive which, however human and natural, must be strictly kept out of the way. It takes all sorts to make a world; and it is not in the least necessary that everybody should have that love of subtle and unobtrusive perfections in the matter of manners or literature which does often go with the type of the ethical idealist. It is not in the least desirable that everybody should be earnest. It is highly desirable that everybody should be honest, but that is a thing that can go quite easily with a coarse and cheerful character. But the ineffectualness of most protests against the abuse of the Press has been very largely due to the instinct of democracy (and the instinct of democracy is like the instinct of one woman, wild but quite right) that the people who were trying to purify the Press were also trying to refine it; and to this the democracy very naturally and very justly objected. We are justified in enforcing good morals, for they belong to all mankind; but we are not justified in enforcing good manners, for good manners always mean our own manners. We have no right to purge the popular Press of all that we think vulgar or trivial. Dr. Horton may possibly loathe and detest Limericks just as I loathe and detest riddles; but I have no right to call them flippant and unprofitable; there are wild people in the world who like riddles. I am so afraid of this movement passing off into mere formless rhetoric and platform passion that I will even come close to the earth and lay down specifically some of the things that, in my opinion, could be, and ought to be, done to reform the Press.

First, I would make a law, if there is none such at present, by which an editor, proved to have published false news without reasonable verification, should simply go to prison. This is not a question of influences or atmospheres; the thing could be carried out as easily and as practically as the punishment of thieves and murderers. Of course there would be the usual statement that the guilt was that of a subordinate. Let the accused editor have the right of proving this if he can; if he does, let the subordinate be tried and go to prison. Two or three good rich editors and proprietors properly locked up would take the sting out of the Yellow Press better than centuries of Dr. Horton.

Second, it's impossible to pass over altogether the most unpleasant, but the most important part of this problem. I will deal with it as distantly as possible. I do not believe there is any harm whatever in reading about murders; rather, if anything, good; for the thought of death operates very powerfully with the poor in the creation of brotherhood and a sense of human dignity. I do not believe there is a pennyworth of harm in the police news, as such. Even divorce news, though contemptible enough, can really in most cases be left to the discretion of grown people; and how far children get hold of such things is a problem for the home and not for the nation. But there is a certain class of evils which a healthy man or woman can actually go through life without knowing anything about at all. These, I say, should be stamped and blackened out of every newspaper with the thickest black of the Russian censor. Such cases should either be always tried *in camera* or reporting them should be a punishable offence. The common weakness of Nature and the sins that flesh is heir to we can leave people to find in newspapers. Men can safely see in the papers what they have already seen in the streets. They may safely find in their journals what they have already found in themselves. But we do not want the imaginations of rational and decent people clouded with the horrors of some obscene insanity which has no more to do with human life than the man in Bedlam who thinks he is a chicken. And, if this vile matter is admitted, let it be simply with a mention of the Latin or legal name of the crime, and with no details whatever. As it is, exactly the reverse is true. Papers are permitted to terrify and darken the fancy of the young with innumerable details, but not permitted to state in clean legal language what the thing is about. They are allowed to give any fact about the thing except the fact that it is a sin.

Third, I would do my best to introduce everywhere the practice of signed articles. Those who urge the advantages of anonymity are either people who do not realise the special peril of our time or they are people who are profiting by it. It is true, but futile, for instance, to say that there is something noble in being nameless when a whole corporate body is bent on a consistent aim: as in an army or men building a cathedral. The point of modern newspapers is that there is no such corporate body and common aim; but each man can use the authority of the paper to further his own private fads and his own private finances.

Chapter 19
Anonymity and Further Counsels

he end of the article which I write is always cut off, and, unfortunately, I belong to that lower class of animals in whom the tail is important. It is not anybody's fault but my own; it arises from the fact that I take such a long time to get to the point. Somebody, the other day, very reasonably complained of my being employed to write prefaces. He was perfectly right, for I always write a preface to the preface, and then I am stopped; also quite justifiably.

In my last article I said that I favoured three things—first, the legal punishment of deliberately false information; secondly, a distinction, in the matter of reported immorality, between those sins which any healthy man can see in himself and those which he had better not see anywhere; and thirdly, an absolute insistence in the great majority of cases upon the signing of articles. It was at this point that I was cut short, I will not say by the law of space, but rather by my own lawlessness in the matter of space. In any case, there is something more that ought to be said.

It would be an exaggeration to say that I hope some day to see an anonymous article counted as dishonourable as an anonymous letter. For some time to come, the idea of the leading article, expressing the policy of the whole paper, must necessarily remain legitimate; at any rate, we have all written such leading articles, and should never think the worse of any one for writing one. But I should certainly say that writing anonymously ought to have some definite excuse, such as that of the leading article. Writing anonymously ought to be the exception; writing a signed article ought to be the rule. And anonymity ought to be not only an exception, but an accidental exception; a man ought always to be ready to say what anonymous article he had written. The journalistic habit of counting it something sacred to keep secret the origin of an article is simply part of the conspiracy which seeks to put us who are journalists in the position of a much worse sort of Jesuits or Freemasons.

As has often been said, anonymity would be all very well if one could for a moment imagine that it was established from good motives. Suppose, for instance, that we were all quite certain that the men on the *Thunderer* newspaper were a band of brave young idealists who were so eager to overthrow Socialism, Municipal and National, that they did not care to which of them especially was given the glory of striking it down. Unfortunately, however, we do not believe this. What we believe, or, rather, what we know, is that the attack on Socialism in the *Thunderer* arises from a chaos of inconsistent and mostly evil motives, any one of which would lose simply by being named. A jerry-builder whose houses have been condemned writes anonymously and becomes the *Thunderer*. A Socialist who has quarrelled with the other Socialists writes anonymously, and he becomes the *Thunderer*. A monopolist who has lost his monopoly, and a demagogue who has lost his mob, can both write anonymously and become the same newspaper. It is quite true that there is a young and beautiful fanaticism in which men do not care to reveal their names. But there is a more elderly and a much more common excitement in which men do not dare to reveal them.

Then there is another rule for making journalism honest on which I should like to insist absolutely. I should like it to be a fixed thing that the name of the proprietor as well as the editor should be printed upon every paper. If the paper is owned by shareholders, let there be a list of shareholders. If (as is far more common in this singularly undemocratic age) it is owned by one man, let that one man's name be printed on the paper, if possible in large red letters. Then, if there are any obvious interests being served, we shall know that they are being served. My friends in Manchester are in a terrible state of excitement about the power of brewers and the dangers of admitting them to public office. But at least, if a man has controlled politics through beer, people generally know it: the subject of beer is too fascinating for any one to miss such personal peculiarities. But a man may control politics through journalism, and no ordinary English citizen know that he is controlling them at all. Again and again in the lists of Birthday Honours you and I have seen some Mr. Robinson suddenly elevated to the Peerage without any apparent reason. Even the Society papers (which we read with avidity) could tell us nothing about him except that he was a sportsman or a kind landlord, or interested in the breeding of badgers. Now I should like the name of that Mr. Robinson to be already familiar to the British public. I should like them to know already the public services for which they have to thank him. I should like them to have seen the name already on the outside of that organ of public opinion called *Tootsie's Tips*, or *The Boy Blackmailer*, or *Nosey Knows*, that bright little financial paper which did so much for the Empire and which so narrowly escaped a criminal prosecution. If they had seen it thus, they would estimate more truly and tenderly the full value of the statement in the Society paper that he is a true gentleman and a sound Churchman.

Finally, it should be practically imposed by custom (it so happens that it could not possibly be imposed by law) that letters of definite and practical complaint should be necessarily inserted by any editor in any paper. Editors have grown very much too lax in this respect. The old editor used dimly to regard himself as an unofficial public servant for the transmitting of public news. If he suppressed anything, he was supposed to have some special reason for doing so; as that the material was actually libellous or literally indecent. But the modern editor regards himself far too much as a kind of original artist, who can select and suppress facts with the arbitrary ease of a poet or a caricaturist. He "makes up" the paper as man "makes up" a fairy tale, he considers his newspaper solely as a work of art, meant to give pleasure, not to give news. He puts in this one letter because he thinks it clever. He puts in these three or four letters because he thinks them silly. He suppresses this article because he thinks it wrong. He suppresses this other and more dangerous article because he thinks it right. The old idea that he is simply a mode of the expression of the public, an "organ" of opinion, seems to have entirely vanished from his mind. To-day the editor is not only the organ, but the man who plays on the organ. For in all our modern movements we move away from Democracy.

This is the whole danger of our time. There is a difference between the oppression which has been too common in the past and the oppression which seems only too probable in the future. Oppression in the past, has commonly been an individual matter. The oppressors were as simple as the oppressed, and as lonely. The aristocrat sometimes hated his inferiors; he always hated his equals. The plutocrat was an individualist. But in our time even the plutocrat has become a Socialist. They have science and combination, and may easily inaugurate a much greater tyranny than the world has ever seen.

Chapter 20
On the Cryptic and the Elliptic

urely the art of reporting speeches is in a strange state of degeneration. We should not object, perhaps, to the reporter's making the speeches much shorter than they are; but we do object to his making all the speeches much worse than they are. And the method which he employs is one which is dangerously unjust. When a statesman or philosopher makes an important speech, there are several courses which the reporter might take without being unreasonable. Perhaps the most reasonable course of all would be not to report the speech at all. Let the world live and love, marry and give in marriage, without that particular speech, as they did (in some desperate way) in the days when there were no newspapers. A second course would be to report a small part of it; but to get that right. A third course, far better if you can do it, is to understand the main purpose and argument of the speech, and report that in clear and logical language of your own. In short, the three possible methods are, first, to leave the man's speech alone; second, to report what he says or some complete part of what he says; and third, to report what he means. But the present way of reporting speeches (mainly created, I think, by the scrappy methods of the *Daily Mail*) is something utterly different from both these ways, and quite senseless and misleading.

The present method is this: the reporter sits listening to a tide of words which he does not try to understand, and does not, generally speaking, even try to take down; he waits until something occurs in the speech which for some reason sounds funny, or memorable, or very exaggerated, or, perhaps, merely concrete; then he writes it down and waits for the next one. If the orator says that the Premier is like a porpoise in the sea under some special circumstances, the reporter gets in the porpoise even if he leaves out the Premier. If the orator begins by saying that Mr. Chamberlain is rather like a violoncello, the reporter does not even wait to hear why he is like a violoncello. He has got hold of something material, and so he is quite happy. The strong words all are put in; the chain of thought is left out. If the orator uses the word "donkey," down goes the word "donkey." If the orator uses the word "damnable," down goes the word "damnable." They follow each other so abruptly in the report that it is often hard to discover the fascinating fact as to what was damnable or who was being compared with a donkey. And the whole line of argument in which these things occurred is entirely lost. I have before me a newspaper report of a speech by Mr. Bernard Shaw, of which one complete and separate paragraph runs like this—

"Capital meant spare money over and above one's needs. Their country was not really their country at all except in patriotic songs."

I am well enough acquainted with the whole map of Mr. Bernard Shaw's philosophy to know that those two statements might have been related to each other in a hundred ways. But I think that if they were read by an ordinary intelligent man, who happened not to know Mr. Shaw's views, he would form no impression at all except that Mr. Shaw was a lunatic of more than usually abrupt conversation and disconnected mind. The other two methods would certainly have done Mr. Shaw more justice: the reporter should either have taken down verbatim what the speaker really said about Capital, or have given an outline of the way in which this idea was connected with the idea about patriotic songs.

But we have not the advantage of knowing what Mr. Shaw really did say, so we had better illustrate the different methods from something that we do know. Most of us, I suppose, know Mark Antony's Funeral Speech in "Julius Cæsar." Now Mark Antony would have no reason to complain if he were not reported at all; if the *Daily Pilum* or the *Morning Fasces*, or whatever it was, confined itself to saying, "Mr. Mark Antony also spoke," or "Mr. Mark Antony, having addressed the audience, the meeting broke up in some confusion." The next honest method, worthy of a noble Roman reporter, would be that since he could not report the whole of the speech, he should report some of the speech. He might say—"Mr. Mark Antony, in the course of his speech, said—

'When that the poor have cried Cæsar hath wept:
Ambition should be made of sterner stuff.' "

In that case one good, solid argument of Mark Antony would be correctly reported. The third and far higher course for the Roman reporter would be to give a philosophical statement of the purport of the speech. As thus—"Mr. Mark Antony, in the course of a powerful speech, conceded the high motives of the Republican leaders, and disclaimed any intention of raising the people against them; he thought, however, that many instances could be quoted against the theory of Cæsar's ambition, and he concluded by reading, at the request of the audience, the will of Cæsar, which proved that he had the most benevolent designs towards the Roman people." That is (I admit) not quite so fine as Shakspere, but it is a statement of the man's political position. But if a *Daily Mail* reporter were sent to take down Antony's oration, he would simply wait for any expressions that struck him as odd and put them down one after another without any logical connection at all. It would turn out something like this: "Mr. Mark Antony wished for his audience's ears. He had thrice offered Cæsar a crown. Cæsar was like a deer. If he were Brutus he would put a wound in every tongue. The stones of Rome would mutiny. See what a rent the envious Casca paid. Brutus was Cæsar's angel. The right honourable gentleman concluded by saying that he and the audience had all fallen down." That is the report of a political speech in a modern, progressive, or American manner, and I wonder whether the Romans would have put up with it.

The reports of the debates in the Houses of Parliament are constantly growing smaller and smaller in our newspapers. Perhaps this is partly because the speeches are growing duller and duller. I think in some degree the two things act and re-act on each other. For fear of the newspapers politicians are dull, and at last they are too dull even for the newspapers. The speeches in our time are more careful and elaborate, because they are meant to be read, and not to be heard. And exactly because they are more careful and elaborate, they are not so likely to be worthy of a careful and elaborate report. They are not interesting enough. So the moral cowardice of modern politicians has, after all, some punishment attached to it by the silent anger of heaven. Precisely because our political speeches are meant to be reported, they are not worth reporting. Precisely because they are carefully designed to be read, nobody reads them.

Thus we may concede that politicians have done something towards degrading journalism. It was not entirely done by us, the journalists. But most of it was. It was mostly the fruit of our first and most natural sin—the habit of regarding ourselves as conjurers rather than priests, for the definition is that a conjurer is apart from his audience, while a priest is a part of his. The conjurer despises his congregation; if the priest despises any one, it must be himself. The curse of all journalism, but especially of that yellow journalism which is the shame of our profession, is that we think ourselves cleverer than the people for whom we write, whereas, in fact, we are generally even stupider. But this insolence has its Nemesis; and that Nemesis is well illustrated in this matter of reporting.

For the journalist, having grown accustomed to talking down to the public, commonly talks too low at last, and becomes merely barbaric and unintelligible. By his very efforts to be obvious he becomes obscure. This just punishment may specially be noticed in the case of those staggering and staring headlines which American journalism introduced and which some English journalism imitates. I once saw a headline in a London paper which ran simply thus: "Dobbin's Little Mary." This was intended to be familiar and popular, and therefore, presumably, lucid. But it was some time before I realised, after reading about half the printed matter underneath, that it had something to do with the proper feeding of horses. At first sight, I took it, as the historical leader of the future will certainly take it, as containing some allusion to the little daughter who so monopolised the affections of the Major at the end of "Vanity Fair." The Americans carry to an even wilder extreme this darkness by excess of light. You may find a column in an American paper headed "Poet Brown Off Orange-flowers," or "Senator Robinson Shoehorns Hats Now," and it may be quite a long time before the full meaning breaks upon you: it has not broken upon me yet.

And something of this intellectual vengeance pursues also those who adopt the modern method of reporting speeches. They also become mystical, simply by trying to be vulgar. They also are condemned to be always trying to write like George R. Sims, and succeeding, in spite of themselves, in writing like Maeterlinck. That combination of words which I have quoted from an alleged speech of Mr. Bernard Shaw's was written down by the reporter with the idea that he was being particularly plain and democratic. But, as a matter of fact, if there is any connection between the two sentences, it must be something as dark as the deepest roots of Browning, or something as invisible as the most airy filaments of Meredith. To be simple and to be democratic are two very honourable and austere achievements; and it is not given to all the snobs and self-seekers to achieve them. High above even Maeterlinck or Meredith stand those, like Homer and Milton, whom no one can misunderstand. And Homer and Milton are not only better poets than Browning (great as he was), but they would also have been very much better journalists than the young men on the *Daily Mail*.

As it is, however, this misrepresentation of speeches is only a part of a vast journalistic misrepresentation of all life as it is. Journalism is popular, but it is popular mainly as fiction. Life is one world, and life seen in the newspapers another; the public enjoys both, but it is more or less conscious of the difference. People do not believe, for instance, that the debates in the House of Commons are as dramatic as they appear in the daily papers. If they did they would go, not to the daily paper, but to the House of Commons. The galleries would be crowded every night as they were in the French Revolution; for instead of seeing a printed story for a penny they would be seeing an acted drama for nothing. But the people know in their hearts that journalism is a conventional art like any other, that it selects, heightens, and falsifies. Only its Nemesis is the same as that of other arts: if it loses all care for truth it loses all form likewise. The modern who paints too cleverly produces a picture of a cow which might be the earthquake at San Francisco. And the journalist who reports a speech too cleverly makes it mean nothing at all.

Chapter 21
The Worship of the Wealthy

here has crept, I notice, into our literature and journalism a new way of flattering the wealthy and the great. In more straightforward times flattery itself was more straightforward; falsehood itself was more true. A poor man wishing to please a rich man simply said that he was the wisest, bravest, tallest, strongest, most benevolent and most beautiful of mankind; and as even the rich man probably knew that he wasn't that, the thing did the less harm. When courtiers sang the praises of a King they attributed to him things that were entirely improbable, as that he resembled the sun at noonday, that they had to shade their eyes when he entered the room, that his people could not breathe without him, or that he had with his single sword conquered Europe, Asia, Africa, and America. The safety of this method was its artificiality; between the King and his public image there was really no relation. But the moderns have invented a much subtler and more poisonous kind of eulogy. The modern method is to take the prince or rich man, to give a credible picture of his type of personality, as that he is business-like, or a sportsman, or fond of art, or convivial, or reserved; and then enormously exaggerate the value and importance of these natural qualities. Those who praise Mr. Carnegie do not say that he is as wise as Solomon and as brave as Mars; I wish they did. It would be the next most honest thing to giving their real reason for praising him, which is simply that he has money. The journalists who write about Mr. Pierpont Morgan do not say that he is as beautiful as Apollo; I wish they did. What they do is to take the rich man's superficial life and manner, clothes, hobbies, love of cats, dislike of doctors, or what not; and then with the assistance of this realism make the man out to be a prophet and a saviour of his kind, whereas he is merely a private and stupid man who happens to like cats or to dislike doctors. The old flatterer took for granted that the King was an ordinary man, and set to work to make him out extraordinary. The newer and cleverer flatterer takes for granted that he is extraordinary, and that therefore even ordinary things about him will be of interest.

I have noticed one very amusing way in which this is done. I notice the method applied to about six of the wealthiest men in England in a book of interviews published by an able and well-known journalist. The flatterer contrives to combine strict truth of fact with a vast atmosphere of awe and mystery by the simple operation of dealing almost entirely in negatives. Suppose you are writing a sympathetic study of Mr. Pierpont Morgan. Perhaps there is not much to say about what he does think, or like, or admire; but you can suggest whole vistas of his taste and philosophy by talking a great deal about what he does not think, or like, or admire. You say of him—"But little attracted to the most recent schools of German philosophy, he stands almost as resolutely aloof from the tendencies of transcendental Pantheism as from the narrower ecstasies of Neo-Catholicism." Or suppose I am called upon to praise the charwoman who has just come into my house, and who certainly deserves it much more. I say—"It would be a mistake to class Mrs. Higgs among the followers of Loisy; her position is in many ways different; nor is she wholly to be identified with the concrete Hebraism of Harnack." It is a splendid method, as it gives the flatterer an opportunity of talking about something else besides the subject of the flattery, and it gives the subject of the flattery a rich, if somewhat bewildered, mental glow, as of one who has somehow gone through agonies of philosophical choice of which he was previously unaware. It is a splendid method; but I wish it were applied sometimes to charwomen rather than only to millionaires.

There is another way of flattering important people which has become very common, I notice, among writers in the newspapers and elsewhere. It consists in applying to them the phrases "simple," or "quiet," or "modest," without any sort of meaning or relation to the person to whom they are applied. To be simple is the best thing in the world; to be modest is the next best thing. I am not so sure about being quiet. I am rather inclined to think that really modest people make a great deal of noise. It is quite self-evident that really simple people make a great deal of noise. But simplicity and modesty, at least, are very rare and royal human virtues, not to be lightly talked about. Few human beings, and at rare intervals, have really risen into being modest; not one man in ten or in twenty has by long wars become simple, as an actual old soldier does by [**Note: Apparent typesetting error here in original.] long wars become simple. These virtues are not things to fling about as mere flattery; many prophets and righteous men have desired to see these things and have not seen them. But in the description of the births, lives, and deaths of very luxurious men they are used incessantly and quite without thought. If a journalist has to describe a great politician or financier (the things are substantially the same) entering a room or walking down a thoroughfare, he always says, "Mr. Midas was quietly dressed in a black frock coat, a white waistcoat, and light grey trousers, with a plain green tie and simple flower in his button-hole." As if any one would expect him to have a crimson frock coat or spangled trousers. As if any one would expect him to have a burning Catherine wheel in his button-hole.

But this process, which is absurd enough when applied to the ordinary and external lives of worldly people, becomes perfectly intolerable when it is applied, as it always is applied, to the one episode which is serious even in the lives of politicians. I mean their death. When we have been sufficiently bored with the account of the simple costume of the millionaire, which is generally about as complicated as any that he could assume without being simply thought mad; when we have been told about the modest home of the millionaire, a home which is generally much too immodest to be called a home at all; when we have followed him through all these unmeaning eulogies, we are always asked last of all to admire his quiet funeral. I do not know what else people think a funeral should be except quiet. Yet again and again, over the grave of every one of those sad rich men, for whom one should surely feel, first and last, a speechless pity—over the grave of Beit, over the grave of Whiteley—this sickening nonsense about modesty and simplicity has been poured out. I well remember that when Beit was buried, the papers said that the mourning-coaches contained everybody of importance, that the floral tributes were sumptuous, splendid, intoxicating; but, for all that, it was a simple and quiet funeral. What, in the name of Acheron, did they expect it to be? Did they think there would be human sacrifice—the immolation of Oriental slaves upon the tomb? Did they think that long rows of Oriental dancing-girls would sway hither and thither in an ecstasy of lament? Did they look for the funeral games of Patroclus? I fear they had no such splendid and pagan meaning. I fear they were only using the words "quiet" and "modest" as words to fill up a page—a mere piece of the automatic hypocrisy which does become too common among those who have to write rapidly and often. The word "modest" will soon become like the word "honourable," which is said to be employed by the Japanese before any word that occurs in a polite sentence, as "Put honourable umbrella in honourable umbrella-stand;" or "condescend to clean honourable boots." We shall read in the future that the modest King went out in his modest crown, clad from head to foot in modest gold and attended with his ten thousand modest earls, their swords modestly drawn. No! if we have to pay for splendour let us praise it as splendour, not as simplicity. When next I meet a rich man I intend to walk up to him in the street and address him with Oriental hyperbole. He will probably run away.

Chapter 22
Science and Religion

n these days we are accused of attacking science because we want it to be scientific. Surely there is not any undue disrespect to our doctor in saying that he is our doctor, not our priest, or our wife, or ourself. It is not the business of the doctor to say that we must go to a watering-place; it is his affair to say that certain results of health will follow if we do go to a watering-place. After that, obviously, it is for us to judge. Physical science is like simple addition: it is either infallible or it is false. To mix science up with philosophy is only to produce a philosophy that has lost all its ideal value and a science that has lost all its practical value. I want my private physician to tell me whether this or that food will kill me. It is for my private philosopher to tell me whether I ought to be killed. I apologise for stating all these truisms. But the truth is, that I have just been reading a thick pamphlet written by a mass of highly intelligent men who seem never to have heard of any of these truisms in their lives.

Those who detest the harmless writer of this column are generally reduced (in their final ecstasy of anger) to calling him "brilliant;" which has long ago in our journalism become a mere expression of contempt. But I am afraid that even this disdainful phrase does me too much honour. I am more and more convinced that I suffer, not from a shiny or showy impertinence, but from a simplicity that verges upon imbecility. I think more and more that I must be very dull, and that everybody else in the modern world must be very clever. I have just been reading this important compilation, sent to me in the name of a number of men for whom I have a high respect, and called "New Theology and Applied Religion." And it is literally true that I have read through whole columns of the things without knowing what the people were talking about. Either they must be talking about some black and bestial religion in which they were brought up, and of which I never even heard, or else they must be talking about some blazing and blinding vision of God which they have found, which I have never found, and which by its very splendour confuses their logic and confounds their speech. But the best instance I can quote of the thing is in connection with this matter of the business of physical science on the earth, of which I have just spoken. The following words are written over the signature of a man whose intelligence I respect, and I cannot make head or tail of them—

"When modern science declared that the cosmic process knew nothing of a historical event corresponding to a Fall, but told, on the contrary, the story of an incessant rise in the scale of being, it was quite plain that the Pauline scheme—I mean the argumentative processes of Paul's scheme of salvation—had lost its very foundation; for was not that foundation the total depravity of the human race inherited from their first parents? ... But now there was no Fall; there was no total depravity, or imminent danger of endless doom; and, the basis gone, the superstructure followed."

It is written with earnestness and in excellent English; it must mean something. But what can it mean? How could physical science prove that man is not depraved? You do not cut a man open to find his sins. You do not boil him until he gives forth the unmistakable green fumes of depravity. How could physical science find any traces of a moral fall? What traces did the writer expect to find? Did he expect to find a fossil Eve with a fossil apple inside her? Did he suppose that the ages would have spared for him a complete skeleton of Adam attached to a slightly faded fig-leaf? The whole paragraph which I have quoted is simply a series of inconsequent sentences, all quite untrue in themselves and all quite irrelevant to each other. Science never said that there could have been no Fall. There might have been ten Falls, one on top of the other, and the thing would have been quite consistent with everything that we know from physical science. Humanity might have grown morally worse for millions of centuries, and the thing would in no way have contradicted the principle of Evolution. Men of science (not being raving lunatics) never said that there had been "an incessant rise in the scale of being;" for an incessant rise would mean a rise without any relapse or failure; and physical evolution is full of relapse and failure. There were certainly some physical Falls; there may have been any number of moral Falls. So that, as I have said, I am honestly bewildered as to the meaning of such passages as this, in which the advanced person writes that because geologists know nothing about the Fall, therefore any doctrine of depravity is untrue. Because science has not found something which obviously it could not find, therefore something entirely different—the psychological sense of evil—is untrue. You might sum up this writer's argument abruptly, but accurately, in some way like this—"We have not dug up the bones of the Archangel Gabriel, who presumably had none, therefore little boys, left to themselves, will not be selfish." To me it is all wild and whirling; as if a man said—"The plumber can find nothing wrong with our piano; so I suppose that my wife does love me."

I am not going to enter here into the real doctrine of original sin, or into that probably false version of it which the New Theology writer calls the doctrine of depravity. But whatever else the worst doctrine of depravity may have been, it was a product of spiritual conviction; it had nothing to do with remote physical origins. Men thought mankind wicked because they felt wicked themselves. If a man feels wicked, I cannot see why he should suddenly feel good because somebody tells him that his ancestors once had tails. Man's primary purity and innocence may have dropped off with his tail, for all anybody knows. The only thing we all know about that primary purity and innocence is that we have not got it. Nothing can be, in the strictest sense of the word, more comic than to set so shadowy a thing as the conjectures made by the vaguer anthropologists about primitive man against so solid a thing as the human sense of sin. By its nature the evidence of Eden is something that one cannot find. By its nature the evidence of sin is something that one cannot help finding.

Some statements I disagree with; others I do not understand. If a man says, "I think the human race would be better if it abstained totally from fermented liquor," I quite understand what he means, and how his view could be defended. If a man says, "I wish to abolish beer because I am a temperance man," his remark conveys no meaning to my mind. It is like saying, "I wish to abolish roads because I am a moderate walker." If a man says, "I am not a Trinitarian," I understand. But if he says (as a lady once said to me), "I believe in the Holy Ghost in a spiritual sense," I go away dazed. In what other sense could one believe in the Holy Ghost? And I am sorry to say that this pamphlet of progressive religious views is full of baffling observations of that kind. What can people mean when they say that science has disturbed their view of sin? What sort of view of sin can they have had before science disturbed it? Did they think that it was something to eat? When people say that science has shaken their faith in immortality, what do they mean? Did they think that immortality was a gas?

Of course the real truth is that science has introduced no new principle into the matter at all. A man can be a Christian to the end of the world, for the simple reason that a man could have been an Atheist from the beginning of it. The materialism of things is on the face of things; it does not require any science to find it out. A man who has lived and loved falls down dead and the worms eat him. That is Materialism if you like. That is Atheism if you like. If mankind has believed in spite of that, it can believe in spite of anything. But why our human lot is made any more hopeless because we know the names of all the worms who eat him, or the names of all the parts of him that they eat, is to a thoughtful mind somewhat difficult to discover. My chief objection to these semi-scientific revolutionists is that they are not at all revolutionary. They are the party of platitude. They do not shake religion: rather religion seems to shake them. They can only answer the great paradox by repeating the truism.

Chapter 23
The Methuselahite

I saw in a newspaper paragraph the other day the following entertaining and deeply philosophical incident. A man was enlisting as a soldier at Portsmouth, and some form was put before him to be filled up, common, I suppose, to all such cases, in which was, among other things, an inquiry about what was his religion. With an equal and ceremonial gravity the man wrote down the word "Methuselahite." Whoever looks over such papers must, I should imagine, have seen some rum religions in his time; unless the Army is going to the dogs. But with all his specialist knowledge he could not "place" Methuselahism among what Bossuet called the variations of Protestantism. He felt a fervid curiosity about the tenets and tendencies of the sect; and he asked the soldier what it meant. The soldier replied that it was his religion "to live as long as he could."

Now, considered as an incident in the religious history of Europe, that answer of that soldier was worth more than a hundred cartloads of quarterly and monthly and weekly and daily papers discussing religious problems and religious books. Every day the daily paper reviews some new philosopher who has some new religion; and there is not in the whole two thousand words of the whole two columns one word as witty as or wise as that word "Methuselahite." The whole meaning of literature is simply to cut a long story short; that is why our modern books of philosophy are never literature. That soldier had in him the very soul of literature; he was one of the great phrase-makers of modern thought, like Victor Hugo or Disraeli. He found one word that defines the paganism of to-day.

Henceforward, when the modern philosophers come to me with their new religions (and there is always a kind of queue of them waiting all the way down the street) I shall anticipate their circumlocutions and be able to cut them short with a single inspired word. One of them will begin, "The New Religion, which is based upon that Primordial Energy in Nature . . . " "Methuselahite," I shall say sharply; "good morning." "Human Life," another will say, "Human Life, the only ultimate sanctity, freed from creed and dogma . . . " "Methuselahite!" I shall yell. "Out you go!" "My religion is the Religion of Joy," a third will explain (a bald old man with a cough and tinted glasses), "the Religion of Physical Pride and Rapture, and my . . . " "Methuselahite!" I shall cry again, and I shall slap him boisterously on the back, and he will fall down. Then a pale young poet with serpentine hair will come and say to me (as one did only the other day): "Moods and impressions are the only realities, and these are constantly and wholly changing. I could hardly therefore define my religion . . . " "I can," I should say, somewhat sternly. "Your religion is to live a long time; and if you stop here a moment longer you won't fulfil it."

A new philosophy generally means in practice the praise of some old vice. We have had the sophist who defends cruelty, and calls it masculinity. We have had the sophist who defends profligacy, and calls it the liberty of the emotions. We have had the sophist who defends idleness, and calls it art. It will almost certainly happen—it can almost certainly be prophesied—that in this saturnalia of sophistry there will at some time or other arise a sophist who desires to idealise cowardice. And when we are once in this unhealthy world of mere wild words, what a vast deal there would be to say for cowardice! "Is not life a lovely thing and worth saving?" the soldier would say as he ran away. "Should I not prolong the exquisite miracle of consciousness?" the householder would say as he hid under the table. "As long as there are roses and lilies on the earth shall I not remain here?" would come the voice of the citizen from under the bed. It would be quite as easy to defend the coward as a kind of poet and mystic as it has been, in many recent books, to defend the emotionalist as a kind of poet and mystic, or the tyrant as a kind of poet and mystic. When that last grand sophistry and morbidity is preached in a book or on a platform, you may depend upon it there will be a great stir in its favour, that is, a great stir among the little people who live among books and platforms. There will be a new great Religion, the Religion of Methuselahism: with pomps and priests and altars. Its devout crusaders will vow themselves in thousands with a great vow to live long. But there is one comfort: they won't.

For, indeed, the weakness of this worship of mere natural life (which is a common enough creed to-day) is that it ignores the paradox of courage and fails in its own aim. As a matter of fact, no men would be killed quicker than the Methuselahites. The paradox of courage is that a man must be a little careless of his life even in order to keep it. And in the very case I have quoted we may see an example of how little the theory of Methuselahism really inspires our best life. For there is one riddle in that case which cannot easily be cleared up. If it was the man's religion to live as long as he could, why on earth was he enlisting as a soldier?

Chapter 24
Spiritualism

I have received a letter from a gentleman who is very indignant at what he considers my flippancy in disregarding or degrading Spiritualism. I thought I was defending Spiritualism; but I am rather used to being accused of mocking the thing that I set out to justify. My fate in most controversies is rather pathetic. It is an almost invariable rule that the man with whom I don't agree thinks I am making a fool of myself, and the man with whom I do agree thinks I am making a fool of him. There seems to be some sort of idea that you are not treating a subject properly if you eulogise it with fantastic terms or defend it by grotesque examples. Yet a truth is equally solemn whatever figure or example its exponent adopts. It is an equally awful truth that four and four make eight, whether you reckon the thing out in eight onions or eight angels, or eight bricks or eight bishops, or eight minor poets or eight pigs. Similarly, if it be true that God made all things, that grave fact can be asserted by pointing at a star or by waving an umbrella. But the case is stronger than this. There is a distinct philosophical advantage in using grotesque terms in a serious discussion.

I think seriously, on the whole, that the more serious is the discussion the more grotesque should be the terms. For this, as I say, there is an evident reason. For a subject is really solemn and important in so far as it applies to the whole cosmos, or to some great spheres and cycles of experience at least. So far as a thing is universal it is serious. And so far as a thing is universal it is full of comic things. If you take a small thing, it may be entirely serious: Napoleon, for instance, was a small thing, and he was serious: the same applies to microbes. If you isolate a thing, you may get the pure essence of gravity. But if you take a large thing (such as the Solar System) it *must* be comic, at least in parts. The germs are serious, because they kill you. But the stars are funny, because they give birth to life, and life gives birth to fun. If you have, let us say, a theory about man, and if you can only prove it by talking about Plato and George Washington, your theory may be a quite frivolous thing. But if you can prove it by talking about the butler or the postman, then it is serious, because it is universal. So far from it being irreverent to use silly metaphors on serious questions, it is one's duty to use silly metaphors on serious questions. It is the test of one's seriousness. It is the test of a responsible religion or theory whether it can take examples from pots and pans and boots and butter-tubs. It is the test of a good philosophy whether you can defend it grotesquely. It is the test of a good religion whether you can joke about it.

When I was a very young journalist I used to be irritated at a peculiar habit of printers, a habit which most persons of a tendency similar to mine have probably noticed also. It goes along with the fixed belief of printers that to be a Rationalist is the same thing as to be a Nationalist. I mean the printer's tendency to turn the word "cosmic" into the word "comic." It annoyed me at the time. But since then I have come to the conclusion that the printers were right. The democracy is always right. Whatever is cosmic is comic.

Moreover, there is another reason that makes it almost inevitable that we should defend grotesquely what we believe seriously. It is that all grotesqueness is itself intimately related to seriousness. Unless a thing is dignified, it cannot be undignified. Why is it funny that a man should sit down suddenly in the street? There is only one possible or intelligent reason: that man is the image of God. It is not funny that anything else should fall down; only that a man should fall down. No one sees anything funny in a tree falling down. No one sees a delicate absurdity in a stone falling down. No man stops in the road and roars with laughter at the sight of the snow coming down. The fall of thunderbolts is treated with some gravity. The fall of roofs and high buildings is taken seriously. It is only when a man tumbles down that we laugh. Why do we laugh? Because it is a grave religious matter: it is the Fall of Man. Only man can be absurd: for only man can be dignified.

The above, which occupies the great part of my article, is a parenthises. It is time that I returned to my choleric correspondent who rebuked me for being too frivolous about the problem of Spiritualism. My correspondent, who is evidently an intelligent man, is very angry with me indeed. He uses the strongest language. He says I remind him of a brother of his: which seems to open an abyss or vista of infamy. The main substance of his attack resolves itself into two propositions. First, he asks me what right I have to talk about Spiritualism at all, as I admit I have never been to a *séance*. This is all very well, but there are a good many things to which I have never been, but I have not the smallest intention of leaving off talking about them. I refuse (for instance) to leave off talking about the Siege of Troy. I decline to be mute in the matter of the French Revolution. I will not be silenced on the late indefensible assassination of Julius Cæsar. If nobody has any right to judge of Spiritualism except a man who has been to a *séance*, the results, logically speaking, are rather serious: it would almost seem as if nobody had any right to judge of Christianity who had not been to the first meeting at Pentecost. Which would be dreadful. I conceive myself capable of forming my opinion of Spiritualism without seeing spirits, just as I form my opinion of the Japanese War without seeing the Japanese, or my opinion of American millionaires without (thank God) seeing an American millionaire. Blessed are they who have not seen and yet have believed: a passage which some have considered as a prophecy of modern journalism.

But my correspondent's second objection is more important. He charges me with actually ignoring the value of communication (if it exists) between this world and the next. I do not ignore it. But I do say this—That a different principle attaches to investigation in this spiritual field from investigation in any other. If a man baits a line for fish, the fish will come, even if he declares there are no such things as fishes. If a man limes a twig for birds, the birds will be caught, even if he thinks it superstitious to believe in birds at all. But a man cannot bait a line for souls. A man cannot lime a twig to catch gods. All wise schools have agreed that this latter capture depends to some extent on the faith of the capturer. So it comes to this: If you have no faith in the spirits your appeal is in vain; and if you have—is it needed? If you do not believe, you cannot. If you do—you will not.

That is the real distinction between investigation in this department and investigation in any other. The priest calls to the goddess, for the same reason that a man calls to his wife, because he knows she is there. If a man kept on shouting out very loud the single word "Maria," merely with the object of discovering whether if he did it long enough some woman of that name would come and marry him, he would be more or less in the position of the modern spiritualist. The old religionist cried out for his God. The new religionist cries out for some god to be his. The whole point of religion as it has hitherto existed in the world was that you knew all about your gods, even before you saw them, if indeed you ever did. Spiritualism seems to me absolutely right on all its mystical side. The supernatural part of it seems to me quite natural. The incredible part of it seems to me obviously true. But I think it so far dangerous or unsatisfactory that it is in some degree scientific. It inquires whether its gods are worth inquiring into. A man (of a certain age) may look into the eyes of his lady-love to see that they are beautiful. But no normal lady will allow that young man to look into her eyes to see whether they are beautiful. The same vanity and idiosyncrasy has been generally observed in gods. Praise them; or leave them alone; but do not look for them unless you know they are there. Do not look for them unless you want them. It annoys them very much.

Chapter 25
The Error of Impartiality

he refusal of the jurors in the Thaw trial to come to an agreement is certainly a somewhat amusing sequel to the frenzied and even fantastic caution with which they were selected. Jurymen were set aside for reasons which seem to have only the very wildest relation to the case—reasons which we cannot conceive as giving any human being a real bias. It may be questioned whether the exaggerated theory of impartiality in an arbiter or juryman may not be carried so far as to be more unjust than partiality itself. What people call impartiality may simply mean indifference, and what people call partiality may simply mean mental activity. It is sometimes made an objection, for instance, to a juror that he has formed some *primâ-facie* opinion upon a case: if he can be forced under sharp questioning to admit that he has formed such an opinion, he is regarded as manifestly unfit to conduct the inquiry. Surely this is unsound. If his bias is one of interest, of class, or creed, or notorious propaganda, then that fact certainly proves that he is not an impartial arbiter. But the mere fact that he did form some temporary impression from the first facts as far as he knew them—this does not prove that he is not an impartial arbiter—it only proves that he is not a cold-blooded fool.

If we walk down the street, taking all the jurymen who have not formed opinions and leaving all the jurymen who have formed opinions, it seems highly probable that we shall only succeed in taking all the stupid jurymen and leaving all the thoughtful ones. Provided that the opinion formed is really of this airy and abstract kind, provided that it has no suggestion of settled motive or prejudice, we might well regard it not merely as a promise of capacity, but literally as a promise of justice. The man who took the trouble to deduce from the police reports would probably be the man who would take the trouble to deduce further and different things from the evidence. The man who had the sense to form an opinion would be the man who would have the sense to alter it.

It is worth while to dwell for a moment on this minor aspect of the matter because the error about impartiality and justice is by no means confined to a criminal question. In much more serious matters it is assumed that the agnostic is impartial; whereas the agnostic is merely ignorant. The logical outcome of the fastidiousness about the Thaw jurors would be that the case ought to be tried by Esquimaux, or Hottentots, or savages from the Cannibal Islands—by some class of people who could have no conceivable interest in the parties, and moreover, no conceivable interest in the case. The pure and starry perfection of impartiality would be reached by people who not only had no opinion before they had heard the case, but who also had no opinion after they had heard it. In the same way, there is in modern discussions of religion and philosophy an absurd assumption that a man is in some way just and well-poised because he has come to no conclusion; and that a man is in some way knocked off the list of fair judges because he has come to a conclusion. It is assumed that the sceptic has no bias; whereas he has a very obvious bias in favour of scepticism. I remember once arguing with an honest young atheist, who was very much shocked at my disputing some of the assumptions which were absolute sanctities to him (such as the quite unproved proposition of the independence of matter and the quite improbable proposition of its power to originate mind), and he at length fell back upon this question, which he delivered with an honourable heat of defiance and indignation: "Well, can you tell me any man of intellect, great in science or philosophy, who accepted the miraculous?" I said, "With pleasure. Descartes, Dr. Johnson, Newton, Faraday, Newman, Gladstone, Pasteur, Browning, Brunetiere— as many more as you please." To which that quite admirable and idealistic young man made this astonishing reply—"Oh, but of course they *had* to say that; they were Christians." First he challenged me to find a black swan, and then he ruled out all my swans because they were black. The fact that all these great intellects had come to the Christian view was somehow or other a proof either that they were not great intellects or that they had not really come to that view. The argument thus stood in a charmingly convenient form: "All men that count have come to my conclusion; for if they come to your conclusion they do not count."

It did not seem to occur to such controversialists that if Cardinal Newman was really a man of intellect, the fact that he adhered to dogmatic religion proved exactly as much as the fact that Professor Huxley, another man of intellect, found that he could not adhere to dogmatic religion; that is to say (as I cheerfully admit), it proved precious little either way. If there is one class of men whom history has proved especially and supremely capable of going quite wrong in all directions, it is the class of highly intellectual men. I would always prefer to go by the bulk of humanity; that is why I am a democrat. But whatever be the truth about exceptional intelligence and the masses, it is manifestly most unreasonable that intelligent men should be divided upon the absurd modern principle of regarding every clever man who cannot make up his mind as an impartial judge, and regarding every clever man who can make up his mind as a servile fanatic. As it is, we seem to regard it as a positive objection to a reasoner that he has taken one side or the other. We regard it (in other words) as a positive objection to a reasoner that he has contrived to reach the object of his reasoning. We call a man a bigot or a slave of dogma because he is a thinker who has thought thoroughly and to a definite end. We say that the juryman is not a juryman because he has brought in a verdict. We say that the judge is not a judge because he gives judgment. We say that the sincere believer has no right to vote, simply because he has voted.

Chapter 26
Phonetic Spelling

correspondent asks me to make more lucid my remarks about phonetic spelling. I have no detailed objection to items of spelling-reform; my objection is to a general principle; and it is this. It seems to me that what is really wrong with all modern and highly civilised language is that it does so largely consist of dead words. Half our speech consists of similes that remind us of no similarity; of pictorial phrases that call up no picture; of historical allusions the origin of which we have forgotten. Take any instance on which the eye happens to alight. I saw in the paper some days ago that the well-known leader of a certain religious party wrote to a supporter of his the following curious words: "I have not forgotten the talented way in which you held up the banner at Birkenhead." Taking the ordinary vague meaning of the word "talented," there is no coherency in the picture. The trumpets blow, the spears shake and glitter, and in the thick of the purple battle there stands a gentleman holding up a banner in a talented way. And when we come to the original force of the word "talent" the matter is worse: a talent is a Greek coin used in the New Testament as a symbol of the mental capital committed to an individual at birth. If the religious leader in question had really meant anything by his phrases, he would have been puzzled to know how a man could use a Greek coin to hold up a banner. But really he meant nothing by his phrases. "Holding up the banner" was to him a colourless term for doing the proper thing, and "talented" was a colourless term for doing it successfully.

Now my own fear touching anything in the way of phonetic spelling is that it would simply increase this tendency to use words as counters and not as coins. The original life in a word (as in the word "talent") burns low as it is: sensible spelling might extinguish it altogether. Suppose any sentence you like: suppose a man says, "Republics generally encourage holidays." It looks like the top line of a copy-book. Now, it is perfectly true that if you wrote that sentence exactly as it is pronounced, even by highly educated people, the sentence would run: "Ripubliks jenrally inkurrij hollidies." It looks ugly: but I have not the smallest objection to ugliness. My objection is that these four words have each a history and hidden treasures in them: that this history and hidden treasure (which we tend to forget too much as it is) phonetic spelling tends to make us forget altogether. Republic does not mean merely a mode of political choice. Republic (as we see when we look at the structure of the word) means the Public Thing: the abstraction which is us all.

A Republican is not a man who wants a Constitution with a President. A Republican is a man who prefers to think of Government as impersonal; he is opposed to the Royalist, who prefers to think of Government as personal. Take the second word, "generally." This is always used as meaning "in the majority of cases." But, again, if we look at the shape and spelling of the word, we shall see that "generally" means something more like "generically," and is akin to such words as "generation" or "regenerate." "Pigs are generally dirty" does not mean that pigs are, in the majority of cases, dirty, but that pigs as a race or genus are dirty, that pigs as pigs are dirty—an important philosophical distinction. Take the third word, "encourage." The word "encourage" is used in such modern sentences in the merely automatic sense of promote; to encourage poetry means merely to advance or assist poetry. But to encourage poetry means properly to put courage into poetry—a fine idea. Take the fourth word, "holidays." As long as that word remains, it will always answer the ignorant slander which asserts that religion was opposed to human cheerfulness; that word will always assert that when a day is holy it should also be happy. Properly spelt, these words all tell a sublime story, like Westminster Abbey. Phonetically spelt, they might lose the last traces of any such story. "Generally" is an exalted metaphysical term; "jenrally" is not. If you "encourage" a man, you pour into him the chivalry of a hundred princes; this does not happen if you merely "inkurrij" him. "Republics," if spelt phonetically, might actually forget to be public. "Holidays," if spelt phonetically, might actually forget to be holy.

Here is a case that has just occurred. A certain magistrate told somebody whom he was examining in court that he or she "should always be polite to the police." I do not know whether the magistrate noticed the circumstance, but the word "polite" and the word "police" have the same origin and meaning. Politeness means the atmosphere and ritual of the city, the symbol of human civilisation. The policeman means the representative and guardian of the city, the symbol of human civilisation. Yet it may be doubted whether the two ideas are commonly connected in the mind. It is probable that we often hear of politeness without thinking of a policeman; it is even possible that our eyes often alight upon a policeman without our thoughts instantly flying to the subject of politeness. Yet the idea of the sacred city is not only the link of them both, it is the only serious justification and the only serious corrective of them both. If politeness means too often a mere frippery, it is because it has not enough to do with serious patriotism and public dignity; if policemen are coarse or casual, it is because they are not sufficiently convinced that they are the servants of the beautiful city and the agents of sweetness and light. Politeness is not really a frippery. Politeness is not really even a thing merely suave and deprecating. Politeness is an armed guard, stern and splendid and vigilant, watching over all the ways of men; in other words, politeness is a policeman. A policeman is not merely a heavy man with a truncheon: a policeman is a machine for the smoothing and sweetening of the accidents of everyday existence. In other words, a policeman is politeness; a veiled image of politeness—sometimes impenetrably veiled. But my point is here that by losing the original idea of the city, which is the force and youth of both the words, both the things actually degenerate. Our politeness loses all manliness because we forget that politeness is only the Greek for patriotism. Our policemen lose all delicacy because we forget that a policeman is only the Greek for something civilised. A policeman should often have the functions of a knight-errant. A policeman should always have the elegance of a knight-errant. But I am not sure that he would succeed any the better in remembering this obligation of romantic grace if his name were spelt phonetically, supposing that it could be spelt phonetically. Some spelling-reformers, I am told, in the poorer parts of London do spell his name phonetically, very phonetically. They call him a "pleeceman." Thus the whole romance of the ancient city disappears from the word, and the policeman's reverent courtesy of demeanour deserts him quite suddenly. This does seem to me the case against any extreme revolution in spelling. If you spell a word wrong you have some temptation to think it wrong.

Chapter 27
Humanitarianism and Strength

omebody writes complaining of something I said about progress. I have forgotten what I said, but I am quite certain that it was (like a certain Mr. Douglas in a poem which I have also forgotten) tender and true. In any case, what I say now is this. Human history is so rich and complicated that you can make out a case for any course of improvement or retrogression. I could make out that the world has been growing more democratic, for the English franchise has certainly grown more democratic. I could also make out that the world has been growing more aristocratic, for the English Public Schools have certainly grown more aristocratic. I could prove the decline of militarism by the decline of flogging; I could prove the increase of militarism by the increase of standing armies and conscription. But I can prove anything in this way. I can prove that the world has always been growing greener. Only lately men have invented absinthe and the *Westminster Gazette*. I could prove the world has grown less green. There are no more Robin Hood foresters, and fields are being covered with houses. I could show that the world was less red with khaki or more red with the new penny stamps. But in all cases progress means progress only in some particular thing. Have you ever noticed that strange line of Tennyson, in which he confesses, half consciously, how very *conventional* progress is?—

"Let the great world spin for ever down the ringing grooves of change."

Even in praising change, he takes for a simile the most unchanging thing. He calls our modern change a groove. And it is a groove; perhaps there was never anything so groovy.

Nothing would induce me in so idle a monologue as this to discuss adequately a great political matter like the question of the military punishments in Egypt. But I may suggest one broad reality to be observed by both sides, and which is, generally speaking, observed by neither. Whatever else is right, it is utterly wrong to employ the argument that we Europeans must do to savages and Asiatics whatever savages and Asiatics do to us. I have even seen some controversialists use the metaphor, "We must fight them with their own weapons." Very well; let those controversialists take their metaphor, and take it literally. Let us fight the Soudanese with their own weapons. Their own weapons are large, very clumsy knives, with an occasional old-fashioned gun. Their own weapons are also torture and slavery. If we fight them with torture and slavery, we shall be fighting badly, precisely as if we fought them with clumsy knives and old guns. That is the whole strength of our Christian civilisation, that it does fight with its own weapons and not with other people's. It is not true that superiority suggests a tit for tat. It is not true that if a small hooligan puts his tongue out at the Lord Chief Justice, the Lord Chief Justice immediately realises that his only chance of maintaining his position is to put his tongue out at the little hooligan. The hooligan may or may not have any respect at all for the Lord Chief Justice: that is a matter which we may contentedly leave as a solemn psychological mystery. But if the hooligan has any respect at all for the Lord Chief Justice, that respect is certainly extended to the Lord Chief Justice entirely because he does not put his tongue out.

Exactly in the same way the ruder or more sluggish races regard the civilisation of Christendom. If they have any respect for it, it is precisely because it does not use their own coarse and cruel expedients. According to some modern moralists whenever Zulus cut off the heads of dead Englishmen, Englishmen must cut off the heads of dead Zulus. Whenever Arabs or Egyptians constantly use the whip to their slaves, Englishmen must use the whip to their subjects. And on a similar principle (I suppose), whenever an English Admiral has to fight cannibals the English Admiral ought to eat them. However unattractive a menu consisting entirely of barbaric kings may appear to an English gentleman, he must try to sit down to it with an appetite. He must fight the Sandwich Islanders with their own weapons; and their own weapons are knives and forks. But the truth of the matter is, of course, that to do this kind of thing is to break the whole spell of our supremacy. All the mystery of the white man, all the fearful poetry of the white man, so far as it exists in the eyes of these savages, consists in the fact that we do not do such things. The Zulus point at us and say, "Observe the advent of these inexplicable demi-gods, these magicians, who do not cut off the noses of their enemies." The Soudanese say to each other, "This hardy people never flogs its servants; it is superior to the simplest and most obvious human pleasures." And the cannibals say, "The austere and terrible race, the race that denies itself even boiled missionary, is upon us: let us flee."

Whether or no these details are a little conjectural, the general proposition I suggest is the plainest common sense. The elements that make Europe upon the whole the most humanitarian civilisation are precisely the elements that make it upon the whole the strongest. For the power which makes a man able to entertain a good impulse is the same as that which enables him to make a good gun; it is imagination. It is imagination that makes a man outwit his enemy, and it is imagination that makes him spare his enemy. It is precisely because this picturing of the other man's point of view is in the main a thing in which Christians and Europeans specialise that Christians and Europeans, with all their faults, have carried to such perfection both the arts of peace and war.

They alone have invented machine-guns, and they alone have invented ambulances; they have invented ambulances (strange as it may sound) for the same reason for which they have invented machine-guns. Both involve a vivid calculation of remote events. It is precisely because the East, with all its wisdom, is cruel, that the East, with all its wisdom, is weak. And it is precisely because savages are pitiless that they are still—merely savages. If they could imagine their enemy's sufferings they could also imagine his tactics. If Zulus did not cut off the Englishman's head they might really borrow it. For if you do not understand a man you cannot crush him. And if you do understand him, very probably you will not.

When I was about seven years old I used to think that the chief modern danger was a danger of over-civilisation. I am inclined to think now that the chief modern danger is that of a slow return towards barbarism, just such a return towards barbarism as is indicated in the suggestions of barbaric retaliation of which I have just spoken. Civilisation in the best sense merely means the full authority of the human spirit over all externals. Barbarism means the worship of those externals in their crude and unconquered state. Barbarism means the worship of Nature; and in recent poetry, science, and philosophy there has been too much of the worship of Nature. Wherever men begin to talk much and with great solemnity about the forces outside man, the note of it is barbaric. When men talk much about heredity and environment they are almost barbarians. The modern men of science are many of them almost barbarians. Mr. Blatchford is in great danger of becoming a barbarian. For barbarians (especially the truly squalid and unhappy barbarians) are always talking about these scientific subjects from morning till night. That is why they remain squalid and unhappy; that is why they remain barbarians. Hottentots are always talking about heredity, like Mr. Blatchford. Sandwich Islanders are always talking about environment, like Mr. Suthers. Savages—those that are truly stunted or depraved—dedicate nearly all their tales and sayings to the subject of physical kinship, of a curse on this or that tribe, of a taint in this or that family, of the invincible law of blood, of the unavoidable evil of places. The true savage is a slave, and is always talking about what he must do; the true civilised man is a free man and is always talking about what he may do. Hence all the Zola heredity and Ibsen heredity that has been written in our time affects me as not merely evil, but as essentially ignorant and retrogressive. This sort of science is almost the only thing that can with strict propriety be called reactionary. Scientific determinism is simply the primal twilight of all mankind; and some men seem to be returning to it.

Another savage trait of our time is the disposition to talk about material substances instead of about ideas. The old civilisation talked about the sin of gluttony or excess. We talk about the Problem of Drink—as if drink could be a problem. When people have come to call the problem of human intemperance the Problem of Drink, and to talk about curing it by attacking the drink traffic, they have reached quite a dim stage of barbarism. The thing is an inverted form of fetish worship; it is no sillier to say that a bottle is a god than to say that a bottle is a devil. The people who talk about the curse of drink will probably progress down that dark hill. In a little while we shall have them calling the practice of wife-beating the Problem of Pokers; the habit of housebreaking will be called the Problem of the Skeleton-Key Trade; and for all I know they may try to prevent forgery by shutting up all the stationers' shops by Act of Parliament.

I cannot help thinking that there is some shadow of this uncivilised materialism lying at present upon a much more dignified and valuable cause. Every one is talking just now about the desirability of ingeminating peace and averting war. But even war and peace are physical states rather than moral states, and in talking about them only we have by no means got to the bottom of the matter. How, for instance, do we as a matter of fact create peace in one single community? We do not do it by vaguely telling every one to avoid fighting and to submit to anything that is done to him. We do it by definitely defining his rights and then undertaking to avenge his wrongs. We shall never have a common peace in Europe till we have a common principle in Europe. People talk of "The United States of Europe;" but they forget that it needed the very doctrinal "Declaration of Independence" to make the United States of America. You cannot agree about nothing any more than you can quarrel about nothing.

Chapter 28
Wine when it is Red

 suppose that there will be some wigs on the green in connection with the recent manifesto signed by a string of very eminent doctors on the subject of what is called "alcohol." "Alcohol" is, to judge by the sound of it, an Arabic word, like "algebra" and "Alhambra," those two other unpleasant things. The Alhambra in Spain I have never seen; I am told that it is a low and rambling building; I allude to the far more dignified erection in Leicester Square. If it is true, as I surmise, that "alcohol" is a word of the Arabs, it is interesting to realise that our general word for the essence of wine and beer and such things comes from a people which has made particular war upon them. I suppose that some aged Moslem chieftain sat one day at the opening of his tent and, brooding with black brows and cursing in his black beard over wine as the symbol of Christianity, racked his brains for some word ugly enough to express his racial and religious antipathy, and suddenly spat out the horrible word "alcohol." The fact that the doctors had to use this word for the sake of scientific clearness was really a great disadvantage to them in fairly discussing the matter. For the word really involves one of those beggings of the question which make these moral matters so difficult. It is quite a mistake to suppose that, when a man desires an alcoholic drink, he necessarily desires alcohol.

Let a man walk ten miles steadily on a hot summer's day along a dusty English road, and he will soon discover why beer was invented. The fact that beer has a very slight stimulating quality will be quite among the smallest reasons that induce him to ask for it. In short, he will not be in the least desiring alcohol; he will be desiring beer. But, of course, the question cannot be settled in such a simple way. The real difficulty which confronts everybody, and which especially confronts doctors, is that the extraordinary position of man in the physical universe makes it practically impossible to treat him in either one direction or the other in a purely physical way. Man is an exception, whatever else he is. If he is not the image of God, then he is a disease of the dust. If it is not true that a divine being fell, then we can only say that one of the animals went entirely off its head. In neither case can we really argue very much from the body of man simply considered as the body of an innocent and healthy animal. His body has got too much mixed up with his soul, as we see in the supreme instance of sex. It may be worth while uttering the warning to wealthy philanthropists and idealists that this argument from the animal should not be thoughtlessly used, even against the atrocious evils of excess; it is an argument that proves too little or too much.

Doubtless, it is unnatural to be drunk. But then in a real sense it is unnatural to be human. Doubtless, the intemperate workman wastes his tissues in drinking; but no one knows how much the sober workman wastes his tissues by working. No one knows how much the wealthy philanthropist wastes his tissues by talking; or, in much rarer conditions, by thinking. All the human things are more dangerous than anything that affects the beasts—sex, poetry, property, religion. The real case against drunkenness is not that it calls up the beast, but that it calls up the Devil. It does not call up the beast, and if it did it would not matter much, as a rule; the beast is a harmless and rather amiable creature, as anybody can see by watching cattle. There is nothing bestial about intoxication; and certainly there is nothing intoxicating or even particularly lively about beasts. Man is always something worse or something better than an animal; and a mere argument from animal perfection never touches him at all. Thus, in sex no animal is either chivalrous or obscene. And thus no animal ever invented anything so bad as drunkenness—or so good as drink.

The pronouncement of these particular doctors is very clear and uncompromising; in the modern atmosphere, indeed, it even deserves some credit for moral courage. The majority of modern people, of course, will probably agree with it in so far as it declares that alcoholic drinks are often of supreme value in emergencies of illness; but many people, I fear, will open their eyes at the emphatic terms in which they describe such drink as considered as a beverage; but they are not content with declaring that the drink is in moderation harmless: they distinctly declare that it is in moderation beneficial. But I fancy that, in saying this, the doctors had in mind a truth that runs somewhat counter to the common opinion. I fancy that it is the experience of most doctors that giving any alcohol for illness (though often necessary) is about the most morally dangerous way of giving it. Instead of giving it to a healthy person who has many other forms of life, you are giving it to a desperate person, to whom it is the only form of life. The invalid can hardly be blamed if by some accident of his erratic and overwrought condition he comes to remember the thing as the very water of vitality and to use it as such. For in so far as drinking is really a sin it is not because drinking is wild, but because drinking is tame; not in so far as it is anarchy, but in so far as it is slavery. Probably the worst way to drink is to drink medicinally. Certainly the safest way to drink is to drink carelessly; that is, without caring much for anything, and especially not caring for the drink.

The doctor, of course, ought to be able to do a great deal in the way of restraining those individual cases where there is plainly an evil thirst; and beyond that the only hope would seem to be in some increase, or, rather, some concentration of ordinary public opinion on the subject. I have always held consistently my own modest theory on the subject. I believe that if by some method the local public-house could be as definite and isolated a place as the local post-office or the local railway station, if all types of people passed through it for all types of refreshment, you would have the same safeguard against a man behaving in a disgusting way in a tavern that you have at present against his behaving in a disgusting way in a post-office: simply the presence of his ordinary sensible neighbours. In such a place the kind of lunatic who wants to drink an unlimited number of whiskies would be treated with the same severity with which the post office authorities would treat an amiable lunatic who had an appetite for licking an unlimited number of stamps. It is a small matter whether in either case a technical refusal would be officially employed. It is an essential matter that in both cases the authorities could rapidly communicate with the friends and family of the mentally afflicted person. At least, the postmistress would not dangle a strip of tempting sixpenny stamps before the enthusiast's eyes as he was being dragged away with his tongue out. If we made drinking open and official we might be taking one step towards making it careless. In such things to be careless is to be sane: for neither drunkards nor Moslems can be careless about drink.

Chapter 29
Demagogues and Mystagogues

 once heard a man call this age the age of demagogues. Of this I can only say, in the admirably sensible words of the angry coachman in "Pickwick," that "that remark's political, or what is much the same, it ain't true." So far from being the age of demagogues, this is really and specially the age of mystagogues. So far from this being a time in which things are praised because they are popular, the truth is that this is the first time, perhaps, in the whole history of the world in which things can be praised because they are unpopular. The demagogue succeeds because he makes himself understood, even if he is not worth understanding. But the mystagogue succeeds because he gets himself misunderstood; although, as a rule, he is not even worth misunderstanding. Gladstone was a demagogue: Disraeli a mystagogue. But ours is specially the time when a man can advertise his wares not as a universality, but as what the tradesmen call "a speciality." We all know this, for instance, about modern art. Michelangelo and Whistler were both fine artists; but one is obviously public, the other obviously private, or, rather, not obvious at all. Michelangelo's frescoes are doubtless finer than the popular judgment, but they are plainly meant to strike the popular judgment. Whistler's pictures seem often meant to escape the popular judgment; they even seem meant to escape the popular admiration. They are elusive, fugitive; they fly even from praise. Doubtless many artists in Michelangelo's day declared themselves to be great artists, although they were unsuccessful. But they did not declare themselves great artists because they were unsuccessful: that is the peculiarity of our own time, which has a positive bias against the populace.

Another case of the same kind of thing can be found in the latest conceptions of humour. By the wholesome tradition of mankind, a joke was a thing meant to amuse men; a joke which did not amuse them was a failure, just as a fire which did not warm them was a failure. But we have seen the process of secrecy and aristocracy introduced even into jokes. If a joke falls flat, a small school of æsthetes only ask us to notice the wild grace of its falling and its perfect flatness after its fall. The old idea that the joke was not good enough for the company has been superseded by the new aristocratic idea that the company was not worthy of the joke. They have introduced an almost insane individualism into that one form of intercourse which is specially and uproariously communal. They have made even levities into secrets. They have made laughter lonelier than tears.

There is a third thing to which the mystagogues have recently been applying the methods of a secret society: I mean manners. Men who sought to rebuke rudeness used to represent manners as reasonable and ordinary; now they seek to represent them as private and peculiar. Instead of saying to a man who blocks up a street or the fireplace, "You ought to know better than that," the moderns say, "You, of course, don't know better than that."

I have just been reading an amusing book by Lady Grove called "The Social Fetich," which is a positive riot of this new specialism and mystification. It is due to Lady Grove to say that she has some of the freer and more honourable qualities of the old Whig aristocracy, as well as their wonderful worldliness and their strange faith in the passing fashion of our politics. For instance, she speaks of Jingo Imperialism with a healthy English contempt; and she perceives stray and striking truths, and records them justly—as, for instance, the greater democracy of the Southern and Catholic countries of Europe. But in her dealings with social formulæ here in England she is, it must frankly be said, a common mystagogue. She does not, like a decent demagogue, wish to make people understand; she wishes to make them painfully conscious of not understanding. Her favourite method is to terrify people from doing things that are quite harmless by telling them that if they do they are the kind of people who would do other things, equally harmless. If you ask after somebody's mother (or whatever it is), you are the kind of person who would have a pillow-case, or would not have a pillow-case. I forget which it is; and so, I dare say, does she. If you assume the ordinary dignity of a decent citizen and say that you don't see the harm of having a mother or a pillow-case, she would say that of course *you* wouldn't. This is what I call being a mystagogue. It is more vulgar than being a demagogue; because it is much easier.

The primary point I meant to emphasise is that this sort of aristocracy is essentially a new sort. All the old despots were demagogues; at least, they were demagogues whenever they were really trying to please or impress the demos. If they poured out beer for their vassals it was because both they and their vassals had a taste for beer. If (in some slightly different mood) they poured melted lead on their vassals, it was because both they and their vassals had a strong distaste for melted lead. But they did not make any mystery about either of the two substances. They did not say, "You don't like melted lead? ... Ah! no, of course, *you* wouldn't; you are probably the kind of person who would prefer beer ... It is no good asking you even to imagine the curious undercurrent of psychological pleasure felt by a refined person under the seeming shock of melted lead." Even tyrants when they tried to be popular, tried to give the people pleasure; they did not try to overawe the people by giving them something which they ought to regard as pleasure. It was the same with the popular presentment of aristocracy. Aristocrats tried to impress humanity by the exhibition of qualities which humanity admires, such as courage, gaiety, or even mere splendour. The aristocracy might have more possession in these things, but the democracy had quite equal delight in them. It was much more sensible to offer yourself for admiration because you had drunk three bottles of port at a sitting, than to offer yourself for admiration (as Lady Grove does) because you think it right to say "port wine" while other people think it right to say "port." Whether Lady Grove's preference for port wine (I mean for the phrase port wine) is a piece of mere nonsense I do not know; but at least it is a very good example of the futility of such tests in the matter even of mere breeding. "Port wine" may happen to be the phrase used in certain good families; but numberless aristocrats say "port," and all barmaids say "port wine." The whole thing is rather more trivial than collecting tram-tickets; and I will not pursue Lady Grove's further distinctions. I pass over the interesting theory that I ought to say to Jones (even apparently if he is my dearest friend), "How is Mrs. Jones?" instead of "How is your wife?" and I pass over an impassioned declamation about bedspreads (I think) which has failed to fire my blood.

The truth of the matter is really quite simple. An aristocracy is a secret society; and this is especially so when, as in the modern world, it is practically a plutocracy. The one idea of a secret society is to change the password. Lady Grove falls naturally into a pure perversity because she feels subconsciously that the people of England can be more effectively kept at a distance by a perpetual torrent of new tests than by the persistence of a few old ones. She knows that in the educated "middle class" there is an idea that it is vulgar to say port wine; therefore she reverses the idea—she says that the man who would say "port" is a man who would say, "How is your wife?" She says it because she knows both these remarks to be quite obvious and reasonable.

The only thing to be done or said in reply, I suppose, would be to apply the same principle of bold mystification on our own part. I do not see why I should not write a book called "Etiquette in Fleet Street," and terrify every one else out of that thoroughfare by mysterious allusions to the mistakes that they generally make. I might say: "This is the kind of man who would wear a green tie when he went into a tobacconist's," or "You don't see anything wrong in drinking a Benedictine on Thursday? . . . No, of course *you* wouldn't." I might asseverate with passionate disgust and disdain: "The man who is capable of writing sonnets as well as triolets is capable of climbing an omnibus while holding an umbrella." It seems a simple method; if ever I should master it perhaps I may govern England.

Chapter 30
The ``Eatanswill Gazette''

he other day some one presented me with a paper called the *Eatanswill Gazette*. I need hardly say that I could not have been more startled if I had seen a coach coming down the road with old Mr. Tony Weller on the box. But, indeed, the case is much more extraordinary than that would be. Old Mr. Weller was a good man, a specially and seriously good man, a proud father, a very patient husband, a sane moralist, and a reliable ally. One could not be so very much surprised if somebody pretended to be Tony Weller. But the *Eatanswill Gazette* is definitely depicted in "Pickwick" as a dirty and unscrupulous rag, soaked with slander and nonsense. It was really interesting to find a modern paper proud to take its name. The case cannot be compared to anything so simple as a resurrection of one of the "Pickwick" characters; yet a very good parallel could easily be found. It is almost exactly as if a firm of solicitors were to open their offices to-morrow under the name of Dodson and Fogg.

It was at once apparent, of course, that the thing was a joke. But what was not apparent, what only grew upon the mind with gradual wonder and terror, was the fact that it had its serious side. The paper is published in the well-known town of Sudbury, in Suffolk. And it seems that there is a standing quarrel between Sudbury and the county town of Ipswich as to which was the town described by Dickens in his celebrated sketch of an election. Each town proclaims with passion that it was Eatanswill. If each town proclaimed with passion that it was not Eatanswill, I might be able to understand it. Eatanswill, according to Dickens, was a town alive with loathsome corruption, hypocritical in all its public utterances, and venal in all its votes. Yet, two highly respectable towns compete for the honour of having been this particular cesspool, just as ten cities fought to be the birthplace of Homer. They claim to be its original as keenly as if they were claiming to be the original of More's "Utopia" or Morris's "Earthly Paradise." They grow seriously heated over the matter. The men of Ipswich say warmly, "It must have been our town; for Dickens says it was corrupt, and a more corrupt town than our town you couldn't have met in a month." The men of Sudbury reply with rising passion, "Permit us to tell you, gentlemen, that our town was quite as corrupt as your town any day of the week. Our town was a common nuisance; and we defy our enemies to question it." "Perhaps you will tell us," sneer the citizens of Ipswich, "that your politics were ever as thoroughly filthy as—— " "As filthy as anything," answer the Sudbury men, undauntedly. "Nothing in politics could be filthier. Dickens must have noticed how disgusting we were." "And could he have failed to notice," the others reason indignantly, "how disgusting we were? You could smell us a mile off. You Sudbury fellows may think yourselves very fine, but let me tell you that, compared to our city, Sudbury was an honest place." And so the controversy goes on. It seems to me to be a new and odd kind of controversy.

Naturally, an outsider feels inclined to ask why Eatanswill should be either one or the other. As a matter of fact, I fear Eatanswill was every town in the country. It is surely clear that when Dickens described the Eatanswill election he did not mean it as a satire on Sudbury or a satire on Ipswich; he meant it as a satire on England. The Eatanswill election is not a joke against Eatanswill; it is a joke against elections. If the satire is merely local, it practically loses its point; just as the "Circumlocution Office" would lose its point if it were not supposed to be a true sketch of all Government offices; just as the Lord Chancellor in "Bleak House" would lose his point if he were not supposed to be symbolic and representative of all Lord Chancellors. The whole moral meaning would vanish if we supposed that Oliver Twist had got by accident into an exceptionally bad workhouse, or that Mr. Dorrit was in the only debtors' prison that was not well managed. Dickens was making game, not of places, but of methods. He poured all his powerful genius into trying to make the people ashamed of the methods. But he seems only to have succeeded in making people proud of the places. In any case, the controversy is conducted in a truly extraordinary way. No one seems to allow for the fact that, after all, Dickens was writing a novel, and a highly fantastic novel at that. Facts in support of Sudbury or Ipswich are quoted not only from the story itself, which is wild and wandering enough, but even from the yet wilder narratives which incidentally occur in the story, such as Sam Weller's description of how his father, on the way to Eatanswill, tipped all the voters into the canal. This may quite easily be (to begin with) an entertaining tarradiddle of Sam's own invention, told, like many other even more improbable stories, solely to amuse Mr. Pickwick. Yet the champions of these two towns positively ask each other to produce a canal, or to fail for ever in their attempt to prove themselves the most corrupt town in England. As far as I remember, Sam's story of the canal ends with Mr. Pickwick eagerly asking whether everybody was rescued, and Sam solemnly replying that one old gentleman's hat was found, but that he was not sure whether his head was in it. If the canal is to be taken as realistic, why not the hat and the head? If these critics ever find the canal I recommend them to drag it for the body of the old gentleman.

Both sides refuse to allow for the fact that the characters in the story are comic characters. For instance, Mr. Percy Fitzgerald, the eminent student of Dickens, writes to the *Eatanswill Gazette* to say that Sudbury, a small town, could not have been Eatanswill, because one of the candidates speaks of its great manufactures. But obviously one of the candidates would have spoken of its great manufactures if it had had nothing but a row of apple-stalls. One of the candidates might have said that the commerce of Eatanswill eclipsed Carthage, and covered every sea; it would have been quite in the style of Dickens. But when the champion of Sudbury answers him, he does not point out this plain mistake. He answers by making another mistake exactly of the same kind. He says that Eatanswill was not a busy, important place. And his odd reason is that Mrs. Pott said she was dull there. But obviously Mrs. Pott would have said she was dull anywhere. She was setting her cap at Mr. Winkle. Moreover, it was the whole point of her character in any case. Mrs. Pott was that kind of woman. If she had been in Ipswich she would have said that she ought to be in London. If she was in London she would have said that she ought to be in Paris. The first disputant proves Eatanswill grand because a servile candidate calls it grand. The second proves it dull because a discontented woman calls it dull.

The great part of the controversy seems to be conducted in the spirit of highly irrelevant realism. Sudbury cannot be Eatanswill, because there was a fancy-dress shop at Eatanswill, and there is no record of a fancy-dress shop at Sudbury. Sudbury must be Eatanswill because there were heavy roads outside Eatanswill, and there are heavy roads outside Sudbury. Ipswich cannot be Eatanswill, because Mrs. Leo Hunter's country seat would not be near a big town. Ipswich must be Eatanswill because Mrs. Leo Hunter's country seat would be near a large town. Really, Dickens might have been allowed to take liberties with such things as these, even if he had been mentioning the place by name. If I were writing a story about the town of Limerick, I should take the liberty of introducing a bun-shop without taking a journey to Limerick to see whether there was a bun-shop there. If I wrote a romance about Torquay, I should hold myself free to introduce a house with a green door without having studied a list of all the coloured doors in the town. But if, in order to make it particularly obvious that I had not meant the town for a photograph either of Torquay or Limerick, I had gone out of my way to give the place a wild, fictitious name of my own, I think that in that case I should be justified in tearing my hair with rage if the people of Limerick or Torquay began to argue about bun-shops and green doors. No reasonable man would expect Dickens to be so literal as all that even about Bath or Bury St. Edmunds, which do exist; far less need he be literal about Eatanswill, which didn't exist.

I must confess, however, that I incline to the Sudbury side of the argument. This does not only arise from the sympathy which all healthy people have for small places as against big ones; it arises from some really good qualities in this particular Sudbury publication. First of all, the champions of Sudbury seem to be more open to the sensible and humorous view of the book than the champions of Ipswich—at least, those that appear in this discussion. Even the Sudbury champion, bent on finding realistic clothes, rebels (to his eternal honour) when Mr. Percy Fitzgerald tries to show that Bob Sawyer's famous statement that he was neither Buff nor Blue, "but a sort of plaid," must have been copied from some silly man at Ipswich who said that his politics were "half and half." Anybody might have made either of the two jokes. But it was the whole glory and meaning of Dickens that he confined himself to making jokes that anybody might have made a little better than anybody would have made them.

Chapter 31
Fairy Tales

ome solemn and superficial people (for nearly all very superficial people are solemn) have declared that the fairy-tales are immoral; they base this upon some accidental circumstances or regrettable incidents in the war between giants and boys, some cases in which the latter indulged in unsympathetic deceptions or even in practical jokes. The objection, however, is not only false, but very much the reverse of the facts. The fairy-tales are at root not only moral in the sense of being innocent, but moral in the sense of being didactic, moral in the sense of being moralising. It is all very well to talk of the freedom of fairyland, but there was precious little freedom in fairyland by the best official accounts. Mr. W.B. Yeats and other sensitive modern souls, feeling that modern life is about as black a slavery as ever oppressed mankind (they are right enough there), have especially described elfland as a place of utter ease and abandonment—a place where the soul can turn every way at will like the wind. Science denounces the idea of a capricious God; but Mr. Yeats's school suggests that in that world every one is a capricious god. Mr. Yeats himself has said a hundred times in that sad and splendid literary style which makes him the first of all poets now writing in English (I will not say of all English poets, for Irishmen are familiar with the practice of physical assault), he has, I say, called up a hundred times the picture of the terrible freedom of the fairies, who typify the ultimate anarchy of art—

"Where nobody grows old or weary or wise,
Where nobody grows old or godly or grave."

But, after all (it is a shocking thing to say), I doubt whether Mr. Yeats really knows the real philosophy of the fairies. He is not simple enough; he is not stupid enough. Though I say it who should not, in good sound human stupidity I would knock Mr. Yeats out any day. The fairies like me better than Mr. Yeats; they can take me in more. And I have my doubts whether this feeling of the free, wild spirits on the crest of hill or wave is really the central and simple spirit of folk-lore. I think the poets have made a mistake: because the world of the fairy-tales is a brighter and more varied world than ours, they have fancied it less moral; really it is brighter and more varied because it is more moral. Suppose a man could be born in a modern prison. It is impossible, of course, because nothing human can happen in a modern prison, though it could sometimes in an ancient dungeon. A modern prison is always inhuman, even when it is not inhumane. But suppose a man were born in a modern prison, and grew accustomed to the deadly silence and the disgusting indifference; and suppose he were then suddenly turned loose upon the life and laughter of Fleet Street. He would, of course, think that the literary men in Fleet Street were a free and happy race; yet how sadly, how ironically, is this the reverse of the case! And so again these toiling serfs in Fleet Street, when they catch a glimpse of the fairies, think the fairies are utterly free. But fairies are like journalists in this and many other respects. Fairies and journalists have an apparent gaiety and a delusive beauty. Fairies and journalists seem to be lovely and lawless; they seem to be both of them too exquisite to descend to the ugliness of everyday duty. But it is an illusion created by the sudden sweetness of their presence. Journalists live under law; and so in fact does fairyland.

If you really read the fairy-tales, you will observe that one idea runs from one end of them to the other—the idea that peace and happiness can only exist on some condition. This idea, which is the core of ethics, is the core of the nursery-tales. The whole happiness of fairyland hangs upon a thread, upon one thread. Cinderella may have a dress woven on supernatural looms and blazing with unearthly brilliance; but she must be back when the clock strikes twelve. The king may invite fairies to the christening, but he must invite all the fairies or frightful results will follow. Bluebeard's wife may open all doors but one. A promise is broken to a cat, and the whole world goes wrong. A promise is broken to a yellow dwarf, and the whole world goes wrong. A girl may be the bride of the God of Love himself if she never tries to see him; she sees him, and he vanishes away. A girl is given a box on condition she does not open it; she opens it, and all the evils of this world rush out at her. A man and woman are put in a garden on condition that they do not eat one fruit: they eat it, and lose their joy in all the fruits of the earth.

This great idea, then, is the backbone of all folk-lore—the idea that all happiness hangs on one thin veto; all positive joy depends on one negative. Now, it is obvious that there are many philosophical and religious ideas akin to or symbolised by this; but it is not with them I wish to deal here. It is surely obvious that all ethics ought to be taught to this fairy-tale tune; that, if one does the thing forbidden, one imperils all the things provided. A man who breaks his promise to his wife ought to be reminded that, even if she is a cat, the case of the fairy-cat shows that such conduct may be incautious. A burglar just about to open some one else's safe should be playfully reminded that he is in the perilous posture of the beautiful Pandora: he is about to lift the forbidden lid and loosen evils unknown. The boy eating some one's apples in some one's apple tree should be a reminder that he has come to a mystical moment of his life, when one apple may rob him of all others. This is the profound morality of fairy-tales; which, so far from being lawless, go to the root of all law. Instead of finding (like common books of ethics) a rationalistic basis for each Commandment, they find the great mystical basis for all Commandments. We are in this fairyland on sufferance; it is not for us to quarrel with the conditions under which we enjoy this wild vision of the world. The vetoes are indeed extraordinary, but then so are the concessions. The idea of property, the idea of some one else's apples, is a rum idea; but then the idea of there being any apples is a rum idea. It is strange and weird that I cannot with safety drink ten bottles of champagne; but then the champagne itself is strange and weird, if you come to that. If I have drunk of the fairies' drink it is but just I should drink by the fairies' rules. We may not see the direct logical connection between three beautiful silver spoons and a large ugly policeman; but then who in fairy tales ever could see the direct logical connection between three bears and a giant, or between a rose and a roaring beast? Not only can these fairy-tales be enjoyed because they are moral, but morality can be enjoyed because it puts us in fairyland, in a world at once of wonder and of war.

Chapter 32
Tom Jones and Morality

he two hundredth anniversary of Henry Fielding is very justly celebrated, even if, as far as can be discovered, it is only celebrated by the newspapers. It would be too much to expect that any such merely chronological incident should induce the people who write about Fielding to read him; this kind of neglect is only another name for glory. A great classic means a man whom one can praise without having read. This is not in itself wholly unjust; it merely implies a certain respect for the realisation and fixed conclusions of the mass of mankind. I have never read Pindar (I mean I have never read the Greek Pindar; Peter Pindar I have read all right), but the mere fact that I have not read Pindar, I think, ought not to prevent me and certainly would not prevent me from talking of "the masterpieces of Pindar," or of "great poets like Pindar or Æschylus." The very learned men are angularly unenlightened on this as on many other subjects; and the position they take up is really quite unreasonable. If any ordinary journalist or man of general reading alludes to Villon or to Homer, they consider it a quite triumphant sneer to say to the man, "You cannot read mediæval French," or "You cannot read Homeric Greek." But it is not a triumphant sneer—or, indeed, a sneer at all. A man has got as much right to employ in his speech the established and traditional facts of human history as he has to employ any other piece of common human information. And it is as reasonable for a man who knows no French to assume that Villon was a good poet as it would be for a man who has no ear for music to assume that Beethoven was a good musician. Because he himself has no ear for music, that is no reason why he should assume that the human race has no ear for music. Because I am ignorant (as I am), it does not follow that I ought to assume that I am deceived. The man who would not praise Pindar unless he had read him would be a low, distrustful fellow, the worst kind of sceptic, who doubts not only God, but man. He would be like a man who could not call Mount Everest high unless he had climbed it. He would be like a man who would not admit that the North Pole was cold until he had been there.

But I think there is a limit, and a highly legitimate limit, to this process. I think a man may praise Pindar without knowing the top of a Greek letter from the bottom. But I think that if a man is going to abuse Pindar, if he is going to denounce, refute, and utterly expose Pindar, if he is going to show Pindar up as the utter ignoramus and outrageous impostor that he is, then I think it will be just as well perhaps—I think, at any rate, it would do no harm—if he did know a little Greek, and even had read a little Pindar. And I think the same situation would be involved if the critic were concerned to point out that Pindar was scandalously immoral, pestilently cynical, or low and beastly in his views of life. When people brought such attacks against the morality of Pindar, I should regret that they could not read Greek; and when they bring such attacks against the morality of Fielding, I regret very much that they cannot read English.

There seems to be an extraordinary idea abroad that Fielding was in some way an immoral or offensive writer. I have been astounded by the number of the leading articles, literary articles, and other articles written about him just now in which there is a curious tone of apologising for the man. One critic says that after all he couldn't help it, because he lived in the eighteenth century; another says that we must allow for the change of manners and ideas; another says that he was not altogether without generous and humane feelings; another suggests that he clung feebly, after all, to a few of the less important virtues. What on earth does all this mean? Fielding described Tom Jones as going on in a certain way, in which, most unfortunately, a very large number of young men do go on. It is unnecessary to say that Henry Fielding knew that it was an unfortunate way of going on. Even Tom Jones knew that. He said in so many words that it was a very unfortunate way of going on; he said, one may almost say, that it had ruined his life; the passage is there for the benefit of any one who may take the trouble to read the book. There is ample evidence (though even this is of a mystical and indirect kind), there is ample evidence that Fielding probably thought that it was better to be Tom Jones than to be an utter coward and sneak. There is simply not one rag or thread or speck of evidence to show that Fielding thought that it was better to be Tom Jones than to be a good man. All that he is concerned with is the description of a definite and very real type of young man; the young man whose passions and whose selfish necessities sometimes seemed to be stronger than anything else in him.

The practical morality of Tom Jones is bad, though not so bad, *spiritually* speaking, as the practical morality of Arthur Pendennis or the practical morality of Pip, and certainly nothing like so bad as the profound practical immorality of Daniel Deronda. The practical morality of Tom Jones is bad; but I cannot see any proof that his theoretical morality was particularly bad. There is no need to tell the majority of modern young men even to live up to the theoretical ethics of Henry Fielding. They would suddenly spring into the stature of archangels if they lived up to the theoretic ethics of poor Tom Jones. Tom Jones is still alive, with all his good and all his evil; he is walking about the streets; we meet him every day. We meet with him, we drink with him, we smoke with him, we talk with him, we talk about him. The only difference is that we have no longer the intellectual courage to write about him. We split up the supreme and central human being, Tom Jones, into a number of separate aspects. We let Mr. J.M. Barrie write about him in his good moments, and make him out better than he is. We let Zola write about him in his bad moments, and make him out much worse than he is. We let Maeterlinck celebrate those moments of spiritual panic which he knows to be cowardly; we let Mr. Rudyard Kipling celebrate those moments of brutality which he knows to be far more cowardly. We let obscene writers write about the obscenities of this ordinary man. We let puritan writers write about the purities of this ordinary man. We look through one peephole that makes men out as devils, and we call it the new art. We look through another peephole that makes men out as angels, and we call it the New Theology. But if we pull down some dusty old books from the bookshelf, if we turn over some old mildewed leaves, and if in that obscurity and decay we find some faint traces of a tale about a complete man, such a man as is walking on the pavement outside, we suddenly pull a long face, and we call it the coarse morals of a bygone age.

The truth is that all these things mark a certain change in the general view of morals; not, I think, a change for the better. We have grown to associate morality in a book with a kind of optimism and prettiness; according to us, a moral book is a book about moral people. But the old idea was almost exactly the opposite; a moral book was a book about immoral people. A moral book was full of pictures like Hogarth's "Gin Lane" or "Stages of Cruelty," or it recorded, like the popular broadsheet, "God's dreadful judgment" against some blasphemer or murderer. There is a philosophical reason for this change. The homeless scepticism of our time has reached a sub-conscious feeling that morality is somehow merely a matter of human taste—an accident of psychology. And if goodness only exists in certain human minds, a man wishing to praise goodness will naturally exaggerate the amount of it that there is in human minds or the number of human minds in which it is supreme. Every confession that man is vicious is a confession that virtue is visionary. Every book which admits that evil is real is felt in some vague way to be admitting that good is unreal. The modern instinct is that if the heart of man is evil, there is nothing that remains good. But the older feeling was that if the heart of man was ever so evil, there was something that remained good—goodness remained good. An actual avenging virtue existed outside the human race; to that men rose, or from that men fell away. Therefore, of course, this law itself was as much demonstrated in the breach as in the observance. If Tom Jones violated morality, so much the worse for Tom Jones. Fielding did not feel, as a melancholy modern would have done, that every sin of Tom Jones was in some way breaking the spell, or we may even say destroying the fiction of morality. Men spoke of the sinner breaking the law; but it was rather the law that broke him. And what modern people call the foulness and freedom of Fielding is generally the severity and moral stringency of Fielding. He would not have thought that he was serving morality at all if he had written a book all about nice people. Fielding would have considered Mr. Ian Maclaren extremely immoral; and there is something to be said for that view. Telling the truth about the terrible struggle of the human soul is surely a very elementary part of the ethics of honesty. If the characters are not wicked, the book is. This older and firmer conception of right as existing outside human weakness and without reference to human error can be felt in the very lightest and loosest of the works of old English literature. It is commonly unmeaning enough to call Shakspere a great moralist; but in this particular way Shakspere is a very typical moralist. Whenever he alludes to right and wrong it is always with this old implication. Right is right, even if nobody does it. Wrong is wrong, even if everybody is wrong about it.

Chapter 33
The Maid of Orleans

considerable time ago (at far too early an age, in fact) I read Voltaire's "La Pucelle," a savage sarcasm on the traditional purity of Joan of Arc, very dirty, and very funny. I had not thought of it again for years, but it came back into my mind this morning because I began to turn over the leaves of the new "Jeanne d'Arc," by that great and graceful writer, Anatole France. It is written in a tone of tender sympathy, and a sort of sad reverence; it never loses touch with a noble tact and courtesy, like that of a gentleman escorting a peasant girl through the modern crowd. It is invariably respectful to Joan, and even respectful to her religion. And being myself a furious admirer of Joan the Maid, I have reflectively compared the two methods, and I come to the conclusion that I prefer Voltaire's.

When a man of Voltaire's school has to explode a saint or a great religious hero, he says that such a person is a common human fool, or a common human fraud. But when a man like Anatole France has to explode a saint, he explains a saint as somebody belonging to his particular fussy little literary set. Voltaire read human nature into Joan of Arc, though it was only the brutal part of human nature. At least it was not specially Voltaire's nature. But M. France read M. France's nature into Joan of Arc—all the cold kindness, all the homeless sentimental sin of the modern literary man. There is one book that it recalled to me with startling vividness, though I have not seen the matter mentioned anywhere; Renan's "Vie de Jésus." It has just the same general intention: that if you do not attack Christianity, you can at least patronise it. My own instinct, apart from my opinions, would be quite the other way. If I disbelieved in Christianity, I should be the loudest blasphemer in Hyde Park. Nothing ought to be too big for a brave man to attack; but there are some things too big for a man to patronise.

And I must say that the historical method seems to me excessively unreasonable. I have no knowledge of history, but I have as much knowledge of reason as Anatole France. And, if anything is irrational, it seems to me that the Renan-France way of dealing with miraculous stories is irrational. The Renan-France method is simply this: you explain supernatural stories that have some foundation simply by inventing natural stories that have no foundation. Suppose that you are confronted with the statement that Jack climbed up the beanstalk into the sky. It is perfectly philosophical to reply that you do not think that he did. It is (in my opinion) even more philosophical to reply that he may very probably have done so. But the Renan-France method is to write like this: "When we consider Jack's curious and even perilous heredity, which no doubt was derived from a female greengrocer and a profligate priest, we can easily understand how the ideas of heaven and a beanstalk came to be combined in his mind. Moreover, there is little doubt that he must have met some wandering conjurer from India, who told him about the tricks of the mango plant, and how it is sent up to the sky. We can imagine these two friends, the old man and the young, wandering in the woods together at evening, looking at the red and level clouds, as on that night when the old man pointed to a small beanstalk, and told his too imaginative companion that this also might be made to scale the heavens. And then, when we remember the quite exceptional psychology of Jack, when we remember how there was in him a union of the prosaic, the love of plain vegetables, with an almost irrelevant eagerness for the unattainable, for invisibility and the void, we shall no longer wonder that it was to him especially that was sent this sweet, though merely symbolic, dream of the tree uniting earth and heaven." That is the way that Renan and France write, only they do it better. But, really, a rationalist like myself becomes a little impatient and feels inclined to say, "But, hang it all, what do you know about the heredity of Jack or the psychology of Jack? You know nothing about Jack at all, except that some people say that he climbed up a beanstalk. Nobody would ever have thought of mentioning him if he hadn't. You must interpret him in terms of the beanstalk religion; you cannot merely interpret religion in terms of him. We have the materials of this story, and we can believe them or not. But we have not got the materials to make another story."

It is no exaggeration to say that this is the manner of M. Anatole France in dealing with Joan of Arc. Because her miracle is incredible to his somewhat old-fashioned materialism, he does not therefore dismiss it and her to fairyland with Jack and the Beanstalk. He tries to invent a real story, for which he can find no real evidence. He produces a scientific explanation which is quite destitute of any scientific proof. It is as if I (being entirely ignorant of botany and chemistry) said that the beanstalk grew to the sky because nitrogen and argon got into the subsidiary ducts of the corolla. To take the most obvious example, the principal character in M. France's story is a person who never existed at all. All Joan's wisdom and energy, it seems, came from a certain priest, of whom there is not the tiniest trace in all the multitudinous records of her life. The only foundation I can find for this fancy is the highly undemocratic idea that a peasant girl could not possibly have any ideas of her own. It is very hard for a freethinker to remain democratic. The writer seems altogether to forget what is meant by the moral atmosphere of a community. To say that Joan must have learnt her vision of a virgin overthrowing evil from *a* priest, is like saying that some modern girl in London, pitying the poor, must have learnt it from *a* Labour Member. She would learn it where the Labour Member learnt it—in the whole state of our society.

But that is the modern method: the method of the reverent sceptic. When you find a life entirely incredible and incomprehensible from the outside, you pretend that you understand the inside. As Renan, the rationalist, could not make any sense out of Christ's most public acts, he proceeded to make an ingenious system out of His private thoughts. As Anatole France, on his own intellectual principle, cannot believe in what Joan of Arc did, he professes to be her dearest friend, and to know exactly what she meant. I cannot feel it to be a very rational manner of writing history; and sooner or later we shall have to find some more solid way of dealing with those spiritual phenomena with which all history is as closely spotted and spangled as the sky is with stars.

Joan of Arc is a wild and wonderful thing enough, but she is much saner than most of her critics and biographers. We shall not recover the common sense of Joan until we have recovered her mysticism. Our wars fail, because they begin with something sensible and obvious—such as getting to Pretoria by Christmas. But her war succeeded—because it began with something wild and perfect—the saints delivering France. She put her idealism in the right place, and her realism also in the right place: we moderns get both displaced. She put her dreams and her sentiment into her aims, where they ought to be; she put her practicality into her practice. In modern Imperial wars, the case is reversed. Our dreams, our aims are always, we insist, quite practical. It is our practice that is dreamy.

It is not for us to explain this flaming figure in terms of our tired and querulous culture. Rather we must try to explain ourselves by the blaze of such fixed stars. Those who called her a witch hot from hell were much more sensible than those who depict her as a silly sentimental maiden prompted by her parish priest. If I have to choose between the two schools of her scattered enemies, I could take my place with those subtle clerks who thought her divine mission devilish, rather than with those rustic aunts and uncles who thought it impossible.

Chapter 34
A Dead Poet

ith Francis Thompson we lose the greatest poetic energy since Browning. His energy was of somewhat the same kind. Browning was intellectually intricate because he was morally simple. He was too simple to explain himself; he was too humble to suppose that other people needed any explanation. But his real energy, and the real energy of Francis Thompson, was best expressed in the fact that both poets were at once fond of immensity and also fond of detail. Any common Imperialist can have large ideas so long as he is not called upon to have small ideas also. Any common scientific philosopher can have small ideas so long as he is not called upon to have large ideas as well. But great poets use the telescope and also the microscope. Great poets are obscure for two opposite reasons; now, because they are talking about something too large for any one to understand, and now again because they are talking about something too small for any one to see. Francis Thompson possessed both these infinities. He escaped by being too small, as the microbe escapes; or he escaped by being too large, as the universe escapes. Any one who knows Francis Thompson's poetry knows quite well the truth to which I refer. For the benefit of any person who does not know it, I may mention two cases taken from memory. I have not the book by me, so I can only render the poetical passages in a clumsy paraphrase. But there was one poem of which the image was so vast that it was literally difficult for a time to take it in; he was describing the evening earth with its mist and fume and fragrance, and represented the whole as rolling upwards like a smoke; then suddenly he called the whole ball of the earth a thurible, and said that some gigantic spirit swung it slowly before God. That is the case of the image too large for comprehension. Another instance sticks in my mind of the image which is too small. In one of his poems, he says that abyss between the known and the unknown is bridged by "Pontifical death." There are about ten historical and theological puns in that one word. That a priest means a pontiff, that a pontiff means a bridge-maker, that death is certainly a bridge, that death may turn out after all to be a reconciling priest, that at least priests and bridges both attest to the fact that one thing can get separated from another thing—these ideas, and twenty more, are all actually concentrated in the word "pontifical." In Francis Thompson's poetry, as in the poetry of the universe, you can work infinitely out and out, but yet infinitely in and in. These two infinities are the mark of greatness; and he was a great poet.

Beneath the tide of praise which was obviously due to the dead poet, there is an evident undercurrent of discussion about him; some charges of moral weakness were at least important enough to be authoritatively contradicted in the *Nation*; and, in connection with this and other things, there has been a continuous stir of comment upon his attraction to and gradual absorption in Catholic theological ideas. This question is so important that I think it ought to be considered and understood even at the present time. It is, of course, true that Francis Thompson devoted himself more and more to poems not only purely Catholic, but, one may say, purely ecclesiastical. And it is, moreover, true that (if things go on as they are going on at present) more and more good poets will do the same. Poets will tend towards Christian orthodoxy for a perfectly plain reason; because it is about the simplest and freest thing now left in the world. On this point it is very necessary to be clear. When people impute special vices to the Christian Church, they seem entirely to forget that the world (which is the only other thing there is) has these vices much more. The Church has been cruel; but the world has been much more cruel. The Church has plotted; but the world has plotted much more. The Church has been superstitious; but it has never been so superstitious as the world is when left to itself.

Now, poets in our epoch will tend towards ecclesiastical religion strictly because it is just a little more free than anything else. Take, for instance, the case of symbol and ritualism. All reasonable men believe in symbol; but some reasonable men do not believe in ritualism; by which they mean, I imagine, a symbolism too complex, elaborate, and mechanical. But whenever they talk of ritualism they always seem to mean the ritualism of the Church. Why should they not mean the ritual of the world? It is much more ritualistic. The ritual of the Army, the ritual of the Navy, the ritual of the Law Courts, the ritual of Parliament are much more ritualistic. The ritual of a dinner-party is much more ritualistic. Priests may put gold and great jewels on the chalice; but at least there is only one chalice to put them on. When you go to a dinner-party they put in front of you five different chalices, of five weird and heraldic shapes, to symbolise five different kinds of wine; an insane extension of ritual from which Mr. Percy Dearmer would fly shrieking. A bishop wears a mitre; but he is not thought more or less of a bishop according to whether you can see the very latest curves in his mitre. But a swell is thought more or less of a swell according to whether you can see the very latest curves in his hat. There is more *fuss* about symbols in the world than in the Church.

And yet (strangely enough) though men fuss more about the worldly symbols, they mean less by them. It is the mark of religious forms that they declare something unknown. But it is the mark of worldly forms that they declare something which is known, and which is known to be untrue. When the Pope in an Encyclical calls himself your father, it is a matter of faith or of doubt. But when the Duke of Devonshire in a letter calls himself yours obediently, you know that he means the opposite of what he says. Religious forms are, at the worst, fables; they might be true. Secular forms are falsehoods; they are not true. Take a more topical case. The German Emperor has more uniforms than the Pope. But, moreover, the Pope's vestments all imply a claim to be something purely mystical and doubtful.

Many of the German Emperor's uniforms imply a claim to be something which he certainly is not and which it would be highly disgusting if he were. The Pope may or may not be the Vicar of Christ. But the Kaiser certainly is not an English Colonel. If the thing were reality it would be treason. If it is mere ritual, it is by far the most unreal ritual on earth.

Now, poetical people like Francis Thompson will, as things stand, tend away from secular society and towards religion for the reason above described: that there are crowds of symbols in both, but that those of religion are simpler and mean more. To take an evident type, the Cross is more poetical than the Union Jack, because it is simpler. The more simple an idea is, the more it is fertile in variations. Francis Thompson could have written any number of good poems on the Cross, because it is a primary symbol. The number of poems which Mr. Rudyard Kipling could write on the Union Jack is, fortunately, limited, because the Union Jack is too complex to produce luxuriance. The same principle applies to any possible number of cases. A poet like Francis Thompson could deduce perpetually rich and branching meanings out of two plain facts like bread and wine; with bread and wine he can expand everything to everywhere. But with a French menu he cannot expand anything; except perhaps himself. Complicated ideas do not produce any more ideas. Mongrels do not breed. Religious ritual attracts because there is some sense in it. Religious imagery, so far from being subtle, is the only simple thing left for poets. So far from being merely superhuman, it is the only human thing left for human beings.

Chapter 35
Christmas

here is no more dangerous or disgusting habit than that of celebrating Christmas before it comes, as I am doing in this article. It
is the very essence of a festival that it breaks upon one brilliantly
and abruptly, that at one moment the great day is not and the
next moment the great day is. Up to a certain specific instant
you are feeling ordinary and sad; for it is only Wednesday. At the next moment
your heart leaps up and your soul and body dance together like lovers; for in one
burst and blaze it has become Thursday. I am assuming (of course) that you are
a worshipper of Thor, and that you celebrate his day once a week, possibly with
human sacrifice. If, on the other hand, you are a modern Christian Englishman,
you hail (of course) with the same explosion of gaiety the appearance of the English Sunday. But I say that whatever the day is that is to you festive or symbolic,
it is essential that there should be a quite clear black line between it and the time
going before. And all the old wholesome customs in connection with Christmas
were to the effect that one should not touch or see or know or speak of something
before the actual coming of Christmas Day. Thus, for instance, children were
never given their presents until the actual coming of the appointed hour. The
presents were kept tied up in brown-paper parcels, out of which an arm of a doll
or the leg of a donkey sometimes accidentally stuck. I wish this principle were
adopted in respect of modern Christmas ceremonies and publications. Especially
it ought to be observed in connection with what are called the Christmas numbers
of magazines. The editors of the magazines bring out their Christmas numbers so
long before the time that the reader is more likely to be still lamenting for the
turkey of last year than to have seriously settled down to a solid anticipation of
the turkey which is to come. Christmas numbers of magazines ought to be tied up
in brown paper and kept for Christmas Day. On consideration, I should favour
the editors being tied up in brown paper. Whether the leg or arm of an editor
should ever be allowed to protrude I leave to individual choice.

Of course, all this secrecy about Christmas is merely sentimental and ceremonial; if you do not like what is sentimental and ceremonial, do not celebrate
Christmas at all. You will not be punished if you don't; also, since we are no longer
ruled by those sturdy Puritans who won for us civil and religious liberty, you will
not even be punished if you do. But I cannot understand why any one should
bother about a ceremonial except ceremonially. If a thing only exists in order to
be graceful, do it gracefully or do not do it. If a thing only exists as something
professing to be solemn, do it solemnly or do not do it. There is no sense in doing
it slouchingly; nor is there even any liberty. I can understand the man who takes
off his hat to a lady because it is the customary symbol. I can understand him, I say;

in fact, I know him quite intimately. I can also understand the man who refuses to take off his hat to a lady, like the old Quakers, because he thinks that a symbol is superstition. But what point would there be in so performing an arbitrary form of respect that it was not a form of respect? We respect the gentleman who takes off his hat to the lady; we respect the fanatic who will not take off his hat to the lady. But what should we think of the man who kept his hands in his pockets and asked the lady to take his hat off for him because he felt tired?

This is combining insolence and superstition; and the modern world is full of the strange combination. There is no mark of the immense weak-mindedness of modernity that is more striking than this general disposition to keep up old forms, but to keep them up informally and feebly. Why take something which was only meant to be respectful and preserve it disrespectfully? Why take something which you could easily abolish as a superstition and carefully perpetuate it as a bore? There have been many instances of this half-witted compromise. Was it not true, for instance, that the other day some mad American was trying to buy Glastonbury Abbey and transfer it stone by stone to America? Such things are not only illogical, but idiotic. There is no particular reason why a pushing American financier should pay respect to Glastonbury Abbey at all. But if he is to pay respect to Glastonbury Abbey, he must pay respect to Glastonbury. If it is a matter of sentiment, why should he spoil the scene? If it is not a matter of sentiment, why should he ever have visited the scene? To call this kind of thing Vandalism is a very inadequate and unfair description. The Vandals were very sensible people. They did not believe in a religion, and so they insulted it; they did not see any use for certain buildings, and so they knocked them down. But they were not such fools as to encumber their march with the fragments of the edifice they had themselves spoilt. They were at least superior to the modern American mode of reasoning. They did not desecrate the stones because they held them sacred.

Another instance of the same illogicality I observed the other day at some kind of "At Home." I saw what appeared to be a human being dressed in a black evening-coat, black dress-waistcoat, and black dress-trousers, but with a shirt-front made of Jaegar wool. What can be the sense of this sort of thing? If a man thinks hygiene more important than convention (a selfish and heathen view, for the beasts that perish are more hygienic than man, and man is only above them because he is more conventional), if, I say, a man thinks that hygiene is more important than convention, what on earth is there to oblige him to wear a shirt-front at all? But to take a costume of which the only conceivable cause or advantage is that it is a sort of uniform, and then not wear it in the uniform way—this is to be neither a Bohemian nor a gentleman. It is a foolish affectation, I think, in an English officer of the Life Guards never to wear his uniform if he can help it. But it would be more foolish still if he showed himself about town in a scarlet coat and a Jaeger breast-plate. It is the custom nowadays to have Ritual Commissions and Ritual Reports to make rather unmeaning compromises in the ceremonial of the Church of England. So perhaps we shall have an ecclesiastical compromise by which all the Bishops shall wear Jaeger copes and Jaeger mitres. Similarly the King might insist on having a Jaeger crown. But I do not think he will, for he understands the logic of the matter better than that. The modern monarch, like a reasonable fellow, wears his crown as seldom as he can; but if he does it at all, then the only point of a crown is that it is a crown. So let me assure the unknown gentleman in the woollen vesture that the only point of a white shirt-front is that it is a white shirt-front. Stiffness may be its impossible defect; but it is certainly its only possible merit.

Let us be consistent, therefore, about Christmas, and either keep customs or not keep them. If you do not like sentiment and symbolism, you do not like Christmas; go away and celebrate something else; I should suggest the birthday of Mr. M'Cabe. No doubt you could have a sort of scientific Christmas with a hygienic pudding and highly instructive presents stuffed into a Jaeger stocking; go and have it then. If you like those things, doubtless you are a good sort of fellow, and your intentions are excellent. I have no doubt that you are really interested in humanity; but I cannot think that humanity will ever be much interested in you. Humanity is unhygienic from its very nature and beginning. It is so much an exception in Nature that the laws of Nature really mean nothing to it. Now Christmas is attacked also on the humanitarian ground. Ouida called it a feast of slaughter and gluttony. Mr. Shaw suggested that it was invented by poulterers. That should be considered before it becomes more considerable.

I do not know whether an animal killed at Christmas has had a better or a worse time than it would have had if there had been no Christmas or no Christmas dinners. But I do know that the fighting and suffering brotherhood to which I belong and owe everything, Mankind, would have a much worse time if there were no such thing as Christmas or Christmas dinners. Whether the turkey which Scrooge gave to Bob Cratchit had experienced a lovelier or more melancholy career than that of less attractive turkeys is a subject upon which I cannot even conjecture. But that Scrooge was better for giving the turkey and Cratchit happier for getting it I know as two facts, as I know that I have two feet. What life and death may be to a turkey is not my business; but the soul of Scrooge and the body of Cratchit are my business. Nothing shall induce me to darken human homes, to destroy human festivities, to insult human gifts and human benefactions for the sake of some hypothetical knowledge which Nature curtained from our eyes. We men and women are all in the same boat, upon a stormy sea. We owe to each other a terrible and tragic loyalty. If we catch sharks for food, let them be killed most mercifully; let any one who likes love the sharks, and pet the sharks, and tie ribbons round their necks and give them sugar and teach them to dance. But if once a man suggests that a shark is to be valued against a sailor, or that the poor shark might be permitted to bite off a nigger's leg occasionally; then I would court-martial the man—he is a traitor to the ship.

And while I take this view of humanitarianism of the anti-Christmas kind, it is cogent to say that I am a strong anti-vivisectionist. That is, if there is any vivisection, I am against it. I am against the cutting-up of conscious dogs for the same reason that I am in favour of the eating of dead turkeys. The connection may not be obvious; but that is because of the strangely unhealthy condition of modern thought. I am against cruel vivisection as I am against a cruel anti-Christmas asceticism, because they both involve the upsetting of existing fellowships and the shocking of normal good feelings for the sake of something that is intellectual, fanciful, and remote. It is not a human thing, it is not a humane thing, when you see a poor woman staring hungrily at a bloater, to think, not of the obvious feelings of the woman, but of the unimaginable feelings of the deceased bloater. Similarly, it is not human, it is not humane, when you look at a dog to think about what theoretic discoveries you might possibly make if you were allowed to bore a hole in his head. Both the humanitarians' fancy about the feelings concealed inside the bloater, and the vivisectionists' fancy about the knowledge concealed inside the dog, are unhealthy fancies, because they upset a human sanity that is certain for the sake of something that is of necessity uncertain. The vivisectionist, for the sake of doing something that may or may not be useful, does something that certainly is horrible. The anti-Christmas humanitarian, in seeking to have a sympathy with a turkey which no man can have with a turkey, loses the sympathy he has already with the happiness of millions of the poor.

It is not uncommon nowadays for the insane extremes in reality to meet. Thus I have always felt that brutal Imperialism and Tolstoian non-resistance were not only not opposite, but were the same thing. They are the same contemptible thought that conquest cannot be resisted, looked at from the two standpoints of the conqueror and the conquered. Thus again teetotalism and the really degraded gin-selling and dram-drinking have exactly the same moral philosophy. They are both based on the idea that fermented liquor is not a drink, but a drug. But I am specially certain that the extreme of vegetarian humanity is, as I have said, akin to the extreme of scientific cruelty—they both permit a dubious speculation to interfere with their ordinary charity. The sound moral rule in such matters as vivisection always presents itself to me in this way. There is no ethical necessity more essential and vital than this: that casuistical exceptions, though admitted, should be admitted as exceptions. And it follows from this, I think, that, though we may do a horrid thing in a horrid situation, we must be quite certain that we actually and already are in that situation. Thus, all sane moralists admit that one may sometimes tell a lie; but no sane moralist would approve of telling a little boy to practise telling lies, in case he might one day have to tell a justifiable one. Thus, morality has often justified shooting a robber or a burglar. But it would not justify going into the village Sunday school and shooting all the little boys who looked as if they might grow up into burglars. The need may arise; but the need must have arisen. It seems to me quite clear that if you step across this limit you step off a precipice.

Now, whether torturing an animal is or is not an immoral thing, it is, at least, a dreadful thing. It belongs to the order of exceptional and even desperate acts. Except for some extraordinary reason I would not grievously hurt an animal; with an extraordinary reason I would grievously hurt him. If (for example) a mad elephant were pursuing me and my family, and I could only shoot him so that he would die in agony, he would have to die in agony. But the elephant would be there. I would not do it to a hypothetical elephant. Now, it always seems to me that this is the weak point in the ordinary vivisectionist argument, "Suppose your wife were dying." Vivisection is not done by a man whose wife is dying. If it were it might be lifted to the level of the moment, as would be lying or stealing bread, or any other ugly action. But this ugly action is done in cold blood, at leisure, by men who are not sure that it will be of any use to anybody—men of whom the most that can be said is that they may conceivably make the beginnings of some discovery which may perhaps save the life of some one else's wife in some remote future. That is too cold and distant to rob an act of its immediate horror. That is like training the child to tell lies for the sake of some great dilemma that may never come to him. You are doing a cruel thing, but not with enough passion to make it a kindly one.

So much for why I am an anti-vivisectionist; and I should like to say, in conclusion, that all other anti-vivisectionists of my acquaintance weaken their case infinitely by forming this attack on a scientific speciality in which the human heart is commonly on their side, with attacks upon universal human customs in which the human heart is not at all on their side. I have heard humanitarians, for instance, speak of vivisection and field sports as if they were the same kind of thing. The difference seems to me simple and enormous. In sport a man goes into a wood and mixes with the existing life of that wood; becomes a destroyer only in the simple and healthy sense in which all the creatures are destroyers; becomes for one moment to them what they are to him—another animal. In vivisection a man takes a simpler creature and subjects it to subtleties which no one but man could inflict on him, and for which man is therefore gravely and terribly responsible.

Meanwhile, it remains true that I shall eat a great deal of turkey this Christmas; and it is not in the least true (as the vegetarians say) that I shall do it because I do not realise what I am doing, or because I do what I know is wrong, or that I do it with shame or doubt or a fundamental unrest of conscience. In one sense I know quite well what I am doing; in another sense I know quite well that I know not what I do. Scrooge and the Cratchits and I are, as I have said, all in one boat; the turkey and I are, to say the most of it, ships that pass in the night, and greet each other in passing. I wish him well; but it is really practically impossible to discover whether I treat him well. I can avoid, and I do avoid with horror, all special and artificial tormenting of him, sticking pins in him for fun or sticking knives in him for scientific investigation. But whether by feeding him slowly and killing him quickly for the needs of my brethren, I have improved in his own solemn eyes his own strange and separate destiny, whether I have made him in the sight of God a slave or a martyr, or one whom the gods love and who die young—that is far more removed from my possibilities of knowledge than the most abstruse intricacies of mysticism or theology. A turkey is more occult and awful than all the angels and archangels. In so far as God has partly revealed to us an angelic world, he has partly told us what an angel means. But God has never told us what a turkey means. And if you go and stare at a live turkey for an hour or two, you will find by the end of it that the enigma has rather increased than diminished.

Book Catalog

Works by Our Authors

- *The Opium of Happiness* by Jeremy Hausotter. This book examines the Church's teachings on drugs and marijuana. It also contains about 70 pages of appendices of hard to find Church documents discussing drugs. ISBN: 978-1-964170-54-1
- *How to Win Tic Tac Toe Like a Champion* by Jeremy Hausotter. ISBN: 978-1-964170-58-9

Theology & Philosophy

- *Select Works* by St. Ambrose. ISBN: 978-1-964170-44-2
- St. Thomas Aquinas
  - *The Summa Theologiae: Prima Pars, Q. 1-119*. ISBN: 978-1-964170-23-7
  - *The Summa Theologiae: Prima Secundae, Q. 1-114*. ISBN: 978-1-964170-24-4
  - *The Summa Theologiae: Secunda Secundae, Q. 1-189*. ISBN: 978-1-964170-25-1
  - *The Summa Theologiae: Tertia Pars, Q. 1-90*. ISBN: 978-1-964170-27-5
  - *The Summa Theologiae: Supplementum, Q. 1-99*. ISBN: 978-1-964170-28-2
- *The Life of St. Anthony* by St. Athanasius. ISBN: 978-1-964170-20-6
- *Select Works and Letters* by St. Athanasius. ISBN: 978-1-964170-67-1
- St. Augustine
  - *On Christian Doctrine*. ISBN: 978-1-964170-74-9
  - *Select Doctrinal and Moral Treatises*. ISBN: 978-1-964170-63-3
  - *The Anti-Donatist Works*. ISBN: 978-1-964170-40-4
  - *The Anti-Manichean Works*. ISBN: 978-1-964170-67-1
  - *The Anti-Pelagian Works*. ISBN: 978-1-964170-65-7
- *The Art of Dying Well* by St. Robert Bellarmine. ISBN: 978-1-964170-62-6
- *Select Letters and Orations* by St. Gregory Nazianzen. ISBN: 978-1-964170-56-5
- St. John Henry Newman
  - *An Essay in Aid of a Grammar of Assent*. ISBN: 978-1-964170-52-7
  - *The Complete Parochial and Plain Sermons*, volumes 1-4. ISBN: 978-1-964170-22-0
  - *The Complete Parochial and Plain Sermons*, volumes 5-8. ISBN: 978-1-964170-66-4
  - *The Complete Historical Sketches*, volumes 1-3. ISBN: 978-1-964170-71-8
  - *On the Development of Christian Doctrine*. ISBN: 978-1-964170-48-0
  - *Sermons Preached on Various Occasions*. ISBN: 978-1-964170-50-3
- *The Problem of Form in Painting and Sculpture* by Adolf von Hildebrand. ISBN: 978-1-964170-60-2

Papal Documents

- The Papal Writings of John Paul II
  - Vol. 1, *The Complete Encyclicals*. ISBN: 978-1-964170-21-3
  - Vol. 2, *Redemptor Hominis*. ISBN: 978-1-964170-00-8
  - Vol. 3, *Dives in Misericordia*. ISBN: 978-1-964170-01-5

- Vol. 4, *Laborem Exercens*. ISBN: 978-1-964170-02-2
- Vol. 11, *Veritatis Splendor*. ISBN: 978-1-964170-09-1
- Vol. 12, *Evangelium Vitae*. ISBN: 978-1-964170-10-7
- Vol. 14, *Fides et Ratio*. ISBN: 978-1-964170-12-1

- The Papal Writings of Benedict XVI

    - Vol. 1, *Select Papal Writings: The Encyclicals, Apostolic Exhortations, and Select Other Writings*. ISBN: 978-1-964170-14-5

Classics

- The G.K. Chesterton Collection

    - Nonfiction

        * *The Defendant, Varied Types, Heretics, All Things Considered*. ISBN: 978-1-964170-79-4
        * *Tremendous Trifles, Orthodoxy, What's Wrong with the World*. ISBN: 978-1-964170-81-7

- The Complete Works of Fyodor Dostoevsky

    - Vol. 8, *The Minor Novels and Novellas: The Insulted and the Injured, The House of the Dead*. ISBN: 978-1-964170-17-6
    - Vol. 9, *The Complete Short Stories*. ISBN: 978-1-964170-18-3

- *The Wind in the Willows* by Kenneth Grahame. ISBN: 978-1-964170-46-6

- Greek and Roman Classics

    - Vol. 1, *Homer's The Iliad and the Odyssey*, translated by Alexander Pope. ISBN: 978-1-964170-15-2
    - Vol. 4, *Commentaries* by Julius Caesar. ISBN: 978-1-964170-72-5

- Norse Classics

    - Vol. 1, *The Poetic and Prose Eddas*. ISBN: 978-1-964170-37-4
    - Vol. 2, *The Heimskringla*. ISBN: 978-1-964170-39-8
    - Vol. 3, *The Nibelungenlied* (prose translation). ISBN: 978-1-964170-33-6
    - Vol. 4, *The Norse Sagas, Part 1*. ISBN: 978-1-964170-35-0
    - Vol. 5, *The Norse Sagas, Part 2*. ISBN: 978-1-964170-29-9
    - Vol. 6, *The Norse Sagas, Part 3*. ISBN: 978-1-964170-31-2

- *20,000 Leagues Under the Sea* by Jules Verne. ISBN: 978-1-964170-42-8

Forthcoming Titles

- A volume on the dogma *no salvation outside of the Church* by Jeremy Hausotter.
- A volume on the hermeneutics of Vatican II by Jeremy Hausotter.
- The *Summa Contra Gentiles* by St. Thomas Aquinas.

Made in the USA
Las Vegas, NV
26 December 2024

15432545R00216